A HISTORY OF
THE
GODDESS
from the
Ice Age
to the
Bible
EDWARD DODGE

Published by:
Trine Day LLC
PO Box 577
Walterville, OR 97489
1-800-556-2012
www.TrineDay.com
trineday@icloud.com

Library of Congress Control Number: 2021901766

Dodge, Edward.
A History of the Goddess: From the Ice Age to the Bible – 1st ed.
p. cm.
Epub (ISBN-13) 978-1-63424-305-6
Kindle (ISBN-13) 978-1-63424-306-3
Print (ISBN-13) 978-1-63424-304-9
1. Godesses -- History 3. Religion -- Prehistoric. 4. Spirituality -- Paganism & Neo-Paganism 5. Mythology -- Assyro-Babylonian. 6. Femininity of God. 7. Bible -- History. 8. Cannabis -- History. 9. Cannabis -- Religious aspects. 10. Cannabis -- Religious aspects -- Christianity -- History. I. Title

FIRST EDITION
10 9 8 7 6 5 4 3 2 1

Printed in the USA
Distribution to the Trade by:
Independent Publishers Group (IPG)
814 North Franklin Street
Chicago, Illinois 60610
312.337.0747
www.ipgbook.com

Publisher's Foreword

Mary had a little lamb
It's fleece was white as snow
Everywhere that Mary went
The lamb was sure to go

– Sarah Josepha Hale, 1830

For nothing is hidden that will not be made manifest, nor is anything secret that will not be known and come to light.

– Luke 8:17

We live in interesting times. The Internet allows us to travel freely around our planet – delve back in time, read ancient texts, connect with other seekers – helping us to understand our existence. Edward Dodge's *A History of the Goddess: From Ice Age to the Bible* delivers an opportunity to examine our hoary past, survive our difficult present, and hopefully appreciate a better and more fruitful future.

There are currently almost eight billion people on Earth, and, according to some, we have been around for about six million years. There are stone tools dated from 2.5 million years ago. *Homo sapiens* emerged around 200,000, cave paintings around 30,000, and human settlements around 12,000 years ago. Seeing the world through the blinders of religious dogma, fundamentalist Christians declare the world is only 6,000 to 10,000 years old. Belief can be used to bully, to mislead people into falsehoods.

Where do religious beliefs come from? How does the past evolve towards today? What were the social interactions that moved us foreword or held us back? Who are we? When did gods become God?

After he commenced researching the direct references to cannabis in the Christian Bible, Dodge began asking deep questions. He wanted to understand: "Why cannabis went from being sacred in the time of Moses to being rejected later on, since we know that cannabis is not part of Judeo-Christian traditions today." A noble endeavor.

Being beyond threescore years and ten, I have experienced a few social changes. When I was a youngster, women could not lead a worship service, they had to wear hats and only men could speak from the pulpit. My world in provincial Northern Virgina was highly segregated, with separate facilities, sundown laws, etc. It was very disconcerting, I didn't have any acculturated prejudices, my family was from out west. We moved to Nashville, there was still prejudice, but it appeared softer – there was more interaction between folks. Then we moved to Oregon, where there were different biases, and as the years went by, the pace of change accelerated.

Coming of age in the 1960s gave me direct experience with marijuana, and a reverence for its use. Cannabis was more than something to get "high" with, there was something deeper, something more profound.

Dr. Sunil K Aggarwal says, "[C]annabis ... happened to make [the] compounds that bind to receptors in the human system which ... goes back 600 million years ... when multicellular organisms were becoming multicellular, and were trying to figure out how to send communication and modulate action.... In *Homo sapiens*, it's a really integrated system for cell communication."

Cannabis is one of the basic building blocks of life – humans share more than 40% of our genome with cannabis. Marijuana and mankind have had a abiding beneficial relationship that was rudely disrupted by religious beliefs several thousands of years ago. Cannabis and the Goddesses in the Bible were concealed by religious zealots – intent on obfuscation.

Edward Dodge tells us how and what happened. Great job!

Onward to the Utmost of Futures,
Peace,
Kris Millegan
Publisher
TrineDay
February 14, 2021

Contents

VOLUME I: Goddess Traditions

VOLUME II: Old Testament

VOLUME III: New Testament

A

When the woman saw that the fruit of the tree was good for food and pleasing to the eye, and also desirable for gaining wisdom, she took some and ate it. She also gave some to her husband, who was with her, and he ate it. Then the eyes of both of them were opened, and they realized they were naked; so they sewed fig leaves together and made coverings for themselves.

-- Genesis 3:6-7

VOLUME I
Goddess Traditions

Artemis, Mistress of Animals

INTRODUCTION

Who is Goddess?

She is the Feminine Divine, she has taken many names and forms through the ages. She is the Mother of God and the Wife of God. We know her today as Mother Earth, Mother Nature, and Gaia. In pagan mythology she manifests as all the goddesses, each of whom represents a piece of her infinite possibilities. She is the Queen of Heaven. She is the Triple Goddess; the mother, maiden, and death – who represents the cycles of life. The philosophers call her Sophia, which is Wisdom. She is the mother of us all who offers beauty, joy, and abundance.

For those who believe in God there is a Goddess to match, and her traditions are far older than monotheism, going back deep into the Ice Age. The Earthly Mother and the Heavenly Father were traditionally seen as the original deities and the parents of all the pagan gods. The rise of monotheism as told in the Old Testament is the story of the divorce of God from the Goddess and the condemnation of her ancient traditions.

The Goddess is in the Bible, but she is whitewashed out of the stories and denounced by the Biblical writers who describe her as shameful and abominable, except where she presents as wisdom. The Bible story is told from only one side though, we don't get to hear her perspective. It is the story of one spouse in an angry and contested divorce. But in their condemnations, the biblical writers make clear the existence of the Goddess, even as they were trying to write her out of history.

Heaven and Earth

The Goddess appears unnamed in the opening lines of Genesis, as shown by the scholar Joseph Campbell.[1]

> *In the beginning God created the heaven and the earth. Now the earth was formless and empty, darkness was over the surface of the deep, and the Spirit of God was hovering over the waters.*
>
> – Genesis 1:1-2 (KJV)

1 *Goddesses: Mysteries Of The Feminine Divine*, Joseph Campbell, New World Library, Novato, California, 2013, p.235.

At the creation of the universe, God moves across the face of the waters. But what are these waters, present in the nothingness? Many ancient cultures believed that the primordial first mover of creation was a goddess, a primeval salt water sea from which everything was born, the virgin Mother of God and Earth, *the waters.*

The Sumerians from Mesopotamia, who were at the root of the Biblical traditions, record these beliefs in the very earliest writing. They also believed that the Heavenly Father and the Earthly Mother were the first manifestations of God and Goddess in the human realm. The Biblical writers refashioned existing mythology when creating their own, by obscuring the identity of the wife of God. Yet her presence remains.

The feminine divine is also seen as wisdom, in addition to being Mother Earth. In the Biblical book Proverbs, wisdom says she was with God at the beginning, guiding his hand at creation. In Hellenistic times, wisdom was given the name Sophia, and she was considered the wife of God in many traditions.

> *By wisdom Yahweh laid the earth's foundations, by understanding he set the heavens in place; by his knowledge the watery depths were divided, and the clouds let drop the dew.*
>
> – Proverbs 3:19-20

Not all cultures have deities, but any culture that believes the Earth is our mother is in the family of Goddess worshippers, including indigenous people with animist beliefs. Goddess shows us that there is a whole other side to spirituality and religion that Western culture is not well acquainted with, but is thirsty for like a man lost in the desert.

The Goddess was knocked off her pedestal in Old Testament days but she never went away. Her traditions are part of the lived human experience and remain with us. We see the Goddess in today's culture wars that pit progressive social values against the traditional moral authority of religious conservatives. Feminism, environmentalism, social justice, cannabis and all sacred plants, sexual freedom, transgenders, and birth control, were all valued in the Goddess temples of the ancient world.

The Goddess traditions were rejected by monotheists who deny the very existence of the independent feminine divine. The logic of monotheism requires that the Goddess not be acknowledged and priestly authorities crushed her worship with violence and prejudice.

GODDESS WORSHIP

Goddess worship is ultimately nature worship and is rooted in the cycles of life. The Goddess traditions achieved their greatest refinement in the Mystery religions, which had at their heart a mythology of a dying and rising god whose tragic death is overturned by the powers of a great goddess who restores the hero to life and majesty. Each resurrection story in its way spoke to the fertility of the Earth and the abundance of agriculture, the springtime renewal of plants and animals after the long winter. These cycle of life traditions were replaced by monotheistic traditions preaching eternal life and separation from nature. The Bible tells us that God created the Earth for us humans to have dominion over, no longer is She seen as our living, breathing, mother. The rape of nature and environmental destruction we live with today is the logical outcome of such a worldview.

Modern scholars dismissively identify the ancient Goddess traditions as fertility cults, primitive religions that fail to appreciate the higher moral values of today's religions. But were these ancient Goddess worshipping cultures really so misguided? There were certainly some Neolithic superstitions that needed to go away eventually as civilization advanced, but the Goddess worshipping cultures also had many insights we would do well to recover.

The ancient Goddess worshippers saw humans as part of nature, not separate from it. They valued wise and independent women and had egalitarian societies based on fair trade rather than dominance and coercion. They saw sex as a source of life and creation and something to celebrated, not shamed. They believed that life begets life and that sex makes the flowers grow. They celebrated transgendered people as shamans and high priests, valued for their mystical insights into the mysteries of creation. They did not see humans as the center of creation, created in the image of God. They had humility and understood that the gods were created in our image to help us tell stories that explain the mysteries of life.

CANNABIS IS A CHARACTER IN THE STORY

This book actually has its origins as a history of the plant. I was researching the five direct references to cannabis in the Hebrew Bible and trying to understand what they meant. The most important reference is that cannabis is an ingredient in Moses' holy anointing oil in Exodus 30:23 (mistranslated as calamus or aromatic cane). I wanted to understand why cannabis went from being sacred in the time of Moses to being rejected later on since we know that cannabis is not part of Judeo-Christian traditions today.

Separately, I had learned that archaeologists have determined that the early Hebrews were pagan and that God had a wife named Asherah, who is named many times in the Bible. I had a theory that cannabis and the Goddess were thrown out of the temple together and that cannabis was part of the earlier pagan Hebrew traditions.

I questioned what the Goddess traditions were since I was never taught them in school or church. Who is the Wife of God? What does it mean to worship her? What exactly was being rejected; when, why, and by whom? It is in seeking to answer these questions that this book came to be written. I learned from teachers like Merlin Stone and Riane Eisler and I saw that there was a consistent pattern of symbols and motifs to the Goddess traditions across cultures.

I also learned that the connection between cannabis and the Goddess was much stronger than I anticipated. I observed that the places where cannabis grows thickest are the cultures where the Goddess traditions are strongest, and this is a consistent trend across time and cultures is still visible today.

Cannabis has been with us since the dawn of the Neolithic Revolution in an unbroken thread of history. Hemp fibers and drugs were always important and the plant was sacred in Goddess traditions. Cannabis was common in the temples of the ancient world where it was used as intoxicating incense, fibers for sacred weaving, and as a medicine. Hemp fibers were used for ropes, canvas, shipbuilding, and a thousand everyday purposes, making the plant critical in laying the foundations of civilization.

Hemp fibers and drugs are all over the Bible, though like the Goddess they are hidden under the whitewash. In the Bible, cannabis is Eve's sacred plant, the Tree of Knowledge in the Garden of Eden, and the hemp threads that sewed the fig leaves together to make the first clothes. Cannabis is Moses' holy smoke, the burning bush, and the Menorah. Cannabis is in sacred incense, strong drink, and holy anointing oil. Hemp ropes served in building every temple, and hemp was used to construct the Phoenician ships King Solomon sent to Ophir to bring back gold. Cannabis even helped Jesus Christ perform miracles.

Ancient wise women knew cannabis' value as an aphrodisiac, as a medicine to reduce spasms, inflammation, and pain, and to induce contractions for midwifery and abortions. Hemp fibers were in the sacred weaving done by the temple priestesses and in the sackcloth worn by grieving kings. Hemp is the alpha and the omega, the fibers that wrap the newborn and the corpse, the sacred plant that binds us to the cycles of life and the Goddess.

Cannabis was highly valued in King Solomon's temple, the first Hebrew temple in Jerusalem, where qedesha priestesses knew the plant's mysteries. King Solomon was a confirmed Goddess worshipper and was criticized for it by the Biblical writers, but considering that he was the wisest, wealthiest, and most successful of all the Biblical kings perhaps Solomon knew more than they.

The father of the wisdom traditions, King Solomon transmuted the feminine divine into wisdom in Proverbs and Ecclesiastes. King Solomon loved women and ganja, and the women loved him. In the Song of Songs, King Solomon compares his beautiful bride to a garden filled with cannabis and all the finest spices (Songs 4:14). Today's ganja praising Rastafarians trace their roots to King Solomon and believe a cannabis plant grows on his grave.

Pagan Hebrews

The early Hebrews were pagan, they were polytheists in a polytheistic world, and monotheism was introduced later. The Hebrews, or Israelites, followed the Canaanite gods and they had a tribal identity as the followers of El, the Heavenly Father and the Creator of the Universe. El was a very ancient god, perhaps the first named god, and was known as An back in Mesopotamia. We see El as Elohim in the Bible, and in the name, Israel.

El was not alone though, he had a wife and family and was the great father of the Canaanite pantheon of gods. The Israelites were monolatrists within the polytheistic Canaanite culture. They elevated El above the other gods, but the entire pantheon was actively worshipped in the community.

The goddesses were very popular and their traditions, or Mystery religions, were at the heart of the biggest festivals and most important holidays every year. The most revered were the Triple Goddess; the mother, maiden, and death – who represent the cycle of life. The Hebrew Triple Goddess was Asherah, Astarte, and Anat – and they were not easily dispatched by the monotheists.

Asherah the mother goddess was the wife of El, the wife of God. The beloved Astarte, goddess of love and war, was the Queen of Heaven. Anat the terrifying, blood-soaked, goddess of vengeance and slaughter was her sister. This Triple Goddess was sometimes combined, particularly in Egypt, into a single, tripartite, cosmic goddess named Qedesh, who is similar to Shakti of the Hindus. Their sacred priestesses were the qedesha, and their holy city was Kadesh (in todays Syria).

Moses introduced the name Yahweh and the new concept of monotheism, which he brought from Egypt. To proclaim that there is only one God meant that the other deities and their worship needed to be eliminated. The introduction of monotheism was a religious reformation that sparked a culture war lasting centuries. The Yahwists were the partisan followers of Yahweh, religious reformers seeking to dismantle the worship of their rivals, particularly the goddesses who were the most popular in the hearts of the people.

The culture war between the Yahwists and the Goddess worshippers played out for over half a millennium, through the entire history of King Solomon's temple. An Asherah pole representing the mother goddess stood beside the altar of God in Solomon's temple for two-thirds of its history. The Asherah pole was occasionally chopped down by the Yahwhists and subsequently restored by the people as soon as they got the chance.

Divorce from the Wife of God

Pure monotheism was only established during the second temple period, when the Hebrews had become the Jews, after the first destruction of Jerusalem and the return from exile in Babylon. Goddess worship continued in the Near East for another thousand years and continues today in many forms around the world.

The divorce of the Hebrew God from the Goddess was finalized on the day in 458 BCE (or 398 BCE) when Ezra the Scribe brought the freshly completed Hebrew Bible to Jerusalem from Babylon. As told in the Old Testament, Ezra read the Book of the Law to the people assembled in front of the newly built second Jewish temple. Ezra was shocked when he discovered how many of the Jewish men were married and had children with Canaanite women.

The Goddess worshipping women could never be proper wives to Jewish men because they did not practice paternity, nor did they practice monogamy. The Canaanite women tracked bloodlines through their mothers and had sex lives independent of their husbands in the goddess temples. This was unacceptable to Ezra and the Jewish leaders who believed in paternity and patriarchy.

To be a Jew one must be born of a Jewish mother they proclaimed. On that day the Jewish men were forced to divorce their Canaanite wives and families and abandon them. This signaled the final act in the divorce between God and the Goddess in the Jewish tradition.

The Jews inspired the Christians and Muslims and together they are the three great monotheistic faiths. Christianity and Islam both claim to possess the exclusive truth about God and are intolerant of other belief systems. They worked for centuries to crush paganism and they see animist peoples as heathens needing conversion, enslavement, or death. When Christianity became the state religion of the Roman Empire in the 4th century CE, pagan religions were banned and the temples were forcibly closed. Christian mobs killed priests, smashed art, and burned books that would remind people of the Goddess traditions.

Christians claim exclusive moral authority based on the inerrancy and infallibility of the Bible and they deny the existence of the Goddess altogether. Yet the Bible shows that the Goddess does exist and the heretical Gnostic Christians knew her. The Goddess has a different moral code than monotheistic priests on matters of sex, sacred plants, and death. For centuries her followers have been persecuted as witches, whores, and homosexuals.

Shakti is the Goddesshead – The Queen

Today we find the Goddess traditions alive and well in India where monotheism never completely took hold. In India, Devi is the Hindu word for goddess and Shakti is the Goddesshead, the supreme creative force of the universe from which all Devi are derived. Hinduism is the oldest of humanity's great religions and the Shakti traditions are one of its original branches. In these ancient and still living traditions it is believed that all is born from Shakti, including the trinity of primary Hindu gods; Brahma, Vishnu, and Shiva, the creator, preserver, and destructor.

The Biblical goddesses Asherah, Astarte, and Anat are directly comparable to the Hindu goddesses Parvati, Durga, and Kali, and are drawn from the same Neolithic roots. This Hindu tridevi, or Triple Goddess, is associated with Shiva and also with the sacred use of cannabis, in traditions that are far older than the biblical Hebrews.

The Devisukta, or Hymn to the Goddess is found in the Rig Veda, the sacred wisdom texts that are the scriptural foundation of Hinduism. The Rig Veda is one of the oldest of all religious texts and dates back to 1500-1200 BCE, a thousand years before the Hebrew Bible.

In the Rig Veda, Devi declares herself Queen, first of those who merit worship. She created the Heaven and the Earth, she brought forth the Heavenly Sky Father, and her home is in the Ocean as Mother.

I am the Queen,
the gatherer-up of treasures,
most thoughtful,
first of those who merit worship.

Thus gods have established me in many places with many homes to enter and abide in.
Through me alone all eat the food that feeds them,
– each man who sees,
breathes,
hears the word outspoken.
They know it not,
yet I reside in the essence of the Universe.
Hear, one and all,
the truth as I declare it.
I, verily,
myself announce and utter the word that gods and men alike shall welcome.
I make the man I love exceedingly mighty,
make him nourished, a sage, and one who knows Brahman.
I bend the bow for Rudra [Shiva],
that his arrow may strike, and slay the hater of devotion.
I rouse and order battle for the people,
I created Earth and Heaven and reside as their Inner Controller.
On the world's summit I bring forth sky the Father:
my home is in the waters,
in the ocean as Mother.
Thence I pervade all existing creatures,
as their Inner Supreme Self,
and manifest them with my body.
I created all worlds at my will,
without any higher being,
and permeate and dwell within them.
The eternal and infinite consciousness is I,
it is my greatness dwelling in everything.

– Devi Sukta, Rigveda 10.125.3 – 10.125.8[2]

2 *The Devi Gita: The Song of the Goddess: A Translation, Annotation, and Commentary,* Cheever Mackenzie Brown, SUNY Press, 1998.

Chapter One

ICE AGE

IO

Long before anyone considered the idea of God, there was nothing other than the great Mother. When early humans emerged in Africa 2,000,000 years ago our distant ancestors lived like all other animals, our awareness was no different from that of a bear, a lion, or a monkey. We lived in nature and we were a part of nature, there was no separation. From the Mother we were born and to the Mother we returned in death.

At some point in time, the ego emerged, "I," the self-aware human mind that first contemplated death, recognized its own mortality, and sought answers to the mysteries of life. We do not know how or why this cognitive leap happened since neither science nor religion has answered this mystery.

Humans developed language, they began telling stories and communicating ideas with one another. They started asking questions about the nature of life. "How was the universe created?" "What happens when I die?" As soon as people began asking these questions they realized they had no answers for them, so they invented stories and mythologies that would help them make sense of the mysteries.

We will never have answers to life's unanswerable questions because the answers lie beyond human comprehension. We are just smart enough to be aware of the mysteries but are unable to resolve them. And for every scientific breakthrough the mysteries remain forever out of reach, like the horizon, and we are eternally plagued by the pain this cognitive dissonance causes us.

Animals have emotions, they feel joy and pain, but they don't spend their time worrying about the ephemeral nature of the cosmos and their role in it, this is the territory of human beings. The human ego and the need for answers to life's mysteries set us apart from the rest of the animal kingdom.

The stories we tell ourselves to answer life's unanswerable questions are the mythologies that form the roots of our cultures and religions. These stories change, and need to change over time, as cultural awareness shifts and the old mythologies cease being serviceable.

Before there was "I," all was "O." "O" is undifferentiated nature, the waters, what the ancients saw as chaos, and today we might call the jungle. Nature is the universal mother, the feminine divine, the mother of us all. "I" is the ego, and from there we created gods in our image. Gods are supernatural, immortal, anthropomorphic, fictional characters that we place in stories and mythologies to help us explain the mysteries of the universe. The gods are poetic allegories that help us to perceive order in the chaos.

"I" was born from "O," the virgin mother of God. Many cultures believe the primordial first mover of creation was feminine, a divine mother, and since she was all alone, she was a virgin. Christians did not invent the idea of the virgin mother of God, they adapted one of humanity's oldest beliefs.

In the Bible, God identified Himself to Moses as "I AM THAT I AM." God is "I" and Goddess is "O." The Earthly Mother was the first goddess and the Heavenly Father was the first god, together they parented all the other gods.

"IO" together forms a cosmic union and appears as a common symbol, the Axis. In 3 dimensions "IO" is like a planetary axis or a gyroscope. We see this symbolism in the Hindu lingam and yoni, the sacred altar that represents the sexual union of Shiva and Shakti and the totality of existence. "IO" is the symbolic union of the Heavenly Father and the Earthly Mother that is the source of all life and creation. Mother and father, yin and yang, order and chaos, spirit and matter, soul and circumstances.

Lingam and Yoni - Axis - IO

Origins of Life

Through the modern sciences of archaeology and geology, we now know much about the origins of human culture and society, including how climate affected our prehistory. We have uncovered ancient human settlements, graves, and artwork. We have found the oldest writing and mythology that goes back to the beginning of civilization, providing us with valuable insight into the beliefs of our ancestors.

200 years ago, most of what we knew of the ancient world came from the Bible. Now we know so much more, including the origins of many Bible stories. We are increasingly able to discern the biblical history from the legend, understanding the natural forces behind some of the more fantastic tales like the flood of Noah. We should never be over-confident about science though – the more we learn the more we realize how little we know.

Life has existed on Earth for millions of years and has been all but wiped out repeatedly by apocalyptic disasters; decimated by volcanic eruptions, earthquakes, tsunamis, disease, and the impacts of objects from space. An asteroid impact 65 million years ago is believed to have killed ¾'s of life on Earth, including the mighty dinosaurs. Scientists believe there were at least 5 such mass extinction events in primordial times, and humanity has been decimated a few times too more recently. We have learned all of this only in the last century or so; in 1820 people would have thought all these notions quite fanciful.

It is paradoxical that in the beginning, life on Earth may have originated with an extraterrestrial impact. A comet crashing into the ocean carrying the seeds of life. Biologists believe that life on Earth began in the ocean and this process may have repeated a few times. A comet crashing into land may decimate life on Earth, while a similar comet falling into the ocean may create life. There were multiple bloomings of primeval life on Earth and multiple catastrophes as well. The forces of creation are also the forces of destruction, cycling over and over again.

The Bull of Heaven mating with Mother Earth

Sumerian Creation Poem

One of the earliest creation myths is a 5,000-year-old poem from Sumer that graphically describes the Heavenly Father mating with Mother Earth and bringing forth life. The story is a perfect metaphor for a comet carrying the seeds of life impregnating the ocean, the womb of Gaia.

Smooth, big Earth made herself resplendent, beautified her body joyously,
wide Earth bedecked her body with precious metal and lapis lazuli,
adorned herself with diorite, chalcedony, and shiny carnelian.
Heaven arrayed himself in a wig of verdure, stood up in Princeship,
Holy Earth, the Virgin, beautified herself for Holy Heaven,
Heaven, the lofty god, planted his knees on wide Earth,
Poured the semen of the heroes Tree and Reed into her womb,
sweet Earth, the fecund cow, was impregnated with the rich semen of Heaven,
joyfully did Earth tend to the giving birth of the plants of life,
luxuriantly did Earth bear the rich produce, did she exude wine and honey.[1]

Ice Age Climate

The Earth's climate cycles through long ice ages that last around 150,000 years, separated by warm interglacial periods of around 15-20,000 years. The last Ice Age reached its maximum 21,000 years ago. A large ice cap glacier, about 2 miles high, extended from the north pole down across North America as far south as New York City. Likewise, much of Northern Europe was covered by the Greenland ice sheet.

During the Ice Age, global temperatures were about 9 degrees colder and sea levels were 410 feet lower than they are today, with vast amounts of water trapped in the ice. The world's coastlines went miles farther out, the Philippines and the British Islands were connected to the mainland, there was a land connection from Asia to North America across the Bering Strait, and the Persian Gulf was nothing but a river.

Primitive human beings (Homo sapiens) and other similar hominids like Neanderthal lived primarily in Africa where it was warm. Homo sapiens migrated out of Ethiopia in waves beginning around 60,000 years ago. They followed pathways from Egypt through the Levant, spreading across Eurasia to the edge of the ice sheets and eventually making their way into the Americas.

These humans lived as hunter-gatherers in small nomadic clans anchored by mothers and followed animal migrations. They used simple stone tools and spears for hunting large animals, managed fire, and cooked foods like meat and simple bread. We call this long period of human history, the Paleolithic, or the Stone Age. We find the earliest examples of human artistic expression and spirituality in this era, in cave paintings dating back over 40,000 years, ritual burials, and ubiquitous Venus figurines demonstrating the antiquity of Goddess worship.

Venus of Hohle Fels

1 *History Begins at Sumer*, Samuel Noah Kramer, UPenn Press, 1956, p.303

Religion

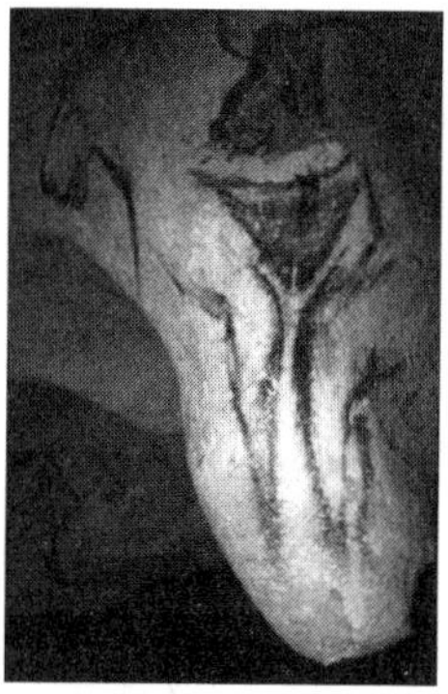
Venus, Chauvet Cave

Paleolithic cave paintings depict animals, hunting, and geometric art; they have been found in hundreds of sites in France, Germany, Indonesia, and in the Americas as well. The cave represents the Mother's womb and a return to the spiritual birth chamber deep in the Earth. Deep down in these dark caves that must have felt like graves, humans worshipped, made art, went on vision quests, and performed cycle of life ceremonies where they experienced their own spiritual rebirth.

On the walls they painted the animals they hunted as a sign of respect and reverence. These people revered the animals in hopes that the animals would thrive so that the humans that depended on them would thrive as well. It was important to ritually confirm the cycle of life so that the animals hunted would be renewed alongside the human spirit, who felt the need to atone for the life taken.

The earliest rituals we know of appear to have been the burying of the dead. The careful arrangements of the corpse, buried with personal possessions and symbolic totems, indicates a thoughtful and heartfelt experience where the living honor the fallen and also confront their own inevitable mortality.

Paleolithic people displayed a form of proto-animism where humans saw themselves as thoroughly a part of nature. They gradually developed the idea of a great Earth mother we were all born from and return to when we die. Animism is the general term for the spirituality and cosmology of indigenous people who believe that humans are a part of nature and that all the animals are brothers and sisters of humans. Animists believe that the invisible spirit world interacts seamlessly with the material world.

Shamans are the spiritual leaders among animists and were the original priests back in the Paleolithic. Shamans are teachers, messengers, and healers; they use a variety of methods to break down the barriers between the material and spirit worlds to bring back visions and messages. Shamanistic methods may include the use of entheogenic plant drugs we now call psychedelics, trances, ecstatic dance, and even states today considered mental illness like seizures or schizophrenia, to close the divide with the spirit world. Gender-bending that bridges the gap between male and female was also commonly considered a trait that brought mystical insights to shamans.

Venus

Paleolithic people made small votive statues known as Venus figurines that are among the most common archaeological finds from the Ice Age. Thousands of Venus figurines have been found across a wide expanse of Eurasia; made from clay, stone, and bone, these statues typically depict a female figure with large breasts and wide hips.

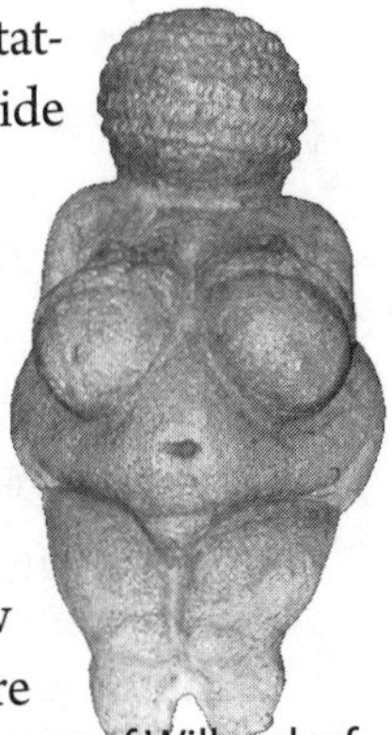

Venus of Willendorf

The famous Venus of Willendorf found in the Danube River valley in Austria is thought to be 30,000 years old, and other figurines are even older. The Venus figurines were made for tens of thousands of years and were still being made by the Biblical Canaanites in the first millennium BCE. These figurines are almost exclusively female, the few statues that depict males seem to be mostly shamans and are often presented as half-man, half-animal.

The implications of these ubiquitous Venus statues are that they represent the oldest human spiritual belief and religion, worship of the Goddess, the Earthly Mother. We can only make inferences since there is no written language from the Paleolithic, but the consistency with which the female is venerated, with no male equals, makes a strong case that the dominant spiritual belief was Goddess worship for tens of thousands of years, perhaps even a monotheism of the universal Mother.

William Blake Richmond, Venus and Anchises

Chapter Two

YOUNGER DRYAS EXTINCTION

21,000 years ago, the Earth began warming and the glaciers melted, forming glacial lakes and inland freshwater seas. This gradual warming was suddenly plunged into reverse in a series of abrupt coolings. 12,800 years ago, global temperatures dropped 4 degrees in a decade and remained cold for 1200 years. And then just as suddenly, temperatures reversed again and quickly climbed 10 degrees to the range we are in now. This period of extreme climate change is known as the Younger Dryas.

It is not known what caused these dramatic turns of events, but comet strikes into the North American ice sheets have been suggested, perhaps multiple strikes over centuries from a large comet that broke into pieces while orbiting through the solar system. A second strike into the ocean may have ejected vast amounts of water vapor into the atmosphere raising global temperatures permanently.

The Younger Dryas was a mass extinction event, most of the large animal species around the world died off and humans were devastated as well. The human population dropped from millions down to tens of thousands. The woolly mammoth, saber-toothed tiger, giant sloth, and many other large animal species that had lived alongside humans went completely extinct. The Clovis people who lived across North America disappeared. It was an apocalypse that nearly wiped us all out, proving

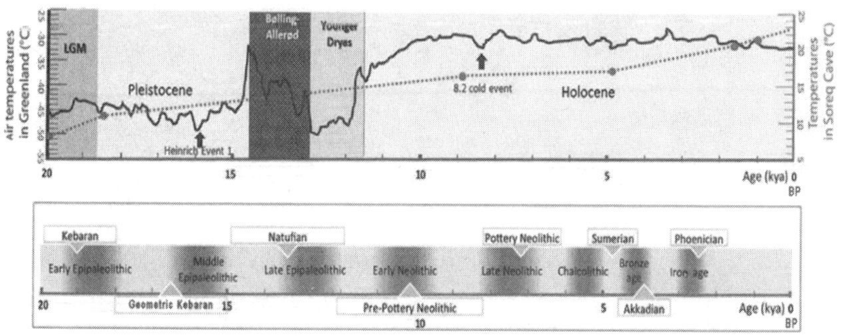

History of global temperatures showing the Younger Dryas period.[1]

1 Credit: Climate and Post-Glacial expansion in the Near East By Daniel E. Platt, Marc Haber, Magda Bou Dagher-Kharrat, Bouchra Douaihy, Georges Khazen, Maziar Ashrafian Bonab, Angélique Salloum, et al.

that humans are not separate from nature, we are a part of it. We do not know exactly what happened or how the human survivors got through the calamity, but the weather may have been violently terrible for centuries, forcing people to extremes to survive.

Glacial meltwater made its way into the oceans where it caused sea levels to rise, but not in a steady, predictable fashion. Geologists have found evidence of massive pulses of meltwater, as though great inland seas suddenly burst their ice dams, generating torrential flooding rivers that tore across entire continents leaving geological scars in the landscape.

Across North America, there is geological evidence of enormous ancient rivers flowing hundreds of miles out to sea and giant cascading waterfalls that dwarf Niagara Falls for size. The meltwater pulses were catastrophic, raising sea levels 40 feet in a 24-hour period on more than one occasion and leaving coastal communities permanently under the seas.

These epic, planetary floods are the source of the oldest tales of mythology, Noah's Ark in the Bible, Manu of the Hindu Vedas, and Utnapishtim from the Mesopotamian Epic of Gilgamesh, among many others. In all these ancient stories, the heroes and their families were the sole survivors of a great flood that wiped out humanity and from whom the entire human race was reborn.

It is not hard to imagine why our ancient ancestors preserved these legendary stories; it is because they tell us about events that truly happened. Humans were nearly wiped out by floods beyond imaging and violent weather that must have felt like angry gods seeking their destruction. We have no idea of how bad life was during the Younger Dryas but the indications are that it was a centuries-long cataclysm with relatively few survivors. When the climate finally improved it was a whole new era for humanity.

The Flood by Léon Comerre

Chapter Three

NEOLITHIC AGE

The Earth warmed rapidly after the Younger Dryas and around 10,000 years ago temperatures and sea levels stabilized into the range we live in today. We call this era of stable climate the Holocene period. The survivors of the cataclysms began to do something new – they learned to plant seeds and harvest crops, establishing surpluses of food that allowed them to survive lean times.

This was the Neolithic Revolution, the end of the Stone Age, and the beginning of agriculture and animal husbandry. Planting led to the first settled communities, which eventually grew into the first cities, while shepherds following animal migration patterns established the first trade routes between settlements.

The Neolithic Revolution that brought us agriculture was the greatest technological breakthrough since the harnessing of fire a million years earlier and fundamentally changed the material status of humanity. The survivors of the Younger Dryas cataclysms had learned to collect seeds and intentionally grow plants for harvest, rather than just relying on what they could gather. With the advent of agriculture, humans established the first permanent settlements that would steadily become more complex societies, and eventually cities and states.

Agriculture first took root in settlements throughout the Fertile Crescent, a horseshoe-shaped territory of the Near East stretching from the shores of the Mediterranean in the Levant, up through Anatolia (modern-day Turkey), across Persia, and down to the Persian Gulf. Notable early Neolithic settlements include Jericho in Canaan, which was inhabited for around 7,000 years before its appearance in the Bible,

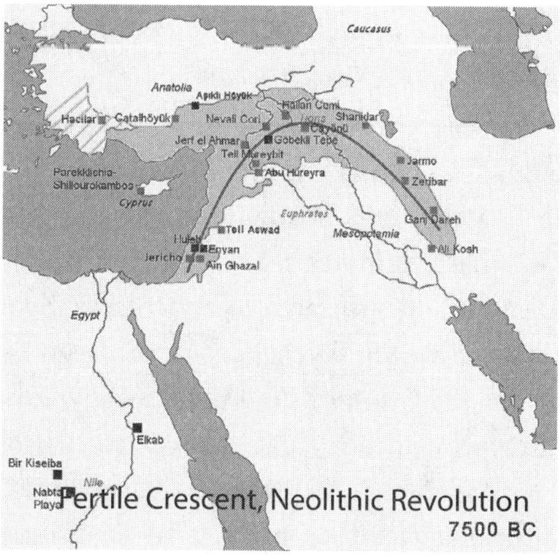

Göbekli Tepe in Anatolia which has the oldest known astronomical temple, and Çatal Hüyük which is one of the best-preserved towns from the era.

Planting and settlements radically transformed day-to-day life compared to living as hunter-gatherers as humans had done for hundreds of thousands of years. Nomadic hunter-gatherers follow available food supplies, never taking more than Mother Earth provides, and not necessarily working very hard. As nomads, they had few possessions, nothing more than they could carry, just a few tools like spears for hunting and fishing, and simple implements to thrash plants for fruits, nuts, seeds, and fiber.

The hunter-gatherers had no surplus stores of food but simply wandered with confidence that bountiful nature would provide their daily needs. This existence sees humans as undifferentiated from nature, and they made little attempt to shape the land to their needs. If the weather turned inhospitable or food and water became difficult to find, then the hunter-gatherers had little margin for survival other than to keep moving in hopes of finding better conditions.

With the Neolithic Revolution and the emergence of agriculture, humans acquired surplus stores of food that allowed them to survive periods of drought and hardship and enabled substantial population growth. As any modern farmer will tell you, working the land by tilling, planting, and irrigating is exceedingly hard work and prone to catastrophe from droughts, disease, or loss of soil fertility.

These agricultural settlements both enabled and required people to specialize their skills and work together to provide for the common good. While some people were busy planting and harvesting, others were managing the storehouses or making crafts. People developed crafts in weaving, basket making, pottery, leatherwork, jewelry, and carving in wood, bone, and stone. Neolithic people also began to trade in crafts and raw materials from distant lands.

Catal Huyuk

Çatal Hüyük is a famous archeological site in Anatolia, it is one of the best examples of a settlement that dates back to the early Neolithic Revolution and the dawn of agriculture. Scholars believe Çatal Hüyük was first established 9500 years ago at the beginning of the Neolithic and occupied for nearly two thousand years by upwards of 8000 people. The people there grew wheat, barley, flax, peas, cannabis, flax, and they domesticated cattle.

At Çatal Hüyük, we find the seeds of civilization that came with the advent of agriculture and settled communities. We find some of the earliest examples of formal religion with complex symbolism and mythology, the birth of architecture and urban planning, flourishing trade and imports of raw materials, and an economy tied to advanced practices in agriculture and stockbreeding.

Çatal Hüyük and other Neolithic settlements show every sign of being egalitarian societies where women were treated with respect as equals to men. There are no signs of dominance, warfare, weapons, or established social hierarchies that would emerge later and that we take for granted today.

No writing has been recovered from Çatal Hüyük that details their beliefs, but we can see from their burial practices that men and women held equal social status. Men and women were buried with equal respect and appear to have had the same diets and health. There were no distinctions based on gender in how the dead were treated or in the apparent quality of their lives. It is a common misconception to label these cultures as *matriarchal* or dominated by women. There is no evidence that women dominated men, but instead that men and women were treated equally and behaved cooperatively.

At Çatal Hüyük, they displayed a sophisticated culture rooted in Goddess worship. Vivid murals and female figurines along with shrines to goddesses were found throughout the settlement. Their art was rich with religious symbols and complex patterns of rituals and divine commandments. The common use of Venus figurines was a direct cultural continuation of the Paleolithic spiritual practices. There were relatively few images of men, but images of bulls, vultures, snakes, and male phalluses proliferated.

The Earth was the center of their spiritual worldview. Their homes were built from mud brick and rose out of the ground, and they buried their dead underneath the floors of their homes. They had unusual burial practices by modern standards. The dead were left outside in the sun to be picked over by vultures until the bones were clean and left to bake in the sun. The bones were then collected and folded into a fetal position and wrapped in a cloth, then buried underneath the home so that they were in close proximity to their family forever.

There is no ego present in the art or ritual of Çatal Hüyük, all the art reflects the cycles of life and sacred animals. There were no lavish tombs or monuments to individuals, no steles celebrating great victories or kings, just simple burials with a few personal possessions. Their artwork prominently featured images of vultures eating humans. These constant ruminations on and acceptance of death, reflect a lack of individualism and personal ego and a sense of the continuity of life through the cycles of death and rebirth.

The bull was a sacred animal; cattle heads and horns were prominent decorations hung on the walls in sacred spaces. One image on a chapel wall shows the Goddess giving birth to a bull. The bull has remained one of humanity's primary religious symbols and has its roots with the first Neolithic shepherds.

Prehistoric cattle cults are well attested in Egypt and India and we see the traditions continue to this day in Hinduism, where cattle are venerated and protected, as well as in the native African Mundari tribal people from South Sudan whose roots go back to antiquity. The Bull of Heaven appears in many myths and was a manifestation of this archetypal symbol that goes back to the dawn of the Neolithic.

The Seated Goddess

Many Venus figurines have been found at Çatal Hüyük, and they typically feature an older, full-figured woman, with rolls of fat and sagging breasts. This indicates that the women portrayed were not young, but were elders who had accumulated years of wisdom. Some of the figures superimpose a skeleton on the fat woman, again indicating the cycle of life, death, and rebirth. The figurines are found all over the site, sometimes they were buried ritually, or placed in a grain bin where they may have served as protective spirits, and other times they were found broken in trash piles.

Seated Goddess of Catal Huyuk

Cybele in Rome 6000 years later

One of the most striking Venus figurines found at Çatal Hüyük is called the "Seated Goddess," it features a plump and well-endowed female sitting on a throne flanked by two lions. Lions were a common symbol of Goddess worship. The image of the Goddess on a throne flanked by a pair of lions would continue to be worshipped into Roman times as the Mother Goddess Cybele, a practice already 6000 years old when it was imported into Rome from Anatolia.

We know much about the ritual practices in later civilizations, and we can project backward into the Neolithic where we see similar symbols and artistic motifs being used.

Goddess symbolism was among the most common, along with bulls and snakes, that is seen in the early Neolithic settlements. We can make inferences about these early cultural belief systems based on what we know those symbols meant later once writing emerged that explained them. Goddesses dominated the Neolithic cosmology and would be slowly and steadily replaced when civilization and militarism emerged thousands of years later.

Goddesses most importantly symbolize the cycles of life, death, and rebirth and were, of course, valued as nurturing mothers. Goddesses embodied nature, the turning of the seasons, and the springtime renewal of vegetation. Goddesses brought wisdom and were widely credited with bringing the gifts of agriculture, planting, and harvesting. In nearly all areas, female deities were valued as healers and dispensers of medicines derived from herbs, plants, and roots. Women were midwives who brought children into the world, and served hospice, holding the hands of the dying. The weaving of fabrics was women's work and a quintessential activity of Goddess worship. Goddesses brought writing, poetry, and were central to music and the arts, as well as mathematics. Later on, after the emergence of warfare, warrior maidens would become another powerful symbol of the Goddess and a reality in some cultures.

The oldest scrap of fabric ever identified was found at Çatal Hüyük in 2013.[1] The 9,000-year-old piece of fabric made of hemp woven with linen was used to wrap the corpse of a baby. Hemp was commonly used throughout history in many cultures to wrap corpses and newborns.

Sacred weaving was practiced in goddess temples through all of ancient history as well as being done at home by women. Weaving was a repetitive and ritualistic act that is a metaphor for the structure of the universe. Weaving involves the binding of pairs of opposites. The warp and the weft threads, one vertical and taught, the other horizontal and loose, are bound together to form fabric. Without these contrasting pairs no fabric can be created, there is just thread and the potential for wholeness. To create material reality these opposite pairs must be bound together like yin and yang, or God and Goddess.

The ancient goddess cults were noted for their open sexuality and drug use. Sex was seen as unequivocally good and was celebrated, not shamed as it is in monotheistic traditions. Ritual sex confirmed the fertility of nature and physical pleasure represented the blessings of the Goddess. It

1 *Hürriyet Daily News*, Centuries-old fabric found in Çatalhöyük, Feb 3, 2014, Dogan News Agency. https://www.hurriyetdailynews.com/centuries-old-fabric-found-in-catalhoyuk-61883

was believed that sex is the source of life and creation, and since life begets life, more sex was good and brought forth more life and vegetation. In their worldview, the more sex the better, and the entire culture could not be having enough sex since it helped the flowers grow. Sexual pleasure meant the Goddess was bestowing her blessings upon you.

These cultures were matrilineal and tracked bloodlines through the mother, so the source of the father's seed did not matter and women's sex lives did not need to be controlled. Women understood their reproductive cycles which are in sync with lunar cycles. They knew when they were fertile and when it was safe to have sex without getting pregnant by tracking the moon.

Goddess worship was centered on nature and they embraced the use of plant entheogens to commune with nature. Entheogenic plants like cannabis, opium poppies, ephedra, mandrake, belladonna, and psychedelic mushrooms such as amanita muscaria and psilocybin, all grew throughout the Fertile Crescent and temples had fully stocked apothecaries of plant drugs for medicine and religion. Worshippers used intoxication and ecstatic dance, music, song, and feasts to celebrate nature and the cycles of life. Hemp thrives in Anatolia and the region is a primary example of how Goddess worship was strongest in the areas where cannabis grew the thickest, a rule that has persisted into the modern-day.

The Dionysian cults with their ritual intoxication and orgiastic sex as well as the Mystery religions probing the cycles of life would later emerge from this region and their roots can be seen early in the Neolithic. At places like Çatal Hüyük, there are many images of men's erect penises, symbolism that would remain common in the Mystery religions and goddess cults in Greek and Roman times. The Roman cult of the mother goddess Cybele was imported from Anatolia and was famous (even scandalous) for its ecstatic, intoxicated, and orgiastic celebrations.

Farmers and Shepherds

Farmers and shepherds represented separate Neolithic communities and they were important symbols in mythology. Farmers were the people living in the settled towns while the shepherds were the nomadic traders following animal migratory patterns. The farmers were worshippers of Mother Earth who brought them bountiful harvests while the shepherds worshipped the Heavenly Father who inhabited the sky.

These two Neolithic communities came together to form Bronze Age civilizations and we know from mythology like the Biblical Cain and Abel story that they did not always get along. Cain was a farmer making offerings of vegetables while Abel was a shepherd making offerings of meat and they had a famous conflict, the first murder.

The Sumerians told stories about farmers and shepherds competing for the love of the goddess Inanna. Inanna's decision to shift her love from the farmer to the newly arrived shepherd symbolized the moment when the shepherds became the kings of Sumer.

The farmers established the first settled communities and towns, which eventually became the first cities. These farming communities, like Çatal Hüyük, were egalitarian and matrilineal; women held leadership roles and were respected as equal to men. They were Goddess-worshipping cultures focused on reproductive cycles of life and modern scholarship describes their religion as fertility cults.

In these farmer communities, family lines were tracked through the mothers. Paternity was not recognized and children were raised communally with no regard to the identity of biological fathers. Mothers chose a social father for her children who might be her brother or other tribal kinsmen. Some cultures practiced sacred prostitution, and the women were encouraged to mate with foreign men to help keep the community's gene pool fresh.

The nomadic shepherds on the other hand raised their families in small, enclosed clans led by the father. The patriarchal shepherd fathers were able to raise their daughters like cattle and practice paternity by controlling their sex lives. In order to pass inheritance from father to son it is crucial to be certain of the identity of a child's biological father, and that means restricting women's sex lives to approved partners only. Marriages were arranged by fathers to promote inter-clan loyalties while in matrilineal communities it did not matter who women's sexual partners were.

Shepherd beliefs focused on the Heavenly Father rather than on the Earthly Mother – they were not farmers concerned with plant growth and the turning of the seasons. The shepherds lived out in the open spaces where they could watch the sky and contemplate the creator of the universe. We see this symbolism in the Bible. The Semitic Hebrews were shepherds and rivals of the Canaanite farmer Goddess worshippers, such as the community in Jericho.

Later, Christians continued the symbolism and commonly refer to themselves as shepherds. As nomadic traders, the shepherds would become the ones to take up weapons and begin raiding the settlements. And as they became warriors, the shepherds came to focus their worship on storm gods, whose thunder and lightning was associated with victory in battle. We know the later pagan storm gods like Zeus, Baal, Indra, Thor, Marduk, and others.

Scholars find evidence of cultural mixing through the study of languages and how they changed over time. There were two broad groups of shepherding people who came in from the outside and joined the settlements, either by invitation or by conquest, and contributed to them developing into robust civilizations.

The first group came from the south around 3000 BCE and spoke Semitic languages; they were shepherding people from around the fertile crescent and Arabian Peninsula whose descendants would eventually become the Hebrews, Arabs, and other Middle Eastern people. Semitic people played an active role in Mesopotamia from the first days of civilization.

The second broad group was the Indo-Aryans who came around 2000 BCE from the north and spoke Indo-European languages. They came in a series of migrations over a thousand years and brought the Sanskrit language to Persia and India. The Indo-Aryans are credited with writing the Vedas around 1500 BCE, the oldest sacred texts of Indian Hinduism, and which were also influential in Persia.

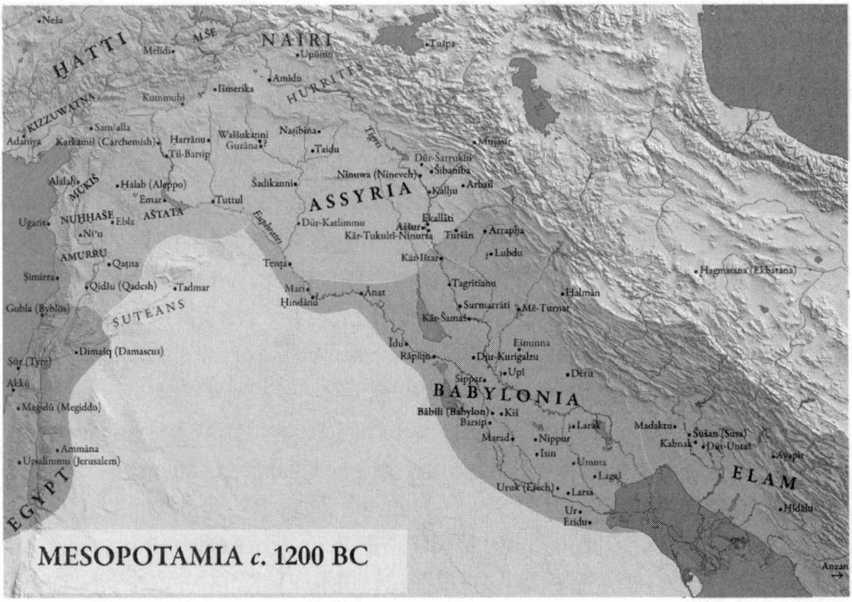

MESOPOTAMIA *c.* 1200 BC

Chapter Four

CANNABIS AND THE GREAT MOTHER

There is an unbroken thread of history that links cannabis and humans all the way back to the Ice Age and cannabis was among the first plants cultivated in the Fertile Crescent at the dawn of the Neolithic Revolution. Cannabis has big, pronounced seeds and easy to recognize fertilization patterns and it may have been the plant that sparked agriculture. Cannabis produces the greatest diversity of products of any plant found in nature and is truly unique in its relationship to humans; providing food, fiber, and medicine. The plant has had an intimate and mutually beneficial relationship with humans and was integral in the establishment of civilization. Humans have been primarily responsible for spreading cannabis around the world, and the plant aided humans in the effort.

Humans initially encountered cannabis in its central Asian homeland during the Ice Age and it was transported back along the migratory pathway into the Levant and Egypt, east into China, and west into Europe. Evidence for the earliest simple weaving of hemp fibers goes back deep into the Paleolithic[1] around the same time as the Venus figurines and cave paintings. Hemp and linen from flax were the first plants cultivated for fibers; linen is finer and more suitable for comfortable clothes while hemp is stronger and used for canvas, sackcloth, lines, nets, and ropes. Finer strands of hemp, particularly from the male plants, are indistinguishable from linen and the fibers were commonly blended together.

Hemp

Cannabis provides the longest and strongest natural fibers; giving hemp a unique role as a primary industrial material through all of

1 Clarke, Robert Connell, and Mark David Merlin. *Cannabis: Evolution and Ethnobotany.* University of California Press, 2013

civilized history in Europe and Asia. Hemp was a common and strategically critical commodity with a thousand everyday uses. Hemp was used to make the ropes that hauled the stones for virtually every ancient temple and road, to bring oxen and horses to heel, for nets to snare fish and game, bowstrings to launch arrows, material for every wooden ship that ever sailed, canvas for awnings and tents, sheets, napkins, and tablecloths, as well as paper for nearly every book ever printed, it was the fabric that wrapped the newborn and the corpse, and the hangman's noose that brought criminals to justice. Hemp was the first crop specifically cultivated for military purposes as it was needed for bowstrings, and later, shipbuilding. Without hemp, civilization as we know it never would have come into being. Hemp's strategic importance only ended with the Industrial Revolution 200 years ago, which sent the fiber's use into decline.

There are distinct varieties of cannabis that produce either fiber or drugs. Hemp varieties are known as *Cannabis Sativa* and are native to the northern latitudes of Europe and China. The drug varieties are little used for fiber and are known traditionally as *Cannabis Indica;* they come from the southern tropical latitudes in India, the Near East, and Africa. Debate raged for centuries among botanists as to whether cannabis should be considered one species or more because of its incredible diversity of attributes.

Spread of Cannabis

It is in the Paleolithic that we find the first speculative evidence of the human use of cannabis. Clay fragments around 26,000 years old found in Czechoslovakia bear the impression of woven textiles pressed into the clay, those textiles were either hemp or nettles, both of which grew in the area and were used as prehistoric fibers[2]. The oldest definitive archaeological evidence of cannabis use as a fiber is around 9,000 years ago at Çatal Hüyük in Turkey, where hemp was actively cultivated in antiquity and has continued to the present day. Hemp fibers and fabrics have been found in hundreds of Neolithic graves, mostly in China. Hemp cord impressed pottery 12,000 years old has been found in Taiwan and the south coast of China in early postglacial fishing settlements.[3]

Nomadic hunter-gatherers routinely investigated plants in search of food and medicine and would have quickly noticed the cannabis plant's pungent aroma and nutritious seeds. As humans came out of Africa and migrated into central Asia and beyond, cannabis became intertwined with them, carried back along the pathway thru the Near East into Africa, and carried for-

2 Gravettian culture, earliest impression of plant-fiber cordage. Clarke and Merlin p.65.
3 *Cannabis: Evolution and Ethnobotany* by Clarke and Merlin, p.65

ward through the Far East and Europe. Cannabis likes fertile, well-drained soil and lots of sun and water. Cannabis thrives on river banks and human dump heaps and the plant effectively followed people wherever they went, becoming native everywhere the conditions were favorable.

Animals like cannabis too and most mammals respond to cannabis medicinally. Horses are from central Asia and they helped spread cannabis seeds when they ate the plant. Horses, elephants, dogs, and other animals will graze on wild cannabis which has anti-inflammatory and analgesic effects. Cannabis is a proven painkiller for animals with a long tradition in veterinary medicine.

Birds may have done the most to spread cannabis besides humans. All sweetly singing birds, especially doves, love hemp seeds which they carried and dropped all over Eurasia. Up until cannabis prohibition in the past century, hemp seeds were the number one item in commercial bird seed mixes, and birdseed retailers were among the few voices to oppose modern hemp prohibition. Hemp seeds help to bring the feathers back and brighten their luster, and most importantly it improves their singing.[4]

5000 years ago, cannabis was already well established with humans and was utilized from the start in all the original Eurasian civilizations; Mesopotamia, China, India, and Egypt. Cannabis came to the Americas with the European colonists 500 years ago; it was not in the Americas before then. Cannabis Sativa hemp varieties grew across Russia and central Europe into Germany and Scandinavia in the Neolithic, eventually spreading through France and Western Europe. Chinese hemp was cultivated across the far east including Korea and Japan. Broad-leaf Afghan hashish types grew along the southern slope of the Himalayan mountains from the Hindu Kush west across Afghanistan and east along the Tibetan Plateau and beyond. Narrow-leaf Cannabis Indica ganja types thrived in India and spread into the tropical lowlands of southeast Asia. Cannabis Indica grew across Persia and Lebanon where it followed the fertile crescent into Egypt and south through Africa.

The central region around Anatolia and the Black Sea was home to cannabis production for both fiber and drugs throughout ancient times. Cannabis is found all along the ancient Silk Road trade routes that travel east-west from China all the way to Europe and down through the Levant into Africa. Hemp ropes and fiber goods were objects of trade from the north into the south since the earliest times, and once hashish became

4 1937 Congressional Hearings on the Marihuana Tax Act, H.R. 6385, Statement of Raymond G. Scarlett, April 30,1937. http://www.druglibrary.org/schaffer/hemp/taxact/scarlett.htm

available it was traded as well. Cannabis was widely dispersed and commonly used for a thousand everyday purposes; ropes, fabrics, and medicines, and it was deeply rooted in human religion and ritual, and once established in a region cannabis remained there permanently.

Female and Male

Cannabis is one of the few plants with distinct male and female plants that must fertilize one another. The female plant is the superior of the two, but both are needed to continue the cycle of life. Only the female plants produce the intoxicating, medicinal resins, and the female plant produces longer and stronger fibers. Fibers from the male plants are softer and more supple and are used for linens, often blended with flax, while the female fibers are used for strong ropes. It has long been understood that removing the male plants before they are allowed to fertilize the females enables the virgin females to grow more robustly. By not diverting any precious energy to seed production the females produce even more potent medicine and stronger fibers, today we call these unfertilized females, sinsemilla, "without seeds".

Cannabis is only modestly psychoactive when consumed raw but it is still medicinal, and for paleolithic people sensitive to plant medicine the effects would have been noticeable. Humans and animals alike benefit from the anti-inflammatory and analgesic effects from eating fresh cannabis, it reduces pain in arthritic joints, it is a muscle relaxant, and is an antiemetic that soothes an upset stomach. Cannabis may have been used for all of these purposes by Paleolithic shamans and healers, and they may have burned it in caves when they made art for intoxication and inspiration.

Cannabis must be heated (decarboxylated) to fully activate its psychoactive potential, when it is eaten raw it does not generate the "high" feeling. When cannabis is burned in a fire, the smoke is psychoactive and when breathed in the effects are felt immediately. The oils can be extracted from the plant into a variety of mediums including animal fats, butter, and milk, all of which were available in the Neolithic.

Simple, yet potent medicines could be made in the earliest days of the Neolithic by cooking cannabis in animal fats and milk as the oily resins are fat-soluble. Cannabis undergoes a remarkable transformation once it has been cooked, unleashing intoxicating properties that can be very intense. Women especially benefit from these medicines as they are particularly useful for reproductive health, they can be taken vaginally to treat painful menstruation, easing contractions during childbirth, and serving as an aphrodisiac and sexual aid. These early recipes were among the first magic potions made by village wise women and midwives and they continue to be effective today.

Shamans and medicine makers used the drugs from cannabis flowers for practical and ritual purposes. Cannabis and other entheogens played important roles in shamanistic ceremonies and Goddess worshipping traditions that connect people to nature and the cycles of life. Ritual intoxication opens pathways to the spirit world and the divine, traditions that are countless thousands of years old.

Cannabis resins can also be absorbed into alcohol, and wine was a common base for mixing medicines and drug cocktails in the ancient world. These drug cocktails were known in the Bible as "strong drink." Intoxicating cannabis confections were commonly eaten and drunk in the ancient world, though the recipes were known under many names and the ingredients are not always clear. Ointments applied externally on the skin were used for pain relief and medicine

Ganja, Charas, Hashish, Bhang

Cannabis drugs come in a variety of forms, and while these terms are fluid, they are suitable for our purposes. Ganja (aka marijuana) is the dried, mature female flowers, cured ganja can be burned in a fire to make intoxicating smoke or cooked and eaten. Charas is the potent resins, collected by rubbing the live plants by hand until a waxy ball is formed. Charas is more concentrated than ganja, but the primitive collection methods lead to dirt and other contaminants getting in. Charas is a simple method available in the Neolithic and has unknown origins.

Superior to charas is hashish which requires more specialized methods that came along later. Hashish is made by rubbing the dried flowers against a silkscreen to separate the resins from the flower. Silk comes from China and was in production 5000 years ago, so the earliest possible dates for hashish go way back in time, though we do not know specifically when it was invented. To make hashish successfully, the flowers must remain cool so the resin never melts. For this reason, hashish is typically made high up in the mountains and it has its origins in Afghanistan. Charas is made in warm areas where the melted resins drip all over the plant.

Cannabis excretes its resin in the form of tiny glandular trichomes that look like mushrooms with a head and a stalk. These trichomes can be broken off from the flower and will hold their form as long as they are kept cool and don't melt. Once collected, the trichome dust is pressed tightly together into a waxy ball, hashish, that can retain its potency for years, making it suitable for the ancient overland spice trade. Hashish was commonly made into sweets and delicacies called majoons, sometimes including other drugs, and was typically eaten in the ancient world.

Charas and hashish have additional uses as incense. The resinous lumps burn and smolder slowly, producing a steady column of intoxicating smoke. Hashish can also be blended with other common ingredients that went into ancient incense like frankincense and myrrh. Incense comes in many varieties and was used in temples for sacred rites throughout the ancient world. Hashish and myrrh look similar and can be mixed, and myrrh was sometimes used as an adulterant for hashish. Both have medicinal uses and were combined in wine, along with other drugs like opium and ephedra in ancient medical texts. Likewise, hashish and opium look similar and were commonly used side by side since ancient times.

Bhang is the sacred cannabis milk drink from India and Persia whose origins are lost in the fog of history thousands of years ago. Bhang is a common intoxicating beverage in India that is used to this day in Hindu festivals, offerings, and rituals, it is poured over the lingam in offerings to Shiva and Shakti. Many scholars regard bhang as the basis for *soma,* the mysterious sacred intoxicating beverage of ancient Persia, though the definition of soma is not clear and may refer to a variety of beverages depending on the text.

Eve

It is women, it is Eve, that had the strongest relationship with cannabis, it is women that did the planting and weaving, staying close to home with the children while the men went out hunting and defending the tribe. Even if cannabis was not the very first plant cultivated we know it was among the first, and it is easy to see why cannabis would have been held sacred in Neolithic Goddess worshipping religions. Every aspect of women's roles and sacred duties can be seen in the use of cannabis; planting, weaving, midwifery, making medicine, potions, and incense. Hemp may have been the first fiber woven into fabric and hemp products were always important, particularly in the cultures where weaving was sacred. Cannabis use as sacred incense in temples is well documented and it is an intoxicant and aphrodisiac in use by cultures where sacred sex, ecstatic dance, and ritual intoxication were common and ceremonial.

Cannabis is a mystery, she reveals her secrets begrudgingly, and the more we learn of her chemical profile the more we see how wildly complex it is. We still don't know why the northern fiber varieties lost their psychoactivity, was it because of human selection, less sun exposure, or some other reason? We have learned just recently thru modern science that humans, and most living things, have a complex network of receptor sites in the body designed to receive cannabinoids called the endocannabinoid system. Cannabinoids are the dynamic chemicals produced by cannabis that regulate homeostasis, the cellular cycle of life, and which make cannabis a powerful and widely effective medicine.

China

China has a rich history with cannabis going back deep into the Neolithic. The Chinese word for hemp is *Ma*, and it is one of their oldest words. China is primarily a hemp culture though they knew the drugs as well in ancient times. China was known as "the land of mulberry and hemp," mulberry being the plant used to feed silkworms. Ancient Chinese used hemp to clothe the masses, string their bows, build ships, and for the invention of paper. The Chinese even have a goddess of love and healing who is closely associated with cannabis named Magu, the "hemp maiden."

Shen Nung, the near-mythic father of Chinese medicine described hemp as "one of the Superior Elixirs of Immortality." Later, the legendary Chinese surgeon Hua Tuo (141-208 CE) used cannabis drugs to make the first surgical anesthetic.

Shen Nung, father of Chinese medicine

The Chinese describe hemp as the alpha and the omega, the fibers that wrap the newborn and the corpse. Confucian funeral rites for grieving the dead involve many elaborate rituals for the wearing of hemp clothes by mourners. Coarse hemp clothes and sackcloth were worn to show respect and piety, and the dead were commonly buried in them. The tradition of burying the dead in hemp is nearly universal in cultures across Europe and Asia, anywhere where hemp was native.

India

India is the country with the oldest and most profound spiritual traditions around cannabis and provides important confirmation of the Goddess traditions. A proper review of the diverse Hindu traditions and their use of cannabis would require a book unto itself. Hinduism is the only one of the world's modern great religions that has robust goddess worship, a sacred role for cannabis, and sacred sex. Hinduism is also the oldest of today's religions and it predates the Axial Age religions by well over a thousand years. Hinduism has its roots in the time when the ancient Goddess traditions were still thriving and were the most popular among the people with the biggest and most important festivals. We touch on China and India only briefly here because they are outside the Biblical traditions and narrative.

Shiva Grinding Bhang in India

Chapter Five

BRONZE AGE

Bronze

The Neolithic Age lasted from roughly 10,000 years ago to around 5,000 years ago when the Bronze Age revolution occurred. The introduction of bronze was the next great technological revolution after planting, and along with some other developments marks the beginning of civilization. Scattered settlements became organized city-states with distinct professions, trades, and class hierarchies. Regional city-states were linked by common language and culture, and would eventually be brought together by force into military empires.

The invention of bronze, an alloy of 90% copper and 10% tin, was a seminal technology revolution that transformed the way people lived. Copper was common in the Ancient Near East, but it is a soft metal with limited value for tools since it does not hold an edge. The addition of tin during smelting hardens the copper, making it suitable for farm tools like plows and pickaxes, as well as for weapons like swords, axes, and chariots.

The introduction of weapons and farm implements in the Bronze Age changed society every bit as much as the Industrial Revolution did in modern times and it brought an end to the Neolithic Age. Farm tools such as the plow and the pickaxe radically transformed planting and turned it into farming. Planting had traditionally been women's work done close to home with children in tow, but with the plow, farming became men's work. The plow needs to be pulled by large beasts of burden, like oxen, that required strong men to manage, and also opened up larger fields which were farther from home. Tools made farming more efficient which led to greater surpluses, more wealth, and an enhanced ability to trade.

Weapons & Raiders

Greater wealth also encouraged theft from rival peoples, and new weapons like the sword and ax gave confidence to raiding tribes that they could defeat the settled communities, steal their lands and wealth, and force the people into slavery. The threat of raiders in turn led to the establishment of city walls, and permanent armies to defend the settlements. Ultimately, these armies would come to be in near-constant conflict, perpetually probing their opponents' defenses while they attempted to protect their own.

Neolithic agriculture created surpluses for trade and the gradual accumulation of wealth, but the fast track to great wealth in the Bronze Age was to conquer your neighbors, plunder their possessions, and force the defeated people into slavery. With bronze weapons and armies, strong men became the leaders of the communities and physical dominance overtook wisdom as the chief characteristic of leadership. Early Neolithic planting cultures had been egalitarian, with equal respect given to men and women, but the Bronze Age civilizations were patriarchal societies run by kings and their armies. Families were led by their fathers and strong men with weapons were in charge of everyone.

Civilization

Civilized society is a wealthy society; it takes wealth to build temples, roads, and city walls, but the nature of wealth is that it is never spread evenly. There were always rich and poor, and slavery was an institution in most of the ancient urban world. Slavery and forced labor were the backbone of Bronze Age economies, allowing the upper classes to avoid manual labor.

It was the nature of society that armies constantly vied to steal lands and take captives from one another. To be strong was to defeat your enemies and to be weak was to be conquered, there was no middle ground. Where equality and egalitarianism remained in the ancient world is where there was no great material wealth, in poor peasant communities, and in nomadic bands living outside the borders of civilization. In this context, women's rights were steadily degraded over 2500 years until women were finally viewed as inferior appendages of men as told in the Bible and Greek mythology.

Domesticated animals on a Sumerian cylinder seal, 2500 BCE

Chapter Six

HISTORY BEGINS AT SUMER

Civilization as we know it first emerged in Mesopotamia, modern-day Iraq, directly south of Anatolia in the Tigris and Euphrates river valley. Neolithic settlements developed into city-states around 3500 BCE that brought us writing, law, hierarchical society, and a recognizable political organization. The Sumerians were the first culture to break through to the Bronze Age, and for Western civilization, it is where history begins, as described by the pioneering scholar of Sumer, Samuel Noah Kramer.

Other early civilizations emerged in China, India, and Egypt and there was trade and interactions among all of them. These other civilizations were every bit as important and sophisticated as the Mesopotamians. We focus on Mesopotamia in this book because it is the culture that leads directly to the Bible.

There were a series of cultures and empires in ancient Mesopotamia; first came the Sumerians who gave us the earliest writing, followed by the Akkadians who were the world's first military empire. Later, during the period of the Old Testament came the mighty Assyrians, and finally the famous Babylonians (Chaldeans).

There were earlier people in Neolithic Mesopotamia, the Ubaids, who began planting and brought in the first civilizing influences in the area. To the west lies the Syrian desert and the Arabian Peninsula, home of the Semitic nomads. The settled Ubaidians thrived and prospered and the nomadic Semites intermingled and joined their settlements.

We do not know whether these infiltrations came as peaceful immigration or war-like conquering. Either way, the linguistic evidence in Sumerian naming conventions shows Semitic influence from the earliest days. The cross-fertilization of the farmer and shepherd cultures brought about civilization.

Uruk

The first big Mesopotamian cities were Ur and Uruk (Erech), both of which appear in the Bible. The original Biblical patriarch, Abraham, led his family from Ur to the promised land in Canaan. But Uruk was the first truly great city anywhere in the world. Uruk is in southern Sumer on the banks of the Euphrates river, on a channel that has since dried up. The city featured two large streams and numerous canals, at the time the region was quite fertile though today it is an arid desert.

First excavated in 1850, Uruk was found to be 1100 acres surrounded by walls 6 miles (10km) in circumference, and contained two ziggurats and several temples. Uruk was the oldest, largest, and most important city in Mesopotamia until it was later surpassed by Babylon. The city was inhabited for thousands of years and its population may have reached 50,000 -80,000 at its peak. Uruk was a major trade hub, it had a full-time bureaucracy and courts, a formal military, and a stratified society with over 100 professions and slavery.

There were two temple districts in Uruk, the older Anu district centered on the temple to An, the Heavenly Father, who would later become El (God) of the Bible. While the Eanna district was dedicated to Inanna, the goddess of love and war, and the Queen of Heaven.

The first monumental temple ever built was a ziggurat dedicated to Inanna which was called the "House of Heaven." Ziggurats were massive stepped pyramids that were the great architectural contribution of the Sumerians. In her various incarnations, Inanna was the most popular goddess in the Ancient Near East for 5000 years or more.

The oldest cuneiform tablets from the initial invention of writing were found in the temple of Inanna, and in this temple were also found the oldest written mythology and pantheon of pagan gods. Uruk was also the home of the oldest known human hero, the king Gilgamesh, who is said to have built the walls around the city. Gilgamesh sought immortality rather than accepting death in the famous epic named for him.

First Writing

The Sumerians invented writing around 3400 BCE which they credited to the goddess Nidaba. Sumerian writing is called cuneiform and was written using the sharp edge of a trimmed reed to make wedge-shaped impressions in a wet clay tablet. Cuneiform was first used to record business transactions and inventory for the temples, but it evolved into a rich vocabulary that could tell stories and communicate abstract ideas like wisdom and justice. Thousands of clay tablet legal documents have been unearthed that are contracts, deeds, wills, promissory notes, receipts, and court documents, as well as sacred prayers and poetry. The Sumerians also invented base 6 math, from which we get time divided in 24 hours, 60 minutes, and 60 seconds, and the circle divided into 360 degrees.

Prior to the archaeological discovery of these oldest cuneiform tablets in the 1800s, the Sumerians were not even known to have existed; they had been completely forgotten. The archaeologists thought they were excavating Assyrian and Babylonian settlements which were well attested by Biblical and Greek sources and they were surprised to discover an older culture with an independent language. The discovery of Sumerian writings and mythology transformed our understanding of ancient history, mythology, and the Bible.

Cuneiform writing was used for over 2500 years until it was replaced by phonetic alphabets. Cuneiform was a great contribution to human development, it made possible the recording of law, business, medicine, astronomy, and mythology. In many ways, writing distinguishes advanced civilizations from mere settlements, and high cultures from low. Cuneiform was widely adopted by succeeding cultures in the ancient Near East; the Akkadians, Assyrians, Babylonians, Hittites, Canaanites, and others borrowed the script and used it to record their own deeds and beliefs. Through the invention of writing, which took many years of schooling to learn, the Sumerians disseminated their culture and religion and remained influential long after they were gone.

Social Organization

Mesopotamia is a dry, arid region that is mostly unsuitable for agriculture except near the great Tigris and Euphrates rivers that could supply water. The Sumerians learned how to do irrigation, building dikes and ditches to channel water where it was needed for farming. Maintaining the irrigation systems was a central concern and activity of Sumerian life, it was an activity that required the organization of large numbers of people to effectively work together, and a system of cooperation to ensure that farmers received their fair share of water. It was this need to organize large groups of people to build complex irrigation systems that led to the first political organizations and professional hierarchies.

In its earliest days, Sumerian society was run as a theocracy where the temple priests directed the work of canal building, collecting the agricultural produce, and redistributing it across society. It was only later, after conflict and hostility between the city-states became the norm, that warrior kings took power permanently. The royal families and the priesthood were closely related and intertwined and were the ruling elite of Mesopotamian society.

Law was divinely provided through the king, and they considered law to be the defining characteristic of an elevated civilization which brought order from chaos. Sumerians wrote no history of their own, just King Lists of uncertain accuracy. They believed the world came into being in full bloom by the gods and they had no sense that there was a time before, or of progress towards a greater future.

The first kings were simply the "big man" appointed in times of conflict, but over time kingship gained its full institutional and hereditary prerogatives and became the very hallmark of civilization. The kings maintained a regular army to defend their territory and engage their rivals. Sumer gained dominance through superior military tactics and weapons; they used chariots as their main offensive weapon and heavily armored infantries. In time, the royal palace came to rival the temples in wealth and influence.

Sumerian civilization was urban in character, with each of its dozen or so city-states featuring a walled city surrounded by villages and hamlets. The greatest building in each city was the main temple situated on a high terrace, which evolved over time into the grand ziggurats. The temple was the tallest and largest building in the city, keeping with the religious principle that each city belonged to its main god, to whom it had been assigned when the world was created.

Black-Headed People

The Sumerians referred to themselves as "the black-headed people" and there were three classes: superiors, commoners, and slaves. Sumerian citizens were free to own land and private property and engage in trade. Artisans sold their wares in the town market, and traders did prosperous business traveling from city to city and to countries as far away as India.

The land was poor in resources, there was very little timber and virtually no precious metals or stones. Yet Sumerian craftsmen were highly skilled, working with imported materials. Jewelers worked in silver and gold, setting semi-precious stones of lapis lazuli, carnelian, and topaz. The temple of Inanna had a limestone base, which was extravagant as the stone had to be hauled in from far away. Mud bricks were used for construction and the temple was decorated with colored clay cones forming geometric patterns. Blue lapis lazuli was among the most precious gemstones, valued by the gods and royalty alike. Lapis lazuli was not found in Mesopotamia though, it was imported from Afghanistan and demonstrates the existence of trade from early times.

Rich and powerful families owned large estates, but the poor were able to own farms and cattle. There were skilled professionals of all types, cattle breeders, boatmen, fishermen, merchants, scribes, doctors, architects, masons, carpenters, smiths, jewelers, and potters. Most payments were made in barter, but standard weights of silver called shekels were also used. Coined money would not be invented for thousands of years.

Free citizens lived in large patriarchal families and clans joined together as communities. Marriages were arranged by the parents, and parents had absolute control over their young children. Families were warm and affectionate, and children were generally treated with great love and care. Women had significant legal rights, they could hold property and engage in business, and divorces were granted with little pretext.

Slavery

Slavery was an institution; temples, palaces, and wealthy families owned slaves and could exploit them for their own benefit. The slave was the property of his owner like any beast of burden, they could be branded, flogged, or raped, and severely punished if they tried to escape. Many slaves were prisoners of war, either foreign or from rival Sumerian city-states.

There was no notion of racial superiority or genetically inherited slavery. Freemen could be reduced to slavery as a form of punishment or for payment of debts, and slaves could purchase their freedom. Slavery was a fluid class system people could go in and out of rather than a fixed hereditary caste system. Parents could sell their children into slavery, and a father might turn over his entire family to a creditor, but for no longer than a period of three years.

It was in a master's interest that his slaves remain healthy and strong, and so slaves were generally treated reasonably well. Slaves even had legal rights, they could engage in business, borrow money, and purchase their freedom. A free person could marry a slave, male or female, and a child born from the marriage was free.

Though market prices varied, a typical price for an adult male slave was twenty shekels, about the same price as a donkey. Slavery would continue to be the economic backbone of civilization throughout history until the Industrial Revolution.

Law & Justice

The Sumerians had a keen sense of truth and justice, the importance of honesty is stressed throughout their literature and they express moral outrage at falsehood and oppression. The Sumerians in their own words cherished goodness and truth, law and order, justice and freedom, righteousness and straightforwardness, mercy and compassion. They abhorred evil and falsehood, lawlessness and disorder, injustice and oppression, sinfulness and perversity, cruelty and pitilessness.

Sumerians pioneered written law, they had courts with judges and lawsuits. Kings boasted that they had established law and order in the land, protected the weak from the strong, the poor from the rich, and wiped out evil and violence. Their laws protected widows and children and leaders were judged on how well they took care of the poor. It was the "Widows and Orphans Rule." The righteousness of the kings was judged by how well they took care of the poorest of the poor.

Kingship was delivered by the gods, and while the position was divine, for the man occupying the role it was considered a heavenly burden. The king was given absolute power but in return, the king had to protect and provide for his people – it was a covenant.

Sumerian kings were judged on their morality and righteousness. The law codes of Ur-Nammu list many of his ethical achievements, he did away with many bureaucratic abuses, regulated weights and measures to ensure fairness in the market, and protected the widows and orphans from ill-treatment and abuse. Other leaders proudly proclaimed that they restored justice and freedom to long-suffering citizens, removed oppressive officials, stopped injustice and exploitation.

Sumerian Cylinder Seal of King Ur-Nammu

Temples

Temples occupied a very important role in society, they received tithes, offerings, and sacrifices from the public that included all manner of agricultural goods, as well as gold, silver, jewels, and valuable commodities. Some temples served as redistribution centers where agricultural goods were brought in and stored, then distributed to the people according to their shares. The larger temples were tended by many priests, officials, and servants.

Each temple was dedicated to its own god, and the patron deity of each city had the largest and most ornate temple. The god lived in the temple in the form of a statue, called an idol, that was carefully dressed and served food every day by the priests. Prosperous cities enlarged their temples to demonstrate the strength and power of their gods. Invaders would ravage the temples to signify their victory, either smashing the idols or taking them away as spoils of war.

Aside from religious duties and rituals, temples served many practical needs for the city; they were granaries and storehouses, and also held the city's archives. If a citizen was kidnapped and could not ransom themselves, then the temple of their city would do so. Poor farmers came to the temple for loans, to borrow seed corn and supplies for their farms, and these loans were repaid without interest. Even the King was obligated to pay back any loans taken from the temple.

Culture

Music was important to the Sumerian culture and they had many instruments, ranging from percussion, like drums and tambourines, to beautiful harps and lyres, and pipes of reed and metal. Poetry and song were celebrated in Sumerian schools and music, song, and dance were common forms of entertainment.

Sumerians may have invented the first sailboats which they used to travel up and down the Tigris and Euphrates and out in the Persian Gulf. The first primitive boats and rafts go back over a hundred thousand years, deep in the Paleolithic, but sailing requires cloth for sails and fiber for ropes, and this means they were using linen and hemp. The Sumerians grew a lot of flax for linen, which was their primary fiber for clothing and also used for sails, but linen does not make as good ropes as hemp.

Sumerian medicine was very practical; their medical texts contain hundreds of recipes, all devoid of mystical incantations so common in later cultures. Beer was their most popular beverage, and they also used it for medicine.

Gardens

Gardens were precious and sacred in Sumer and throughout Mesopotamian history as an outgrowth of their success with irrigated agriculture. Gardens were cultivated by kings as a sign of their wisdom and mastery of the lands and all those that dwelt in them. These artificial landscapes mimicked nature and were designed to be pleasing while also adding to the prestige of the royal patron responsible for its creation. Mesopotamians planted gardens in cities, palace courtyards, and temples with fragrant trees and edible fruits that recreated their concept of paradise. A garden of the gods and a tree of life were common mythological themes that carried over to the biblical Garden of Eden.

Akkadian Cylinder Seal - Inanna with lion and her aide Ninshubur, 2300 BCE

Winged Inanna (left), sun god Shamash rising, Enki with streams of water and his aide Usimu, 2300 BCE

Chapter Seven

FIRST GODS

It is from the Sumerians that we get the first written descriptions of pagan deities. Sumerian mythology is particularly instructive because it is the oldest we have on record and it speaks to the time when writing was invented and civilization was first established.

As simple Neolithic settlements developed into complex societies so too did human awareness and cognition grow in complexity. Simple depictions of a universal Mother Goddess were not suitable for expressing the ideas of an urban, professionalized people. Just as a single biological cell splits repeatedly and goes through the process of mitosis on the way to becoming a complex organism, so too did human consciousness and language advance, leading to the use of more complex vocabulary to represent the world they lived in.

New words were needed to express new ideas and to account for new human activities, such as skilled trades and professions. They also expanded their pallet of symbols to communicate wisdom about the divine and supernatural, creating a pantheon of gods and goddesses to represent every visible object as well as human ideas and emotions.

Pagan is a general term for polytheism and idolatry, and we use it here specifically to describe cultures whose gods are not part of a single cosmological unity. There were no cultures that called themselves pagan, it was a name applied to them by Roman-era Christians. Pagan cosmology is inchoate, each god is driven by its own divine purpose and they operate independently from one another.

Modern-day Hindus have countless gods and goddesses, but they are not pagan, because the Hindus believe all their gods are manifestations of a single cosmic unity they call Brahma, or Shakti, depending on one's tradition. Likewise, Christians have a trinity of father, son, and holy ghost, but they are all understood to be aspects of the same universal God.

Heaven & Earth

To the Sumerians, the world was known as An-Ki, Heaven-Earth, the Heavenly Father and Earthly Mother. The Earth was a flat disk enclosed by a solid domed vault that contains the atmosphere. The stars and heavenly bodies existed on the surface of the dome, and the netherworld was underneath. Surrounding the An-Ki on all sides was a boundless chaotic sea in which the An-Ki remained fixed and immovable like a bubble. This cosmology was common throughout the Ancient Near East, including in the Bible.

These basic facts were accepted as self-evident and from there the Sumerians developed a cosmology to fit. Supervising and organizing this universe was the pantheon of gods and goddesses, living beings, human-like in form, but invisible, superhuman, and immortal, who guided and controlled the cosmos in accordance with duly prescribed divine laws, called the *Me's*.

Sumerians created gods in the image of humans and they assumed that the gods were organized in a hierarchy that mirrored human culture, with a king in the lead and multitudes of gods with specific jobs to do. The Sumerians believed that humans were created by the gods to serve them and relieve them of their labors. The Sumerian gods were immortal, human-like masters to be feared and obeyed. The gods could be malevolent and cruel, their reasons inexplicable to mortals.

Humans lived in a mysterious, unpredictable, and perilous world where the gods may strike the people down with no warning by an earthquake, a flood, or fire from the sky. These beliefs reflect a world of cataclysms, where entire cultures could be wiped from existence in a single day, experiences that their ancestors had survived. Mesopotamian gods exhibited the full range of human emotions; they could be kind or cruel, capricious or benevolent, wise or vain, selfish or magnanimous.

Sumerian mythology was not devotional; most of the surviving stories are not liturgical or intended for direct use as prayers in rituals. The mythological stories continued the traditions of the spoken word bards who retold the old tales for inspiration and entertainment. The stories were meant to be enjoyed and impart inherited wisdom, but they are not fixed

Sumer Ur mosaic royal tombs

by logic and reason, they rely on imagination and fantasy to impart their message. The poets were free to expand the folklore, add chapters and embellish details. Fidelity to dogma was not a concern for the Sumerian poet – the gods were inscrutable and unknowable, therefore the poet had license to imagine them however they chose.

Religion

All of the great realms of heaven, earth, sea, and air had their own deities to represent and guide their actions in accordance with established rules. The visible heavenly bodies; the sun, moon, Venus, Jupiter, Saturn, Mercury, and Mars; the atmospheric forces like wind and storms; natural features like rivers and mountains; cultural entities like city and state; even common implements like pickaxe and plow had their own gods to guide their actions.

There were thousands of gods and their mythological tales combined cosmology, entertainment, and politics. The major gods had their own temples, festivals, and priests, and when new political powers rose their patron deities were elevated over their rivals.

There was no fixed doctrine or dogma in pagan cultures and there was always room for new gods to become popular and find a place for themselves. New gods could absorb the powers and the worshippers of the old gods. The stories of great kings' victories could also become mythology, featuring their favorite gods guiding the hero.

Individuals also had their own personal gods to intercede on their behalf with the great gods who were far too busy to take notice of one person's troubles. The gods had their own hierarchy just as humans did – the god of the brick could not be expected to compare to the god of the sun.

The Sumerian gods inhabited a meta-divine realm, but they did not wield unlimited power, they were subject to forces that limited their actions. In pagan belief, there was a fluid boundary between the human and divine realms. Gods and humans could meet, speak, mate, and have conflict. Gods mating with humans produced semi-divine humans who were the heroes of many mythological tales.

The anthropomorphic nature of the gods meant that they could be sick to the point of death, they fought and could be wounded and even killed. Immortality in the Sumerian mind was not the same as omnipotence. The Sumerians did not have an ordered, codified theology that addressed its own internal contradictions; they seemed to have accepted many assumptions about the gods and the order of the universe.

The Sumerians believed that the gods had begun the work of building the irrigation canals, but that humans were created to relieve them of the burden of their labors. Humans were effectively slaves to the gods. Sumerians did not place man on a pedestal, they were convinced that man was fashioned out of clay and created for only one purpose, to serve the gods by providing them with food, drink, and shelter, so that the gods may be relieved of their work and have leisure.

After death, the human spirit descends to the dreary underworld where life is a dismal reflection of earthly life. Reincarnation was a belief that emerged later in other cultures, particularly Egypt, though the Sumerians did recognize the cycles of life, death, and rebirth in nature.

Sin

Sumerian thinkers accepted their dependent status and that it was the gods who planned, while humans followed divine orders. The will and motives of the gods were inscrutable, and all the Sumerian could do to avoid misfortune was to plead and wail, lament, and confess their sins and failings. Human life was haunted by insecurity and uncertainty, at the whim of unpredictable gods.

Man's misfortunes were the result of his own sins and misdeeds, there was no unjust human suffering, no man is without guilt and only he is to be blamed for his suffering, not the gods. The proper response to illness or misfortune was to go humbly before your gods with tears and lamentations, prayer and supplication, in hopes of pleasing your god and moving him to compassion so that the deity may turn your suffering into joy.

All Sumerian deities were extolled as lovers of the good and just, the ethical and moral, and disdained the unethical and immoral. The kings and priests were the gods' divine representatives on Earth, and common people were obligated to serve the gods through labor and ritual, providing the gods with food and placating them with sacrifices.

A number of deities supervised the moral order; in particular, the sun god Utu, who was the god of truth and justice. It was a common pagan theme for the sun god to represent honesty and justice, as it was believed that the light of the sun washes away the darkness of deceit and exposes all.

Idols

The temple was the home of its god who was represented by a statue, called an idol, that was carefully tended by the priests. The idols were dressed in clothes and meals were served to them every day. Offerings of food and animal sacrifices were made daily at the temples and at home altars, the goal of sacrifice and ritual was to placate the gods' mercurial whims by demonstrating humble servitude. By modern standards, pagan cultures were primitive and superstitious. In the Judeo-Christian and Islamic traditions, idolatry is considered one of the greatest of sins and a sign of false religion.

There was an exchange that was central to the relationship between gods and people. Humans needed to make heartfelt sacrifices of crops and animals to please the gods, who in turn protected the people from misfortune. Any misfortune that did occur was strictly the fault of the individuals and never the fault of the gods. The proper response to droughts, illnesses, and military defeats was to make additional sacrifices and humble yourself before the gods until they were satisfied and reversed your suffering.

Magic was accepted as real and it involved the manipulation of substances like crystals, amulets, and totems that can tap directly into the meta-divine realm. Humans were generally powerless to thwart the capricious behavior of the gods that could make life miserable, but magic could be used to try and at least influence the gods, while divination helped to discern their intentions.

Stele of Ur-Nammu who holds the measuring rod and cord

The "Queen of Night Relief," which dates to the Old Babylonian Period and is believed to represent either Ereshkigal or Ishtar.

Chapter Eight

SUMERIAN PANTHEON

Creation

First, the Sumerians believed that everything emerged from the primeval sea, a goddess named Nammu that was the first cause and prime mover, the primordial virgin mother of all. The great Mother Nammu gave birth to An and Ki, who were the gods' Heaven and Earth, as well as Enki, the god of water and wisdom.

An separated from Ki who gave birth to Enlil, the air god. An carried off the heavens, while Enlil carried away the Earth. The union of Enlil and his mother led to the creation of other gods, animals, plants, and the establishment of civilization. Nammu and Enki were responsible for the creation of humans, who were made from clay and created to relieve the gods of their labors.

The four creator gods were the most important and popular in Sumerian worship. Ninhursag (Ki), was the Earth and the Mother Goddess, An was the Heavenly Father, Enlil was the king of the gods, and Enki was the god of water and of wisdom. Three more gods rounded out the council of the "*7 Who Decreed the Fates*." Utu, the sun, was the god of truth and justice. The moon god Nanna was the prince of the gods. And the beloved Inanna, the goddess of love and war, was represented by Venus, the third brightest object in the sky.

After the 7 who decreed the fates, there were 50 great gods, hundreds of minor gods, and an endless number of personal gods. Finally, there were the Annunaki, about whom not much is known but are subject to great amounts of modern-day speculation. The Annunaki appear in myths as judges, both in the underworld and in the terrestrial world. In all, scholars have identified over 2000 Sumerian gods by name, because every known object had its own god.

Ki

Ninhursag is the great Mother Goddess, Ki, also known as Ninmah, "the exalted lady." In the earliest god lists, she was always listed first, but as civilization progressed and the soldiers asserted themselves socially, the Goddess was reduced in rank. She is also called Nintu, "the lady who gave birth," the mother of all living things. She is represented by a symbol that looks like the letter Omega, Ω, or a womb.

An

Most scholars believe that An, the Heavenly Father, was the high god in the early days of Sumer, but by 2500 BCE, Enlil had become the king of the pantheon. This pattern would repeat throughout many pagan traditions. The great heavenly father god would retreat to the background like a retired and respected elder, while his vigorous son, the storm god, takes the throne as the active king of the gods.

Enlil

Enlil was by far the most important Sumerian god, the King of Heaven and Earth, and he played a dominant role in politics, ritual, and myth. Kings and rulers boasted that it was Enlil who gave them kingship and the strength to conquer. Enlil is sometimes portrayed by scholars as a cruel and destructive god, as he is the one who released the great flood that nearly destroyed humanity, but in most of his myths, he is a friendly and fatherly god who watched over the safety and well-being of all humans.

Enki

Enki is the water god but more importantly the god of wisdom; he was widely popular and was the husband of Ninhursag, the mother goddess. Enki organized the Earth in accordance with the plans laid out by Enlil. Enki is the resourceful and skillful god responsible for all the cleverness in the Earth's natural phenomena. Enki was the keeper of the "*me*'s," the divine laws that govern the order of the universe. The Sumerians were not interested in uncovering the fundamental origins of natural processes in the way that obsesses modern science, they were satisfied with the explanation that "Enki did it" by mere word and command.

TRINITIES

Triads, trinities, and the Triple Goddess are all important symbolic archetypes that repeat through cultures and religions. A triad is three ruling gods, typically male, one of whom one is the alpha, the leader. These three gods simultaneously compete and cooperate, they can be rivals or partners. Like three staffs' forming a tripod, one leg of the triad can be taller and they still work together, even on uneven ground.

An, Enlil, and Enki form a triad of leading gods. The brothers Zeus, Poseidon, and Hades from the Greek Olympian pantheon are a familiar god triad. Isis, Osiris, and Horus were the Egyptian trinity of mother, father, and child known as the Abydos Triad.

A trinity is three gods who are inextricably linked together, like the Hindu Brahma, Vishnu, and Shiva. Brahma is the creator, Vishnu is the preserver, and Shiva is the destroyer, and together they form a cosmic life cycle for the entire universe. For Christians, the trinity is the Father, the son Jesus, and the Holy Spirit. A trinity must be linked like a triangle or circle.

TRIPLE GODDESS

The Triple Goddess is one of the most important symbolic archetypes of the Goddess and repeats across many cultures. The Triple Goddess is the mother, maiden, and death, and she represents the full cycle of life. She is often portrayed as a mother and two sisters. The Hindu Tridevi; Parvati, Durga, and Kali, are an important Triple Goddess still worshipped today as a manifestation of Shakti, the cosmic force underlying the universe. The Sumerian Triple Goddess consisted of Inanna as the maiden, along with her mother Ninhursag, and her sister Ereshkigal, the Queen of the Underworld.

Kali

Virtually every pagan culture had a Triple Goddess that was central to their worship. Demeter, Persephone, and Hecate were the Greek Olympian Triple Goddess central to the Eleusinian Mysteries. In some cases, the Triple Goddess was reduced to a single goddess who had three forms such as Qedesh, a popular Egyptian goddess who equated to Asherah, Astarte, and Anat, the Biblical Triple Goddess of the Canaanites.

The mother goddess represents all manifestations of nurturing motherhood for all life. She is Mother Earth, Mother Nature, and mother of all the plants and animals. The loving wife of God, she manifests as the nurturing goddess of hearth and home, the patron of human mothers, wives, and homemakers. The mother goddess also manifests as wisdom, which the Greeks called Sophia. Mothers and mother goddesses were greatly respected for their sage advice.

The maiden is a young woman and was often the most popular and important goddess in the culture. The maiden was commonly called "Virgin" in honor of the primeval mother and as a sign of her youth and independence. She manifests in various forms, sometimes she was a goddess of beauty and eroticism who was the most perfect and sensuous lover, other times she was chaste. Diana, a Roman goddess who remained popular in medieval Christian Europe, was a virginal huntress and midwife. She may be a warrior maiden riding a lion who leads the kings to victory in battles, such as Babylonian Ishtar or the Hindu Durga. The maiden could also be a goddess of divination and prophecy, and she was often portrayed with serpents.

Death is the sister of the maiden, sometimes presented as an old woman, the crone. For the Sumerians, she was Ereshkigal, Queen of the Underworld. Death is not always confined to the underworld and the elderly, sometimes she takes the form of a blood-soaked warrior maiden like the Canaanite Anat, or the Hindu Kali. Hecate, a widely worshipped goddess of night time and magic who led the dead to the underworld played this role in many European Triple Goddess formations.

Hecate

Chapter Nine

INANNA/ISHTAR/ASTARTE

A Prayer to Ishtar

Unto Her who renders decisions, Goddess of all things,
Unto the Lady of Heaven and Earth who receives supplication;
Unto Her who hears petition, who entertains prayer;
Unto the compassionate Goddess who loves righteousness;
Ishtar the Queen, who suppresses all that is confused.

To the Queen of Heaven, the Goddess of the Universe,
the One who walked in terrible Chaos and brought life by the Law of Love;
And out of Chaos brought us harmony, and from Chaos Thou has led us by the hand.
– Ancient Babylon, author unknown[1]

The many-named goddess in her various incarnations was the most popular goddess in the Ancient Near East, the Queen of Heaven, for some 5000 years. She is the goddess of love and war, the virgin and the harlot, the most beautiful, sensuous, and desirable of all the immortals. She had great power and delivered justice to the kings and common folk alike. She led the kings to glorious victory in battle and she directed the oracles who oversaw divination and prophecy. She is the goddess of sex, beauty, and desire who brings fertility and abundance through ritual sex and wild, decadent celebrations full of life, music, dancing, drinking, feasting, and intoxicated ecstasy.

We are not taught about this goddess in Western schools or in church. Her rituals and character are among the most alien to Western civilization and perhaps the most threatening. She is the archetype of the independent, sexually free young woman who has the capacity to win in battle and also deliver prophetic counsel, yet who is so beautiful that men and women alike fall down before her in desirous lust. Modern Western women, at least until the present era, were not taught to embrace or harness these powers, they were taught to

1 *Babylon, Eighteenth to Seventh Century BCE*. Merlin Stone, *When God Was a Woman,* Harcourt Brace Jovanovich, 1978.

be submissive to men and sexually passive, yet this goddess was dominant in all aspects of life, from the battlefield to the bedroom to the royal halls.

She was first named in Sumer as Inanna, but there were Neolithic images of her thousands of years earlier. She was often drawn nude with a pronounced pubic triangle. In Babylon, she was worshipped widely and known as Ishtar. The Canaanites of the Bible, who were also the Phoenicians, called her Astarte and they spread her worship throughout the Mediterranean through their far-flung trade colonies. The Hebrews saw Astarte as a great rival and she is insulted and denigrated in the Bible. The Goddess never forgives or forgets an insult.

Queen of Heaven

The Queen of Heaven was a title given to the most important goddess in any culture, the counterpart to the King of the Gods, though not necessarily his wife or consort. In Uruk, the first great city in history 5000 years ago, the first great temples were built to the Heavenly Father An and his daughter Inanna. Isis was the Queen of Heaven in Egypt, Hera in Greece, and the Virgin Mary still carries the title in the Catholic traditions.

Inanna was called "the Virgin" as a title of respect. In many ancient languages, the words "virgin" and "maiden" are synonymous and have nothing to do with chastity, leading to much confusion for scholars in later centuries. For the ancients, the word virgin meant a childless, unmarried, independent woman, and did not refer to her sexual history. The conflation of the words "virgin" and "maiden" had a major impact on later religious traditions, particularly around the Catholic Virgin Mary.

The contrast between the Virgin Mary and the Virgin Inanna could not be starker. The Virgin Mary's sexual chastity and actual virgin birth is seen to this day as a moral ideal, an impossible standard all mothers fail to live up to. While the Virgin Inanna's promiscuous sex life was celebrated and graphically portrayed.

Inanna is the archetype of all maiden love goddesses that followed, she was syncretized into every successive pagan culture and had many names. Besides Ishtar and Astarte, the Greeks syncretized her as Aphrodite, the Romans called her Venus, the Norse Freya, and the Assyrians called her Mylitta.

The patriarchal Greeks distinguished between two Aphrodites, the older and foreign Aphrodite Urania ("celestial") who was the Asian Queen of Heaven, and Aphrodite Pandemos ("common"), who was the Olympian goddess of sex, beauty, and prostitution, but who lacked the powers of war and divination. In school we are taught about Aphrodite

Pandemos, but we are not taught about her more powerful incarnation as Aphrodite Urania, the Queen of Heaven.

Inanna is the original role model for the ambitious, sexually free, and independent young woman, that was embodied by the Amazon warrior maidens, a role model that does not exist for young women in modern societies. The practices of the cult of Inanna carried directly over into the later Babylonian cult of Ishtar and Phoenician Astarte. Inanna and Ishtar are virtually identical and many scholars conflate the two. The only significant difference is that the later Ishtar stories have more literary detail and more often depict warfare.

Hieros Gamos

Inanna/Ishtar/Astarte was notoriously promiscuous, the "hierodule of heaven" and the "courtesan of the gods," she did not believe in monogamy as a matter of principle. She generally had no children, though each culture had its own stories about her. The cult of Inanna/Ishtar/Astarte was extremely sexual by modern standards and this is perhaps the most misunderstood aspect of her worship.

Her religion is generally described as a fertility cult. Sexuality was understood to be the source of all life and there was nothing shameful about it. Ritual sex confirmed the fertility of nature and sexual pleasure was believed to be the blessing of the goddess. Sex was used in agricultural rituals to promote plant growth and bring about the rains.

The *hieros gamos* was Inanna's most important public ritual, the sacred marriage between the king and the goddess, represented by a sacred hierodule. The hieros gamos was central to the most important festival of the year, the springtime New Year that celebrated the rebirth of plants after the long winter. This annual sexual ritual consecrated the king's rule by demonstrating his vitality and virility and ensured the fecundity of nature and the crops. The passionate sexual embrace between the king and Inanna brought forth the blooming flowers and bursting of springtime life, confirming the covenant between the King, the Goddess, and the community. The hieros gamos inspired a genre of sacred love poetry, most famously seen in the Biblical Song of Solomon.

Sacred Sex

The Mesopotamians practiced temple prostitution, but the word has modern connotations of transactional sexual services that would be foreign to the Sumerians. In the cult of Inanna, men came bearing gifts to the goddess, hoping to win her favor and be blessed with her embrace. In the temple the women were in control of the situation, they could choose the men they partnered with and the temples generated considerable wealth from their sanctified sexuality. While some of the hierodules were temple slaves, free women took part in ritual sex as well. In a culture that was sexually wide open and permissive, the exchange of gifts for sex was accepted as a perfectly normal part of day-to-day life.

It is from the word hierodule that we get the words, "harlot," and "whore." Long before these words became slurs to shame women for their sexual lives, Inanna was known as the "Holy Harlot," and Ishtar was the "Whore of Babylon"; these were not insults but proudly proclaimed titles. These cultures would laugh at the idea that is was sinful to accept gifts in exchange for sex, and to be fair, the modern dating world is not far off from these temple practices – men still come bearing gifts to women, hoping to gain their favor and sexual blessings. The difference then was that there was no obligation or expectation of monogamy in the culture and free women had complete autonomy in their sexual lives, at least within the temple. In the Bible, the Hebrew prophets discuss and condemn these practices at length, giving evidence of their existence in Jerusalem at that time in the cult of Astarte.

The circumstances of temple prostitution would change over time and it would eventually become an international sex market. Temple prostitution still exists today in India, though it is not respected and the women are considered to be at the bottom of society. But in the Neolithic and the early days of civilization, temple prostitution was a sacred act that confirmed the fertility of nature.

Pleasure was the blessing of the Goddess and the Goddess' only requirement was to be righteous and do your allotted work. The righteous and honorable were given all the pleasures in life; sex, music, dance, art, ecstasy, feasts, love, beauty, springtime renewal, flowers blooming, abundant harvests. For the unrighteous there was no sympathy, no reward, Inanna sent her one and only husband to the underworld for his lack of righteousness, and that message applied to all people.

Maiden

Over the course of her mythology, Inanna had no clear parentage as so many stories were written about her. Inanna/Ishtar appeared in far more mythology than any other Mesopotamian deity. Inanna was not a mother goddess, she had no children of her own and only one husband who met an infamous fate. Inanna was known for her promiscuity and many lovers. Independent and free-spirited, she could be cruel to any lover who became attached to her.

Inanna was ambitious for power, often challenging the other gods and attempting to trick or subvert them to gain their powers for herself. And while innocents might suffer for her vainglory, Inanna remained firmly beloved by all. Inanna would be considered a nightmare role-model for modern-day parents of daughters. In stories, Inanna lies to her mother about sneaking off with her lovers and openly challenges her father's authority, all while gallivanting around nude with a line of suitors trailing her. The Sumerians intimately understood the power of sex in human relations and they celebrated it.

As Ishtar, she would lead the kings to victory in war. In battle, she rides a lion, nude but for her armor. The modern comic book character Wonder Woman with her raven hair and bare legs looks just like Ishtar in battle (though Ishtar was not Caucasian) and was inspired by Amazon warrior women who worshipped the spirited goddess. Her weapons are the bow and arrow, ax, and lasso. Ishtar could also sprout wings and fly around the battlefield like a sparrow. The early Sumerians were not as warlike as those that followed and the very earliest myths do not portray much conflict and war, but over time the most popular deities, like Ishtar, were portrayed as heroic warriors.

Symbols

Inanna's symbols include the eight-pointed star, the rosette, that represents the planet Venus. Venus is the third brightest heavenly body after the sun and moon and is associated with the goddess of love in many cultures. Venus has an unusual orbit and appears both as the Morning Star and as the Evening Star. Many people did not recognize that both stars were the same object, but the Mesopotamians excelled at astronomy and they recognized the orbital transit of Venus from an early time. Love and war were reflected in the Morning Star and the Evening Star, day time was for battle and night time was for love.

Inanna's animals were lions, doves, and serpents. These are three very important symbols that were used in many ancient goddess cultures and carried on in Biblical beliefs. Even Jesus instructs his disciples to "be wise as serpents and innocent as doves" (Matthew 10:16). There are many images of Inanna with lotus flowers in one hand and snakes in the other, surrounded by doves, and sometimes with the magical Tree of Life.

Transgendered

Ishtar is transgendered and sometimes sports a beard in battle. She was tended by eunuch and transvestite priests and she celebrates gender fluidity. Ishtar says:

> *I make right into left. I make left into right. I turn a man into a woman. I turn a woman into a man. I am the one who causes the man to adorn himself as a woman. I am the one who causes the woman to adorn herself as a man.*
>
> – Lamentation Uru- Amirabi[2]

Eunuchs were the transgenders of the ancient world and chose self-castration as a sign of their devotion to the goddess. Gender fluidity was a mark of the Goddess and believed to impart divine wisdom and magic. Flamboyant gender-bending priests were a common feature of goddess worship well into Greek and Roman times. The Galli priests served Cybele in Rome, while the Megabyzi served at the grand temple to Artemis in Ephesus, and the Enaree roamed with the Scythian Amazons.

Wild Worship

The worship of Inanna/Ishtar/Astarte included sacrifices of animals, music, food, and drink as well as orgiastic sex, ecstatic dance, and bloody self-flagellation. Inanna's celebrations could be wild and frenzied, and it was believed that "nothing is prohibited to Inanna." Transgressions of normal social and physical limitations including gender and celebrations of physical abnormality enabled worshippers to cross over from everyday consciousness into the world of spiritual ecstasy. Handicapped, crippled, and deformed people were welcome and involved in the life of the temple. Shamans and oracular divination were important features of temple life.

Entu

Sumerian royalty and the priesthood were closely intertwined. The *Entu* was the High Priestess, and she may be the wife or daughter of the King, and the King often was often referred to as the Priest of Inanna. The Entu wore special caps, jewelry, and ceremonial clothing that distinguished them from common people. Long clothes that hung to the ground were the sign of royalty and high priests.

Many men and women served in the temple, the names and titles of all the priests and temple functionaries are known, but not all of their roles

2 Launderville, Dale, *Celibacy in the Ancient World: Its Ideal and Practice in Pre-Hellenistic Israel, Mesopotamia, and Greece*. Liturgical Press, 2010.

are fully understood. It is accepted that in any temple, the high priest, the *En,* was usually the opposite sex of the deity. So, the temple of Inanna was headed by a man, possibly the king, while the temple of Enlil was usually led by a woman, and often the daughter of the king.

Naditu

The Sumerian *Naditu* were consecrated women who lived at the temple, ranking second only to the Entu. The Naditu were committed to remaining childless and unmarried and were not involved in ritual sex. The Naditu were highly respected and took part in business, they came from leading families and were sent by their fathers to represent them in the temple. The Naditu had legal protections and were known for their business acumen, they lived full and active lives in the community; they bought and sold land and slaves, imported and exported products, and managed lands and businesses.

Gala

The *Gala* are notable, they may have been singers and poets, as their job was to perform lamentations in the temple. Their name is derived from the word "ga" meaning penis, and "la" meaning anus, and they were portrayed graphically in literature performing sex acts.

Sumer Gala priests

Assinnu and Kurgarru

The *Kurgarru* were transvestite priests who dressed like the opposite sex, while the *Assinnu* were full-fledged transgenders much loved by Inanna. These priests and their later equivalents throughout Near-Eastern goddess cults adopted female clothes and manners and engaged in passive anal sex. Homosexuality was perfectly normal and anal sex was encouraged in Sumerian culture; it was good luck to give anal sex to a temple priest and for women, it was a recommended form of birth control.

Ishtaritu

Ishtaritu were female devotees of Ishtar; they specialized in music, dance, and the arts, especially the sensual, undulating belly dance that is still popular to this day. The belly dance is evocative of snakes and imitates their movements with vigorous hip and pelvic gyrations.

Stele of the goddess Qedesh ('the saint') she was a singular manifestation of Asherah, Astarte, and Anat and was popular in Egypt and Syria. New Kingdom, Dynasty XIX (1292-1186 BC)

Chapter Ten

QEDESHA & SACRED SEX

Qedesha

The *qaditsu (Sumerian)*, or *qedesha (Hebrew)*, were a class of sacred sex priestesses, or hierodules, and the *qadesh* were their male counterparts. The hierodule is the physical embodiment of the Goddess herself, and they were prominent in goddess temples throughout the ancient Near East for thousands of years. They are misunderstood in our day and are usually referred to as cult prostitutes by scholars, which is semantically true as gifts were received for sexual activity but diminishes the sacred and respected aspect of their duties. The qedesha were known as the *holy ones*, or the *set apart*, which spoke to their respected spiritual purity, and *virgins*, which referred to their autonomous, unmarried status in service to the Triple Goddess.

We use the biblical Hebrew term qedesha throughout this text for consistency, just as one might use the word monk generically to describe a type of priest across many cultures. Qedesha were a type of priestess common in many Near Eastern cultures and they had many different names. Qedesha, naditu, and other consecrated women had special protections under law, they lived together in the temple where they attended school and were trained in the arts, and given special privileges and responsibilities.

The qedesha were mystical women; healers and midwives, sorceresses, prophetesses, and oracles. Sacred harlots trained in all the arts of sex and love, they explored the mysteries where the sacred meets the profane. The qedesha were the highest rank of healers and to lie with one was a special occasion, and not for simple pleasure of the flesh. Common prostitutes and sex slaves were normal parts of society, so the qedesha occupied a separate role from routine sex. It was a great honor to make love within the precincts of the Goddess, cleanliness and respect were paramount rules and there was no encouragement to either promiscuity or attachment. The qedesha were known for their charity and powers of divination and prophecy. They were among the most respected and mysterious women.

Ishtar

Qedesha were anonymous so that worshippers would not form an attachment to them. They were hidden behind veils and concealed in public. They wore long flowing caftans of mixed colors, interwoven with gold and silver. The qedesha were prized for their weaving, and they ritually wove hemp, linen, and yarn into sacred linens for the devotees. Masters of mystery potions, they made strong drink, lotions, ointments, perfumes, and incense. As midwives they helped women through pregnancy and birth, using cannabis medicines to ease the birth pains and nourish mother and child.

As the goddess of war and strategy, soldiers would come to the temple before battle to receive Ishtar's blessings, divinations, and prophecies. Upon returning from battle the men would immediately return to the temple where they could be cleansed of their battle wounds, nourished with the healing arts and divine sexuality. The qedesha would bathe, soothe, and massage their physical, emotional, and spiritual wounds, cleansing the soldier of the nightmare of war. This ritual was called "Taking the War out of Man" and would probably benefit modern soldiers as well.

It was a common practice for free women to devote themselves to the temple in service of Ishtar for a day, a week, or a year. Hidden behind veils and anonymous, sexual ecstasy offered a path to the divine. Sex with foreigners was encouraged because it kept the bloodlines fresh and paternity was not a concern. Abortions by means of herbal medicine were available if needed and women tracked their fertility cycles; women were in control of their own cycle of life.

Babylonian Marriage Market, by Edwin Long

It was a woman's choice to become a qedesha and it seems to have been a calling. A father could not refuse his unmarried daughter's request to serve the Goddess and the qedesha were free to leave the service of the temple at any time. There was no shame or scandal for serving in the temple, and the children born from the service belonged to their mothers.

Children of the qedesha were said to be *virgin-born* and these children appear in many legends, often fathered by gods. Virgin-born children inherited the names and properties of their mother, in contrast to the rest of the patriarchal society. The qedesha's rights and good name were protected under law, they could own and inherit property, and were free to return to secular life to marry and have children, though it was said that their independence made them difficult wives. The qedesha were also forbidden by law from opening taverns – due to their mastery of mystery potions.

Law Codes of Hammurabi

We learn many important details about the qedesha and naditu from the law codes of Hammurabi, written in Babylon, (ca.) 1750 BCE. The devoted woman could inherit property from her father and do with it as she pleased, and she shared with her brothers an equal portion of their father's estate upon his passing (*Hammurabi's Laws* 178-182)[1]. Children born to qedeshas inherited their name and property from their mother, and the biological father had no claim over the child (law 187). Qedeshas were banned from opening a tavern, or from even entering one, due to their mastery of mystery potions. The penalty for a qedesha who opened a tavern was to be burned to death (law 110). If anyone were to "point the finger" (slander) a devoted woman, or any man's wife, and can not prove his claim, this man shall be taken before the judges and his brow shall be marked (by cutting the skin, or perhaps hair) (law 127).

Ritual Prostitution

The evidence is not clear as to the precise activities of the qedesha and their sexual rituals, and there is much debate over the subject among modern scholars. But the cultures of the Ancient Near East were openly sexual, using sex in magic and agricultural rituals, and the basic existence of ritual temple prostitution is well established. There is certainly no doubt about the existence of conventional prostitution in brothels

1 King, L.W., translator, *The Code of Hammurabi*, The Avalon Project, Yale Law School, Lillian Goldman Law Library, New Haven, CT. https://avalon.law.yale.edu/ancient/hamframe.asp

and taverns, which was legal, common, and taxed throughout the ancient world. Greek and Roman law was expansive on the behavior and taxation of prostitutes, concubines, and slaves, and children born to them.

It is disputed by some modern academics whether consecrated women in goddess cults took part in ritual sexual activities, particularly by third-wave feminists who portray earlier generations of scholarship as prurient sexual fantasy. Prudish scholars dismiss the accounts of the Greek historians, particularly Herodotus, as fiction. Yet these "feminist" scholars generally fail to appreciate just how different the view of sex was in these agricultural communities, for whom sex was public and celebrated, compared to modern cultures who often treat sex as private and shameful.

The patriarchal, Hellenistic Greek culture that came much later did not celebrate women's sexuality in the way their west Asian rivals did – and Greek writers uniformly described ritual prostitution as a foreign practice that was strange to them. The Greek goddess of love, Aphrodite, was the patron of prostitutes and her temples were centers of prostitution throughout Greek history. In Greek culture, prostitutes were not celebrated as hierodules or given special legal protections. Educated, high-class Greek prostitutes were courtesans; some were noted artists and they could become wealthy, famous, and influential, but they were not considered sacred or set apart.

Herodotus

The famous Greek historian Herodotus writing in the 5th century BCE, 1200 years after Hammurabi, described ritual prostitution in Babylon as the most vile of traditions. His account is very famous and has been referenced ever since by scholars. Many modern critics dismiss Herodotus' account as slander or conjecture and claim that this single passage has been overly influential in shaping views of Near Eastern culture. But Herodotus was not alone; Greeks, Romans, and early Church Fathers all described the sexually "licentious" goddess worshipping traditions that existed in many countries, and the biblical Hebrews prophets went to great lengths to vilify them.

> *The foulest Babylonian custom is that which compels every woman of the land to sit in the temple of Aphrodite (Ishtar) and have intercourse with some stranger once in her life. Many women who are rich and proud and disdain to mingle with the rest, drive to the temple in covered carriages drawn by teams, and stand there with a great retinue of attendants. But most sit down in the sacred plot of Aphrodite, with crowns of cord on their heads; there is a great multitude of women coming and*

going; passages marked by line run every way through the crowd, by which the men pass and make their choice. Once a woman has taken her place there, she does not go away to her home before some stranger has cast money into her lap, and had intercourse with her outside the temple; but while he casts the money, he must say, "I invite you in the name of Mylitta" [Assyrian for Aphrodite]. It does not matter what sum the money is; the woman will never refuse, for that would be a sin, the money being by this act made sacred. So she follows the first man who casts it and rejects no one. After their intercourse, having discharged her sacred duty to the goddess, she goes away to her home; and thereafter there is no bribe however great that will get her. So then the women that are fair and tall are soon free to depart, but the uncomely have long to wait because they cannot fulfill the law; for some of them remain for three years, or four. There is a custom like this in some parts of Cyprus.

– Herodotus, *Histories* 1.199[2]

It seems cruel for the unattractive woman to be stuck in the temple if no man was willing to have intercourse with her; it must have been deeply shameful for the poor woman. In another passage, Herodotus wrote about Lydia, a kingdom in eastern Anatolia that included Troy. The Lydians invented coined money, and young Lydian women earned their dowries through temple sex.

All the daughters of the common people of Lydia ply the trade of prostitutes, to collect dowries, until they can get themselves husbands; and they themselves offer themselves in marriage.

– Herodotus, *Histories* 1.93

The customs of the Lydians are like those of the Greeks, except that they make prostitutes of their female children. They were the first men whom we know who coined and used gold and silver currency; and they were the first to sell by retail.

– Herodotus, *Histories* 1.94

Jeremiah

Jeremiah was a Biblical prophet who witnessed the fall of Jerusalem and the destruction of the Hebrew temple at the hands of the Babylonians. In exile, he castigated the pagan Hebrews for their sexual behavior and issued a divorce to the goddess worshippers.

2 Herodotus, *The Histories, with an English translation* by A. D. Godley. Cambridge. Harvard University Press. 1920. http://www.perseus.tufts.edu/

> *Yahweh said to me, "Have you seen what faithless Israel has done? She has gone up on every high hill and under every spreading tree and has committed adultery there ... I gave faithless Israel her certificate of divorce and sent her away because of all her adulteries.*
>
> – Jeremiah 3:6,8

Ezekiel

The Hebrew prophet Ezekiel in the Bible went with the first wave of exiles to Babylon around 589 BCE. Ezekiel condemned the women for their generous sexual practices and he described the custom of women bringing gifts to their lovers rather than receiving them that was also attested by the Greek writer Strabo.

> *You adulterous wife! You prefer strangers to your own husband! All prostitutes receive gifts, but you give gifts to all your lovers, bribing them to come to you from everywhere for your illicit favors. So in your prostitution you are the opposite of others; no one runs after you for your favors. You are the very opposite, for you give payment and none is given to you.*
>
> – Ezekiel 16:32-34

Strabo

Strabo was a Greek writer who lived 64 BCE-24 CE, contemporary with Rufus, and 500 years after Herodotus. Strabo wrote in his book *Geographica* about cult prostitution among the Persians and Armenians, where the exchange of gifts was mutual between men and women. Acilisene was an Anatolian city now known as Erzincan, and Anaitis was a Persian goddess considered to be a manifestation of Ishtar.

> *Now the sacred rites of the Persians, one and all, are held in honour by both the Medes and the Armenians; but those of Anaïtis are held in exceptional honour by the Armenians, who have built temples in her honour in different places, and especially in Acilisenê. Here they dedicate to her service male and female slaves. This, indeed, is not a remarkable thing; but the most illustrious men of the tribe actually consecrate to her their daughters while maidens; and it is the custom for these first to be prostituted in the temple of the goddess for a long time and after this to be given in marriage; and no one disdains to live in wedlock with such a woman.*
>
> *Something of this kind is told also by Herodotus in his account of the Lydian women, who, one and all, he says, prostitute themselves. And*

they are so kindly disposed to their paramours that they not only entertain them hospitably but also exchange presents with them, often giving more than they receive, inasmuch as the girls from wealthy homes are supplied with means. However, they do not admit any man that comes along, but probably those of equal rank with themselves.

– Strabo, *Geographica*, Book XI, Chapter 14, verse 16[3]

RUFUS

Quintus Curtius Rufus (died 53 CE) was a Roman senator and author of an important history of Alexander the Great that described the sexually permissive culture in Babylon, where Alexander died in 323 BCE. Rufus does not describe ritual prostitution, but he makes it clear that Babylon was a sexually free society.

Alexander's stop in Babylon was longer than anywhere else, and here he undermined military discipline more than in any other place. The moral corruption there is unparalleled; its ability to stimulate and arouse unbridled passions is incomparable.

Parents and husbands permit their children and wives to have sex with strangers, as long as this infamy is paid for. All over the Persian empire kings and their courtiers are fond of parties, and the Babylonians are especially addicted to wine and the excesses that go along with drunkenness.

Women attend dinner parties. At first they are decently dressed, then they remove their top-clothing and by degrees disgrace their respectability until (I beg my reader's pardon for saying it) they finally throw off their most intimate garments. This disgusting conduct is characteristic not only of courtesans but also of married women and young girls, who regard such vile prostitution as "being sociable."

– *History of Alexander the Great of Macedonia* [5.1.36-38][4]

Modern scholars who seek to downplay the possibility of sacred sex and ritual prostitution typically fail to acknowledge just how sexually open these cultures were in general. These societies celebrated promiscuous sexuality and pleasure as the blessings of the Goddess, and the exchange of gifts for sex was perfectly normal and common. The idea of a sacred sex priestess is not hard to imagine in this context, nor is it hard to imagine how these practices became increasingly exploitive and disreputable over time as civilization be-

---

3 *The Geography of Strabo,* published in Vol. V of the Loeb Classical Library edition, 1928. http://penelope.uchicago.edu/Thayer/E/Roman/Texts/Strabo/11N*.html

4 Curtius Rufus' *History of Alexander the Great of Macedonia,* translated by John Yardley. https://www.livius.org/sources/content/curtius-rufus/the-rape-of-the-babylonian-women/

came more warlike and globalized and lost its original connections to nature. These cultural practices existed for thousands of years, and the last vestiges were only finally extinguished when Christianity became the state religion of the Roman Empire under Emperor Constantine in the 4th century CE.

Eusebius

Eusebius of Caesarea (c. 265-c. 340) was an early Church Father who wrote histories of early Christianity and a biography of Emperor Constantine, the first Roman emperor to convert to Christianity and who began the systematic and violent purging of pagan religions. In his *Life of Constantine*, Eusebius described in critical terms the Phoenicians from Lebanon. Eusebius praised Constantine for closing the goddess temples and forcing the people to behave themselves.

> *... a hidden and fatal snare of souls in the province of Phœnicia. This was a grove and temple, not situated in the midst of any city, nor in any public place ... [on] the summit of Mount Lebanon, and dedicated to the foul demon known by the name of Venus. It was a school of wickedness for all the votaries of impurity, and such as destroyed their bodies with effeminacy. Here men undeserving of the name forgot the dignity of their sex, and propitiated the demon by their effeminate conduct; here too unlawful commerce of women and adulterous intercourse, with other horrible and infamous practices, were perpetrated in this temple as in a place beyond the scope and restraint of law.*
>
> *Meantime these evils remained unchecked by the presence of any observer, since no one of fair character ventured to visit such scenes. These proceedings, however, could not escape the vigilance of our august emperor, who, having himself inspected them with characteristic forethought, and judging that such a temple was unfit for the light of heaven, gave orders that the building with its offerings should be utterly destroyed. Accordingly, in obedience to the imperial command, these engines of an impure superstition were immediately abolished, and the hand of military force was made instrumental in purging the place. And now those who had heretofore lived without restraint learned self-control through the emperor's threat of punishment.*
>
> – Chapter 55. *Overthrow of an Idol Temple, and Abolition of Licentious Practices, at Aphaca in Phœnicia.*[5]

5 *Life of Constantine*, Eusebius of Caesarea (c. 265-c. 340). Source. Translated by Ernest Cushing Richardson. *From Nicene and Post-Nicene Fathers, Second Series, Vol. 1.* Edited by Philip Schaff and Henry Wace. (Buffalo, NY: Christian Literature Publishing Co., 1890.) Revised and edited for New Advent by Kevin Knight. <http://www.newadvent.org/fathers/2502.htm>.

> *We may instance the Phœnician city Heliopolis, in which those who dignify licentious pleasure with a distinguishing title of honor, had permitted their wives and daughters to commit shameless fornication. But now a new statute, breathing the very spirit of modesty, proceeded from the emperor, which peremptorily forbade the continuance of former practices.*
>
> – Chapter 58. *How he destroyed the Temple of Venus at Heliopolis, and built the First Church in that City.*

Maimonides

12th-century Jewish philosopher Maimonides wrote commentary on the superstitious practices the biblical Hebrews sought to stamp out in Canaan. Maimonides had access to books long lost to us, and he described the gender-bending and bizarre nature-based sexual beliefs of the goddess worshippers.

> *You find it in the book Tomtom, that a male person should wear coloured woman's dress when he stands before Venus, and a female, when standing before Mars, should wear a buckler and other armor. I think that this precept has also another reason; namely, that the interchange of dress creates lust and leads to immorality.*
>
> – *Guide for the Perplexed,* part 3, ch. 37, v. 5[6]

Maimonides wrote about the agricultural sex rituals of the Canaanites and their innovative methods of plant breeding. Perhaps the ancients knew something we don't and some modern experiments need to be conducted on these methods in a proper laboratory setting.

> *They also said that when one species is grafted upon another, the branch which is to be grafted must be in the hand of a beautiful damsel, whilst a male person has disgraceful and unnatural sexual intercourse with her; during that intercourse the woman grafts the branch into the tree. There is no doubt that this ceremony was general, and that nobody refused to perform it, especially as the pleasure of love was added to the (supposed) future results of the grafting.*
>
> *Guide for the Perplexed,* part 3, ch. 37, v.10

---

6 *Maimonides, Guide for the Perplexed,*1190 CE, English Translation, Friedlander (1903) https://www.sefaria.org/Guide_for_the_Perplexed%2C_Part_3.49.2?lang=bi&with=all&lang2=en

Gilgamesh slays the Bull of Heaven

Chapter Eleven

MESOPOTAMIAN MYTHOLOGY

Great Flood

The Hebrews had their roots in Mesopotamia and there are many parallels to Biblical imagery and Old Testament stories found in Sumerian mythology. The Sumerians had a flood myth, very similar to the biblical story of Noah, and one of the most common themes of all ancient mythology. Many old religions have a myth about a great flood that nearly destroys humanity but for the efforts of a hero who rides out the storm in a boat with his family and animals. For the Hindus, the hero is Manu, the Greeks told of Deucalion, the Babylonians retold the story with Utnapishtim in the Epic of Gilgamesh, and variations of the story can be found in China, Europe, and the Americas. It is not hard to see that these common myths preserve a widely held memory of the Younger Dryas cataclysms. The old Sumerian version of the story is the oldest. It is fragmented and many details are missing, but the story would be retold many times over.

The Sumerian gods An and Enlil decided to destroy the human race with a great flood for unknown reasons. The human king Ziusudra was warned by the gods and instructed to build an enormous boat. Upon surviving the flood, the hero was granted immortality for his efforts and permitted to live in Dilmun, a Garden of Eden.

After An, Enlil, Enki, and Ninhursag
Had fashioned the black headed people,
Vegetation luxuriated from the earth,
Animals, four legged (creatures) of the plain,
were brought artfully into existence.

After the ... of kingship had been lowered from heaven,
After the exalted tiara and the throne of kingship had been lowered from heaven,
He perfected the rites and the exalted divine laws...

Founded the five cities in ... pure places,
Called their names, apportioned them as cult centers.

All the windstorms, exceedingly powerful, attacked as one,
At the same time, the flood sweeps over the cult centers.
After, for seven days and seven nights,
The flood had swept over the land,
And the huge boat had been tossed about by the windstorms on the great waters,

Utu came forth, who sheds light on heaven and earth,
Ziusudra opened a window on the huge boat,
The hero Utu brought his rays into the giant boat.
Ziusudra, the king, prostrated himself before Utu,
The king kills an ox, slaughters a sheep.

An and Enlil uttered "breath of heaven," "breath of earth," by
their... it stretched itself,
Vegetation, coming up out of the earth, rises up.

Ziusudra, the king, prostrated himself before An and Enlil.
An and Enlil cherished Ziusudra, life like a god they give him:
Breath eternal like a god they bring down for him.

Then, Ziusudra the king,
The preserver of the name of vegetation and of the seed of mankind,
In the land of crossing, the land of Dilmun,
the place where the sun rises, they caused to dwell.

– Samuel Kramer, *History Begins at Sumer*[1]

Enki and the World Order

This story demonstrates Inanna's desire for power and authority. After Enki had completed fulfilling his creations and inventions, following the instructions of Enlil, Inanna came to complain that she had not been given enough prerogatives. Enki responded that she has been given divine order over battles, she was the chief oracle, and she was responsible for spinning, weaving, dyeing, and making garments. What more did she want?

Enki was dismayed by her boundless ambition, "*Inanna, you have destroyed the indestructible, you have made perish the imperishable. You whose admirers do not grow weary to look at.*" But the text is incomplete so we do not know the end of the story, but we do see that she was honored among the gods with some of the most important duties.

1 Kramer, Samuel Noah. *History Begins at Sumer: Thirty-Nine Firsts in Recorded History.* University of Pennsylvania Press, 1956.

Inanna Takes the Divine Laws

The *me's* were the divine laws that provided an explanation for how the universe operated continuously and harmoniously, without conflict or confusion, and without spinning off into chaos and oblivion. The precise definition of the *me's* has not been unearthed, but in general, they represent the rules and regulations that governed the behavior of each cosmic entity and cultural phenomena that were laid down by the deity that created it. The existence of the *me's* was considered self-evident and offered a satisfactory, albeit superficial, cultural explanation for the origins of human experiences.

The goddess Inanna, in one of her many moments of ambition, decided that she wanted more *me*'s for her city, Uruk, so that it may be more prosperous and to exalt her name and fame. She went to visit Enki, the god of wisdom, and also her father in this story, who was responsible for all the divine laws fundamental to civilization.

Inanna and Enki sat down to feast and drink, and Enki got drunk. The Sumerians brewed and loved beer. In his sloppy cheerfulness, he gave the divine laws to Inanna who happily accepted them. She loaded the *me*'s into her Boat of Heaven and returned to Uruk. Enki woke from his drunkenness to find the *me*'s missing and dispatched his messengers and sea monsters to seize the boat before it arrived home. Inanna's faithful helper Ninshubur came to her rescue and she brought the *me*'s to Uruk triumphantly, cementing the city's preeminence.

Farmer and Shepherd Compete

There are many symbols, motifs, and images that appear in the Bible but were presented in Sumer first. One of the oldest stories is the courtship of Inanna, which shows the competition between the wandering shepherds and the settled farmers.

This conflict would show up again in the biblical story of Cain and his brother Abel. In that story, Cain was a farmer who made offerings of plants and vegetables to God, which were rejected for unknown reasons. Abel the shepherd's offerings of meat on the other hand were accepted, showing that the Hebrew God preferred the shepherds over the farmers. The farmer Cain then killed the shepherd Abel in an act of jealousy that is seen as the first murder.

In the Sumerian story, the goddess Inanna is the deity in contention. The sun god Utu tries to convince his sister Inanna that she should marry the shepherd Dumuzi (also Dumuzid), but she resists as her heart was already pledged to the farmer Enkimdu. The goddess came from the farming communities but now the shepherds wanted to join them and Dumuzi was determined to win her love.

Dumuzi was a prominent human king from the early days of Uruk who became mythologized. This story immortalizes the ascension of the shepherds to the throne after they entered the farmer community.

Her brother, the hero, the warrior, Utu
Says to the pure Inanna:
"O my sister, let the shepherd marry you,
O maid Inanna, why are you unwilling?
His cream is good, his milk is good,
The shepherd, everything his hand touches is bright,
O Inanna, let the shepherd Dumuzi marry you,
O you who are bedecked with jewels, why are you unwilling?
His good cream he will eat with you,
O protector of the king, why are you unwilling?"

Inanna refuses,

"Me the shepherd shall not marry,
In his new garment he shall not drape me,
His fine wool shall not cover me,
Me, the maid, the farmer shall marry,
The farmer who makes plants grow abundantly,
The farmer who makes grain grow abundantly…"

Dumuzi steps forward to proclaim his superior qualities.
"What more does the farmer have than I?
Should he give me his garment, I will give him my ewe, should he give me his beer,
I will give him my milk, should he give me his good bread, I would give him my honey-cheese,
if he gives me his beans, I will give him my cheese,
and I after I have eaten, I will leave my extra cream and my extra milk.
What more does the farmer have than I?"

Apparently, Dumuzi's offerings were sufficient to impress Inanna. The shepherd rejoiced on the riverbank after he finally convinced the goddess to change her mind. There he met Enkimdu and started a quarrel with him. But Enkimdu refused to fight, instead he encouraged Dumuzi to pasture his flocks on his lands. One might think the jilted lover would be jealous and angry, but Enkimdu was friendly, perhaps he was ready to be free of the burdens of his demanding mistress.

The farmer welcomed the shepherd into Uruk.

"Against you shepherd, why shall I strive?" asks Enkimdu,
"let your sheep eat the grass of the riverbank,
in my cultivated lands let your sheep walkabout,
in the bright fields of Uruk let them eat grain,
let your kids and lambs drink the water of my canal."

The shepherd Dumuzi says,

"farmer, at my marriage you may be counted as my friend,
farmer Enkimdu, may you be counted as my friend."

Enkimdu offered to bring his farm products as a wedding gift.

"I will bring you wheat,
I will bring you beans,
I will bring you lentils,
O maid Inanna,
I would bring you whatever there is . . . "

The poet concludes,

"In the dispute which took place between the shepherd and the farmer,
O maid Inanna, your praise is good."

This story comes to a very different result for the farmer and shepherd from the Biblical Cain and Abel who would remain in conflict. For the Sumerians, this story is a celebration of the peaceful union of farmer and shepherd.

Courtship of Inanna and Dumuzi

Dumuzi may have been the first shepherd king to perform the sacred marriage. Centuries later, Dumuzi had been immortalized in the nation's myths as a full god and the husband of Inanna. In the Bible, Dumuzi is identified by his Babylonian name, Tammuz, the consort of Astarte.

The most important Mesopotamian holiday was the spring New Year festival celebrated annually over several days. The significant rite and climax of the holiday was the hieros gamos, the sacred marriage between the king representing the god Dumuzi, and a priestess, the hierodule of heaven, representing the goddess Inanna. The union of the king and priestess, the union of Inanna and Dumuzi, ensured the fecundity and prosperity of nature and society.

This next story follows the first and proceeds to the bridal chamber where Inanna declares herself to be the armor-bearer of the king and his advocate among the gods, the important role confirmed annually by the hieros gamos. This story is worth detailing at length, it is a good example of the graphic sexuality of Sumerian myth and the intrinsic connection between sex, nature, and planting.

The brother spoke to this younger sister
The Sun God, Utu, spoke to Inanna, saying:
'Young Lady, the flax in its fullness is lovely,
Inanna, the grain is glistening in the furrow.
I will hoe it for you, I will bring it to you
A piece of linen, big or small, is always needed.
Inanna, I will bring it to you.'

'Brother, after you've brought my bridal sheet to me,
Who will go to bed with me?
Utu, who will go to bed with me?'
'Sister, your bridegroom will go to be with you
He who was born from a fertile womb,
He who was conceived on the sacred marriage throne
Dumuzi, the shepherd! He will go to bed with you.'

Inanna bathed and anointed herself with scented oil.
She covered her body with the royal robe
She arranged her precious lapis beads around her neck
She took the royal seal in her hand
Dumuzi waited expectantly
Inanna opened the door for him
Inside the house she shone before him
Like the light of the moon
Dumuzi looked at her joyously
He pressed his neck close against hers
He kissed her
'Let the bed that rejoices the heart be prepared!
Let the bed that sweetens the loins be prepared!
Let the bed of kingship be prepared!
Let the bed of queenship be prepared!
Let the royal bed be prepared!'
'The bed is ready!'
'The bed is waiting!'
'What I tell you, let the singer weave into song
What I tell you, let it flow from ear to mouth
Let it pass from old to young.
'My vulva, the horn, the Boat of Heaven,
Is full of eagerness like the young moon
As for me, Inanna, who will plow my vulva?
Who will plow my high field?

Who will plow my wet ground?
As for me, the young woman, who will plow my vulva?
'Great Lady, the king will plow your vulva.
I, Dumuzi, the King, will plow your vulva!'
'Then plow my vulva, man of my heart!
Plow my vulva!'
'O Lady, your breast is your field
Inanna, your breast is your field.
Your broad field pours out plants
Your broad field pours out grain.
Water flows from on high for your servant
Bread flows from on high for your servant
Pour it out for me, Inanna,

I will drink all you offer!
'I bathed for the wild bull
I bathed for the shepherd Dumuzi
Now I will caress my high priest on the bed
I will caress the faithful shepherd Dumuzi
I will decree a sweet fate for him!'

The Queen of Heaven who was presented the Sacred Measures by Enki
Inanna, the first daughter of the moon, decreed the fate of Dumuzi.
'In battle, I am your leader
In combat, I am your armor-bearer
In the assembly, I am your advocate
On the campaign, I am your inspiration
You, the chosen shepherd of the holy shrine
You, the king, the faithful provider of Uruk,
You, the light of An's great shrine
In all ways you are fit
To hold your head high on the lofty dais
To sit on the lapis lazuli throne
To cover your head with the holy crown
To wear long clothes on your body
To bind yourself with the garment of kingship
To race on the road with the holy scepter in your hand
And the holy sandals on your feet
You, the sprinter, the chosen shepherd
In all ways I find you fit
May your heart enjoy long days.
That which An determined for you – may it not be altered
That which Enlil has granted – may it not be altered
You are the favorite of Ningal

Inanna holds you dear.'

Ninshubur, the faithful servant of the holy shrine of Uruk
Led Dumuzi to the sweet thighs of Inanna and spoke:
'My queen, here is the choice of your heart
The king, your beloved bridegroom
May he spend long days in the sweetness of your holy loins
Give him a favorable and glorious reign!
O my Queen of Heaven and Earth
Queen of all the Universe
May he enjoy long days in the sweetness of your holy loins!'
The king went with lifted head on the holy loins
Dumuzi went with lifted head to the loins of Inanna
He went to the Queen with lifted head
He opened his arms to the Holy Priestess of Heaven[2]

Inanna's Descent To the Underworld

Inanna's Descent to the Underworld is one of the most significant Sumerian myths and the prototype for the cycle of life resurrection traditions that lasted thousands of years. Here, Inanna is the first of the dying and rising gods central to many pagan religions. This story tells the tragic second act of Inanna's marriage to Dumuzi, which does not go so well for him.

Though she was already the Queen of Heaven, Inanna was ambitious and sought even greater power and glory. She decided that she would challenge her older sister, Ereshkigal, over her rule of the underworld. Inanna adorned herself in her Queenly robes and jewels, and gathered up the divine laws in preparation for entering the land of no return.

Inanna gave instructions to her vizier and faithful lady-servant Ninshubur. If Inanna failed to return after three days then Ninshubur must set up a lament for her in the assembly of the gods. Ninshubur was to then go visit Enlil and plead with him to save her. If Enlil refused, then Ninshubur is to go visit the moon-god Nanna and repeat her plea. If Nanna also refuses, then Ninshubur was to go visit Enki, the god of wisdom who "*knows the food of life*" and "*the water of life,*" and who would surely come to Inanna's rescue.

Inanna descended to the nether world and approached the gate of the lapis lazuli castle, demanding to be let in. Inanna spoke with the gatekeeper who had been given instructions by his mistress. Ereshkigal was no fool, she knew her sister's intentions. The gatekeeper insisted that Inanna was bound by the same rules as everyone else and must remove one piece

2 Wolkstein, Diane, and Samuel Noah Kramer. *Inanna: Queen of Heaven and Earth ; Her Stories and Hymns from Sumer*. Harper & Row, 1983.

of her clothing at each of the seven gates. The seven gates are highly symbolic of the journey to mystical enlightenment and are reflected in many other traditions.

At the first gate, her crown was removed. Inanna protested but was told that she must respect the laws of the underworld. At the second gate, the measuring rod and line was removed and again she protested. At the third gate, her lapis lazuli necklace was removed. At the fourth gate, more jewelry was removed. At the fifth gate, the gold ring from her hand was removed. At the sixth gate, her breastplate was removed. At the seventh gate, her garment was removed, leaving her naked.

Bowed low and humbled, yet furious, Inanna was brought naked before her sister Ereshkigal who was seated on her lapis lazuli throne. The Annunaki, the seven judges of the underworld, pronounced judgment upon Inanna. Death!

Inanna was struck down and her corpse hung on a hook.

After waiting three days and nights, the faithful Ninshubur set up the lamentation and beat a drum in mourning. She traveled to visit Enlil, who would not help. Ninshubur then traveled to visit Nanna, who would also not help her. But Enki was greatly disturbed by the news and immediately jumped to aid the beloved Inanna.

What now has happened to my daughter! I am troubled,
What now has happened to Inanna! I am troubled,
What now has happened to the queen of all the lands! I am troubled,
What now has happened to the hierodule of heaven! I am troubled.

He brought forth dirt from his fingernail and fashioned the kurgarru,
He brought forth dirt from the red painted fingernail and fashioned the kalaturru,
To the kurgarru he gave the "food of life"
To the kalaturru he gave the "water of life"

The kurgarru and the kalaturru were sexless eunuchs who traveled to the underworld with the food of life and the water of life and are symbolic of eunuch priests. They met with Ereshkigal and requested the corpse of Inanna.

In some versions of the story, when Inanna died all sexual activity on Earth came to an abrupt halt, greatly concerning the gods and interfering with the cycle of life. When the eunuchs met Ereshkigal they found her in agony, as though she was in labor even though she was not with child.

The eunuchs requested the corpse of Inanna and it was removed from the hook; they sprinkled on her the food of life and the water of life, and she rose from the dead.

Before Inanna could ascend from the underworld, the servants of Ereshkigal reminded her of her obligations. No one can leave the underworld without sending down a replacement. Vicious demons followed Inanna to ensure that she returned a suitable substitute.

The first deities that Inanna met upon ascending prostrated themselves before her, showing their humility and servitude. This pleased Inanna and they were spared, and she continued the journey to her home.

When she arrived at Uruk, she found her husband Dumuzi sitting proudly on her throne, dressed in his finest regalia, and celebrating his ascension. Inanna was enraged at his lack of respect and mourning for her, she cast upon him the "*eye of death!*"

Inanna gave her one and only husband to the demons and the underworld.

Dumuzi wept and pleaded to Utu, his brother-in-law, for deliverance from this cruel fate. Utu felt mercy and changed Dumuzi to a gazelle so he could escape, but the demons caught and beat him. All his attempts to escape failed, and ultimately the demons killed poor, terrified Dumuzi, the tragic victim of Inanna's ambition and rage and his own unrighteousness.

Inanna then deeply regretted her actions, she wept and mourned for Dumuzi, along with his mother, and his sister, Geshtinanna, the goddess of vegetation. The three goddesses worked to bring Dumuzi back from the netherworld, but since there must always be a replacement it was agreed that Geshtinanna would take his place half the year. The annual transfer from Dumuzi to Geshtinanna back to the underworld represented the turning of the seasons and was at the heart of the annual springtime New Year festival.

Inanna's descent to the Underworld is an archetypal story that was taken up by many other cultures and would live on for thousands of years. These stories of a dying and rising god brought back from the underworld for half the year were retold in the Mystery religions as the myths of Demeter and Persephone, Isis and Osiris, Cybele and Attis, Orpheus and Eurydice, Ishtar and Tammuz, Dionysus, and others. These stories symbolize the lean winter months followed by the bountiful spring and summer. Jesus Christ would of course become the ultimate dying and rising god, but that story comes later.

The Sumerian version of the story is unique, not only because it is the oldest we know, but because it is Inanna's ambitions for power that cause her husband to be killed. In other versions of the story, the hero dies in more innocent circumstances, such as in a hunting accident.

For Goddess religions, these cycle of life myths and their springtime resurrection festivals are central to their beliefs and are every bit as important as Easter is for Christians. Easter is a Christian springtime resurrection holiday with Jesus as the dying and rising god that was explicitly syncretized from these older traditions. The difference for Christians is that the ritual is separated from nature and the seasons and was instead converted into a celebration of eternal life rather than the Earth's vegetative cycle of life.

Epic of Gilgamesh

The discovery of the Sumerians, with their writing and elaborate mythologies that reflect many stories in the Old Testament, completely reshaped our views on the origins of human civilization and the lives of ancient people. The *Epic of Gilgamesh* was translated in 1872 to great acclaim; not only is it the world's oldest complete work of epic literature, but it is also a series of tales reflecting the life, conflict, and spiritual growth of humanity's first literary hero. Gilgamesh appears as a character in the oldest Sumerian tales, and scraps of the *Epic* have been found in Uruk, but the more complete versions of the story came from Babylon and Nineveh later on. This translation comes from Babylon and some of the gods have new names, Inanna is Ishtar, An is Anu, Dumuzi is Tammuz, Utu the sun god is Shamash, and Enki is Ea.

Prior to Gilgamesh, there are no examples from archaeology of any individual human being celebrated as a hero, their names living on beyond them. Gilgamesh is our first legendary hero and his name remains immortal to this day.

Gilgamesh is believed to have been the fifth king of Uruk who reigned 4600 years ago and is listed on the primeval portion of the Sumerian Kings List right after Dumuzi, who also went to mythological glory. The Sumerian Kings List is very similar to the listing of patriarchal generations in the Bible from Adam to Noah. In both traditions, the early patriarchs lived for centuries or even over a thousand years.

Gilgamesh was a great king of Uruk, the world's first major city, and sought to glorify his name through heroic adventures, eventually seeking immortality. When one compares this desire for immortality against the Neolithic Goddess traditions of Çatal Hüyük, where death is a constant reminder and there appears to be no acknowledgment of individual heroes, one can see the emergence of the human ego coalescing into form, emerging from the chaos of undifferentiated nature.

A critical aspect of the epic is the presentation of women and the goddesses. Ishtar plays an important role in the story but is treated antagonistically by Gilgamesh. This marks a moment when human cultures shifted and the status of the feminine divine was slowly degraded while the status of the warrior kings began their ascent. Other contemporary stories like the Enuma Elish, the Babylonian creation myth, also portray the feminine divine negatively.

We also see in the epic presentations of sexuality that contrast starkly with Judeo-Christian ethics. Female sexuality is shown to have the power to civilize the untamed man, while homosexuality is embraced and not seen as sinful or ignoble. Judeo-Christian traditions encourage sexual asceticism and seek to restrain women's sexuality as much as possible, making it acceptable only within the context of monogamous marriage and childbearing. Judeo-Christian traditions also condemn homosexuality, but the Mesopotamian cultures embraced sexuality broadly, recognizing the connection to nature.

Gilgamesh was semi-divine, the child of the Priest-King Lugalbanda and the goddess Ninsun, giving him extraordinarily long life and superhuman strength. He was a mighty king, awesome to perfection, who ruled with great strength and confidence for many years. Gilgamesh was a man of great appetites, fighting with all the men and taking all the women for himself, he ruled roughly, generating resentment and complaints. For one example, Gilgamesh was fond of bedding brides on their wedding day before they were able to lie with their husbands.

Hearing these complaints, the gods decided to craft a match for Gilgamesh, a man of great strength who could engage him and allow the children of Uruk to live in peace. They created Enkidu, a wild man of the forest who ran with the beasts, naked and covered in hair. Enkidu ate grass and drank from watering holes, racing as swift as the wind.

A hunter came across Enkidu and was frightened, he reported to Gilgamesh that he has seen a man who is the biggest and the best, who roams tirelessly across the land, wrecking traps and letting the animals go free.

Gilgamesh instructed the hunter to set a trap for the wild man, "take back with you a fine lover, Shamhat, the sacred temple harlot who might let him see what charm and force a girl can have. When Enkidu comes to the watering hole, let her strip nearby in isolation to show him all her grace. If he is drawn toward her and leaves the herd to mate, the beasts on high will leave him behind."

Shamhat spied Enkidu near the watering hole, she said, *"That is he, Shamhat! Release your clenched arms, expose your sex so he can take in your voluptuousness. Do not be restrained – take his energy! When he sees you, he will draw near to you. Spread out your robe so he can lie upon you, and perform the task of womankind! His animals, who grew up in his wilderness, will become alien to him, and his lust will groan over you."*[3]

Shamhat unclutched her bosom, exposed her sex, and he took in her voluptuousness. She was not restrained, but took his energy. She spread out her robe and he lay upon her, she performed the task of womankind. His lust groaned over her; for six days and seven nights Enkidu stayed aroused, and had intercourse with the harlot[4] *until he was sated with her charms.*

But when he turned his attention to his animals, the gazelles saw Enkidu and darted off, the wild animals distanced themselves from his body. Enkidu was diminished, his running was not as before. But then he drew himself up, for his understanding had broadened. Turning around, he sat down at Shamhat's feet, gazing into her face, his ears attentive as the harlot spoke.

Shamhat said to Enkidu: "You are beautiful, Enkidu, you are become like a god. Why do you gallop around the wilderness with the wild beasts? Come, let me bring you into Uruk, to the Holy Temple, the residence of Anu and Ishtar, the place of Gilgamesh, who is wise to perfection, but who struts his power over the people like a wild bull." What she kept saying found favor with him. Becoming aware of himself, he sought a friend.

"Come, let us go, so he may see your face. I will lead you to Gilgamesh – I know where he will be. Look about, Enkidu, inside Uruk, where the people show off in skirted finery, where every day is a day for some festival, where the lyre and drum play continually, where harlots stand about prettily, exuding voluptuousness, full of laughter and on the couch of night the sheets are spread.

"Enkidu, you who do not know how to live, I will show you Gilgamesh, a man of extreme feelings.

Look at him, gaze at his face – he is a handsome youth, with freshness, his entire body exudes voluptuousness. He has mightier strength than you, without sleeping day or night!"

Enkidu and Shamhat traveled to Uruk. On the way Enkidu learned the civilized ways, herding sheep, and using weapons for the first time to chase away lions and predators; he put on clothes and became like a war-

3 Kovacs, Maureen Gallery (translator), *The Epic of Gilgamesh*, Stanford University Press; 1st Edition, 1989. Electronic Edition by Wolf Carnahan, 1998. http://www.ancienttexts.org/library/mesopotamian/gilgamesh

4 The original word *harimtu* does not have a precise translation in English, Shamhat's identity has been debated ever since the *Epic* was discovered.

rior. Enkidu learned to eat bread and drink beer as men and women do; he learned all the customs a man needs to know in the city.

When Enkidu entered Uruk, he was hailed as a hero, as one who might rival the king who treats the gentlefolk unfairly. The people rallied around and adored him, for so it is when one comes from nowhere to do what no one thought could be done.

Enkidu came to a wedding party Gilgamesh was attending and stood before the bridal chamber, he stopped Gilgamesh from having sex with the bride as was his custom. Gilgamesh met the challenge and the two fought throughout the night, round about Uruk's walls, which they chipped and wrecked in places.

After many hours of fighting, they were evenly matched. Enkidu finally sued for rest saying, "Gilgamesh, enough! I am here to match some fate with you, not to destroy or rival any king." Then Enkidu and Gilgamesh joined in sacred friendship and sealed their solemn bond with a noble kiss – Gilgamesh embraced him like a wife.

Enkidu and Gilgamesh became fast friends, making many plans for the future together. Gilgamesh proposed that they go kill Humbaba-the-awful, a mighty demon who lived deep in the Cedar Forest. Enkidu objected as the Cedar Forest is the domain of the gods, but no one could dissuade Gilgamesh from his desire for glory and they prepared for the journey. Gilgamesh had bad dreams along the way, but Enkidu encouraged him on. After a fearsome battle, Humbaba was killed.

Ishtar was impressed with the virility of Gilgamesh and attempted to seduce him. *"Come to me," she whispered. "Come to me and be my groom. Let me taste all parts of you, treat you as husband, be treated as your wife… Come to my home, most sweetly scented of all places, where holy faces wash your feet with tears as do the priests and priestesses of gods like Anu. All mighty hands of kings and queens will open doors for you."*

Gilgamesh addressed Princess Ishtar saying: "What would I have to give you if I married you! Do you need oil or garments for your body! Do you lack anything for food or drink! I would gladly feed you food fit for a god, I would gladly give you wine fit for a king."

"Where are your bridegrooms that you keep forever? See here now, I will recite the list of your lovers. Tammuz, the lover of your earliest youth, for him you have ordained lamentations year upon year!

"You loved the colorful 'Little Shepherd' bird and then hit him, breaking his wing, so now he stands in the forest crying 'My Wing'!

"You loved the supremely mighty lion, yet you dug for him seven and again seven pits.

You loved the stallion, famed in battle, yet you ordained for him the whip, the goad, and the lash, ordained for him to gallop for seven and seven hours, ordained for him drinking from muddled waters,' you ordained for his mother Silili to wail continually.

"You loved the Shepherd, the Master Herder, who continually presented you with bread baked in embers, and who daily slaughtered for you a kid. Yet you struck him, and turned him into a wolf, so his own shepherds now chase him and his own dogs snap at his shins.

"You loved Ishullanu, your father's date gardener, who continually brought you baskets of dates, and brightened your table daily. You raised your eyes to him, and you went to him: 'Oh my Ishullanu, let us taste of your strength, stretch out your hand to me, and touch our vulva. Ishullanu said to you: 'Me! What is it you want from me! Has my mother not baked, and have I not eaten that I should now eat food under contempt and curses and that alfalfa grass should be my only cover against the cold? As you listened to these his words you struck him, turning him into a dwarf, and made him live in the middle of his (garden of) labors, where the mihhu do not go up, nor the bucket of dates go down.

"And now me! It is me you love, and you will ordain for me as for them!"

When Ishtar heard this, in a fury she went up to the heavens, going to Anu, her father, and crying, going to Anrum, her mother, and weeping: "Father, Gilgamesh has insulted me over and over, Gilgamesh has recounted despicable deeds about me, despicable deeds and curses!"

Ishtar spoke to her father, Anu, saying: "Father, give me the Bull of Heaven, so he can kill Gilgamesh in his dwelling. If you do not give me the Bull of Heaven, I will knock down the Gates of the Netherworld, I will smash the doorposts, and leave the doors flat down, and will let the dead go up to eat the living! And the dead will outnumber the living!"

Ishtar led the Bull of Heaven down to the earth. When it reached Uruk It climbed down to the Euphrates… At the snort of the Bull of Heaven a huge pit opened up, and 100 Young Men of Uruk fell in. At his second snort a huge pit opened up, and 200 Young Men of Uruk fell in. At his third snort a huge pit opened up, and Enkidu fell in up to his waist.

Then Enkidu jumped out and seized the Bull of Heaven by its horns. the Bull spewed his spittle in front of him, with his thick tail he flung his dung behind him. Enkidu stalked and hunted down the Bull of Heaven. He grasped it by the thick of its tail and held onto it with both his hands, while Gilgamesh, like an expert butcher, boldly and surely approached the Bull of Heaven. Between the nape and the horns, he thrust his sword.

After they had killed the Bull of Heaven, they ripped out its heart and presented it to Shamash. They withdrew bowing down humbly to Shamash. Then the brothers sat down together. Ishtar went up onto the top of the wall of Uruk, cast herself into the pose of mourning, and hurled her woeful curse: "Woe unto Gilgamesh who slandered me and killed the Bull of Heaven!"

When Enkidu heard this pronouncement of Ishtar, he wrenched off the Bull's hindquarter and flung it in her face: "If I could only get at you I would do the same to you! I would drape his innards over your arms!" Ishtar assembled the (cultic women) of lovely-locks, joy-girls, and harlots, and set them to mourning over the hindquarter of the Bull.

Gilgamesh said to the palace retainers: "Who is the bravest of the men? Who is the boldest of the males! Gilgamesh is the bravest of the men, the boldest of the males! She at whom we flung the hindquarter of the Bull of Heaven in anger, Ishtar has no one that pleases her in the street." Gilgamesh held a celebration in his palace.

The gods were angered that Enkidu and Gilgamesh had killed the Bull of Heaven and Mumbaba of the Cedar Forest. Enlil said, "let Enkidu die, but Gilgamesh must not die!"

Enkidu became sick and grieved that he was dying. Gilgamesh was devastated by Enkidu's death, realizing that he too will die.

Over his friend, Enkidu, Gilgamesh cried bitterly, roaming the wilderness. "I am going to die! Am I not like Enkidu?! Deep sadness penetrates my core, I fear death, and now roam the wilderness – I will set out to the region of Utnapishtim, son of Ubartutu, and will go with utmost dispatch!"

Utnapishtim was the hero of the great floods, like Noah, who survived with his family and restored humanity after it was devastated by the cataclysms. Utnapishtim and his wife had pleased the gods and were given the gift of immortality. Gilgamesh hoped to learn their secret.

It was a very long and perilous journey to get to Utnapishtim, much of which is missing from the broken tablets. Gilgamesh had to cross over mountain passes and great rivers, slaying monstrous lions, bears, and beasts. Eventually, he arrived at the end of the world, crossing the river of death (similar to the River Styx from Greek mythology) to reach the island of Dilmun where Utnapishtim lives.

Gilgamesh told his story and asked for help, but Utnapishtim reprimanded him because he knew that fighting the fate of humans is futile and ruins the joy in life. Utnapishtim told Gilgamesh how the great storm and flood was brought by the god Enlil, who wanted to destroy all of mankind for the noise and confusion they brought. But the god Ea (Enki) warned Utnapishtim, telling him to abandon wealth and build an ark and to load onto it his family and all the living things.

The frightful rains came as promised and the whole world was covered with water, killing everything except those with Utnapishtim on his boat. The boat came to rest on top of the mountain of Nisir, where they waited for the waters to subside, releasing first a dove, then a swallow, and then a raven to check for dry land. They made it to shore and Utnapishtim made sacrifices and burned incense to the gods. Enlil was angry that someone had survived his flood but Ea advised him to make his peace. So Enlil blessed Utnapishtim and his wife and granted them everlasting life, taking them to live in the land of the gods on the island of Dilmun.

Despite his reservations, Utnapishtim told Gilgamesh he would give him a chance at immortality if he could stay awake for seven days and nights, but Gilgamesh fell asleep immediately, exhausted by his long and difficult journey. Utnapishtim mocked Gilgamesh and told him to go back to Uruk. But Utnapishtim's wife had mercy, and they told Gilgamesh of a plant that grows at the very bottom of the ocean that will make him young again.

Gilgamesh obtained the plant of immortality by binding stones to his feet to allow him to walk under the sea. He found the plant and brought it to shore, planning to bring it back to Uruk. But while Gilgamesh was bathing, the plant was stolen by a serpent who ate it. The serpent then shed its skin and was reborn, the ancient symbol of the cycle of life.

Gilgamesh wept at his failure and returned to Uruk empty-handed. And that is the end of the Epic of Gilgamesh, the quest for glory and immortality and disappointment at the ultimate futility of it all.

Enuma Elish

The *Enuma Elish* is the Babylonian creation myth, it introduced the warrior storm god Marduk, as the new king of the pantheon, pushing aside Enlil, who was not eliminated but sent into retirement. Marduk was an entirely new god, not simply a renaming of an old god, and likely represented the rise of a new political dynasty and the ascendency of Babylon as the new capital over Uruk. Compared to Enlil, who was a rather kindly god for the most part, Marduk was violent and wielded terrible weapons of war, reflecting the shifts in society since the advent of Bronze Age weapons. The Enuma Elish is believed to date back to the 18th century BCE when Babylon rose to prominence under Hammurabi.

The Enuma Elish is a typical mythological tale where the younger gods rise up to defeat the older generations of gods and become pre-eminent. The Greeks told stories of the Olympian gods battling the Titans, leading to the rise of Zeus as the king of the gods, and the Phoenicians had stories of Baal rising to lead his pantheon.

The Enuma Elish is part of a trend in mythology of the era when the goddesses were losing their paramount status as male storm gods ascended as heroes. In the Enuma Elish, the primeval mother goddess, now named Tiamat, had been converted into a villain who must be defeated by the hero, in contrast to the kindly Nammu of the Sumerians.

Similarly, in the Epic of Gilgamesh, the hero insulted Ishtar and rejected her seductions. Gilgamesh speaks to Ishtar as though she is a source of trouble that should be ignored. Gilgamesh was not alone in this attitude towards women. The Hebrews portrayed Eve as the cause of the fall of man in the Garden of Eden, while the Greeks presented Pandora, also the first woman, in a similar light when she opened the jar that unleashed all the world's ills.

The Enuma Elish describes two primeval gods; Apsu, who represents the upper, fresh waters, and Tiamat, goddess of the lower, salt waters. Apsu and Tiamat join to generate creation and parent a generation of gods. In time, disharmony prevailed and Apsu decided to move against the younger gods. Ea (Enki), the wisest of the young gods, learned of the plan and managed to kill Apsu by drowning him. Ea then reigned in Apsu's stead and with his wife Damkina conceived Marduk, the strongest and most able of the gods.

Tiamat wanted revenge for the death of her husband and created an army of titanic monsters and gods. Even the great Ea could not withstand the attack. Tiamat elevated Kingu and gave him the Tablets of Destiny which gave him dominion, and made him her new husband. The gods who opposed them were powerless against Tiamat and Kingu. The gods then elected Marduk as their new champion, with kingship over the entire universe, and they gave him great weapons to slay Tiamat.

Then the lord raised up the flood-storm, his mighty weapon.
He mounted the storm-chariot irresistible and terrifying.
He harnessed and yoked to it a team-of-four,
The Killer, the Relentless, the Trampler, the Swift.
Sharp were their poison-bearing teeth.
They were versed in ravage, skilled in destruction.
On his right he posted the Smiter, fearsome in battle,
On the left the Combat, which repels all the zealous.

His cloak was an armor of terror,
His head was turbaned with his fearsome halo.
The lord went forth and followed his course,
He set his face Towards the raging Tiamat.

Marduk commenced a mighty battle, destroying Tiamat with mighty winds, killing her, and splitting her in half like a shellfish into two parts. One half of Tiamat was set up as the ceiling of the sky while Marduk formed the world from her corpse. The gods then killed Kingu, and Ea used his blood to create humankind for the purpose of serving the gods with their labor. Babylon was established as the residence of the chief gods. The gods confirmed Marduk's kingship, singing a hymn to his glory and hailing him with 50 titles. Marduk then reigned as the supreme deity, ordering heaven and the earth and controlling the Tablets of Destiny.

New Year Festival

Akitu, the Mesopotamian New Year festival was the most important holiday of the year. The twelve-day festival served to establish harmony with nature and was indispensable to ensuring a good harvest and prosperity for the community. Rituals also reconfirmed the relationship between the people and the gods, as exemplified by the king's rituals, who represented the people, and his presence was critical otherwise certain rituals could not be performed.

The New Year Festival was typically held in the spring following the Spring equinox, though in some communities the festival was held in the fall. These festivals were held for thousands of years starting in ancient Sumer, or even earlier, and continued into Roman times. Rituals acted out important mythologies, including the Enuma Elish, Ishtar's Descent, and the Courtship of Ishtar and Tammuz. The best descriptions we have of the Akitu Festival come from Babylon.

The king had important duties including his ritual humiliation and the sacred marriage. During the first five days of the Festival, the rites focused on bereavement and uncertainty for the future. The people of the city were given over to lamentations, misery, and ritual wailing. On the evening of the fourth day, the Enuma Elish was recited in its entirety, reconfirming the sacred connection back to the beginning of creation.

The fifth day was the Day of Atonement for the king, and the contrast in this important ritual compared to the reverential treatment of rulers we are accustomed to could not be starker. The temple was purified and many preparations were made for offerings. The king entered Marduk's shrine, the Esagila, escorted by the chapel priests, who left him alone. The high priest emerged from inside the Holy of Holies where the statue of Marduk stood. The high priest took the king's scepter, ring, scimitar, and crown and placed them before the god. The king humbled himself before the gods, begging for forgiveness for his sins and shortcomings.

The priest then approached the king, stripped of all his emblems of royalty, and struck him hard across the face. It was important that he hit the king hard enough to make the king cry, for without tears the ritual was invalid. Tears were signs of the king's humility, penance, and confession. Through his penance the king was cleansed of his sins, thus cleansing the entire community. The king was then coronated anew, his insignias were restored, and he sat upon the throne that represented the connection of Heaven and Earth. The ritual cycle of the king's degradation and reinstatement signified the chaos out of which civilization and kingship were first created.

On day six the god idols were brought by barge down to Babylon from other cities, Nippur, Uruk, Kish, and Eridu, for a series of rituals that culminated on day seven as the liberation of Marduk. On day eight, the gods gathered together and bestowed their combined powers on Marduk who gained a "destiny beyond compare." Day nine featured a triumphal procession down the grand boulevard led by the king to the Bit Akitu, the House of the New Year's feast, to celebrate his victory and the renewal of nature. Day ten was the climax of the festival with a great celebration and banquet at the Bit Akitu. The Bit Akitu was located outside the city walls and was surrounded by rich gardens. These elaborate gardens represented the god's conquering of chaos, and also personified nature itself. Following the feast, the King returned inside Babylon to take part in the sacred marriage.

The sacred marriage, the hieros gamos, was the most important ritual of all. The king and the high priestess disappeared behind the curtains for a private ceremony that presumably involved sexual intercourse. The king had to annually prove his vitality in order to retain the right to rule while the sex ensured that the goddess would bring forth the spring blossoming of the flowers. The hieros gamos confirmed the renewal of the seasons and the divine union between the king, who represents all the people, and the Goddess who represents nature and the fertility of life, and the restoration of harmony and order.

Scholars dispute whether the hieros gamos ritual involved actual physical sex between the king and a hierodule. There is no doubting the sexual imagery and metaphor, but it is unknown to us what specifically occurred behind the curtains in the temple between the king and the priestess. It is conceivable that in the early era the ritual was genuinely sexual, but over time the physical act was replaced by a symbolic act. The Akitu festival was celebrated for thousands of years, so it stands to reason that specific rituals varied over time.

On days eleven and twelve, the gods were assembled a final time to determine the destiny of the community for the coming year, attuning the community to the gods' designs, and reflecting the requirement that humans were created to serve the gods, and their happiness was dependent on carrying out the gods' wishes. On the last day, the various gods returned to their temples and the people returned to the life of everyday normalcy, planting, sowing, and harvesting for the coming year.[5]

SYMBOLS FROM THE GARDEN OF EDEN

Serpents

The serpent is one of the most ancient and enduring symbols of the Goddess and represents wisdom and prophetic counsel. The serpent who sheds its skin and is seemingly reborn symbolized the cycle of life. Snakes were common in pottery and art throughout the ancient world, often shown with goddesses, coiled around a sacred tree of life, or in an endless circle eating its tail.

The symbolism of the wise serpent remains with us today as the caduceus, the symbol of medicine featuring two snakes coiled around a staff. Serpents were valued in agricultural communities rather than feared because they protected the granaries from rodents and other vermin. There is also speculation that poisonous snake bites induced hallucinations that produce shamanic visions and insights. Snake tubes were a feature at many goddess temples, where snakes were kept, cultivated, and revered.

The Sumerian goddess Nidaba, the first patron of writing, was often depicted as a serpent and was described as "the Divine Serpent Lady." Inanna, Ishtar, and many other goddesses were associated with serpents and their priestesses in the temples often served as oracles and interpreters of dreams. Ishtar was known as "She who Directs the Oracles" and was commonly portrayed holding snakes.

The Mediterranean island of Crete was a Bronze Age Goddess worshipping culture where artifacts of females and snakes abound. A cobra

5 Frankfort, Henri (1978) *Kingship and the Gods: a study of Ancient Near Eastern Religion as the Integration of Society and Nature* (with a preface by Samuel Noah Kramer). The University of Chicago Press, Chicago, London. http://www.gatewaystobabylon.com/religion/akitu.htm

goddess was also pre-eminent in pre-dynastic Egypt and the cobra continued to be an important symbol through their entire ancient history. In classical Greece, serpents were associated with Athena, the goddess of wisdom, and were especially important at the Oracle of Delphi where the oracular priestesses were known as the Pythia, named for the python. In the Bible, the serpent was one of Moses' most powerful symbols, but was later rejected during the monotheistic reforms of King Hezekiah. In the Biblical Garden of Eden myth, the serpent was transformed into a villainous instrument of Eve's denial of God's law.

Tree of Life

The Tree of Life was a common image in Mesopotamian art and religion. On some levels the Tree of Life is clearly a symbolic mythological archetype, a plant providing immortality to whoever partakes of it such as in the Epic of Gilgamesh. In other cases, the Tree of Life may be referring to an actual sacred plant, one whose identity is intentionally obscured and kept secret for only initiates to know.[6]

Kiskanu was the name for the Sumerian tree of life that appeared in many artworks and legends. In a myth called *The Incantation of Eridu,* the city of Eridu was described as having a House of Wisdom, a sacred grove, and a Kiskanu tree with the appearance of lapis lazuli. Scholars have debated the meaning of the Kiskanu tree for decades with no clear consensus about its true meaning. Some scholars have suggested that Kiskanu is cannabis.[7] The *-kanu* suffix is phonetically similar to the Assyrian *qunubu,* Sanskrit *kana*, Persian *canna*, and *cannabis.*

Though stylized, Assyrian images of the Tree of Life show a plant with a seven-bladed leaf being used in rituals. The images also show shamanic priests handling pine cone-like objects that can easily be seen as cannabis buds. Considering that cannabis was arguably the first plant cultivated and was being used for food, fiber, and drugs since the dawn of the Neolithic Revolution, there is a strong case to be made for its importance as a ritual plant in a culture that celebrated nature.

CANNABIS IN MESOPOTAMIA

Mesopotamian religion was deeply tied to nature and the annual growth of plants, and cannabis is a truly special and unique plant

6 Bennett, Chris, *Cannabis and the Soma Solution*, Trine Day, 2010. Images 10.9, 10.12, 10.16
7 Bennett, Chris, "Cannabis the Once and Future Tree of Life," *Cannabis Culture*, May 19, 2018. https://www.cannabisculture.com/content/2018/05/19/cannabis-the-once-and-future-tree-of-life/

they were intimately familiar with. No other plant provides such an array of valuable products for people, and cannabis was spread around the world by humans, both the plant and people have benefited from the relationship. Cannabis was present when plants were first cultivated and may have been that seminal plant.

It is reasonable to think that in Bronze Age religions they still remembered their Neolithic roots and celebrated cannabis ritually. We know that the most important recipes for ritual intoxicants, medicines, and incense were secrets kept only for initiates and intentionally left a mystery to those outside. There may never be conclusive enough evidence to satisfy critics, but the idea that cannabis was sacred in the Ancient Near East and through history as a Tree of Life has many believers.

Cannabis was cultivated in Mesopotamian gardens for ritual and temple purposes with irrigated water and presumably did not grow wild to any great degree since the country is too arid. Cannabis thrived just to the north in Anatolia and also grows well in the mountains of Persia immediately to the east. The Mesopotamians were known for growing linen extensively for clothes and did not grow much hemp for fiber. High-quality hemp fiber and rope production is a specialty task, hemp ropes and fiber products were always valuable objects of trade throughout history and were imported as needed. The Mesopotamians did not need a lot of cannabis if they only used it for ritual and medicine and could grow enough for those purposes in gardens.

Reginald Campbell Thompson was a famed British archaeologist who translated many Assyrian and Sumerian texts. Thompson provides an extensive discussion of cannabis in his book, *A Dictionary of Assyrian Botany.* Cannabis is the 48th most mentioned herb, indicating that the Sumerians may not have grown a lot of it, which makes sense considering the location and climate. Many of the old cuneiform texts still need to be translated, and there remain debates among scholars over specific translations. Plant names in particular have been tricky for scholars to identify and a great deal of uncertainty remains over plants named in various medicinal recipes.

Though detailed evidence of cannabis use in Sumerian times is limited, it was known as *azallu,* a drug for grief that was also used for spinning and making cables, which shows they accurately understood its use as an industrial fiber and as a psychoactive drug. There are explicit accounts of cannabis' ritual use by the later Assyrians and others. The Assyrians called cannabis,[8] *qunubu or kunubu,* etymologically close to their contemporaries' names, He-

8 Thompson, Campbell R., *A Dictionary of Assyrian Botany*, The British Academy, Burlington Gardens, London, 1949.

brew *qaneh bosm,* Scythian *kannabis,* Greek *konabos,* and the later English *cannabis.*[9] Cannabis is an ancient name that has been passed down through time. Cannabis was used medicinally and as a sacred incense mixed with myrrh. Durable hemp fibers came from Anatolia, as they had for a long time.

There is an herb identified as *Sim.Ashara,* "aromatic of the goddess Ishtar," that many scholars equate to *qunubu,* cannabis.[10] The priestesses of Ishtar mixed cannabis with other aromatic resins like myrrh, balsam, frankincense, and perfumes, and used the mixture to anoint their skins and burn as incense. Qunubu was identified as among the aromatics to be used in rituals in a number of texts, such as the Kettledrum Ritual. Mesopotamian holy men used a variety of enchanted intoxicants to achieve heightened states of excitement and add power and mystery to their rituals.

Recipes for sacred incense were found in the royal libraries of Assyrian King Ashurbanipal, who reigned from 669-631 BCE. The Assyrian capital city was Nineveh in the north of Mesopotamia, near modern-day Mosul, and it was destroyed in 612 BCE. When the city was sacked the library was burned and buried under rubble. It remained untouched until it was found by archaeologists in one of their most important discoveries. There were a large number of recipes for medicines and incense found, that were recognized to be copies of much older texts, but scholars have not translated them all.

In a letter written in 680 BCE to the mother of Assyrian king Esarhaddon, in response to her question, "What is used in the sacred rites," a high priest named Neralsharrani responded that *"The main items for the rites are fine oil, water, honey, odorous plants, myrrh, and qunubu (cannabis)."*[11] In another letter from the same library, qunubu was among a list of spices, and as an ingredient in a perfume recipe, as a name used for girls, and as a term of endearment.[12]

Sacred recipes for medicines, incense, and magic were closely guarded secrets in most cultures, making it a challenge, if not impossible, for modern scholars to discern what was being used in the temples. Magic revealed is magic lost. The recipe for *Kykeon,* the sacred intoxicating beverage of the Greek Eleusinian Mysteries remains unknown today, despite the religion being popular for two thousand years. Many ancient Mesopotamian texts included lines like the following. *"Let the initiate show the initiate; the non-initiate shall not see it. It belongs to the tabooed things of the great gods."*

Cannabis was used in midwifery as a medicinal painkiller and to help aid contractions. Women continue to use cannabis in this way today. Can-

9 Russo 2007, noting R.C. Thompson, *A Dictionary of Assyrian Botany,* 1948.
10 Bennett, Chris, *Cannabis and the Soma Solution,* Trine Day, 2010.
11 Russo 2007, Royal Correspondence at Kouyunjik, letter 368.
12 Russo 2007, Letters and Contracts, No. 162.

nabis was referenced for midwifery in one of the oldest medical texts ever found, from Egypt in 1550 BCE.

> Another (to cool the uterus and eliminate its heat): s^ms^m-t [cannabis]; ground in honey; introduced into her vagina. This is a contraction.
> – Ebers Papyrus 821[13]

One archaeological find from Israel provides some proof of this, although it is from a later era. A burial tomb found in Beit Shemesh, Israel, between Jerusalem and Tel Aviv, with coins dating to the 4th century CE, was discovered containing the skeleton of a pregnant 14-year-old girl who died late in her term or while giving birth. The full-size fetus was still in her mother's womb and was too large for a safe birth. Inside of her abdominal area, scientists found a gray material that upon analysis showed the chemical remains of cannabis. Scholars believe that cannabis was used medicinally to assist the doomed mother to give birth, but in this case, the midwives were not successful.[14]

Cannabis could also be used in abortions as an ingredient in a potion and was documented in the Zend Avesta, the sacred texts of the Zoroastrians from Persia. The texts are of unknown antiquity since it is said that Alexander the Great burned the Persian libraries at Persepolis. The Zend Avesta has a significant reference to cannabis as an abortifacient and speaks to the drug being acquired from an old woman, the crone, or the village wise woman. By itself, cannabis does not cause abortions, but it is a painkiller that eases contractions, and it could be blended with toxic drugs to induce the miscarriage. In this text, abortions are seen as sinful but they existed nonetheless.

> *And the damsel goes to the old woman and applies to her for one of her drugs, that she may procure her miscarriage; and the old woman brings her some Banga [bhang, cannabis], or Shaeta, a drug that kills in the womb or one that expels out of the womb, or some other of the drugs that produce miscarriage and [the man says], "Cause thy fruit to perish!" and she causes her fruit to perish; the sin is on the head of all three, the man, the damsel, and the old woman.*[15]
> Zend-Avesta: Venidad, Fargard XV, verse 14

13 Russo 2007
14 Russo 2007
15 Darmesteter, James (translator), *Sacred Books of the East*, American Edition, 1898. Zend-Avesta: Venidad, Fargard XV, verse 14. http://www.avesta.org/vendidad/vd15sbe.htm

Ashurbanipal and the Assyrian Tree of Life

Chapter Twelve

BABYLON

Babylon was the premier Mesopotamian city for over 1500 years, from the 18th to the 4th centuries BC. The city was a cultural center, the largest and most prosperous city in the ancient world, a hub for religion, trade, the arts, and likely the first city whose population exceeded 200,000 people. Babylon was legendary in its time for its beauty and antiquity, and the city would play an important role in the fortunes of some of the world's most powerful leaders.

Babylon's influence is felt all over the Hebrew Bible, the city was the dominant cultural force during the entire history of the Hebrews from Abraham thru Moses and the first temple period. The first Hebrew temple was of course destroyed by the Babylonians and the Israelites sent into exile. It is in Babylon where the Hebrew Bible was compiled, edited, and completed in the form we read today. The Hebrew scribes worked in the shadow of the great ziggurat dedicated to Marduk while resisting the temptations of Ishtar's wild sex cult.

Sargon The Great

Legendary accounts assert that Babylon was first founded by Sargon of Akkad around 2300 BCE, though it was a minor city at that time. Sargon of Akkad (2334-2284 BCE) is not well known today but he should be. Sargon the Great was the world's first military emperor, thousands of years before Cyrus the Great, Alexander the Great, the Romans, or modern aspirants like Napoleon. Sargon defeated all of Sumer and introduced the Akkadian language, ending the Sumerian era and establishing the Akkadian Empire.

Sargon united all of Sumer under his Akkadian banner and extended his military conquests deep into Anatolia. This was the first military empire in history that united numerous hostile city-states under a single ruler. Sargon's empire extended from the Persian Gulf to the Mediterranean, from the upper sea to the lower sea as they were called. Sargon utilized an effective bureaucracy and administration that would be a model for centuries. Later tales would extend his conquests far and wide, claiming

Sargon sent his armies to Egypt, Ethiopia, and India. Sargon was a legend in the ancient world, his name was hailed for 1500 years as the patron saint of all subsequent empires.

Sargon was a Semite, who began his career serving as the king's cup-bearer, a high official for Ur-Zababa, the King of Kish. The king of Kish was deposed by the evil Lugal-Zage-Si, king of Uruk, who was cursed for having burned and looted all the holy sites in the city of Lagash when he took power. Sargon raised an army and destroyed Uruk, Lugal-Zage-Si's capital, in a surprise attack. Sargon ultimately captured Lugal-Zage-Si, parading him in a neck stock in front of the city gates of Nippur to be reviled and spat upon by those who walked by for his sins against the gods.

Like all great heroes, Sargon had a legendary birth. He was virgin-born and elements of his story would be repeated in the biblical story of Moses' birth.

My mother was a high priestess, my father I knew not.
The brothers of my father loved the hills.
My city is Azupiranu, which is situated on the banks of the Euphrates.
My high priestess mother conceived me, in secret she bore me.
She set me in a basket of rushes, with bitumen she sealed my lid.
She cast me into the river which rose over me.
The river bore me up and carried me to Akki, the drawer of water.
Akki, the drawer of water, took me as his son and reared me.
Akki, the drawer of water, appointed me as his gardener.
While I was a gardener, Ishtar granted me her love,
and for four and ... years I exercised kingship.
The black-headed [people] I ruled, I governed;

This story has many important details, Sargon's mother was a qedesha and he did not know his father, making him virgin-born. We do not know why his mother felt the need to hide him, but the virgin-born were often heroes in myths and legends. Irrigation and gardening were sacred duties in Sumer and being appointed as a gardener was a great honor. He must have done something right because Ishtar gave him her love, consecrating his kingship in the hieros gamos.

It is during the rule of Sargon that the Akkadian language was first used for writing and administration, and we see a shift in names for cities and gods. Inanna became Ishtar around this time (they may have been separate goddesses who were merged for political reasons) but none of Inanna's myths or rituals changed at all, they were only embellished and reinforced.

Enheduanna, The First Named Poet

Sargon made another contribution to world history and culture. His daughter Enheduanna was the High Priestess of An and she is the first named poet in all of human history, long before Homer and the biblical writers. Enheduanna wrote many hymns and praises to Inanna, and she is credited with establishing many of the formats for prayers, hymns, and psalms that would be replicated for thousands of years. Enheduanna was to literature what her father was to empires, she was the first. The most famous of Enheduanna's hymns are, "The Great Hearted Mistress," "The Exaltation of Inanna," and "Goddess of the Fearsome Powers."

A sample adapted from one of Enheduanna's many hymns to Inanna:

The great-hearted mistress, the impetuous lady,
proud among the gods and pre-eminent in all lands...
The magnificent lady who gathers up the divine powers
of heaven and earth and rivals great An.

... is mightiest among the great gods -- she makes their verdicts final.
She changes her own action, and no one knows how it will occur.

Without Inanna, great An makes no decisions, and Enlil determines no destinies.
Without you no destiny at all is determined, no clever counsel is granted favor.

My lady, let me proclaim your magnificence in all lands, and your glory!
Let me praise your ways and greatness!
Who rivals you in divinity?
Who can compare with your divine rites?
Your great deeds are unparallelled, your magnificence is praised!
Young woman, Inanna, your praise is sweet![1]

City of Babylon

Babylon first came to dominance under King Hammurabi in the 18th century BCE who defeated the neighboring city-states and united them into his empire. Hammurabi is known to us today for his famous law codes, written on a large stele in the center of the city. Hammurabi's sons did not hold the empire together, and as typical of Mesopotamian history, warring city-states battled constantly and political formations ebbed and flowed.

Over the centuries Babylon would fall under a number of different empires. When the Assyrians ruled Mesopotamia, they had their capital in the great city of Nineveh. More than a thousand years after Hammurabi

1 *A hymn to Inana* (Inana C), ETCSL translation : t.4.07.3, The ETCSL project, Faculty of Oriental Studies, University of Oxford. http://etcsl.orinst.ox.ac.uk/cgi-bin/etcsl.cgi?text=t.4.07.3#

the Neo-Babylonian (Chaldean) empire emerged and left its mark on history in the events of the Hebrew Bible.

Babylon was rich in culture and religion; it was a beautiful city filled with many temples and teeming with artisans. The city was a center for the arts, education, and intellectual pursuits. Women held a relatively high status compared to neighboring cultures and had strong legal rights and personal autonomy. Babylon was known for its tolerance and many religions flourished there. Ishtar was the pre-eminent goddess and her cult with its wild and extravagant celebrations was at the heart of Babylon's culture.

The walls of Babylon at their peak reached a height of 25 meters, with towers another three meters taller. The walls were made of small baked bricks cemented with bitumen and they surrounded the entire city. There were enough fields inside the walls to allow the people to withstand a siege and continue to farm. The wall was ten meters wide and it was said that two chariots could pass by each other safely.

The Euphrates river ran under the walls and through the city, contained by large levees and moats to protect the residents from floods. The river was crossed with bridges that were an engineering challenge as the flow of the Euphrates undermined their foundations, great flows of sand and mud routinely smashed violently against the support pillars, requiring frequent repairs.

King Nebuchadnezzar

In the Old Testament days, The Chaldean Nabopolassar came to power in Babylon after defeating the Assyrians and sacking their capital. The great city of Nineveh, also dedicated to Ishtar, was burned and the residents massacred during a famous battle in 612 BCE.

Nabopolassar's son, King Nebuchadnezzar II (ruled 605-562 BCE) raised the Neo-Babylonian empire to its greatest heights. Nebuchadnezzar is a famous character in the Bible, he was the king of Babylon who burned down Jerusalem, destroyed King Solomon's temple, and sent the Hebrews into the Babylonian exile. In the Bible, Nebuchadnezzar was troubled by bad dreams and counseled by the Hebrew prophet Daniel. It may be hard to imagine, but the ferocious Nebuchadnezzar was thoroughly dedicated to his gods, including Ishtar and Marduk, and took part in the hieros gamos ceremony in every year of his reign, including the ritual humiliation and recitation of his sins.

Nebuchadnezzar rebuilt Babylon after it had been flooded and desecrated by the Assyrians. Babylon was elevated to the greatest heights of influence at this time, even though it was already over a thousand years old. Nebuchadnezzar improved the great walls of Babylon and built the famous Ishtar Gate. The gates were part of the grand walled processional way leading into the city and the walls were finished in blue glazed bricks depicting animals and deities. The animals on the wall were lions, bulls, and dragons, representing the most important gods in the city, Ishtar, Adad, and Marduk (Adad was a god of storms and rains). The blue color is evocative of lapis lazuli, the color of Mesopotamian royalty.

Lion from the Ishtar Gate, Babylon

The Ishtar Gate and the ½ mile-long Processional Way were used every year in the New Year Akitu festival as a parade route. The Ishtar Gate was excavated by archaeologists and carefully reconstructed at the Pergamon Museum in Berlin, Germany. This was a very impressive feat even though they only reconstructed one of the smaller, inner gates.

Nebuchadnezzar also renovated and restored the Etemenanki ziggurat and the Imperial grounds. The Etemenanki, the "House of the Foundation of Heaven on Earth" was the giant ziggurat in Babylon dedicated to the god Marduk. The Etemenanki was one of the largest ziggurats ever built and was the most important, as it was dedicated to the most important god in the most important city. This temple tower was considered by the Babylonians to be the center of the universe, and it was the inspiration in the Hebrew Bible for the Tower of Babel.

The Etemenanki was believed to reach all the way to heaven, though in reality the tower was 91 meters tall, and was made up of seven terraces with stairs on the outside. The ziggurat was located at the end of the processional way that extended through the center of the city from the Ishtar Gates, where it appeared as a stairway to heaven. On the highest terrace was the temple to Marduk.

The Hanging Gardens of Babylon were reportedly built by King Nebuchadnezzar II and were said to be one of the Seven Wonders of the Ancient World. They were made to honor and please his young Queen, who missed her Persian homeland. The complex was described as covering two hectares, as high as the city walls, and resting on heavy stone foundations. The Hanging Gardens were reported by ancient Greek writers, but modern archaeologists have been unable to confirm their location, and many believe they were actually in Nineveh.

Nebuchadnezzar II ruled for 43 years and when he died, he was the most powerful monarch in the Near East. The Neo-Babylonian empire did not last long though, despite their capital city's sophistication and influence. Nebuchadnezzar's sons could not hold the empire together and it was soon defeated by King Cyrus II and the Persians. The Persian Empire under Cyrus the Great then took over from the Babylonians as the most powerful empire in the world.

King Cyrus protected Babylon and continued the practice of religious tolerance, although he made his capital in Persepolis. Cyrus is hailed in the Bible for liberating the Hebrews and allowing them to return to Jerusalem. Later Persian kings sponsored Hebrew priests remaining in Babylon to assemble their holy texts into what we know today as the Hebrew Bible and the Old Testament.

Babylon had its final moments of significance under the short-lived reign of the Macedonian Alexander the Great. Alexander invaded Persia, crossing the Hellespont from Greece, and established an even greater empire, uniting Greece, Persia, Egypt, and Afghanistan under his rule after a ten-year military campaign of unprecedented and brutal success.

Alexander had planned to restore Babylon to its former glory and make it the capital of his new Hellenistic empire. But his sudden death at age 33 in Babylon in June of 323 BC marked the point when the city went into terminal decline. A few centuries later the great metropolis was completely abandoned and left to be buried under the desert sands.

Climate change and failing agricultural fertility contributed to the broad decline of Mesopotamia. The region became increasingly arid and once-fertile lands dried up and turned into the desert it is today, forcing the people to leave.

Chapter Thirteen

EGYPT

Egyptian History

Egypt, in North Africa, had the next oldest civilization after the Sumerians. It was famous in the ancient world for its grand pyramids, temples, knowledge of science and medicine, and deep spirituality. Egypt was a primary pathway for early humans as they migrated out of Africa into Asia and Europe, making it a place with some of the deepest connections to ancient human history.

The mighty Nile river was at the heart of Egyptian civilization, culture, and wealth. Egypt is a desert country, but every year the Nile River would flood, leaving behind a deposit of fresh alluvial soil that enabled agriculture to flourish. Egyptians considered their land to be the most blessed and that they were the most blessed people by the gods because of their connection with the land.

Egyptian history is identified by the ruling dynasty of the era. There were thousands of years of Paleolithic and Neolithic history before Dynasty 0 and the beginning of established civilization around 3100 BCE. The Egyptians did not have kings but were ruled by Pharaohs who carried a much greater religious import than the militarized warrior kings of Mesopotamia and other neighboring cultures. The Pharaohs were considered to be direct emissaries of the gods and were worshipped as god-like figures.

The Egyptians shunned long military campaigns beyond their borders lest they die on foreign land and be denied a proper burial. So, while Egypt constantly interacted with the other great empires of antiquity, they rarely attempted to expand their borders beyond an immediate buffer in the Levant, nor did the royalty like to marry their daughters off to foreign powers.

There were over 30 Egyptian dynasties, extending into Greek and Roman times. The 30th Dynasty was the last native leadership before Egypt was conquered by the Persians. Alexander the Great defeated the Persians in 332 BCE and liberated Egypt from their hated rule.

Alexander was welcomed in and declared Pharaoh. He established the city of Alexandria n 331 BCE which went on to become the most important city for religion, learning, and philosophy after Babylon went into decline. Alexander ushered in the Hellenistic era and his general Ptolemy fathered the last Dynasty that ended with the reign of Queen Cleopatra's death in 30 BCE. At this time Egypt fell under the direct rule of the Roman Empire, which endured until the Arab Conquest in the 7th century CE.

Religion

The Egyptians had a full pantheon of gods and a distinctive culture all their own. Similar to their neighbor civilizations, the Egyptians placed goddesses, particularly Isis, at the heart of their worship systems, but there were many details that made their beliefs unique.

For instance, in Egyptian mythology, the Earth is male and the sky is female, in contrast to most other cultures where the Earth is a mother goddess. The most politically important deity through most of Egypt's history was the sun god Ra who was the king of the gods and the patron of the Pharaoh.

The Egyptians were the first people to codify the idea of an immortal soul whose journey continued after the death of the physical body. The bodies of Pharaohs and royalty were mummified for preservation and buried with elaborate written instructions and wisdom literature that would help guide them through the perilous journey of the afterlife. Living a virtuous life was of central importance if one hoped to reach a blissful eternal afterlife. After death, one's virtue was judged by having their heart weighed on a scale by the goddess Ma'at and if that person's heart was weighed down with sins and self-interest then they could not pass through.

Ma'at was both the name of the goddess and of the principle of the harmony of the universe. People were expected to be virtuous and they were judged for their virtue after death. Pharaohs and individuals both were expected to maintain balance and harmony in society through their interdependence and mutual reliance. Harmonious existence pleased the gods and brought pleasure and happiness to humans and enabled the gods to perform their tasks. The goddess Ma'at held the white feather of truth that was used to judge the weight of a person's heart after they had died to determine if they had been virtuous and were deserving of a blissful afterlife.[1]

1 Mark, Joshua, J. *Ancient Egyptian Religion, Ancient History Encyclopedia,*

ISIS

Isis was one of the most popular and enduring of all the Egyptian deities and certainly the most important goddess. Isis was the great Egyptian mother goddess, the Queen of Heaven, and the throne upon which the pharaoh sat. Isis' name means, "the seat," she was the throne that represented the stability of the Egyptian people and culture.

Isis was portrayed as the selfless, giving, mother, wife, and protector who placed the well-being of others ahead of her own. She was known for having great powers of magic and healing and being the patron of the magic arts. Isis' great powers of magic gave her pre-eminence among the gods, but these powers were only used as needed and she often took a supportive role behind her husband Osiris and son Horus. In one famous story, Isis tricked the sun god Ra into telling her his secret true name, which gave her his powers, by having him bit by a poisonous snake for which only she had the cure.

Isis first appeared in the Pyramid Texts from around 2350 BCE, which are the oldest religious texts found anywhere in the world. But Isis would achieve some of her greatest popularity and influence during the Greek and Roman era. There were many cults to Isis in Alexandria and her worship was exported throughout the Roman Empire.

Isis was worshipped across the known world from England and France all the way to India. Isis was demure and respectable and was readily syncretized into the patriarchal Hellenistic world, unlike the lascivious and unbridled cults of Ishtar and Cybele who did not reflect the acceptable behavior of honorable Greek and Roman wives.

Isis had a well-established Mystery religion that emphasized the cycles of life, death, and rebirth and promised initiates to guide their souls to a blissful afterlife. Initiates into Mystery religions were sworn to secrecy and very little is known about their sacred rites or specific beliefs. Whatever happened behind closed doors at the temple remained a mystery to outsiders.

The Temple of Isis at Philae in the south of Egypt was first built in 690 BCE and was the last major goddess temple to be shut down in 550 AD after Christians rose to power in Rome and banned all pagan religions.

Abydos Triad

The story of Isis and Osiris is one of the great resurrection cycles of ancient mythology and confirms Isis' role as master of the cycle of life, death, and resurrection. This story appeared in the Pyramid Texts, the oldest known sacred texts in the world, from around 2350 BCE.

Isis was married to Osiris who ruled as Lord of the Earth with Isis as his queen and consort. Isis, Osiris, and their child Horus are a trinity known as the *Abydos Triad.* Abydos was a sacred city filled with many temples and tombs of pharaohs. Osiris was the dying and rising resurrected god similar to Dumuzi, Tammuz, Dionysus, Baal, and many others.

Images of Isis holding the infant Horus on her lap were very common in art. Isis and Horus were the model for later iconography of the Christian Madonna and child, Mother Mary holding the baby Jesus. These images of Isis and Horus were syncretized as the Black Madonna and predate Christianity by a millennium.

Isis, Orirus, Horus

Osiris and Isis ruled wisely during primordial times and it was a golden age. Humans lived in paradise with lush vegetation and cool running waters, men and women were equals, and peace prevailed in all the land.

Osiris' brother Set was jealous and arranged to murder Osiris. Set had a coffin made and tricked Osiris into climbing inside. Set shut the lid and threw the coffin into the Nile where it floated out to sea, eventually making its way to Byblos in Phoenicia. Osiris died while trapped in the coffin. Isis was distraught when she discovered her husband missing and searched all over for him.

The coffin came to shore in Byblos and was quickly engulfed by a great Tamarisk tree that grew around it. The sweet-smelling tree was discovered by the king and queen, named Astarte, and brought into their home. The king and queen had no idea about the coffin trapped inside the tree.

Isis meanwhile had made her way to Byblos in search of her husband, and through a series of interactions she ended up in the royal court, disguised as an old woman brought in to tend to the children. Isis was fond of the royal baby and decided to grant him immortality by burning away his weakness in holy fire. One night, Astarte discovered the nursemaid holding her child in the fire, the Queen screamed and startled Isis, who revealed her true form as the Goddess. (This scene is replicated almost exactly in the Greek story of Demeter in the Eleusinian Mysteries).

The King and Queen were terrified of the Goddess and bowed low before her, offering her anything she asked. Isis merely asked for the return of the tree, which they happily granted. Isis left the court and cut the body of Osiris out. Isis hid her husband's body in a swampy region of the Nile and left to gather herbs to make a potion to return him to life.

Set meanwhile, had discovered Isis' plans and found the body while she was gone. Set hacked Osiris up into pieces and scattered them across the land. Isis was horrified but quickly worked to gather up all the body parts. Isis found all the parts of Osiris but one, his penis, which had been thrown in the Nile and eaten by a fish. Like many goddesses, Isis was tended by eunuchs and transgendered priests, symbolized by the loss of Osiris' genitals.

With her great magic, Isis was able to restore Osiris to life. Again with her magic, Isis extracted a seed from Osiris and became pregnant, despite his lack of a penis, making Isis the virgin mother of Horus (Black Madonna). Osiris could not stay in the land of the living because he was incomplete, so he descended to the underworld to become Lord and Judge of the Dead, though still the loving husband and father of his family.

Isis hid the baby Horus away from Set until he grew into adulthood. Once he was grown, Horus became a mighty warrior who killed Set and restored his family to kingship, with Isis as Queen Mother, the throne upon which the pharaoh sits.

IMMORTALITY

The cult of Isis evolved into a Mystery Religion, like the Eleusinian Mysteries of Greece, whose initiates were promised the secrets of life and death, but sworn to secrecy. The cult promised eternal life to those who knew its secrets, but little was ever revealed about the inner workings of the worship.

The Greeks associated Isis with their goddess Demeter, the goddess of grains and nature, and Osiris was the equivalent of Dionysus who was also a resurrected god. The Greek historian Herodotus said the Egyptians were the first to establish a doctrine of reincarnation and immortality.

> *No gods are worshipped by all Egyptians in common except Isis and Osiris, who they say is Dionysos; these are worshipped by all alike.*
>
> Herodotus, *Histories* 2.42[2]

> *The Egyptians say that Demeter [Isis] and Dionysos [Osiris] are the rulers of the lower world. The Egyptians were the first who maintained*

2 Herodotus, *The Histories*, English translation by A. D. Godley.

the following doctrine, too, that the human soul is immortal, and at the death of the body enters into some other living thing then coming to birth; and after passing through all creatures of land, sea, and air, it enters once more into a human body at birth, a cycle which it completes in three thousand years. There are Greeks who have used this doctrine [the Orphics], some earlier and some later, as if it were their own; I know their names, but do not record them.

– Herodotus, *Histories* 2.123

SESHAT

Seshat was another important Egyptian goddess, though not as well-known as Isis in modern popular culture. Seshat was the goddess of writing and the patron of scribes, as well as the goddess of wisdom, knowledge, and mathematics. Seshat was the consort of Thoth, the god of measuring, numbers, and the calendar. Seshat was the Mistress of the House of Life and her priests were librarians who preserved the most sacred scrolls.

Seshat, Karnak Temple, Luxor

Seshat was one of Egypt's oldest and most enduring gods, but she was not a center of worship. Rather than having temples to Seshat, the goddess appeared in all the other temples as the patron of the priests and scribes who worked inside. In Mesopotamia, goddesses were also credited with inventing and preserving writing.

Thoth was one of the oldest Egyptian deities, first appearing in Neolithic imagery. Thoth has a very distinctive look with the head of an ibis bird on a human body. In Egypt, there were numerous creation myths, attributable to the cults of various gods. In one of the myths, Thoth was the original self-creating god who laid an egg that contained the universe and all of creation, including the other deities.

Thoth was credited with inventing mathematics and writing, along with other important roles. It seems that over time his duties were passed to his sister-wife Seshat who was a very active deity throughout the Dynastic history of Egypt.

Seshat was among the most important and widely recognized Egyptian deities and had certain indispensable duties and responsibilities. As the patron of scribes and the goddess of writing, books, and libraries, Seshat was very influential in Egyptian culture.

Egyptian writing was unique and used hieroglyphics, a complicated system of pictographs that were considered to be deeply sacred, "the Gods' Words." Writing was not merely a system for record-keeping or preserving stories. Writing was seen as the act of creating reality, bringing the unseen into the visible world, and establishing it as a truth. Words carried the power to create, sustain, heal, curse, and protect – and the written word was even more powerful because it endured. Scribes were a celebrated profession, among the most highly respected, and it was a role that some women could aspire to. Women also were respected as doctors and healers in Egypt.

Seshat was said to grant eternal life to authors through their works, and this author prays to her for guidance and success.

Seshat was responsible for the temple layout and the "Stretching of the Cord" ritual, the act of sacred geometry that was required when engineering a new temple and laying the cornerstone. The measuring rod and cord were important in the ancient world, these were the official measuring tools used to certify lengths and properties, calculate taxes and tithes, and were critical in architecture to lay out the temples. Kings and gods were often depicted holding the measuring rod and cord as a sign of authority.

Another unique aspect of Seshat is her explicit association with cannabis, which had been growing in Egypt since Neolithic times, having followed the human migratory pathways backward from Central Asia into Africa. Seshat is depicted with a big and venerable cannabis leaf growing directly out of her headdress. Scholars have typically identified the symbol as a seven-pointed star. Above the cannabis leaf is the figure of a bow over a bow that has challenged scholars. A single bow represents the number 10 and the double bow may represent 10 over 10 and Seshat's mastery of mathematics.

Hemp lines were commonly used for the measuring cord and rod because the fibers are long and stiff, without stretch, making them suitable for the important and sacred task of measuring. Cannabis drugs have long been associated with writers and poets, an association that persisted in Egyptian culture through the Middle Ages and into the modern-day.

CANNABIS IN EGYPT

Cannabis grew in Egypt from the very early days of their civilization, and it has remained a heart of hashish culture into the modern-day (though Islamic law discourages its use). Cannabis indica drug types predominated in Egypt while growing hemp for fiber was relatively rare, though they were aware of it.

Ancient Egypt was a great producer of linen, which they exported throughout the world and for which they were famous. Linen is described in great detail in Egyptian records while references to cannabis are slim. It is likely that the Egyptians grew small amounts of cannabis for medicine and ritual, and traded for hemp ropes and canvas which were routinely exported from Anatolia.

Egypt was known in ancient times for its expertise in medicine and a rich variety of medicinal drugs. Scholars have identified the Egyptian hieroglyphic word *shemshemet* (s^ms^m-t) as cannabis, and it is described as a plant used in rope making and as medicine.[3] Passages carved into stone dated to 2350 BCE in the city of Memphis during the Old Kingdom may be the oldest written references to cannabis found anywhere.

Cannabis is mentioned in a few different ancient Egyptian medical texts, but the texts were not very detailed and the instructions are cryptic. Though the Ebers Papyrus from 1550 BCE provides clear evidence of the ancient use of cannabis as an obstetric and birth aid.

> Another (to cool the uterus and eliminate its heat): s^ms^m-t; ground in honey; introduced into her vagina. This is a contraction.
>
> – Ebers Papyrus 821, 1550 BCE

> A treatment for the eyes: celery; hemp; is ground and left in the dew overnight. Both eyes of the patient are to be washed with it early in the morning.
>
> – Papyrus Ramesseum III, A 26, ca. 1700 BCE

Hemp fibers were found in the tomb of Akhenaten at Amarna, from ca. 1350 BCE, and confirmed in two separate scientific analyses. Akhenaten was the controversial heretic Pharaoh who attempted to impose monotheism on the unwilling Egyptian people. Mummies were wrapped in linen. Several cannabis pollen grains were found inside the mummy of Rameses II, who died around 1213 BCE. Cannabis pollen has been found in geological strata dating to the mid-third millennium BCE.

Diodorus of Sicily was a Greek historian who wrote in the first century BCE how Egyptian women of Thebes employed a potion like the legendary *Nepenthe*, "a drug of forgetfulness," that "chases away sorrow," that was

3 Ethan Russo, "History of Cannabis and Its Preparations" in *Saga, Science, and Sobriquet, Chemistry & Biodiversity* · November 2007 Russo describes all the ancient Egyptian medical entries in detail and considers the medicinal qualities of the recipes.

used by Helen of Troy in Homer's *Odyssey*. Many scholars have suggested cannabis as the basis for Nepenthe, it is impossible to prove definitively, but cannabis is known in modern science to affect memory and can be used therapeutically by victims of trauma.

> *Then Helen, daughter of Zeus, took other counsel. Straightway she cast into the wine of which they were drinking a drug to quiet all pain and strife, and bring forgetfulness of every ill.*
>
> – Homer's Odyssey, Book 4, v. 219–221

According to Francois Rabelais, the famous 16th-century French writer, physician, and occultist, the altars and priests of Isis were always adorned with cannabis. He then states that all newborns are likewise shrouded in hemp cloth – yet another reference to hemp as the cloth that wraps the newborn (and the dead) and deeply associated with cycles of life, death, and rebirth

> *The altars of Isis are adorned therewith, the Pastophorian priests are therewith clad and accoutred, and whole human nature covered and wrapped therein at its first position and production in and into this world.*
> – Francois Rabelais, *Gargantua and His Son Pantagruel*, Book 3, Chapter 3.LI.

Rabelais dedicated four chapters of his masterwork, *Gargantua and Pantagruel,* to cannabis which he called *the Herb Pantagreulion.* Rabelais extolled the virtues of the noble plant, which he called "the King of the Plants" and inspired the name for his hero. Rabelais wrote in satire and code to avoid accusations of heresy, a capital crime at the time.

Francois Rabelais said cannabis was king of the plants and adorned the altars of Isis

Minoan fresco from Knossos palace,16th C BCE Crete

Chapter Fourteen

MINOANS

The Minoans on the Greek island of Crete were the first great civilization in Europe and they were one of the important Goddess worshipping cultures of the ancient world. The Minoans had a sophisticated and advanced culture and were the last great Bronze Age civilization that maintained an ethic of egalitarianism with women in leadership roles rather than martial dominance by militant kings.

The Minoans are known for having a wealthy, redistributive, and peaceful society that excelled in the arts and trade while having no signs of war. Women were revered and the culture may have been led by a queen as there are no indications in their art of any kings or military leaders.

Goddess Worship

On the protected island of Crete, the Goddess-centric worship held out much longer than in the mainland Bronze Age cultures where rule by Kings and male warrior gods had steadily displaced the primacy of the Goddess. The Minoans had one of the last cultures where male dominance was not the norm. There were no signs of war on Crete in the Minoan era. Their economy prospered and the arts flourished while their culture remained egalitarian and cooperative with women occupying a place of reverence and sharing equal status with men.

Crete was first settled around 6000 BCE and had 4000 years of Neolithic settlements until they entered the Palace period around 2000 BCE. For roughly 500 years during the middle Bronze Age, the Minoans were the masters of trade throughout the Mediterranean, particularly in tin. They had a great fleet of merchant ships and interacted with all the neighboring cultures.

Minoan art has been found throughout the ancient Near East from Egypt to Mesopotamia and beyond. As seafarers, the Minoans were able to travel around while maintaining their home island as a safe refuge. The Minoans were badly hurt by the huge volcanic eruption of Thera (modern-day Santorini) around 1500 BCE and were later displaced by the Mycenaeans from mainland Greece.

The Minoans were literate but their script has not been translated so we do not know the details of their religion or beliefs, but it is known that they celebrated their goddesses and had a great Goddess at the head of their pantheon. We also know from their highly imaginative and skilled art, which has been found in abundance, that men and women were treated equally and both participated in sports, dance, and ritual. Their Goddess worship was deeply imbued by a love and deep spiritual connection to nature and there was a spirit of harmony between men and women as joyful and equal participants in life.

Women were high priestesses and held many roles of authority in the culture. There are no signs of a king in their art, but there are many images of women receiving tribute, sometimes seated in thrones, leading many scholars to speculate that the Minoans were a matriarchal culture led by women.

Fine Art

Minoan art displayed an abiding love of nature and the sea and featured many images of dolphins and fish as well as many of the characteristic symbols of the goddess cultures; bulls, snakes, lions, and doves. Their imaginative art delighted in beauty, grace, and athletic movement. Bulls were central to their art and culture and bull-leaping was a celebrated and risky sport in which teams of men and women took part in grabbing the bulls horns and somersaulting over the bulls back.

The Minoans produced some of the finest art and goddess sculptures in all the ancient world including many images of females holding snakes and stylized double-axes. Among the most famous pieces is a small faience statue called the Minoan Snake Goddess showing a bare-breasted woman who may have been a priestess holding snakes.

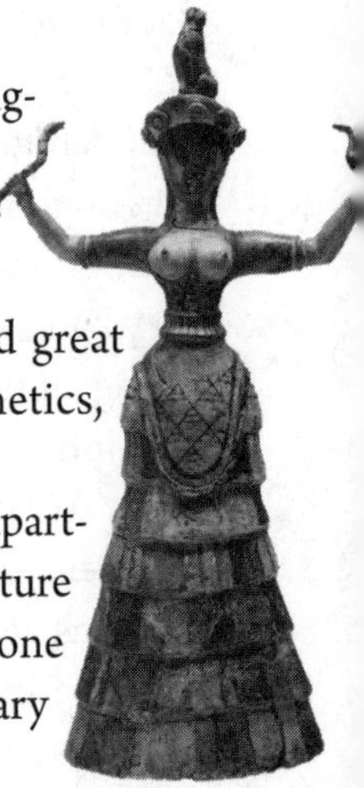

The Minoans were skilled craftsmen who built increasingly spectacular palaces with a distinctive architectural style. The famed palace at Knossos from around 1700 BCE was the largest, with over 1000 rooms arranged in multiple stories built around a central courtyard. The Minoans paid great attention to detail in their architecture, emphasizing aesthetics, natural light, and a high degree of refinement and comfort.

The people in the palaces lived in pleasant multi-story apartments spread around open courtyards. Minoan architecture stood in contrast to the walled fortresses and monumental throne rooms celebrating royal authority typical of their contemporary neighboring cultures.

LABYRINTH

The Minoans were highly organized and practiced advanced city planning, they built aqueducts for running water and complex drainage systems for the palaces. The Minoan palace structures were said to be "labyrinthine" and it is from the Minoans that we get the later Greek myth of the half-man, half-bull Minotaur who was kept in a maze-like labyrinth from which victims could not escape.

The Minoans were generally peaceful people as evidenced by the lack of defensive walls around their palaces which were open to nature and allowed the free flow of people. There may have been 100,000 residents on Crete whose communities were linked by an integrated network of paved roads. These were the first paved roads in all of Europe and were well engineered with drainage systems. The highway network and lack of internal defenses indicate the Cretan communities were peaceful with each other.

The Minoans had a palace economy in which the palaces served as storage and redistribution centers where agricultural goods were consolidated and shared, like a big community center. The Minoans had a very high standard of living and practiced an equitable sharing of wealth. And while there was an affluent ruling class, even the peasants lived well. There was a bureaucracy but no evidence of coercive domination or large armies.

SEX AND SPIRITUALITY

The Minoans had an openly sexual culture and their clothing revealed women's breasts and men's genitals. They loved sports and dancing for both men and women, and combined with liberated sexual mores contributed to a relaxed society free of many of the social anxieties and tensions that permeate dominator cultures into the modern-day.

Minoan spirituality embraced death through the joy of life, and fear of death was vanquished through the ubiquitous joy of living. Worship of nature and the cycle of life pervaded everything. The Minoans may have practiced human sacrifice, though this opinion is controversial. But it is a common theme among some native cultures globally who see themselves as part of nature, and for whom life is cyclical, to not fear death and even embrace it based on the idea that their life will be regenerated anew.

Nikolaos Platon, a renowned Greek archaeologist who discovered palaces on Crete, described Minoan culture. "The whole of life was pervaded by an ardent faith in the goddess Nature, the source of all creation and harmony. This led to a love of peace, horror of tyranny, and a respect for the law."[1]

1 Eisler, Riane, *The Chalice and the Blade: Our History, Our Future*, Harper One, 1987, p.36

Destroyed by Earthquake

The Minoans were devastated by earthquakes caused by the dramatic volcanic eruption on the nearby island of Thera somewhere around 1500 BCE. This was one of the largest volcanic eruptions ever known in recorded history. A settlement on Thera was entombed by a layer of pumice and later excavated by archaeologists.

The Minoans, saved by the prevailing winds, initially survived the catastrophe but were severely weakened, leading to their eventual conquest by the warlike Mycenaeans from mainland Greece, who took control of Crete and most of the other islands in the Aegean Sea. Mycenean palaces were all walled fortresses designed to withstand attack. The circumstances of their takeover of Crete are not known. We don't know if the Mycenaeans attacked and defeated the Minoans or whether the Minoans had simply emigrated from natural disaster, leaving the island unattended and undefended.

Mycenaeans

The Mycenaeans remain well known today as the Greeks of the Trojan War. We remember King Agamemnon, Achilles, Odysseus, and others in the classic stories of Homer; the *Iliad* and the *Odyssey*. These stories tell of the Mycenean Greeks who attacked and ultimately desecrated the Anatolian city of Troy in a ten-year-long war, and the trials of Odysseus on his 10-year journey home.

Long thought to be a legend, the city of Troy was discovered and excavated by archaeologist Heinrich Schliemann in the late 1800s who found evidence of fire and slaughter around the year 1184 BCE, now believed to be the year that Troy fell to the Mycenaeans.

The Mycenaeans would ultimately fall during the Bronze Age collapse shortly after the Trojan War. Greece and the rest of the Near East entered a two-hundred-year Dark Age at this time during which trade, writing, record-keeping, and political authority all broke down.

Chapter Fifteen

BRONZE AGE COLLAPSE

Near East Apocalypse

At the turn of the 12th century BCE, there was a series of disasters from around 1225-1175 BCE that brought down all of the Mediterranean and Near Eastern powers in what scholars call the Bronze Age Collapse.

These disasters included waves of earthquakes, droughts, and famine that forced refugees to migrate, causing cataclysmic wars and conflict. Surprise assaults on coastal cities by a still-unidentified group called the Sea Peoples devastated numerous cultures including the Mycenaeans in Greece, the Hittites in Anatolia, and the Egyptians, while the Assyrians retreated to their homeland in Mesopotamia. Political uprisings and opportunistic invasions on top of crop failures and drought all contributed to a Mediterranean apocalypse.

The Bronze Age collapse ushered in a Dark Age that lasted roughly 200 years where trade was disrupted, empires receded, and written language broke down. There was widespread trauma for refugees who fled one disaster only to find themselves in another. Earthquakes struck throughout the region, leveling cities in Greece, Anatolia, and the Levant.

Many palaces and cities were burned and destroyed. Centralized political and economic control in the palaces amplified the impacts of the disasters. Since all administrative control was tightly held, entire kingdoms were unable to survive when the palaces lost their grip. This created a domino-effect of collapsing cultures that were deeply intertwined through treaties, intermarriages, and trade. Once the kingdoms started to fall, they brought down the others until they all collapsed.

Drought and climate change contributed to the misery and helped create a perfect storm that brought down multiple empires. There is speculation that a dramatic volcanic eruption in Iceland called Hekla 3 around 1100 BCE caused an 18-year period of global cooling and crop failures. Whether these droughts reflect a permanent shift in climate from a more verdant period to the arid semi-desert that the region is now, remains a matter of scholarly debate.

Letters from the prosperous city-state of Ugarit on the Syrian coast document the disasters, giving clear evidence of famine and mass starvation, uprisings, and revolts. Fighting in many cities and widespread unrest undermined trade and had a terrible impact on people dependent on imports like the Mycenaeans.

Trade and contact continued right to the end when cities fell in dramatic fashion to invasions and natural disasters. It took decades and even centuries in some cases for regions to be rebuilt and repopulated. The entire Near East changed dramatically between 1200 BCE and 1100 BCE and was unrecognizable by 1000 BCE. It was a complete systems' collapse, a Dark Age lasting two centuries.[1]

The Bronze Age Collapse also marks the beginning of the Iron Age. New metallurgy techniques were introduced to make iron and carbon into steel tools and weapons which were cheaper and stronger than bronze. The introduction of steel eliminated the strategic importance of tin. Iron enabled new people carrying new weapons to defeat the old Bronze Age powers. The shift to iron permanently altered trade routes and hastened the demise of cultures who profited from the tin trade.

Sea Peoples

The Sea Peoples were a wave of migrants/invaders yet to be properly identified by scholars, who may have been invaders or who may have been desperate refugees, or both. The Sea Peoples assaulted a series of coastal city-states in surprise attacks featuring vast hordes of invaders arriving by ship in huge numbers with formidable force, possibly carrying steel weapons.

The Sea Peoples worked their way down the Mediterranean coast, attacking and sacking cities in Anatolia, Syria, Cyprus, Phoenicia, and Canaan before finally being held off by the Egyptians. The Sea Peoples defeated the Hittites and caused their empire to completely disappear, after which they devastated Ugarit. The Sea Peoples attacked Egypt twice in 1207 and 1177 BCE and were repelled both times in dramatic and costly battles recorded by Egyptian scribes.

After the 200-year Dark Age, new peoples and powers emerged, the Classical Greeks (the Hellenes), the Phoenicians in Lebanon, and the Israelites first appeared on the world stage. The Neo-Assyrians in Mesopotamia became a dominant military power in the 10th century BCE, while Egypt slowly came out of its slumber.

1 Cline, Eric H. *1177 B.C. – the Year Civilization Collapsed*. Princeton University Press, 2015, p.161

Some of the Sea Peoples settled on the Mediterranean coast in Gaza (modern-day Israel) where they became the Philistines of Biblical fame, occupying the same strip of territory where the Gaza Strip is today and giving us the name Palestine.

CLASSICAL ANTIQUITY

1000 BCE marks the beginning of Classical Antiquity, where we see the emergence of the cultures that are the foundation of Western Civilization; the Hebrews, Greeks, and later Romans. The Bronze Age collapse also brought the end of cuneiform writing and the eventual introduction of phonetic alphabets.

To put the timelines into context: The Biblical Hebrews, or Israelites, first entered the archaeological record around 1200 BCE during the Bronze Age collapse. King David is believed to have taken the city of Jerusalem for the Hebrews around the year 1000 BCE. David's son King Solomon built the first Hebrew temple and it was ultimately destroyed by the Babylonians in 586 BCE, who sent the Hebrews into exile. The Hebrew Bible we read today was completed in Babylon around 458 BCE.

The Greek city-states like Athens, Sparta, and Corinth emerged in the 9th century BCE and the first Olympic Games were held in 776 BCE. The epics of Homer, the *Iliad* and the *Odyssey*, were written around this time. They were the first literature of Western Civilization and used the new Greek alphabet. Athens reached its cultural apex with the introduction of representative democracy and the golden age of philosophers and writers such as Socrates and Herodotus in the 5th century BCE, the same time the Hebrew Bible was being worked out.

For most of the first millennium BCE, the Phoenicians from Lebanon were the dominant trading power in the Mediterranean. The Phoenicians and Greeks both established colonies throughout the coastal regions, the Greeks focused on the Aegean and the Black Sea while the Phoenicians ventured westward and established Carthage in North Africa, Cadiz in Spain, Marseille in France, and others.

The Roman Republic was established in 509 BCE and the Roman Empire in 27 BCE by Octavius Caesar. The defeat of the Phoenicians, first by the Greek Alexander the Great with the siege of Tyre in 332 BCE, followed by the Punic Wars between Rome and Carthage from 264 to 146 BCE marked the ascendance of those cultures into international powers during the Hellenistic Age.

The Neo-Assyrians from Mesopotamia had the first Near Eastern military empire of the Iron Age and were dominant from 911 BCE until their defeat in 605 BCE by an alliance of Medes, Persians, Scythians, and the Babylonian Chaldeans. The Neo-Assyrian empire at its peak covered Mesopotamia, parts of Persia and Anatolia, and the whole of the Levant and Egypt.

The Chaldeans followed briefly, for less than a century, before falling to Cyrus the Great and the Persians. Cyrus created the Achaemenid Empire, seizing Babylon in 539 BCE and freeing the Hebrews from exile. Cyrus and his successors ruled the Near East, Egypt, and eventually parts of Greece for two centuries. These empires provided the political backdrop behind the events of the Old Testament. Each of these empires was the largest the world had seen and each grew larger than the last, building on the infrastructure and political dynamics of the former.

Entry of Alexander the Great into Babylon by Charles Le Brun

Alexander the Great, from the Greek kingdom of Macedon, defeated the Persians in an unprecedented ten-year military campaign that went even farther, extending his rule from Greece and Egypt all the way to India, before dying young in 323 BCE. Alexander's influence lasted centuries as he introduced the Hellenistic Age of cultural diffusion and East to West religious syncretism. The Roman Empire in its time dominated the entire Mediterranean but never extended into Mesopotamia or Persia.

Buddha, Socrates, Confucius

Axial Age

The middle of the first millennium BCE also marks the Axial Age, the period when all of our modern religions and philosophies were born. The time when Confucius in China, Buddha in India, the Hebrew prophets, and the Greek philosophers all lived. Hinduism took its modern form, while Buddhism, Taoism, Confucianism, Judaism, and western moral philosophy all emerged. These philosophies appeared separately and in parallel, with cross currents of influence on one another.

The Axial Age religions all broke away in common from older belief systems rooted in nature and cycle-of-life traditions. Human morality took center stage in religions around the world, supplanting superstitious Neolithic belief systems that saw humans as victims of cruel and unreliable gods. The Axial Age is the period when women were completely subordinated to men in society. This transition was centuries in the making and was ultimately codified in Greek mythology and the Bible.

Though unique in their own ways, each of the modern religions born in the Axial Age shares a sensibility that we humans are responsible for our own behavior, and that ethics and morals dictate our ultimate fates in this life and beyond. The Golden Rule was invented, "Do unto others as you would have them do unto you."

Philosophy was elevated over superstition and humans were given greater control over their own destinies rather than being seen as the victims of inscrutable deities and the vagaries of nature. Even the Mystery religions that appeared in this era, while maintaining strong connections to the Neolithic goddesses and the cycles of life, emphasized morality and knowledge as keys to a happy afterlife.

Raw sexuality believed to make the plants grow, shamanism, and nature worship came to be seen as antiquated and unrespectable. Indigenous animist peoples were viewed as uncivilized heathens capable only of living in the jungles and hinterlands.

Diana by Auguste Renoir

Chapter Sixteen

OLYMPIAN GREEKS

Hellenes

The Classical Greeks, or Hellenes, were one of the foundational cultures of Western Civilization alongside the Biblical Hebrews and the Romans. The Greeks built on the accomplishments of their Bronze Age forebears and developed a uniquely European culture with sophisticated philosophy, science, medicine, and mathematics.

Greece is where we had the birthplace of democracy and western moral philosophy, and where we trace many of our traditions in literature and theater. Greek culture and religion would directly influence the Romans who created an early republic and later became the greatest military empire in the ancient world. These accomplishments have continued to inspire European and American leaders into the modern-day.

The Greeks knew the Earth was round and they built on the astronomy of Egypt and Mesopotamia. Greek mathematicians such as Pythagoras and Archimedes discovered many of the seminal algebraic and geometric formulas we still rely on today.

The Greeks created beautiful art and architecture and we continue to see their influence today. Greek sculpture is famous for its majestic realism and elevation of the human form. Greek artists idealized perfection of the human body, reflecting their philosophical attitudes that elevated human reason over ignorant superstition.

Philosophy

The seminal Greek philosopher Socrates (470-399 BCE) lived in Athens at the height of Athenian hegemony, around the same time the Hebrew Bible was being completed in Babylon. Socrates observed that the gods often engage in immoral behavior; they lie, cheat, steal, commit murder, and adultery, and if these actions are immoral for man then why were they not immoral for the gods?

Socrates concluded that either the gods are cruel and unjust with a twisted sense of humor, or else they did not exist. And how can you respect unjust gods? All you can do is bribe them or appease them with sacrifices and prayers, but that has limited benefits. Either there are no gods, or else they take no care of men.

Greek culture gained its great influence on western culture when it elevated human reason and philosophy over superstitious fealty to the pagan gods. Socrates is considered to be the father of moral philosophy and Western ethics, whose influence helped to transition from an era of superstitious belief in unknowable gods into an era when the gods were understood to be metaphors for the natural world.

Greece would eventually fall under the political rule of the Romans, but Greek art, philosophy, and religion were hugely influential on the Romans. The Romans began with a rather unrefined culture of their own and eagerly absorbed the finer points of the peoples they defeated such as the Etruscans. Between Alexander's Hellenistic Empire and the Roman Empire, Greek art and culture spread far and wide beyond the Greek homeland.

Graeco-Roman culture was religiously tolerant and open-minded, importing religious cults from throughout the known world. You were allowed to believe what you wanted and worship whatever gods you pleased as long as you weren't seditious and honored your duties as a citizen to the local civic gods.

Greek philosophers first created the idea of Sophia, the feminine personification of wisdom that was adopted into Judeo-Christian mystical traditions. Sophia was not a goddess in the pagan sense, but she is a personification of the divine feminine in the monotheistic traditions. Sophia is the voice of wisdom in Jewish wisdom literature and the holy spirit and the Bride of Christ in Gnostic Christianity.

New Gods

After the recovery from the Bronze Age Collapse, the Greek descendants of the Mycenaeans rebuilt their society, complete with an entirely new pantheon of gods that was a mix of old and new, native, and imported deities.

The Greek Olympians led by Zeus were later adopted by the Romans and are the most familiar pagan gods to modern Western audiences. The Olympian pantheon shares many characteristics with other polytheistic cultures but there were important differences as well, particularly in how they portrayed their goddesses.

The Classical Greeks and Romans were deeply patriarchal and sexist societies, they kept their women on very short leashes with few legal and political rights. Women were generally confined to their homes where they tended to the children, homemaking, and weaving.

All the Iron Age cultures severely restrained women's rights and freedoms compared to their Neolithic forebears. But even by Iron Age standards, the Greeks were particularly restrictive of their women. This treatment of women is reflected in the Greek goddesses, who were far more chaste and demure than the wild and unbridled goddesses beloved from this period in Phoenicia, Mesopotamia, and among the Scythians.

Homer and Hesiod

The earliest and most important Greek writers of mythology were Homer and Hesiod. Homer is the timeless author of *the Iliad* and *the Odyssey,* epic poems of the Trojan War and its aftermath that are the oldest pieces of literature in Western Civilization. Hesiod wrote the story of creation and the biographies of the gods in the *Theogony* and other works. Hesiod and Homer's writings date back to around the 8th century BCE when literacy reappeared in Greece with the advent of the new phonetic Greek alphabet (which was copied from the Phoenicians).

Homer and Hesiod were the first authors to describe the Greek gods' appearance and character. The Greek gods were not derived from an inspired teacher or any particular set of doctrines or dogma, they were a reflection of Greek thought and culture and arrived at by a consensus of the people. The stories, plays, and literature that spoke to the people were remembered and retaught, while portrayals of the gods that did not resonate with the public were soon forgotten.

The Greek myths were not obscure works discovered in some dusty old cave. Greek plays were staged in major contests and the winning authors earned fame and fortune. The works of Homer, Hesiod, Aeschylus, and others were living and breathing features of Greek cultural life and played a central role in popular entertainment, much like Hollywood movies do today for modern audiences.

ILIAD

The *Iliad* and the *Odyssey* are epic poems that were told orally for centuries before being written down. The precise identity of Homer, where and when he lived, and even if he was one person, has been disputed since antiquity but his stories were profoundly influential on Greek culture and remain significant today.

The Mycenaeans and their ten-year-long war against Troy formed a backdrop for Greek literature for centuries. It was a rich framework from which countless stories were drawn of adventurous characters both human and immortal.

Troy was located on the northwest shore of Anatolia on the approach to the Bosporus Strait, the narrow channel that joins the Mediterranean to the Black Sea and separates Europe from Asia Minor. The Trojan War took place during the Bronze Age collapse. Troy, Ugarit, and other important cities were destroyed around the same time and the Mycenaeans did not last much longer either.

The *Iliad* tells the story of the last days of the Trojan War and the fall of Troy. The *Iliad* includes the tale of the famous Trojan Horse, the large wooden statue that was used as a subterfuge to sneak the Greek soldiers inside Troy's gates and burn the city. The *Odyssey* is a companion piece to the *Iliad* and details the ten-year return voyage of the Greek hero Odysseus to his home in Ithaca. These epics are considered to be the first great works of European literature.

The story of the Trojan War is well known. The backstory of the war began with a beauty contest between three of the primary Greek goddesses, Hera, Athena, and Aphrodite. Paris, the young prince of Troy was chosen by Zeus to be the judge, after all the immortals wisely declined to choose between the vindictive goddesses.

Each of the three goddesses worked to bribe Paris with gifts to earn his favor. Athena offered wisdom and skill in war, Hera offered to make Paris

Judgement of Paris by Joseph Hauber

the king of Europe and Asia, while Aphrodite offered the love of the most beautiful woman in the world. The Judgement of Paris was a popular subject of medieval art, particularly because the artists had license to portray the beautiful goddesses in the nude.

Paris famously chose Aphrodite; who offered him the love of Helen, who was unfortunately already married to the Mycenaean King Menelaus of Sparta. Aphrodite helped Paris spirit Helen away from her husband and by these actions launched the Trojan war. Menelaus rallied his brother Agamemnon and other Greek leaders to attack Troy and bring back the wayward woman. Athena and Hera were angered by Paris' decision and worked to assist the Greeks while Aphrodite was on the side of the Trojans.

Over the course of the war, the gods fought amongst themselves and intervened on the battlefield to assist their favored humans. Divine intervention in the stories reflects the common pagan belief that the universe was mysterious and inexplicable. Mere mortals were fated to suffer at the hands of mercurial gods whose intentions were unknowable.

For humans, the greatest fate was to achieve immortality thru glory. This is exemplified by the Greek hero Achilles, who was born of a goddess and given the choice to live a long and happy life in obscurity, or die young gloriously and be remembered through the ages. The fact that we still talk about Achilles today tells you what choice he made.

THEOGONY

Creation

Greek writer Hesiod was the most significant after Homer, he recorded many of the classical myths of the Greeks in his books, *Theogony*, and *Works and Days*, sometime in the 8th century BCE. Hesiod was a poor farmer far removed from the royal courts and their lives of luxury and wrote from the perspective of a humble peasant living in a harsh world.

Hesiod's works exalted justice and disdained hubris, he believed that man should gain his livelihood through strenuous and persistent work. For Hesiod, hard work was the only way to prosperity and distinction, in opposition to the ideals of glory and immortality portrayed by Homer.

The *Theogony* was an explanation of the creation of the universe and the gods. For the Greeks, the universe was born from a primordial mother, Gaia, who gave birth to the universe and all the gods. In the beginning, there was the spontaneous generation of four beings: first came Chaos, then the Earth (Gaia), Tartarus (the Abyss), and Eros (Desire) "the fairest of the deathless gods."

Gaia

Gaia (Earth) first bore equal to herself starry Uranus (Heaven) so that he may cover her all over like a veil, to be always the unshakable seat for the blessed gods.

Hesiod, *Theogony* (126-128)

The Homeric Hymns were from the same period and had unknown authors. Each of the 33 hymns was dedicated to an individual god. This is the Hymn to Gaia.

Mother of us all, oldest of all, of the earth, the sacred ground,
nourishing all out of her treasures- children, fields, cattle, beauty...
Mistress, from you come our fine children and bountiful harvests;
Yours is the power to give mortals life and to take it away
Hail to you, mother of gods.[1]

– Homeric Hymn to Gaia

Gaia, the primordial mother Earth goddess, gave birth to her own husband, Uranus, the heavenly father. Uranus mated with Gaia, and she gave birth to the twelve Titans, the three Cyclops (giant one-eyed monsters), and the three Hecatoncheires (monsters with a hundred hands and fifty heads). Uranus was cruel and hated his monstrous children, he imprisoned the Hecatoncheires in a secret place within the Earth, greatly angering their mother.

Gaia, groaning with pain, appealed to her children for help and her youngest, the Titan Cronus responded. Cronus hated his lusty father and took the sickle his mother prepared for him. Gaia hid Cronus away, and when Uranus came to visit her for some lovemaking, Cronus reached out with the sickle and castrated his father, throwing the testicles over his shoulder. From the drops of blood were born the Furies, Giants, and Nymphs. The testicles fell into the sea and a foam formed around them, out of which was born Aphrodite, the goddess of the foam (foam being a euphemism for semen). This speaks to the belief that Aphrodite was one of the oldest gods.

1 Sargent, Thelma (translator), *The Homeric Hymns*, W. W. Norton & Company, New York,1973. p.79

Gaia gave birth to many children; gods, monsters, and forces of nature, and she remained an active character in Greek myth. Cronus ruled the universe with his sister-Queen Rhea. Cronus learned that one of his children was destined to unseat him, so his response was to eat all of his children as soon as they were born. When Rhea gave birth to her sixth child, Zeus, she secreted him away to safety and gave Cronus a stone wrapped in swaddling cloths as a trick for him to eat, which he did. Rhea later came to be associated with the Anatolian mother goddess Cybele.

Zeus Becomes King

When Zeus was grown, he led a rebellion against Cronus, he forced him to disgorge the stone and his five siblings Hera, Hestia, Demeter, Poseidon, and Hades. By tradition, the stone was kept at the Oracle at Delphi where the priests anointed it every day.

Zeus and his brothers and sisters waged a mighty war against Cronus and the Titans that shook the universe to its core. Zeus and the gods prevailed and he punished his enemies terribly, binding them in chains deep down in Tartarus, the abyss. Among the Titans was Atlas, who was punished by having to bear the weight of the world on his shoulders.

Some Titans had joined Zeus and were rewarded for their loyalty. Prometheus and his brother Epimetheus were given the task of creating man and animals. Absent-minded Epimetheus gave all the great gifts to the animals; speed, strength, and flight, leaving nothing left for man. It was wise Prometheus who made man noble, standing upright, and intelligent. And to make up for their lack of physical gifts, Prometheus gave man fire, stealing it from the gods. Men were not created to serve the gods, the Greeks considered man to be the noblest of creatures. At this time on earth there were no women, the Greek mythical Golden Age was men only.

Zeus was greatly angered at Prometheus, not only had he had given man fire, but he had also tricked Zeus into accepting inferior offerings of fat and bones, leaving the good meat for man to eat, the custom of the Greeks. Zeus swore to be revenged, Prometheus was taken away and chained to a rock where an eagle swooped down every day to eat his liver, only to have it restored every night. Prometheus endured this torture for a long time until he was eventually freed by Hercules in another story.

Pandora, The First Woman

Pandora

Hesiod's Theogony was deeply misogynistic, reflecting Greek culture and their regressive attitudes towards women. Hesiod told a story similar to Eve in the Garden of Eden, of how the first woman brought ill upon the men of the world.

Zeus in his anger with Prometheus created the most clever punishment of all for man, he created the first woman, Pandora. She was a sweet and lovely young maiden, her beauty modeled on Aphrodite. All the gods gave her gifts; wisdom, beauty, kindness, peace, generosity, and health, as well as silver and gold, bright garlands of blooming flowers, and a shining crown. Her name Pandora means, "the one who bears all gifts."

Zeus, delighted in his stratagem, brought her out and all the gods and men held her in wonder. From Pandora was born the race of women, who according to the Greeks are evil to men, with a nature to do mischief.

Zeus had Pandora delivered to Epimetheus, who immediately fell in love and wanted to marry her, despite Prometheus' warnings of Zeus' trickery and not to accept gifts from the Gods. As a wedding present, Zeus gave Pandora a beautiful storage jar (often mistranslated as a "box") but warned her not to open it.

Pandora was curious, she could not help herself, she tried to avoid temptation but, in the end, she opened the jar, unleashing Zeus' curses on humanity. Out of the jar streamed all of life's miseries; greed, envy, hatred, pain, disease, hunger, poverty, war, and death. Pandora was terrified by all the evil spirits and closed the jar as fast as she could, but it was too late.

Zeus in his wisdom had left behind one spirit who remained in the jar, one last boon to humanity; hope. Against the onslaught of life's unending suffering there remains the constant flickering candle of hope, and as long as hope burns humans still stand a chance.

OLYMPIAN GODS

By tradition, there were 12 great gods who lived on Mt. Olympus, but there were other important deities as well. Six of the oldest and most important Olympians were the siblings born to the Titan mother goddess Rhea and the Titan King Cronus.

Zeus

Zeus was the King of the Gods and the supreme deity in Greek religion. Zeus took power over the older generation of cruel Titans with the help of his brothers and sisters. He was a prototypical warrior storm god, lord of thunder, and master of lightning. In later periods Zeus would be elevated by Greek philosophers to something approaching monotheism, called Zeus Hypsistos.

Poseidon

Poseidon was the powerful god of the sea, he was Zeus' brother and among the most primeval of Greek gods, having been worshipped in Mycenaean times or earlier. For seafaring people like the Greeks, the god of the sea was always vital.

Hades

Hades was the King of the Underworld, the god of death. The third brother of Zeus and Poseidon, together they formed a triad of leading gods. Hades was not considered to be an Olympian since he did not reside on the mountaintop with the other gods but instead ruled from his underworld kingdom of the dead. At his side stood the lovely Queen Persephone, the goddess of spring.

Hera

Hera was the Queen of the Gods, the Queen of Heaven, and the sister-wife of Zeus. Hera had roots in older Minoan traditions, but in Olympian myth, she was rarely displayed in a flattering light. Though obviously powerful, in most stories Hera was reduced to being a jealous scold who pursued and tormented the many women with whom Zeus had extramarital affairs.

Hera's wrath was legendary and her pursuit of revenge against Zeus' lovers was the backbone of many tales of Greek mythology. This came despite the fact that most of the women had been unwilling participants who were either raped or abducted by Zeus in the first place, only then to be persecuted by his wife – speaking to the poor prospects faced by pretty young women in Greek society. Hera was also seen as the scourge of unfaithful husbands.

Demeter

Demeter was "the Good Goddess" and arguably the most popular deity in Greek religion alongside Zeus. The goddess of agriculture and grains had roots going back to the Minoans and the Neolithic and had perhaps the most ancient and sustained worship in all of Greek culture.

Demeter and her daughter Persephone were at the heart of the Eleusinian Mysteries, the most well attended of all Greek religious festivals. Demeter, Persephone the goddess of spring, and Hecate the goddess of night and magic, were the Greek Triple Goddess.

Hestia

Hestia was the virgin goddess of the hearth and home. Hestia was a minor character in Greek myth and in time gave up her seat to the youngest Olympian, Dionysus the god of wine, ecstasy, and ritual intoxication.

Athena

Athena was the goddess of wisdom, war strategy, the arts, weaving, and civilization. She was among the most highly esteemed and the most uniquely native Greek deity. Athena most closely represented Classical Greek values and she was not imported from foreign lands or earlier cultures (though the name was used by the Mycenaeans). The city of Athens was named for Athena and the Parthenon in Athens was a great temple dedicated to her.

Athena was notably asexual and virginal, routinely dismissing and even punishing would-be suitors, demonstrating parochial Greek values towards women's sexuality. It was Athena who judged that children belonged to their father only, the mother being nothing more than an anonymous vessel for the father's all-important seed. This ruling codified Greek values, patriarchal bloodlines, and confirmed women's subordinate role in society.

Athena was born directly from the skull of Zeus, with no mother, fully grown and armed. Athena sat at the right hand of Zeus, providing him with counsel. This mythic birth symbolized an enduring Hellenistic philosophical ideal that wisdom sprouted directly from the Godhead as seen in the ideals of Sophia.

Aphrodite

Aphrodite was the goddess of love, sex, beauty, and desire. Aphrodite was the most beautiful of the immortals, the golden one who was always smiling. The Greeks considered Aphrodite to be imported from Asia and she was among the oldest deities in their culture.

Aphrodite was born in the sea and protected sailors. The patron of prostitutes, she was commonly depicted nude. Aphrodite was the patron goddess of Corinth, a wealthy trading city famous for its seaports and brothels.

Aphrodite had the same beautiful looks and symbolism as Inanna, Ishtar, and Astarte, such as the planet Venus and the dove, but Aphrodite had none of the great powers over war and divination, or the political influence, as her West Asian counterparts. The Greeks reduced Aphrodite to romance and sexuality and little else, she was not one to lead the generals into battle, nor was there a hieros gamos ceremony to consecrate the king.

By Greek standards, Babylonian Ishtar combined the powers of Aphrodite (sex and love), Athena (war strategy and weaving), and Apollo (divination). But Ishtar's personification of female power and independence did not fit with Iron Age Greek values nor would she be transmitted into the culture of Western Civilization.

Aphrodite Urania

The Greeks actually recognized two separate Aphrodites. They distinguished Aphrodite Urania (from heaven, or the Queen of Heaven) from Aphrodite Pandemos (common Aphrodite). Aphrodite Urania was the older Asian import who was the Queen of Heaven with the full complement of powers over sex, war, and divination and was presented in her temples wearing armor. Aphrodite Pandemos had no war powers and was basically just the patron of brothel prostitutes who had no sacred role in Greek society. In the Iliad, Aphrodite won the beauty contest judged by Paris and rewards him with the love of Helen of Troy. During the ensuing war, Aphrodite steps on the battlefield only once – she cries and flees after being wounded on her wrist. The connection between love and war was seen in the form of the illicit romance between Aphrodite and Ares, the Greek god of war.

> *[Zeus] the father of men and gods smiled, and calling to him golden Aphrodite, said: "Not unto thee, my child, are given works of war; nay, follow thou after the lovely works of marriage, and all these things shall be the business of swift Ares and Athena."*
>
> Homer, Iliad 5. 429[2]

2 Homer. *The Iliad* with an English Translation by A.T. Murray, Ph.D. in two volumes. Cam-

Apollo

Apollo, another native Greek deity, was the highly popular god of divination, music, medicine, and the bow. Apollo was the patron of the civilized arts and the epitome of youth and beauty; he was a central character in many tales and was widely worshipped.

Apollo was most famously associated with the Oracle at Delphi, the most important temple for divination in the ancient world. The Oracle at Delphi had existed long before the era of the classical Greeks and was renamed in honor of Apollo. Pilgrims traveled from all over the Mediterranean to hear the cryptic messages delivered by the Pythia, the female oracle priestesses. The Pythia take their name from the python, yet another reference to serpents in the context of divination.

Artemis

The Olympian Artemis was the twin sister of Apollo, she was the virginal goddess of the hunt who protected wildlife and young girls. She was depicted as a maiden hunter with a bow and arrow who guarded her virginity carefully.

Artemis was also the patron of midwives and assisted the birth of her own twin brother. Their mother was the Titan Leto, a favorite lover of Zeus, who impregnated her before marrying Hera. Hera was extremely jealous and she pursued and hounded Leto. Leto was protected by her children Apollo and Artemis, who grew into powerful gods in order to defend their mother's honor.

In the Trojan War, Artemis played a brief but important role before the Greeks ever set sail to Troy. Angered by King Agamemnon for hunting her sacred deer, Artemis calmed the winds and would not allow the Greek fleet to set sail. To appease the goddess, Agamemnon proceeded to sacrifice his lovely, chaste, daughter Iphigenia. In some versions of the story, Artemis rescues the girl at the last moment, while in other versions the girl dies.

Artemis is commonly confused with and was later syncretized with Artemis of Ephesus, the great West Asian goddess, both of whom would later be known as Diana in Roman times. Ephesus on the Anatolian coast was one of the major sites for goddess worship for thousands of years. Artemis of Ephesus was extremely powerful and popular.

The great temple to Artemis at Ephesus was the single largest temple ever built and was one of the seven wonders of the ancient world. The

---

bridge, MA., Harvard University Press; London, William Heinemann, Ltd. 1924. http://www.perseus.tufts.edu/hopper/text?doc=Perseus%3Atext%3A1999.01.0134%3Abook%3D5%3Acard%3D416

Greek Artemis and the Ephesian Artemis were originally completely different deities, but they overlapped later in the Hellenistic and Roman periods and were eventually combined into one.

The remaining Olympian gods include Hermes the messenger, Hephaistos the blacksmith, and Ares the god of war.

GOOD GODDESS DEMETER

Not all of the gods were cruel to humans, some were very kind, particularly those associated with the Earth and the cycles of life. The Olympian Demeter was the goddess of agriculture, grain, and the harvests, and her daughter Persephone was both the goddess of Spring and Queen of the Underworld. Demeter and Persephone were the patrons of the Eleusinian Mysteries and were among the most popular and widely worshipped Greek gods. Some scholars describe Greek religion as being centered on Zeus and Demeter.

Demeter was one of the oldest and most esteemed of the Greek gods and was especially popular with women; she was one of the six Olympians born to Cronus and Rhea and was far more noble and sympathetic than her sister Hera. Their third sister was Hestia, the virginal goddess of the hearth, home, and domesticity. Demeter was a goddess of childbirth and marriage and as the patron of the Mystery religions, she guided the passage to Elysium, the blessed afterlife.

The Return of Persephone by Leighton

The sacred rites of the nature goddesses Demeter and Persephone speak to most mysterious experiences in life – birth, sexuality, death, and enduring love. Men and women both expressed their joy in the beauty and abundance of nature and in the rebirth of the human spirit through suffering and death. These rituals were the Greek equivalent of West Asian nature goddess worship.

Demeter and Persephone's most important myth was the basis for Mystery festivals and was one of the most well-known resurrection cycles. This story parallels Inanna's Descent to the Underworld and others that represent the turning of the seasons through a dying and rising god. This story is told in the Homeric Hymns from the 7th century BCE, but its roots are far older.

Persephone

Demeter had only one daughter who was fathered by Zeus, the lovely Persephone, maiden of the spring. Zeus promised Persephone to his brother Hades the god of the underworld without informing Demeter since he knew she would oppose the marriage.

While out on a walk one day with her nymphs, Persephone was lured by the wondrous bloom of a narcissus flower. When Persephone was distracted, Hades, the King of the Dead, rose up through a chasm in the Earth and grabbed her by the wrist, taking her down to his realm to be his wife and queen. Persephone cried out and wept as she was taken away but the only divinities who heard the maiden's cries were Hecate and Helios, the sun. The *Rape of Persephone* was one of the most famous motifs in classical Greek art.

Rape of Persephone by Bernini

Hecate

Hecate was the enduring goddess of magic, witchcraft, the night, moon, and ghosts. To the Greeks, she was a Titan who was honored by the Olympians. Hecate was one of the main protective goddesses of households rather than being worshipped in major temples. Hecate was often depicted in triple form and shrines to her were placed at three-way crossroads and in doorways, a tradition that lasted into Medieval times.

Hecate is thought to have originated in Thrace or Anatolia and was closely associated with Artemis of Ephesus. Hecate is very old and was worshipped over a wide area of Europe and West Asia, she was a mystical goddess whose character overlapped with many other goddesses in various traditions. For the Greeks, she was the handmaiden of Demeter and central to the Mysteries. Hecate, Persephone, and Demeter were the Greek Triple Goddess.

Demeter sensed that something was wrong with Persephone, but no one could help her. Demeter wandered the Earth for nine days in grief, taking no food or drink. On the tenth day, she met Hecate, who told her that she had heard Persephone's cries but not seen what had taken place. Hecate took torches in both hands and led Demeter on the search until they came to Helios, the watchman of both gods and men. Helios informed them that Hades had taken the girl with the consent of Zeus. Demeter was angered and avoided Olympus, dwelling on the Earth where she gave out blessings wherever she was welcomed, and punishing those who did not receive her gifts with proper reverence.

Eleusis

In this manner during her wanderings in the guise of an old woman, Demeter arrived at the Greek city of Eleusis and was introduced to King Keleos and Queen Metaneira. The Queen thought the old woman was noble and they invited her to nursemaid her infant child. Demeter loved the child and he grew quickly feeding on the ambrosia of the Goddess. Demeter wanted to give the child immortality and at night she would hold the child in the fire so that he might live like a god.

Then one night, Queen Metaneira became suspicious and stole upon the Goddess. The Queen screamed when she saw her baby in the fire. Demeter was angered, and the child lost his chance at immortality. Demeter then revealed herself in all her power and glory and said, "Witless are you mortals and dull to foresee your lot, whether of good or evil, that comes upon you."

The King and Queen were terrified and dedicated themselves to her, so Demeter taught them her sacred rites and they built a temple to her at Eleusis. This parallels the story of Isis in Byblos with Queen Astarte. Dangling infants over a candle may have been a ritual in Mystery religions.

Zeus

In her anger at losing Persephone, the goddess had caused a great famine on Earth by not allowing the fields to produce any fruit. Zeus became gravely concerned that the entire human race may perish and sent out the gods to entreat Demeter with presents, but the goddess would not be conciliated. Demeter vowed that she would not restore fertility to the Earth until she had her daughter back. Zeus eventually realized that he must convince Hades to allow his bride to return to her mother or else all humans would perish.

Zeus sent the messenger Hermes to visit the underworld where he found Hades and Persephone sitting side by side, the maiden crestfallen, missing her mother as much as she was missed. Hermes delivered Zeus' message and Persephone was overjoyed. Hades knew he must obey Zeus' command, but he prayed that Persephone not think harshly of him, and to not be sad that she was married to one of the greatest of the immortals.

But Persephone had taken a fateful step, in her hunger she had eaten seeds from a pomegranate. It was a rule of the Fates that whoever consumed food in the Underworld was doomed to spend eternity there.

Demeter ran to meet her daughter like a Maenad running down a hillside. They rejoiced to be reunited, but Demeter grieved to learn of the pomegranate seeds, knowing what it meant. Zeus sent a revered messenger, none other than their own mother, the Titan Rhea, to inform them of his judgment. For having eaten six seeds, Persephone was to return to Hades for ½ of the year, 6 months (in some versions 4 months), and remain with her mother Demeter the rest of the year. During those six months, winter descends and the vegetation dies off, to be reborn each spring with Persephone's return.

Demeter sadly conceded, and every year she watches her daughter return to her husband, where she reigns as Queen of the Underworld. When she returns, Persephone is the goddess of the spring and rebirth. Demeter was kind, the "Good Goddess," and she was sorry for the desolation she had brought. She made the fields rich again with abundant grain and fruit, the world bright with the blooming spring. Demeter went to the temple at Eleusis where she taught them how to sow corn and established the sacred rites that would be known as the Eleusinian Mysteries.

ELEUSINIAN MYSTERIES

There were numerous Mystery religions in other countries that had similar precepts, and they were all said to be originated by the mythical poet Orpheus. Orpheus was a prince of Thrace who was so devastated by the death of his beloved wife Eurydice that he followed her to the underworld. Orpheus played his harp directly to Hades and Persephone and begged them to honor his love for Eurydice.

Persephone was moved to tears and Hades agreed to allow Eurydice to leave the underworld. Orpheus was instructed to walk ahead of his love and not turn around until they had returned above. But Orpheus could not help himself and he turned around and Eurydice was lost to him. Orpheus then wrote the Orphic Hymns, all the great songs of doomed and tragic love, and traveled around teaching rites of Demeter, Dionysus, Isis, and the other Mysteries.

Demeter's chief festival took place at harvest time and evolved into one of the most enduring, sacred, and famous of the Mystery traditions. The Eleusinian Mysteries were one of the most popular religions in Greece; it was a respected state religion and well attended by the most prominent philosophers and politicians. Lesser and Greater Mystery festivals were held for over two thousand years and pilgrims flocked from all over to take part in the festivities.

The Mysteries were open to all people from slaves to kings, the only requirements were that the initiates spoke Greek and that their hands were free from the sin of murder. There were large public festivals that took place over a number of days, as well as sacred rites performed inside the temple. The public festivals had great feasts filled with dancing, drinking, and merriment.

Initiates were sworn to secrecy about the sacred rites and little is known about them despite being performed for a long time, as the vows were enforced by law. These rites spoke to the mysteries of life and the afterlife and no one knows what the central revelations were. The rituals were reported to have elements that were sexual and filled with ecstatic dance and intoxication. It is thought by some that the hieros gamos ceremonies, once performed publicly, had been taken private.

We do know that they consumed a mysterious intoxicating drink, the *kykeon,* whose recipe has never been revealed. These rituals had their roots in the ancient goddess cultures of Minoan Crete, Anatolia, and Thrace, all areas thick with cannabis and the full apothecary of ancient drugs and psychedelics like opium, ergot, belladonna, and psilocybin.

For the initiates, the rites put them in touch with the divine, recognizing their own immortality and divinity. The annual rebirth of Persephone symbolizes immortality and it is believed that they gained visions of Elysium, the glorious afterlife, through their ecstasies.

Ritual objects found in Eleusis included images of wheat and barley, pomegranates – a symbol of fertility, poppies – a symbol of sleep and death, and snakes – the symbols of rebirth and divination. Snakes protected grain harvests from rodents and were welcome around granaries and temples, and of course, were long associated with goddess worship. Doves, bees, and pigs were also important symbols to Demeter.

In the Mystery celebrations of the Goddess, men and women renewed their beliefs in the fundamentally loving nature of the universe, with the emphasis on regeneration and rebirth as the pathway to overcoming death.

Warlike patriarchal religions, particularly the monotheistic Biblical faiths, denigrated these beliefs and reduced them to mere "fertility cults," while their jealous God demanded absolute fealty to him alone, with no room for any goddess to share in the reverence.

Goddess worship was fundamentally egalitarian and peaceful, whose morals rejected the values of rape and plunder, the primary means of achieving wealth and power in the ancient world. The requirement that initiates be free from the stain of murder speaks to the emphasis on peace in the Mystery traditions.

Some parts of the Mystery festivals were for women only, and these celebrations were filled with merriment and laughter. In these ritual communities' older women instructed young women with knowledge of menstruation, sex, marriage, pregnancy, childbirth, and motherhood. These rites created deep bonds of loyalty and friendship among the women.

An important characteristic of the cycle of life festivals present in both Babylon and Greece were the ritual lamentations and crying over the death of the central character, whether it was Persephone or Dumuzi/Tammuz. One part of the ritual was dedicated to crying and weeping, followed by joy and celebrations at the return from death.[3]

DIONYSUS

Dionysus

Dionysus, also known as Bacchus in Roman times, was the god of wine, vegetation, pleasure, ecstatic frenzy, and ritual intoxication. Dionysus was widely worshipped as a fertility god and was commonly presented nude. Phallic images and elaborate processions were common parts of his festivities which also included theater performances and drama competitions. Wild Bacchic orgies were a famous aspect of his rituals and were scandalous at times. Dionysus was worshipped in many countries and he was among the most popular gods, as shown by the Roman temple to Bacchus at Baalbek, Lebanon beside Jupiter (Zeus) and Venus (Astarte).

Dionysus was worshipped alongside Demeter in the Mystery religions though his roots were in Thrace where he was the patron of wine. Thrace was not only thick with cannabis but was also one of the first places to cultivate grapes for winemaking, which they introduced to

3 Mara Lynn Keller, "The Eleusinian Mysteries of Demeter and Persephone: Fertility, Sexuality, and Rebirth." *Journal of Feminist Studies in Religion*, 1988 vol 4, no 1.

Greece. Though considered to be the youngest Olympian, Dionysus was actually quite old and his religion was imported into Greece. There are multiple conflicting myths about his parentage and youth and there were many variations of his cult.

Dying and Rising God

In Greece, Dionysus was the last god introduced to the Olympian pantheon and was the only one born to a mortal. His mother Selene was one of those poor women loved by Zeus and tormented by the jealous Hera.

Hera tricked Selene while she was pregnant to ask Zeus to reveal his full glory to her. Zeus had promised Selene her heart's desire and warned her that no human could survive contact with the Godhead. But she insisted and the moment Selene saw his full godly splendor she was instantly vaporized. Zeus saved the unborn child by sewing him into his thigh until he was mature, making Dionysus twice-born.

Hera, angered that the child survived, incited the Titans to tear Dionysus to shreds. By some traditions, his body was restored by Demeter, but there are many versions of the myth. What is important is that Dionysus is a god who dies and is reborn, like so many others we have discussed.

Grapevines represent the dying and rising god because the grapevine is pruned down to its bare stalk after harvest, to be reborn again in the spring, demonstrating the resurrection cycle in very practical terms to humans.

God of Wine

When Dionysus grew up, he discovered how to culture grapes and extract the precious juice, being the first to do so. Once again Hera intervened; she struck Dionysus with madness, forcing him to wander widely in foreign lands. In Anatolia, he was cured by the goddess Cybele, whom the Greeks knew as Rhea, and taught her religious rites.

Dionysus then continued through Asia teaching people to make wine and worship the Mother, continuing as far as India where his cult was well established. There are many tales of Dionysus and his travels, he was one of the most popular gods. Among his legacies, Dionysus is the god who gave King Midas the golden touch. He also had a brief affair with Aphrodite, and a child, Priapos, who was cursed with ugliness by Hera.

Dionysus eventually returned to Greece in triumph, making peace with Hera, and is considered to be the originator of the triumphal procession. Wild Dionysian parades were annual drunken festivals featuring sculptures of giant penises. Many of the Dionysus myths depict the resistance to his arrival in new towns, in some cases, Dionysus had to kill the king before he was ultimately welcomed.

In Rome, the Bacchic cults sparked a moral panic and were outlawed throughout Italy in a Senatorial edict of 186 BCE, *Senatus consultum de Bacchanalibus.* 7000 people were arrested and many leaders were executed, it was the greatest religious persecution in Rome until the time of the Christians, but the cult did survive.

Maenads

Dionysus was depicted as either an older, bearded god or as an effeminate, long-haired youth. He was served by maenads, satyrs, and nymphs.

The maenads were the female followers of Dionysus and the most important members of his retinue. They were known as the "Raving Ones" who were inspired by the god into a state of ecstatic frenzy through dancing and intoxication. Dressed in animal skins and often handling snakes, they were famous for maniacally running through the forests, killing animals they caught with their bare hands, tearing them apart and eating the raw flesh, symbolizing the death and rebirth of the god. Maenads came to be known as a variety of supernatural women, both historical and mythological, that followed Dionysus.

Nymphs

Nymphs were semi-divine female spirits associated with air, seas, woods, or water who maintained nature. Nymphs are like fairies and are depicted as beautiful, young, graceful maidens and are popular in art and literature.

Satyrs

Satyrs were male nature spirits, depicted as half-man, half-goat, or as a man with a horse tail. Satyrs were known for their ribald behavior; typically depicted naked with comically large erections, they were known as lovers of wine, music, dancing, and women. Satyrs were known for their bawdy humor and attempts to seduce women and nymphs, often unsuccessfully.

GREEK SEX

The Greeks had a sexually open culture. Depictions of graphic sex with images of nudity and men's erections were common in Greek art and were often on display in public and in people's homes. Prostitution was legal, common, and taxed.

Homosexuality

Dionysus was also the god of homosexuality and effeminacy. Described as androgynous and soft, he was not shy about perfuming his flowing locks and walking with a mincing gait, his robes gay and shining with gold. Dionysus was known to be receptive in homosexual intercourse and to be a friend of eunuchs. The Greeks had a rather unique view of homosexuality, even for the times, and accepted it only in certain circumstances, contributing to Dionysus' scandalous, yet oh-so-popular reputation, like a modern-day rock star.

> *[The infant] Dionysus was hidden from every eye ... a clever babe. He would mimic a newborn kid; hiding in the fold ... Or he would show himself like a young girl in saffron robes and take on the feigned shape of a woman; to mislead the mind of spiteful Hera, he molded his lips to speak in a girlish voice, tied a scented veil on his hair. He put on all a woman's many colored garments: fastened a maiden's vest about his chest and the firm circle of his bosom, and fitted a purple girdle over his hips like a band of maidenhood.*
>
> Nonnus, *Dionysiaca* 14.143 ff[4]

In Greek culture, homosexual pederasty was normal and accepted but there were severe lines of etiquette that needed to be maintained. Greek culture was chauvinistic and patriarchal and any behavior that made a masculine man effeminate was frowned upon. Public nudity and prostitution were common so there was no shortage of outlets for people's sexual energies.

Pederastic relationships were honored as a coming of age tradition, where an adult man mentored a young adolescent male in a relationship that was intimate and affectionate, while serving to introduce the young man into the professional social networks that he would need in adulthood. These pederastic relationships were traditional and the participants were all family friends. The older man was always dominant and the young man passive, these roles were important as they spoke to the cosmic and social order.

4 Nonnus, *Dionysiaca*. Translated by Rouse, W H D. Loeb Classical Library Volumes 344, 354, 356. Cambridge, MA, Harvard University Press, 1940. (Greek epic C5th A.D.) https://www.theoi.com/Text/NonnusDionysiaca1.html

In these pederastic relationships, it was typical to kiss and share a bed, but the physical affection stopped short of sexual penetration as this was a critical line of etiquette. It was acceptable to be aroused and achieve orgasm so long as neither man was penetrated, which was degrading to a masculine man. Similarly, sexual relationships between adult men of the same age were discouraged, as the proper homosexual relationships were purely pederastic in nature.

Alexander the Great Libertine

The Greek emperor Alexander the Great was scandalous for his open homosexuality. A terror on the battlefield, Alexander was a flamboyant diva off of it who flaunted his transgressive sexuality and lovers both male and female. Alexander was also a heavy drinker and carouser who likely used his share of hashish. He led his armies through the heart of hashish country in Afghanistan, visiting Samarkand and Tashkent.

Alexander took his behavior too far for his Macedonian troops when he demanded to be worshipped like a god in the Persian manner. The Greeks refused to bow down and prostrate themselves to their king – "No man is a god," they said, in a defining moment of western civilization which has always valued the individual human over the collective.

Prostitution

The Greeks did not practice sacred temple sex, and they placed a much higher emphasis on female chastity than the West Asians. Aphrodite was primarily the patroness of prostitutes and the pleasures of the flesh with none of the overt political importance held by her West Asian counterparts. Inanna, Ishtar, and Astarte were all goddesses of sacred sex whose qedesha priestesses were honored in their communities and consecrated the kings in the hieros gamos ceremonies.

Temples to Aphrodite on the other hand were widely regarded throughout the ancient world as homes to common prostitution. The famous temple in Corinth was said to have 1000 prostitutes dedicated to the goddess (not all in the building at once, but throughout the town).

Prostitution was common, legal, and taxed in ancient Greece and Rome. Street prostitutes, called *pornai*, were found in brothels and taverns, and sex slaves were owned by the temples. Concubines were servant sex partners from a lower social class, or slaves, who were not eligible for a respectable marriage to an upper-class man, but they could have warm, romantic relationships, albeit with one-sided power dynamics. There were little to no expectations of monogamy for men, but married women's sexuality belonged to their husbands, and girls were expected to remain intact virgins until marriage.

The Greeks did not have qedesha priestesses, but they did have many courtesans, called *hetaira,* upper class independent women who had semi-exclusive sexual relationships with wealthy men. Courtesans were educated and sophisticated, many were artists and musicians, who were able to socialize at the most elite levels of society and support themselves through their relationships.

Artists, actors, and musicians of both sexes often supplemented their income through paid sex. Courtesans were not sacred but they did have legal property rights, and some were famous and influential, though they had mixed and somewhat scandalous reputations in Greek society. It is safe to say that married women did not think highly of the courtesans who slept with their husbands and received valuable gifts from them.

ORESTEIA

Hellenistic Greek culture was regressive in their views towards women. Greek literature and mythology served a role similar to the Hebrew Bible in codifying the diminished stature for women and the Goddess in their society.

In 458 BCE, around the same time Ezra completed the Hebrew Bible, the famous Greek playwright Aeschylus won first prize at the Dionysia festival for his trilogy, the *Oresteia.* The *Oresteia* tells the story of an escalating cycle of familial violence that culminates in matricide. In order to halt the retribution, the gods Athena and Apollo convened the first trial by jury. Athena famously ruled that killing the mother is no crime, because the child belongs solely to the father.

Aeschylus was deeply religious and was born in Eleusis, home of the Mystery religion of Demeter. The playwright was very influential and by arguing that matricide is not a blasphemous crime because no matrilineal relationship exists, he implicitly argued in favor of sole patrilineal descent, just as the Hebrew Bible does.

This story codifies the moment in Greek culture when the ancient ways of the Goddess were finally overthrown by male dominance. It details the clash between matriarchal and patriarchal cultures and the establishment of the Greek legal system. The Greeks sought to bring order from chaos, by ending the cycles of clan vengeance for murders that had existed for millennia.

Queen Clytemnestra

The story begins with the return of King Agamemnon from the Trojan War. Agamemnon was the thuggish leader of the Greeks who had succeeded in defeating Troy. In doing so, Agamemnon had committed sacrilege by desecrating the Trojan temples, women, and people. When we meet his wife, Queen Clytemnestra is shown eagerly awaiting his return after ten long years of absence. Clytemnestra does not love Agamemnon though; she has murder on her mind.

Prior to leaving for Troy a decade earlier, Agamemnon had insulted the goddess Artemis by hunting her sacred deer. The angry goddess then becalmed the winds which prevented the Greek ships from setting sail. In order to appease the goddess, Agamemnon arranged to sacrifice his daughter Iphigenia. He told his daughter that she was to marry the hero Achilles, and when she arrived at the altar, he killed her. In some versions of the story Artemis rescues the maiden, but in this influential version of the story the girl dies. The winds then returned and the ships made the journey to Troy.

Clytemnestra never forgave her husband for killing their daughter, and in her role as matriarch she was obligated to avenge her. Clytemnestra is a dominant figure who represents the old ways, the primal traditions of the Goddess. She is portrayed by Aeschylus as deceitful and murderous. Clytemnestra was also the sister of the beautiful Helen, whose affair with prince Paris initially led to the Trojan War.

In the play, Clytemnestra greets Agamemnon with fulsome praise and invites him into the palace. Agamemnon has brought along his war prize, the slave concubine Cassandra, a tragic figure who was given the divine gift of prophecy but cursed so that no one would ever believe her. Despite Cassandra's warnings, Agamemnon steps right into his wife's trap. Clytemnestra kills Agamemnon and Cassandra both and publicly announces the act, declaring her right to revenge as matriarch and Queen.

The Murder of Agamemnon

Orestes

The second play, *The Libation Bearers,* tells the story of Orestes, the son of Agamemnon and Clytemnestra. Orestes had been ordered by the god Apollo to return to his homeland and seek revenge upon his mother. He joined up with his sister Electra, who shared his desire to avenge their father.

At the fateful moment, Clytemnestra begged her son to spare her life and Orestes hesitated, knowing that killing his mother was a great crime. But Orestes followed through on Apollo's instructions and cut his mother down.

No sooner had he slain his mother, Orestes began to see visions of the Furies, three ancient goddesses of vengeance and justice who punish those who have done evil acts, particularly familial murder. Driven by madness, Orestes flees, ending the second play.

First Jury Trial

The third play, the *Eumenides,* opens at Apollo's temple at Delphi. The temple is famous to this day for being home to the Pythia, the oracles and prophetesses of Apollo. One of the Pythia finds Orestes clinging to the center stone in the temple, seeking sanctuary, his hands still dripping with blood. Around Orestes sit the fearsome, terrifying Furies.

Apollo enters and tells Orestes that he will protect him and that he should leave and head to the temple of Athena in Athens. Apollo argues with the Furies, they express their disgust with this new and unjust god who would both encourage Orestes to murder a parent and then also offer him sanctuary in his temple. The Furies vow revenge upon Orestes for his blood crime – it is the ancient way.

The scene shifts to the temple of Athena where Orestes begs the goddess for protection. Athena arrives and listens to both Orestes and the Furies plead their cases. Athena announces that the matter is too great for her to decide so she institutes the first homicide court and holds a trial with a jury of oath bound citizens to render a verdict.

This play mythologizes the origins of the Greek legal system which was set up to replace the traditional path of blood vengeance. The trial is to be held with Orestes as the defendant, Athena as the judge, and a group of Athenian citizens as the jury. The Furies, despite their misgivings, act as the prosecutors, while Apollo is Orestes' defense lawyer.

Apollo makes an unusual argument in Orestes defense, an argument that would be as profound in establishing the role of women in society as the tale of Eve in the Garden of Eden.

Apollo argues that the Furies are charged with avenging familial murders. But the mother cannot be considered family because the mother merely safeguards the father's seed, and the child belongs to the father only. "*The mother of what is called her child is not the parent, but the nurse of the newly-sown embryo,*" says Apollo. A child only has a father and the mother is of no significance. So Orestes has not committed the grave sin of familial murder, argues Apollo.

Ruling

Apollo states that proof of his claim can be seen in none other than the goddess Athena, who was born fully grown directly from the skull of Zeus with no mother. The jury is split so it is up to Athena to cast the deciding vote. Athena says that she agrees with Apollo and will always favor the men over the women.

Apollo: This too I answer; mark a soothfast word,
Not the true parent is the woman's womb
That bears the child; she doth but nurse the seed
New-sown: the male is parent; she for him,
As stranger for a stranger, hoards the germ
Of life; unless the god its promise blight.

And proof hereof before you will I set.
Birth may from fathers, without mothers, be:
See at your side a witness of the same,
Athena, daughter of Olympian Zeus,
Never within the darkness of the womb
Fostered nor fashioned, but a bud more bright
Than any goddess in her breast might bear.

Athena: Mine is the right to add the final vote,
And I award it to Orestes' cause.
For me no mother bore within her womb,
And, save for wedlock evermore eschewed,
I vouch myself the champion of the man,
Not of the woman, yea, with all my soul,--
In heart, as birth, a father's child alone.

Furies: Woe on you, younger gods! the ancient right
Ye have o'erridden, rent it from my hands.

– Aeschylus, *The Oresteia*[5]

5 Aeschylus, *The Oresteia*, Translated by E. D. A. Morshead. Project Gutenberg. http://gutenberg.net.au/ebooks07/0700021h.html

Orestes is acquitted on the grounds that he has not shed kindred blood and returns to his city as the new king. The Furies are shocked and dismayed, they vow vengeance on the entire city of Athens. But Athena manages to dissuade them by offering them a position in the new order, from now on they would defend Greek democracy and justice and be known by a new name, the Eumenides, "the kindly ones." She gives them a cave to live in under the city, symbolizing how they were driven underground.

This marks the Axial Age conversion from the ancient ways of superstition into something more philosophical and institutional. From the Greek perspective, this was a just and ethical correction of societies' moral structure marked by the advent of formal legal systems.

Greek Athenian democracy and legal systems laid the foundation for the best aspects of liberal governance in the western tradition. But like so many things it comes as a paradox. In this case the advancement towards democracy was directly attached to the repression of women and denial of their most important roles, as mothers.

Clytemnestra was defending her clan by killing Agamemnon, but she was denied the right to take revenge, for a woman held no standing in Greek society. The original killing of Iphigenia was completely forgotten, her murder dismissed.

Athena and Apollo were both original Greek deities, they were not imported nor were they historical archetypes from earlier cultures. Athena, in particular, represents Greek views of femininity, she is wisdom, civilization, and the patron of weaving, she is chaste and celebrates her virginity and restrained sexuality. Her birth from the skull of Zeus represents wisdom being derived directly from the godhead. Apollo held the role of oracle and master of divination, which was generally a goddess' role, even as the Pythia who worked in his temple were all women.

GREEK AND ROMAN CANNABIS

Hemp

Cannabis did not grow much in classical Greece and the drugs were not a part of their culture or mythology. The lack of cannabis drugs can be seen in their enfeebled goddesses. Greece has a rocky landscape that is not as lush in vegetation as other regions. Cannabis did grow wild in some parts of Greece. Judging from the medical texts, which lack many references to intoxication, it appears to have been the *cannabis sativa* fiber types and not the *cannabis indica* drug types.

The Greeks and Romans both needed a lot of hemp for shipbuilding. Hemp was a critical raw material for wooden shipbuilding for over 3,000 years in both Europe and China, only ending with the industrial revolution and the invention of modern steel ships and engines. Hemp fibers provided all the ropes, the rigging that holds up the masts, the anchor cables, the caulking between the wooden boards, and some of the sails (which were mostly made from linen). Cannabis sativa accounted for ¼ of the weight or more of every wooden ship that ever sailed from Europe and China for untold centuries.

Hemp was a critical strategic commodity for every powerful nation that relied on its navy, and securing adequate supplies of hemp was an important concern of Admirals, ministers, and kings. Hemp's importance remained consistent until 1900 CE, when the graceful Clipper ships became the last great wooden merchant sailing ships to ply the world's oceans.

The quality of the hemp is important in shipbuilding because hemp is a natural fiber that degrades in the harsh conditions at sea. Even the highest quality materials needed to be replaced every other year at best but low-quality hemp could fail within months, putting the ship, cargo, and lives of the sailors at perilous risk. Hemp producers in certain regions specialized in making the strongest marine grade hemp, using sophisticated techniques to cure the fibers in a manner that optimized their strength. In the colonial era, only Russian hemp was trusted for British and American ships, and shipbuilders would not touch other sources, including American hemp.

Imports

The Greeks imported their hemp from around the Mediterranean, in particular from the Babylonian city of Sura and the Anatolian cities of Alabanda and Cyzicus.[6] The Romans needed hemp for many purposes and systematically spread the cultivation of it through Italy and western Europe all the way to the British Isles. In medieval times, Italian hemp was the finest in the world and there was a trade guild in Venice that controlled for quality.

The Greek geographer Strabo described Colchis, a region on the eastern shore of the Black Sea in modern-day Georgia, that exported hemp, linen, timber, and pitch, all the materials needed for shipbuilding to the Greeks. High-quality hemp has been produced in Anatolia and around the Black Sea into the modern day. The cities of Ephesus and Colchis on

6 Clarke, Robert Connell, and Mark David Merlin. *Cannabis: Evolution and Ethnobotany.* University of California Press, 2013, p.160.

the Black Sea were major centers of hemp industries, and centers of goddess worship.

> *The country is excellent both in respect to its produce... and in respect to every thing that pertains to shipbuilding; for it not only produces quantities of timber but also brings it down on rivers. And the people make linen in quantities, and hemp, wax, and pitch. Their linen industry has been famed far and wide; for they used to export linen to outside places;*
>
> – Strabo, *Geography* (11.12.17)

Syracusia

The story and documentation of a famous Greek ship provide us evidence of how the Greeks valued fine hemp. King Hiero II ruled the Greek city-state of Syracuse from 270 to 215 BCE. Hiero ordered the famous mathematician Archimedes to design for him one of the largest and grandest ships ever built, the *Syracusia.*

Archimedes was from Syracuse and is known for having said, "*Give me a place to stand, and I shall move the world,*" in describing leverage. As well as, "*Eureka! I have found it!*" when running naked from his bath after discovering the mathematics describing displacement and buoyancy.

The colossal *Syracusia* was fabled for having a sumptuous decor of exotic woods and marble. Hiero spared no expense for his pride, which was over 180 feet long and took more than a year to build (some sources say the ship was larger, at 360 ft).

Hiero imported the finest materials including hemp cables from Spain, and hemp and pitch from the Rhone Valley in France, as recorded by the Greek writer Athenaeus.[7] This is the earliest mention of hemp being grown in France and it has continued to be cultivated there into modern times.

The *Syracusia* was built in the seafaring port city of Corinth, Aphrodite's famous city of luxury and sin. The ship was so large that the shipbuilders had a problem when they realized they could not get the boat from the land into the water.

Necessity being the mother of invention, Archimedes personally invented the windlass to move the heavy ship single-handedly. A windlass is a tool with a winch and pulleys that has been used ever since to move heavy objects. The *Syracusia* was so large that most ports could not accommodate her. She sailed just once to the Egyptian city of Alexandria and was never mentioned again in surviving texts.

7 Athenaeus, *The Deipnosophistae*, published in Vol. II of the Loeb Classical Library edition, 1928. http://penelope.uchicago.edu/Thayer/E/Roman/Texts/Athenaeus/5C*.html vol. Book V, p. 435.

Medicinal Cannabis

The classical Greek and Roman herbalists Dioscorides, Galen, and Pliny all wrote about cannabis in their works, and primarily referenced hemp types, and not the indica drug types.

De Materia Medica Published In 77 CE Entry On Cannabis Sativa

Pedanius Dioscorides was a physician from Asia Minor employed in the Roman army who wrote *De Materia Medica* around 77 CE, the classic medical reference book that was consulted for 1500 years. The book was a 5-volume pharmacopeia covering herbal medicine and related medicinal substances and methods.

Dioscorides has two entries for cannabis, one for cultivated cannabis, and one for wild cannabis. Cultivated cannabis, he says, is a plant useful in life for the braiding of strong ropes and appears to be cannabis sativa. The seeds are edible but if taken to excess dry up the man's procreation. The seeds can be instilled and used for pain in the ears. Wild cannabis, Dioscorides says, is short, dark, and reddish in color, but he makes no mention of intoxicants, so it is likely feral hemp, what we call "ditchweed" today. He says the boiled roots are useful for treating inflammation and the fibers can be used for ropes.

Pliny the Elder was a Roman naturalist and contemporary of Dioscorides. Pliny wrote the encyclopedic *Naturalis Historia,* multiple books about natural philosophy and topics of agriculture, medicine, and magic. Pliny discussed hemp as being useful for ropes and the regions it grew best.

> *Then, too, there is hemp, a plant remarkably useful for making ropes, and usually sown after the west winds have begun to prevail: the more thickly it is sown, the thinner are the stalks. The seed is gathered when ripe, just after the autumnal equinox, and is dried by the agency of the sun, the wind, or smoke. The hemp itself is plucked just after vintage-time, and is peeled and cleaned by the labourers at night.*

The best hemp is that of Alabanda, which is used more particularly for making hunting-nets, and of which there are three varieties. The hemp which lies nearest the bark or the pith is the least valuable, while that which lies in the middle, and hence has the name of "mesa," is the most esteemed. The hemp of Mylasa occupies the second rank. With reference to the size to which it grows, that of Rosea in the Sabine territory, equals the trees in height.

– Pliny the Elder, *Naturalis Historia: Book XIX*[8]

Alabanda and Mylasa are cities in present day Turkey, while Rosea in the Sabine Territory is near Praeneste in modern day Italy. Variances in grades of hemp were important, and certain regions produced the best hemp both because of the climate and their production methods.

Hemp seed, it is said, renders men impotent: the juice of this seed will extract worms from the ears, or any insect which may have entered them, though at the cost of producing head-ache. The virtues of hemp, it is said, are so great, that an infusion of it in water will cause it to coagulate: hence it is, that if taken in water, it will arrest looseness in beasts of burden. A decoction of the root in water, relaxes contractions of the joints, and cures gout and similar maladies. It is applied raw to burns, but it must be frequently changed, so as not to let it dry.

– Pliny the Elder, *Naturalis Historia*: Book XX

Galen was one of the most influential medical writers of the ancient world and the personal physician of multiple Roman emperors. Writing around 199 CE, Galen did not have much to say about cannabis, repeating the earlier prescriptions and adding that it was used as a casual intoxicant in after-dinner desserts.

And still nevertheless, some people, after drying it, consume it along with other desserts. And it sufficiently warms and on account of this (property) it overtakes the head, if an abundance is taken in a short (period of time), while sending up hot vapor to the head, it is also medicinal.

– Galen, *De Alimentorum Facultatibus*, 6.550[9]

8 Pliny the Elder, *The Natural History*, John Bostock, M.D., F.R.S. H.T. Riley, Esq., B.A. London. Taylor and Francis, Red Lion Court, Fleet Street. 1855. http://www.perseus.tufts.edu/hopper/text?doc=Perseus:abo:phi,0978,001:19

9 Sumler, Alan. *Cannabis in the Ancient Greek and Roman World*. Lexington Books, 2018 p. 87

Amazons and Scythians by Otto van Veen

Chapter Seventeen

SCYTHIANS

Horse Lords

Farmers and shepherds were not the only communities when civilization emerged from the Neolithic, there were also the horse lords. Horses were first domesticated and ridden in the same region of central Asia where cannabis originated.

The original horse lords were the Botai people who lived in the cannabis homeland of Kazakhstan. The Botai were the first people to domesticate and ride horses around 5,000 years ago at the dawn of the Bronze Age. The Yamnaya people were also in the central Asian steppe, riding horses, and using cannabis around the same time.

These people learned to domesticate and ride horses in order to help them hunt over wide ranges of the Eurasian steppes. Their nomadic descendants became the mighty Scythians of classical antiquity whose Goddess worshiping warrior women remain famous today, the Amazons.

There is a deep connection between cannabis, horses, and the Bronze Age horse lords, a connection that extends into their Goddess worshipping cultures. The first horse riders likely used hemp ropes to corral the animals, and perhaps horse and rider were sharing the ganja as well. Horses are fond of eating cannabis and gain medicinal benefits from its nutritional, anti-inflammatory, and pain killing properties.

Humans and horses may have developed their first personal connections while traversing the vast fields of cannabis they both enjoyed. Hemp ropes were used for reins and woven hemp may have been used for riding blankets and pants. The horse lords did as much as anyone to spread cannabis seeds across the continent from central Asia to India and Europe.

Noble Barbarians

The nomadic Scythians were widely feared and respected in the ancient world and they cast a forbidding shadow. Stampedes of fierce men and women barbarian warriors, riding side by side, covered head to toe in elaborate tattoos. With their horses dressed and adorned, the Scythians were an intimidating presence.

The Scythians ranged and raided across Europe and Asia for thousands of years, and demonstrated the clearest example of a culture with strong independent women, powerful goddesses, and an extensive use of cannabis.

"Scythians" is an umbrella term for a loose confederation of tribes; we do not know what they called themselves, much about their history, or relations between them. They ranged across the steppes of central Asia, from Siberia and Mongolia to eastern Europe and the Black Sea, periodically fighting with the Persians, Mesopotamians, and Greeks.

They were nomads who had cattle and oxen, pulling wagons that they lived in, and following the good grasslands. The Scythians left no writing behind. Most of what we know about them is from Greek and Persian sources who were their traditional enemies, and from archaeological excavations of their graves.

Amazon Warrior Women

In the nomadic tribes, it was important that the women be mobile and independent. Girls were trained from childhood to ride, fight, and hunt alongside the boys. Scythian women were masters of the bow and arrow and kept birds of prey for hunting. On horseback, a woman with a bow and arrow was just as deadly as a man. The Scythians invented the powerful recurve bow, which they strung with hemp string.

All young Scythian women took part in hunting and raiding, while childbearing women were given the choice to continue being a warrior or to stay in the wagons with the children. Of the hundreds of Scythian graves that have been found, around twenty percent were women warriors buried with weapons and war wounds. Scythian graves also featured censers used for burning cannabis and charred cannabis seeds.

The Scythian women were the mighty Amazons of Greek legend, warrior women who fought with and against men. Greek legends say the Amazons were a women-only society but that is unlikely. There may have been woman-only bands of lesbian fighters. But in general, the Amazons were warrior women who fought alongside their men and lived in an egalitarian society with them. Some Greek legends claimed the Amazons would cut off one of their breasts to assist them in using a bow, but there is no evidence that is true.

Greek History

Herodotus wrote about the Scythians and the Amazons, attempting to explain their origins and culture to his native Greek audience. The Greeks knew the Scythians as barbarians who dwelled in the lands around the Black Sea and had existed since the most ancient times. Wars with the Scythians were pivotal moments in Greek history, and they were fascinated by the exotic foreigners whose women were equal to men and fierce in battle. The Greeks thought of the Scythians as noble barbarians, among the most honest and forthright in their dealings, yet a terrifying enemy.

The firmly patriarchal Greeks were both awed by and disdainful of the Amazons – they were a popular motif in art and legend and children played with Amazon dolls. Heroes in Greek myths, like Hercules, tested themselves against mighty Amazon Queens who were skilled slayers of men. The Greeks saw themselves as masculine compared to the feminine Persians, their primary Asiatic rivals. The female Amazon warriors, on the other hand, challenged Greek masculinity by fighting them head-on and winning many battles.

Greek women were kept on a tight leash and mostly stuck indoors, tending to the weaving and children, so the contrast with the tough nomadic warrior women was stark. The Amazon women were heroic and beautiful, spirited, courageous, and brave. Bold barbarian archers on horseback who gloried in fighting, hunting, and sexual freedom.

The Scythians were known for having elaborate tattoos all over their bodies, and the women wielded battle axes, used lassos, trained eagles to hunt, and trained dogs too. The Scythians dressed in an unusual fashion foreign to the Greeks, they wore pants, which were invented for the purpose of riding horses. In general, the Scythians wore clothes of leather, wool, hemp, and silk.

Scythian Cannabis

The Scythian horse lords were famous in the ancient world for their love of cannabis. The Persians called the Scythians soma drinkers, indicating that they drank bhang. Herodotus gives us the oldest written description of people getting high when he wrote about the elaborate Scythian funeral rituals for their kings. These rituals included honoring the corpse for 40 days, keeping it in a wagon, and holding feasts until the final burial.

The Scythians burned cannabis inside a small tent which was filled with intoxicating smoke, causing them to "howl with joy." Herodotus also mentions the Thracians producing fine hemp fabrics indistinguishable from linen, and the mixing of cannabis with other aromatics to make skin-cleansing perfumes.

> *After the burial the Scythians cleanse themselves as follows: they anoint and wash their heads and, for their bodies, set up three poles leaning together to a point and cover these over with wool mats; then, in the space so enclosed to the best of their ability, they make a pit in the center beneath the poles and the mats and throw red-hot stones into it. (4.73.2)*
>
> *They have hemp growing in their country, very like flax, except that the hemp is much thicker and taller. This grows both of itself and also by their cultivation, and the Thracians even make garments of it which are very like linen; no one, unless he were an expert in hemp, could determine whether they were hempen or linen; whoever has never seen hemp before will think the garment linen. (4.74.1)*
>
> *The Scythians then take the seed of this hemp and, crawling in under the mats, throw it on the red-hot stones, where it smolders and sends forth such fumes that no Greek vapor-bath could surpass it. The Scythians howl in their joy at the vapor-bath. This serves them instead of bathing, for they never wash their bodies with water. (4.75.1-2)*
>
> *But their women pound cypress and cedar and frankincense wood on a rough stone, adding water also, and with the thick stuff thus pounded they anoint their bodies and faces, as a result of which not only does a fragrant scent come from them, but when on the second day they take off the ointment, their skin becomes clear and shining. (4.75.3)*
>
> – Herodotus, *Histories*

The Scythians used cannabis ritually to both cleanse themselves and to forget their sorrow. Many Scythian tombs had the burnt remains of cannabis, showing that they fumigated before and after the burials. The method of consuming cannabis smoke inside a small tent or cave is so simple that one can only speculate about how far back in time the practice goes.

Archaeological Proof

Herodotus's descriptions were confirmed when small censers and tents for burning cannabis, along with charred seeds, were found by archaeologists in frozen tombs, ca. 500 BCE, from the Pazyryk culture. These tombs were from a Scythian tribe present in the Altai mountains of Siberia, on the border with Mongolia, China and Kazakhstan. These unique tombs were frozen completely in ice, which allowed spectacular preservation.

Archaeologists found two complete mummies with intricate tattoos, a chief and a warrior maiden, and numerous textiles including the oldest pile rug. Inside one tomb they found a small wooden tent frame with copper containers that held charred stones and charred cannabis seeds. The archaeologists also found a leather pouch that contained cannabis seeds, coriander, and yellow sweet clover. [1]

Herodotus also wrote about another nomadic tribe, the Massagetae, who were related to the Scythians and their use of intoxicating herbs rather than alcohol. This passage does not name cannabis but the description fits. Roman writers also described Scythian customs of burning intoxicating herbs in the fire as a foreign and curious practice.

> *... and they know (it is said) of trees bearing a fruit whose effect is this: gathering in groups and kindling a fire, the people sit around it and throw the fruit into the flames; then the fumes of it as it burns make them drunk as the Greeks are with wine, and more and more drunk as more fruit is thrown on the fire, until at last they rise up to dance and even sing. Such is said to be their way of life. (1.202.2)*
>
> – Herodotus, *Histories*

> *There is laughing weed in Bactria and along the Borysthenes river. If this plant is consumed with myrrh and wine, different hallucinations are observed and there is no end of laughing until you drink the kernel of pine nuts with pepper and honey in palm wine.*
>
> – Pliny the Elder, *Naturalis Historia* (24.102.16)[2]

1 The Pazyryk tombs are well documented. M. Ren, Z. Tang, X. Wu, R. Spengler, H. Jiang, Y. Yang, N. Boivin, "The origins of cannabis smoking: Chemical residue evidence from the first millennium BCE" in the *Pamirs. Sci. Adv.* 5, eaaw1391 (2019).

2 Translation Alan Sumler, *Cannabis in the Ancient Greek and Roman World*. P. 63

Scholars have long identified the Bactrian laughing weed as cannabis, and here we see another example of cannabis being mixed with myrrh in wine. Bactria is in Central Asia, north of the Hindu Kush, in the cannabis homeland. The Borysthenes river is the Dnieper river in Ukraine that flows into the Black Sea, it is one of the great rivers of Europe and was very important to the Scythians as a center for agriculture.

Another reference to cannabis use around the Black Sea by Scythian tribes comes from Greek Geographer Strabo. The Mysians were known as the "*kapnobatai,*" the "smoke-walkers" or "smoke-eaters," who were peaceful, vegetarian, and burned cannabis ritually as part of their daily life.

> *Poseidonius goes on to say of the Mysians that in accordance with their religion they abstain from eating any living thing, and therefore from their flocks as well; and that they use as food honey and milk and cheese, living a peaceable life, and for this reason are called both "god-fearing" and "kapnobatai";*[3]
>
> – Strabo, *Geography* (7.3.3)

Scythian Goddess Religion

Only limited amounts are known about Scythian religion but it was clearly Goddess-centric. They had a pantheon of deities led by a Goddess Queen named Tabiti, Papaios was the Earth Mother, and Api was the Heavenly Father.

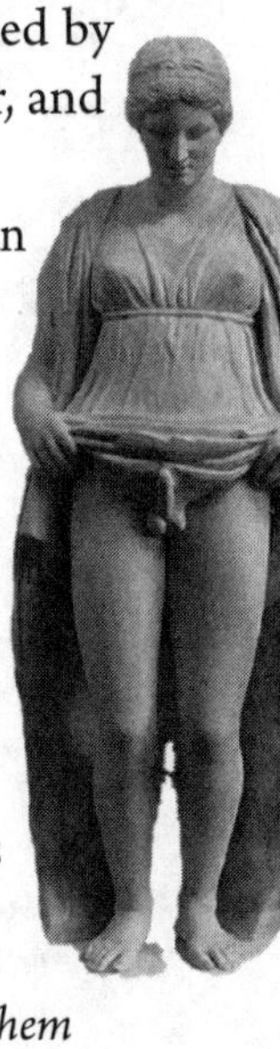

Argimpasa was a maiden love goddess, similar to Ishtar, and an oracular deity associated with the practice of shamanism. She was served by the Enarei, a class of gender-fluid priests. The Enarei were soothsayers and magicians who practiced fortune-telling using bones, along with cannabis to induce trance and divination.

In all, there were eight primary Scythian deities, three female and five male, with a Queen at the head. Herodotus documented the existence of the shamanic transgender oracles among the Scythians. Stating that the practice was hereditary and given to them by the goddess of love. This is consistent with Goddess traditions throughout the Ancient Near East.

> *The Enarees, who are hermaphrodites, say that Aphrodite gave them the art of divination.*
>
> – Herodotus, *Histories*, 4.67.2

3 Strabo. ed. H. L. Jones, *The Geography of Strabo*. Cambridge, Mass.: Harvard University Press; London: William Heinemann, Ltd. 1924.

Tree of Life

The Tree of Life was a common motif in Scythian artwork, often featuring a serpent twining itself around it. Both of these symbols appear in the Biblical Garden of Eden story and are important and widespread.

The Tree of Life has had many different meanings. In Mesopotamia, the Tree of Life grew in the heart of their garden paradise. The Hebrews represented it in the Menorah, while the Jewish Kabbalists use it as a mystical diagram of the human psyche. In China, the Tree of Life symbolizes the eternity of the spirit and the continuity of life. For the Christians, it represents immortality. For the Celtics it is a symbol of balance and harmony. For Muslims it represents life taken to its highest level of perfection. For Native Americans, it encompasses all of life. And for the Norse, it is Yggdrasil, the world tree that connects the heavens to the Earth to the underworld; the Axis Mundi, the pillar of the cosmos.

Serpents

Serpents are believed to be very wise and are closely associated with Goddesses, especially in the context of oracles, divination, and wisdom. The serpent lives down in the Earth and emerges to shed its skin, continually renewing itself like the cycle of life. Temple oracles were almost exclusively women throughout ancient times, like the famous Oracle at Delphi. Eurasian shamans would carve serpents into the handles of whips and drums which they used for their journeys to the spirit world.

A serpent-entwined staff is another powerful symbol, the Greeks called it the Rod of Asclepius and it represented doctors and medicine. Moses made one of brass for the wandering Hebrews and they burned cannabis incense to it. Our modern symbol for medicine is called the Caduceus, with two serpents wrapped around a winged staff.

In mythical imagery, the good serpent is always presented standing vertically. If the serpent is presented horizontally, slithering on the ground, then it is a negative, or evil presentation.

Temple of Artemis At Ephesus

The Amazon warrior women were credited with establishing the original worship of Artemis at Ephesus. Ephesus was one of the most important cities in Asia Minor, a wealthy port of 100,000 residents with important roads leading to the interior, which made it a strategic location and center of governance and commerce.

Ephesian Artemis was a great goddess related to the Anatolian Mother Goddess Cybele. Artemis' famous statues depict her with rows upon rows of breasts, that upon closer inspection appear to be a coat of gourds or bull testicles, such as may have been worn by a priestess, though interpretations vary.

Artemis was a midwife who protected fertility and childbirth. Her statue featured many animals; lions, leopards, goats, griffins, bulls, and bees, and she was called the Lady of the Animals. Her priests were eunuchs, the highly honored Megabyzi, similar to the eunuch Galli priests who tended to Cybele in Rome.

The grand temple of Artemis at Ephesus was the biggest and most magnificent pagan temple ever built. It was the largest building in the world at the time, four times as large as the Parthenon in Athens, and one of the Seven Wonders of the Ancient World. Worship began there around 800 BCE with a sacred meteorite.

The temple was destroyed and rebuilt multiple times. In 356 BCE it was burned down by an arsonist seeking immortality through glory and the Ephesians were so angry that they made a law forbidding his name from ever being mentioned. It was said that Alexander the Great was born the day the temple burned; the story is that the great goddess was distracted attending to his safe birth and could not save her own temple from destruction.

The temple was rebuilt grander than ever and no expense was spared. It was constructed completely from marble with 127 columns 60 feet high. Aside from priceless works of art, there were four huge bronze statues of Amazon warrior women, to honor the legend that Ephesus was founded by the Amazons.

> *I have gazed on the walls of impregnable Babylon along which chariots may race, and on the Zeus by the banks of the Alpheus, I have seen the Hanging Gardens, and the Colossus of the Helios, the great man-made mountains of the lofty Pyramids, and the gigantic tomb of Mausolus; but when I saw the sacred house of Artemis that towers to the clouds, the others were placed in the shade, for the sun himself has never looked upon its equal outside Olympus.*
>
> – Antipater of Sidon, *Greek Anthology* IX.58 (140 BCE)

The cult of Artemis at Ephesus was one of the most popular in the ancient Near East and the city of Ephesus was uniquely devoted to her. Pilgrims from all over the Near East would purchase small statuettes of the goddess Artemis as souvenirs and they have been found all over the Mediterranean.

Apostle Paul's Visit

In the New Testament of the Bible, the Apostle Paul visited Ephesus and caused a near riot at the temple. This is the only mention of a goddess in the New Testament and demonstrates her importance at the time.

> *A silversmith named Demetrius, who made silver shrines of Artemis, brought in a lot of business for the craftsmen there. He called them together ... and said: "You know, my friends, that we receive a good income from this business. And you see and hear how this fellow Paul has convinced and led astray large numbers of people here in Ephesus and in practically the whole province of Asia. He says that gods made by human hands are no gods at all.*
>
> *There is danger not only that our trade will lose its good name, but also that the temple of the great goddess Artemis will be discredited; and the goddess herself, who is worshipped throughout the province of Asia and the world, will be robbed of her divine majesty."*
>
> *When they heard this, they were furious and began shouting: "Great is Artemis of the Ephesians!" Soon the whole city was in an uproar. The people seized ... Paul's traveling companions from Macedonia, and all of them rushed into the theater together. Paul wanted to appear before the crowd, but the disciples would not let him. They all shouted in unison for about two hours: "Great is Artemis of the Ephesians!"*
>
> *The city clerk quieted the crowd and said: "Fellow Ephesians, doesn't all the world know that the city of Ephesus is the guardian of the temple of the great Artemis and of her image, which fell from heaven? Therefore, since these facts are undeniable, you ought to calm down and not do anything rash.*
>
> – Acts 19:24-36 (NIV)

The temple of Artemis at Ephesus was ultimately destroyed by a Christian mob in the year 401 CE. Most of the marble was hauled away to be used for other building projects and today barely a trace remains of the largest and grandest temple that ever stood in the ancient world. But the Christians would continue the Goddess traditions at Ephesus in their own fashion. Ephesus became the center of Catholic veneration for the Virgin Mary. It was in Ephesus in the year 431 CE that the Virgin Mary was declared to be the "Mother of God," a title she holds to this day.

Venus Astarte by Dante Gabriel Rossetti

CHAPTER EIGHTEEN

PHOENICIANS

GODDESS WORSHIPPERS

The Phoenicians were an important Goddess-worshipping culture that arose on the coast of Lebanon after the Bronze Age Collapse. The Phoenicians were wealthy and successful and were the dominant merchants in the Mediterranean for most of the first millennium BCE. The famed "traders in purple," the Phoenicians embodied luxury, fine arts, and sumptuous living. They were commercial rivals of the Greeks and Romans for control of the Mediterranean. The Phoenicians were also the Biblical Canaanites who were the great religious rivals of the Hebrews. As we will see, the Phoenician/Canaanite gods were very important to the Biblical story.

The coast of Lebanon had been inhabited for thousands of years since early in the Neolithic. Ugarit had been a prosperous city-state but it fell around the same time as Troy, presumably at the hands of the Sea Peoples during the Bronze Age Collapse. The Iron Age Phoenicians emerged around 1000 BCE and their leading cities were Tyre, Sidon, and Byblos, and they also lived in Canaan (today's Israel/Palestine).

The Phoenicians had a pronounced Goddess-worshipping culture that shared many affinities with the Minoans and syncretized deities from both Mesopotamia and Egypt. The Etruscans in Italy at this same time were similar to the Phoenicians and they were trade allies. Both were artistic, wealthy, sexually expressive Goddess cultures with Neolithic roots. Etruscan women were equals to men, they had great independence and played leadership roles in society. The Etruscans were ultimately defeated by and assimilated into the Roman Republic.

In keeping with the egalitarian ethos of Goddess cultures, the Phoenicians were not a dominator society. They were merchants and craftsmen, skilled artisans, not militants, who operated on principles of fair trade and not one of assault and plunder. The Phoenicians had no military empire, but were a confederation of independent city-states that shared language and culture.

Mediterranean Colonies

The Phoenicians were great sailors and from the period 900-600 BCE they established colonies all over the Mediterranean; on the islands of Sicily, Sardinia, and Corsica, they founded the city of Marseille, France, and the Spanish cities of Barcelona, Cadiz, Malaga, and Algeciras. The most famous and important Phoenician colony was Carthage, on the north coast of Africa in what is now Tunisia. The network of colonies served as trading posts, warehouses, and ports, and Phoenician merchants were respected throughout the civilized world.

The Phoenicians were trading partners and rivals to both the Greeks and Romans. The destruction of Tyre at the hands of Alexander the Great and the defeat of Carthage by the Romans were turning points when those cultures achieved international dominance, but those events were centuries in the future.

> *Tyre, the crowning city, whose merchants are princes, whose traffickers are the honourable of the earth.*
>
> – Isaiah 23:8 (KJV)

The Phoenicians are important characters in the Hebrew Bible but they are not described as Phoenicians. They were identified by their home regions, as Canaanites, Tyrians, Sidonians, Carthaginians, etc. King Hiram of Tyre was one of King Solomon's greatest allies and helped build the first Hebrew temple in Jerusalem. King Hiram supplied Lebanese cedar and craftsmen, though relations soured under later Kings. The notorious Queen Jezebel of Israel was a Phoenician princess from Sidon. Hebrew prophets preached doom upon Tyre for their "abominable" goddess worship and licentious, sexually free lifestyles.

Tyre & Carthage

Tyre was famed throughout the world, not only for its luxury markets and fine crafts, but also because the city was built on an island 1 km from shore, in addition to the mainland city. The island featured two sheltered ports that were among the best in the Mediterranean, and was capped by an impregnable fortress with walls 150 feet over the sea and robust battlements. Tyre had already been occupied for over 2000 years, but it rose to international prominence under the Phoenicians.

In the 9th century BCE, Pygmalion was king of Tyre and paid tribute to Assyria. Pygmalion's legendary sister Dido stole his treasure and fled.

She first went to Cyprus where they picked up a high priest of Astarte and some hierodule women to keep the soldiers' company. The company eventually arrived in Libya, in North Africa.

Dido asked the local Berber chief for permission to settle on his land, to which he replied that she could take all the land covered by a single ox hide. Clever Dido took the ox hide and cut it into narrow strips which she then used to encircle enough land for a city.

In this way, Dido founded the grand city of Carthage in 814 or 825 BCE. Carthage would rise to become the most important Phoenician colony in the Mediterranean and one of the wealthiest, most cosmopolitan trading centers in the world. Carthage was ultimately destroyed by the Romans in the Punic Wars over half a millennium later.

PHONETIC ALPHABET

The Phoenicians made many important contributions to global civilization and culture, but perhaps their most long-lasting contribution was the invention of what became our modern alphabet. We still refer to it as a "phonetic" alphabet, because it is based on letters, "22 magic signs" that correspond to sounds and arranged to make words (vowels were invented later).

The phonetic alphabet replaced the pictographic alphabets used in Sumerian cuneiform and Egyptian hieroglyphics. The word "biblio" meaning "books," as in bibliography or bibliophile, as well as Bible, comes from the city of Byblos. Pictographic writing disappeared in the Bronze Age Collapse and after the 200-year Dark Age phonetic writing was invented.

The Phoenician alphabet was modified and improved to form many of our modern written languages. It directly influenced the development of Hebrew and Aramaic, and the Greeks did not hide the fact that they created their alphabet from the Phoenician model, which in turn led to Latin.

By virtue of being traders who used their written script to record business transactions, the Phoenicians spread their written language throughout the civilized world. The Phoenician script was widely adopted because it was much easier to master than the pictographic scripts with thousands of possible characters.

Ironically, despite their contributions to writing the Phoenicians wrote little about themselves, at least that survives. Most of what we know about the Phoenicians comes from the writings of their rivals, and discoveries by archaeologists.

Luxury

Lebanon was famed for its cedar forests from which the Phoenicians both exported lumber and used for shipbuilding and temples. The Phoenicians were known for producing fine textiles, carpets, and were manufacturers of luxury goods and glassware. They produced fabulous faience, an efflorescent glazed ceramic. Objects created with faience were considered magical, the shiny blue glaze reflects the undying shimmer of the sun, and imbues the object with the powers of fertility, life, and rebirth.

The Phoenicians gained their greatest wealth and built the basis of their trading empire on the color purple. Specifically, from the rare and valuable murex dye used to create the color purple for textiles that was reserved only for the wealthiest and royalty. The dye was derived from murex shellfish, and each mollusk only produced one or two drops of dye. To make a single gram of purple dye required between 10,000 and 20,000 murex shellfish and this made the mollusks more valuable than gold.

Phoenician seacoast colonies were largely dedicated to harvesting murex and they traded cloth colored in the "Tyrian Purple" for all manner of valuable goods, particularly tin, copper, gold, and silver, as well as other raw materials. Even today, true "Tyrian Purple" dye remains fantastically expensive, thousands of dollars per gram.

Fair Trade

The Phoenicians were a peaceful people by nature, scrupulous about fair trade, and not seeking conquest or domination, though they did have slavery and trade in slaves. They did not maintain a standing army and relied on mercenaries to do their fighting.

The Phoenicians valued family, spirituality, Mother Earth, and respected women and their trading partners. They were known for their tight communities and placed a high value on solidarity and partnership, and families shared in the prosperity generated by trading ventures.

They were explorers of distant shores and were known for admiring the customs and traditions of the people they encountered. The Phoenicians developed long-lasting friendships and trade relationships and always sought interactions of mutual benefit; it was the Phoenician way. Though the Greeks and Romans often described them as pirates, cheats, and liars.

> *Another story is told by the Carthaginians. There is a place in Libya, they say, where men live beyond the Pillars of Heracles; they come here and unload their cargo; then, having laid it in order along the beach,*

> *they go aboard their ships and light a smoking fire. The people of the country see the smoke, and, coming to the sea, they lay down gold to pay for the cargo, and withdraw from the wares.*
>
> *Then the Carthaginians disembark and examine the gold; if it seems to them a fair price for their cargo, they take it and go away; but if not, they go back aboard and wait, and the people come back and add more gold until the sailors are satisfied. In this transaction, it is said, neither party defrauds the other: the Carthaginians do not touch the gold until it equals the value of their cargo, nor do the people touch the cargo until the sailors have taken the gold.*
>
> – Herodotus, *The Histories,* 4.196.1-3

Phoenix

The Phoenicians were skilled in the arts of diplomacy and sought to avoid armed conflict. At times when invasion or conflict became inevitable, the Phoenicians would initiate peace offerings, lavishing gifts on their would-be attackers in hopes of achieving a mutually beneficial settlement. Commitment to peace processes enabled the Phoenicians to avoid many painful conflicts.

On the occasions that negotiations failed and their cities were poised to come under attack, the Phoenicians would leave their cities by boat taking all their valuables with them. When the attackers had departed after looting and burning the city to the ground, the Phoenicians would return and rebuild.

From this we get the legends of the Phoenix, the majestic red and gold birds who perish and burn in fire, only to rise and live again. The Phoenicians were very wealthy and every few centuries their cities were inevitably plundered and burned – such annihilations being common in the ancient world. The Phoenicians displayed an extraordinary response to these calamities that distinguished them from other peoples. They would return to their land in unity and rebuild within five or ten years. Phoenician cities would rise from the ashes and become even richer than before, a process that was repeated numerous times over the centuries. To this day Lebanon has been a land of strife, resilience, and pride.

Phoenician Cannabis

The Phoenicians were very intimate with cannabis. They used hemp fibers for shipbuilding and the drugs influenced their Goddess worship. Cannabis drugs help people spiritually connect to nature and empower the divine feminine in worship. The regions where cannabis grows thickest is where goddess worship is the most pronounced, and the Phoenicians exemplified this relationship as well as anyone. Lebanon is identified in the Bible as a source of cannabis and the country continues to be an important producer today.

The Phoenicians were great shipbuilders and sailors, they were the ancient mariners. By virtue of being shipbuilders, the Phoenicians were ensured of the active use of cannabis for ropes, cable, rigging, caulk, and some sails, in the same manner as the Greeks. The Phoenicians were not the first to sail, but they did the most to establish the Mediterranean as a routine transit zone, and they mastered the arts of navigation.

The Phoenicians explored beyond the Straits of Gibraltar into the Atlantic, south down the west African coast, and north to Britain, known as the Tin Isles, where they engaged in an active tin trade. The Phoenicians were the first to circumnavigate Africa around 600 BCE, a thousand years before the Europeans. They sailed from the Red Sea in a trip sponsored by Egyptian Pharaoh Necho II (who appeared in the Bible). There is reasoned speculation that the Phoenicians may have made it to the Americas as well. It was certainly within their capabilities to catch the same ocean currents that brought Christopher Columbus to the Caribbean.

Phoenician ships were constructed from Lebanese cedar and displayed sophisticated engineering techniques. The Phoenicians were renowned for being able to build ships quickly, and archaeologists who have found sunken ships have observed notations on the boards indicating that they were prefabricated following a model, and joined using mortise and tenon methods.

Unfortunately for the Phoenicians, the Romans reverse-engineered this technique and duplicated the Punic shipbuilding methods. Despite not being a traditional seafaring people, the Romans quickly built their own navy when they decided to challenge and ultimately defeat the Carthaginians in the Punic Wars. The Romans in turn spread hemp culture throughout Italy and Europe to satisfy the Empire's insatiable demand for the durable fibers.

The Marsala shipwrecks are Punic warships from the third century BCE discovered off the coast of Sicily, that were likely sunk during the Punic wars. Among the interesting items archaeologists have found were a bundle of cannabis stems preserved in an amphora, that were likely the remains of flowers used to get high.

Baalbek

Lebanon remains famous today for the quality of the cannabis indica and hashish grown in the Bekaa Valley, the fertile agricultural region that is also home to the ancient city of Baalbek. Cannabis was grown there in Biblical times and armed Lebanese farmers proudly continue to grow excellent cannabis today.

Modern outlaw cannabis farmers in the Bekaa Valley maintain their independence, growing what they consider to be a sacred plant, despite the threats from corrupt governmental prohibitionists, bloody civil war, and violent religious extremists.

Baalbek was originally inhabited 9,000 years ago early in the Neolithic, and it was home to one of the most important and remarkable temple sites in the ancient world. The grand temples at Baalbek were dedicated by the Phoenicians to Baal and Astarte, the King of the Gods and the Queen of Heaven. The Romans called the city Heliopolis and they rebuilt it with three temples dedicated to Jupiter (Baal), Venus (Astarte), and Bacchus (Dionysus). The Temple to Jupiter was the largest and grandest temple ever built by the Romans, surpassing any in the city of Rome itself.

Trilithon Stones

The Temple to Jupiter at Baalbek features unusual megalithic stones and architectural details. There are three enormous 900-ton limestone foundation blocks, called the *Trilithon* that were carefully and precisely placed in position. They are the largest stone blocks ever cut, moved, or lifted in human history.

The Trilithon stones are each 70 feet long, 14 feet high, and 10 feet wide. They were moved uphill from the quarry a kilometer away and elevated 30 feet off the ground. Two more even larger stones were cut but never moved from the quarry, including the single largest cut-stone block ever found, that weighs an astonishing 1,650 tons.

It is an enduring mystery how the Trilithon stones were put in position, since the Romans left no records of the feat and never claimed to have done it. The Romans never moved any other stones that were anywhere close to as large and did not have the technology to do so. Nor were the Phoenicians known for such engineering feats. The evidence indicates that the Romans found the stones in place and built their temples on top of them.

The Trilithon are the largest carved stones ever used in construction anywhere in the world. They baffle modern engineers who can't understand how or why the oversized stones were cut and moved. The effort would be extremely challenging today using modern technology. The Trilithon blocks are truly of unknown origin and antiquity. According to local folklore, the stones were cut by giants in the time of the Great Flood.[1]

CANAANITE GODS

The Bible's Other Gods

In the Old Testament of the Bible, the chief nemesis of the Hebrews were the Canaanites, the native peoples of the Levant who practiced folk religions and worshipped in the traditional ways. The Canaanites had the same culture and worshipped the same gods as the Phoenicians, but we only know limited amounts about their religion.

The oldest evidence of these traditions were found in the city of Ugarit, which was a prosperous trading and port city that had been occupied since 6000 BCE. It fell during the Bronze Age collapse around 1200 BCE. Ugarit was destroyed by fire and warfare, and unlike neighboring cities, it was not rebuilt and remained abandoned.

In 1928 Ugarit was unearthed by archaeologists who discovered an important trove of cuneiform tablets. The tablets included dramatic and distressing royal letters requesting aid during the fall of the city. Even more remarkably they found previously unknown mythology of the Phoenician gods that appear in the Bible.

The Phoenician myths include El, who would later become Yahweh, the Judeo-Christian God. The early Hebrews emerged out of the Canaanite culture and were originally monolatrists before they became monotheists, but we will get to that story later.

The Phoenician/Canaanite pantheon predates the Bronze Age collapse and represents the older traditions with roots in the Neolithic that would come into conflict with the new philosophical and religious ideals of the Axial Age.

The Phoenicians syncretized deities from both Mesopotamia and Egypt and they had particularly powerful goddesses. Goddesses were central to Phoenician mythology and as we will see, the Phoenician goddesses stand out for their power and ferocity. Particularly in contrast to the Greeks who devalued their goddesses, and the Hebrews who deny the existence of the Goddess altogether. It is a notable paradox that the Phoenicians were peaceful people, yet they had some of the most fearsome deities.

1 Hancock, Graham. *Fingerprints of the Gods: The Evidence of Earth's Lost Civilization*. Three Rivers Press (CA), 1996. https://www.megalithicbuilders.com/asia/lebanon/baalbek-baalbek-temple-complex

EL

El is the most important god we discuss in this book because he became God of the Bible. El was the grandfatherly patriarch of the Phoenician pantheon. To the Phoenicians, El was the Heavenly Father, the Creator of the Universe, Creator of Creatures, the Father of Time, the Bull of Heaven, and many other titles. El has a wife, Asherah the Mother Goddess, and their children were the prominent deities in the pantheon.

El is pictured with the same type of imagery we have for God today, as an old gray-bearded man reaching down from the heavens. Unlike the Biblical presentations though, the Phoenician El is very sexual and numerous stories depict him seducing women. We only have a limited amount of Phoenician mythology and we don't have their creation story. We don't know who their primordial deities were, or of a primeval mother goddess.

El was derived directly from the Sumerian An, who was the first male god worshipped in Sumer. So, it is fair to say that the Judeo-Christian God, the Heavenly Father, has a worship practice going back deep into pre-history; it is just that, for most of that time, he was part of a polytheistic pantheon. Monotheism was a new idea for a very old God.

El presided over the heavenly council of gods, but he was mostly removed from human affairs and provided his authority to the active king, similar to the Sumerian An. El was seen by the Greeks as the equivalent of the Cronos. A big difference though is that El was a kind and generous god who had a ribald sense of humor and cared for the fates of humans and the other gods, while Cronos was cruel.

The name El appears throughout the Bible as Elohim, which is both the name of God and a generic name for gods generally. El is seen in the biblical names El Shaddai (God Almighty), Elyon (God Most High), in the town name of Bethel, in the name of the nation Israel (wrestles with God), and many other places. In the book of Genesis (33:20), Jacob builds an altar and calls it "El Elohe Israel," which translates to, "El is the God of Israel."

BAAL, YAMM, & MOT

The god triad of Baal, Yamm, and Mot are direct equivalents of the Greeks' Zeus, Poseidon, and Hades. Baal, Yamm, and Mot are all the sons of El and rivals for power. Baal was the king of the gods, Yamm the god of the sea, and Mot the god of death and the underworld.

It is instructive that the male gods of the Greeks and the Phoenicians were very similar, while the Goddesses were dramatically different. There is no equivalent to the Phoenician Triple Goddess in the Olympian pantheon. The Phoenician pantheon was said to live on Mt. Zaphon, similar to the Greek gods on Mt. Olympus.

Baal was the king of the Phoenician pantheon and the chief opponent of the Hebrews in the Bible. Baal was depicted as a warrior storm god with a club in one hand and a lightning bolt in the other. Baal is the god of agricultural fertility and the lord of rain and dew, critical sources of water in the arid Levant, which lacks any great rivers. The Baal Cycle was the most important mythological story recovered at Ugarit; it tells of how Baal came to be the King of the Gods with the crucial assistance of the goddesses.

Baal was considered to be an equivalent to the Greek Olympian Zeus, the Roman Jupiter, the Babylonian Marduk, and the Vedic Indra. Baal was vilified in the Hebrew Bible as the great rival to Yahweh, the Hebrew god. Many cities were named for Baal including Baalbek in Lebanon and the Biblical towns of Baal-Hamon and Baalath.

Baal was also a euphemism for "Lord" that was used in general conversation, a wife might call her husband, 'my Baal'.

Yamm is the god of the sea, and the equivalent of the Greek Poseidon. Both were seafaring cultures for whom the sea was very important, and both elevated the god of the sea as the brother of the ruler.

Mot is the god of death and the equivalent of the Greek Hades. Baal and Mot were rivals locked in an unending struggle between life and death, barrenness and fertility.

Phoenician Triple Goddess

Asherah, Astarte, and Anat (or Anath) were the Phoenician Triple Goddess, the mother, maiden, and death. The Phoenician goddesses appear repeatedly in the Bible and are always denounced, dismissed, and defamed by the Biblical writers, though they were incredibly popular in Canaan. Try as they might, the Hebrews were powerless against these fearsome goddesses and as we will see, the Hebrews ultimately chose to simply ignore them and pretend they did not exist.

The goddesses were the true rivals of the Yahwists (followers of Yahweh) because they were the most popular in the hearts of the people and they had the major festivals with the wild celebrations. Their popularity was no doubt related to the practices of ritual sex which they performed in sacred groves to promote the fertility of nature.

ASHERAH, THE WIFE OF GOD

Asherah was the Mother Goddess and the wife of El, the wife of God, with whom she was the mother of 70 gods. In the Baal Cycle story, El and Asherah do not live together and Asherah was far more active in the lives of the other gods. Asherah was called 'She who Walks on the Sea', and the 'Lady of the Sea'.

Like the Sumerian, Ninhursag (Ki), Asherah may have been the oldest deity in the pantheon. She was widely revered and worshipped throughout Lebanon, Syria, and the Levant. There have been many archaeological pieces found that depict Asherah, often nude with a prominent pubic triangle in the images, and she was associated with lions.

Asherah plays an important role in the Hebrew Bible and is mentioned over 40 times. She was worshipped with an Asherah pole that represents a sacred tree or a sacred grove. The Asherah pole is like a maypole or a totem pole, ancient symbols representing the Earth and the divine feminine. Asherah poles could be carved and may have been similar to Native American totem poles, but there are no images or precise descriptions that have survived.

An Asherah pole stood in front of Solomon's Temple for most of its history and they were commonly placed next to altars throughout the countryside. The Biblical Hebrews were always keen to chop the Asherah poles down, and the common folk would put them back up as soon as they were able.

ASTARTE, THE QUEEN OF HEAVEN

Astarte was the maiden, the Queen of Heaven, and she was a continuation of Ishtar and Inanna. Astarte performed the same role for the Phoenicians as Ishtar did for the Babylonians; she presided over the hieros gamos and confirmed the fecundity of nature. They believed that lovemaking in the name of the goddess makes the flowers bloom, and that logic leads to a very sexually permissive culture.

The Phoenicians practiced sacred sex and the Greeks mocked them for prostituting their daughters. Astarte only played a passing role in the Baal Cycle, but she is mentioned many times in the Bible. The Hebrews call her Ashtoreth, the epithet '-eth' means shame, as in 'shameful Astarte.' The Bible also names her as the Queen of Heaven.

In Carthage, Astarte was called Tanit and she was considered to be the consort of Baal. She developed an independent mythology in Carthage and was central to their worship. In pagan religions there is no doctrine or dogma, and communities remade their mythologies as they saw fit.

Generally, Astarte/Ishtar was considered to be the courtesan of the gods and only ever had one husband, Dumuzi/Tammuz. As a matter of principle, Astarte did not believe in monogamy for herself or anyone else. She had many lovers and got around quite a bit.

Anat the Terrible

Anat was the most unique goddess in the Phoenician pantheon, she is a beautiful, blood-soaked warrior maiden and the sister/lover of Baal. She plays a crucial role in the Baal Cycle, rescuing Baal from death, and killing many humans. Anat was syncretized from Egypt where she was a popular goddess of the Hyksos. Similar to how Isis restored Osiris; without Anat, Baal would not be King.

Anat is a hunter who favors her bow and arrow and has a fierce temper aimed at humans and gods alike. She is a Canaanite Kali, except that Anat is drop-dead gorgeous with long hair black as bitumen, alabaster skin white as a ghost, ruby red lips, and piercing emerald eyes. Anat was dressed to kill with macabre stylings, a garland skull necklace and a belt of human hands.

Anat is never mentioned in the Bible though, probably because she was too terrifying. Her favorite activity was slaughtering the enemies of Baal and wading up to her vulva in their blood and gore, cheered by the carnage. And the Hebrews of course, were the greatest of all enemies of Baal. Anat must have had great bloodlust for the Biblical prophets.

Anat is the sister of Astarte, her rival in beauty and equal in combat. Both sisters were addressed with the honorific title, "Virgin," and both are warrior maidens, often depicted nude with a pronounced pubic triangle. The maidens rush into battle together riding lions, nude but for their armor. Lions are their sacred animals, and both favor a bow and arrow but are skilled with many weapons.

While Astarte is a goddess of strategy who leads the kings to victory and glory, Anat is the goddess of slaughter and vengeance. Wherever the enemy was thickest is where Anat went first, cutting down soldiers ten at a time with her broadsword. Anat delights in battle, chopping off limbs with a laugh and making jewelry from the body parts.

QEDESH

Asherah, Astarte, and Anat were a Triple Goddess worshipped for thousands of years. The Phoenician Triple Goddess had no equivalency among the Greek and Roman Olympians, though they are quite similar to the Hindu Devi; Parvati, Durga, and Kali. Both sets of goddesses were intimate with cannabis, which influenced the potency of their depictions.

Limestone stela of Qeh depicting Qedesh flanked by Min and Reshep. In lower register, Qeh and his family shown worshipping the goddess Anat.

In Egypt, Asherah, Astarte, and Anat were consolidated into a single cosmic goddess named Qedesh, a Semitic goddess of the Hyksos. Qedesh was known as "the Holy One" and was a goddess of nature, beauty, and sexual pleasure. Qedesh was often depicted naked riding a lion and holding snakes. Like the Phoenician goddesses, she was served by qedesha priestesses and eunuch transgender priests, which her name evokes. One of their holy cities was Kadesh in Syria, which makes a notable appearance in the Bible as the location for the burial of Miriam, the sister of Moses.

UGARITIC TEXTS

CANAANITE MYTHOLOGY

Phoenician/Canaanite religion has roots that predate the Bronze Age Collapse and connects to the older Neolithic Goddess traditions. The biblical Hebrews emerged out of this culture and became rivals with the Canaanites with the introduction of monotheism. It is important to understand the Canaanites in order to understand the hostility they faced from the Hebrews as this contentious relationship lays at the foundation of Western Civilization.

For centuries little was known of the Canaanite religion that is denounced in the Bible. The biblical writers provided no context to understand the worship practices they condemned in Canaan. These sections of the Hebrew Bible are written as a harsh, one-sided, political polemic and the native residents of Canaan almost never get a chance to defend themselves against the Hebrew prophets.

The discovery of cuneiform texts from Ugarit in 1928 offered the first examples of Canaanite mythology. These texts bring radical new insights into the beliefs of the people prior to the introduction of Hebrew monotheism.

The texts used here were first published in 1978,[2] with a second edition in 2012 in *Stories from Ancient Canaan* by Michael D. Coogan and Mark S. Smith. Both authors are renowned professors and experts in biblical studies, Coogan from Harvard and Smith from New York University.

These texts have not gotten the attention they deserve outside of scholarly circles, and by the historical standards of the Bible, this is brand new information. If people were paying attention these stories should be controversial, but conservative religious traditionalists have no desire to challenge long-held views and liberal secularists have little interest in religion.

Scholars recognize that these stories portray an earlier iteration of "God" before he took the familiar form in the Bible. But most scholars in the west are polite, respectable, Christians and do not make the obvious logical leap to describe these texts as direct contradictions of traditional monotheistic interpretations of God.

God Among the Gods

There are many remarkable details to the Ugaritic stories that should give pause to Western audiences. We now see El, (God) in an entirely different light. For the first time, we get to see El among the entire pantheon of gods.

There are many tantalizing clues in the biblical text that indicate the polytheistic roots of the Hebrews. One of the most well-known examples comes in the first chapter of Genesis when God created human beings. In this verse God is clearly speaking to other gods – gods we are never introduced to in the Bible.

Then Elohim said, "Let Us make man in Our image, according to Our likeness."
– Genesis 1:26

In Psalms, God presides over the great assembly of the gods, which is the role played by El in the Canaanite pantheon.

Elohim presides in the great assembly; he renders judgment among the gods.
– Psalm 82

2 Coogan, Michael David., and Mark S. Smith. *Stories from Ancient Canaan*. Westminster John Knox Press, 2012.

In the Ugaritic texts, we see El among his wife and children, and he shows them great love. Baal is vilified in the Bible, but here we see that Baal is El's favored son and King of the Gods. In the Bible we never properly meet El's wife Asherah and daughter Astarte, they are simply denounced and condemned. Even though one of the 12 Tribes of Israel is named Asher in honor of Asherah.

Anat is never even mentioned in the Bible even though she is the consort of Baal and was obviously known to the biblical writers. We can see why – Anat is terrifying, violent, and powerful above the other gods.

Anat challenges her father El and threatens to smash his skull in if she does not get what she wants. Anat then proceeds to destroy Death, cleaving him in half with a sword, grinding him up like grain, and feeding him to the birds. This is not a goddess who fits in the biblical framework.

We even see El try to sexually seduce Asherah, who denies him. Throughout it all, El is kind and generous and takes his trials in stride with a sense of humor and genuine concern for the fates of humans and gods alike.

This is the culture of the golden calf, the old-fashioned idolatrous practices of the pagan Hebrews. Moses worked to wipe these traditions out after coming down from Mt. Sinai with the Ten Commandments, and a new name for God – Yahweh.

EL'S DRINKING PARTY

One short story from Ugarit shows why Moses may have wanted to move away from the name El, and why early Church fathers had all these stories burned.

In *El's Drinking Party,*[3] El gets dead drunk, defecates and urinates on himself, and must be helped home. The next morning, El is fed a hangover cure by his daughters' Astarte and Anat, which they called the "hair of the dog." Ironically, this expression is still used today to describe a hangover cure. If you ever wondered where the expression came from, now you know.

This is all too strange to believe and shocks the sensibilities of anyone raised in the Church who thinks of Elohim/Yahweh/God as the all-powerful and omnipotent creator of the universe whose existence goes back to the beginning of time. Truth is truly stranger than fiction.

3 Coogan, Michael David., and Mark S. Smith. *Stories from Ancient Canaan*. Westminster John Knox Press, 2012.

BAAL CYCLE

The Baal Cycle, or the Epic of Baal, is the longest and most important piece of Canaanite mythology that has been discovered. It is a central piece of their religion, it is both the story of how Baal became King of the Gods, and also their resurrection story. The Baal Cycle was found on six tablets in Ugarit, that are mostly preserved but with chunks missing throughout the text.

Baal is the dying-and-rising god whose death brings a barren landscape and disaster to humanity. Anat is the all-powerful goddess who defeats death and restores her brother Baal to life and kingship, bringing fertility back to the land.

Baal first rose to be King of the Gods after fighting with his brother Yamm the sea god for supremacy. But after achieving kingship, Baal oversteps his authority and is ordered to submit to Mot, the god of death, who kills him. Anat then confronts Mot, demands her brother's return, and destroys the King of the Underworld in dramatic fashion.

This cycle of life tale shares the common characteristics of other pagan dying and rising god traditions that tie the fate of the gods to the fertility of Earth. We have seen this story repeated with Inanna in Sumer, Isis and Osiris in Egypt, Dionysus in Greece, Demeter and Persephone, and so many others. But these Phoenician stories stand unique for the raw unbridled power of the goddess Anat, who is more powerful than the other gods.

King of the Gods

The story begins with a conversation between Yamm, the god of the sea, and his father El about Yamm's enemy Baal. The two great gods are competing to be king and Yamm says that Baal must be defeated. The reasons behind the conflict are not clear, though the god of the sea was typically one of the most primeval and powerful deities and a natural rival to the god of storms.

El and Asherah proclaim Yamm's kingship. El sends messengers to Anat, telling her to desist from war. The violent Anat is Baal's sister and greatest defender.

Yamm sends messengers to the Assembly of the Gods, ordering them to surrender Baal to him.

The gods were alarmed by Yamm's rudeness, and while Baal was ready for a fight, El agreed to send Baal to Yamm to pay him tribute. Baal was angry, he had a weapon in each hand and had to be restrained. Anat seized one hand and Astarte seized the other.

Baal had two special clubs made – for he had no intention of submitting to his brother. Baal's clubs were named "Driver" and "Chaser." In a fierce battle, Baal struck Yamm on the skull and defeated him.

Astarte shouted, *"Hail Baal the Conqueror! Hail Rider on the Clouds!"*

ANAT'S BLOODY GLORY

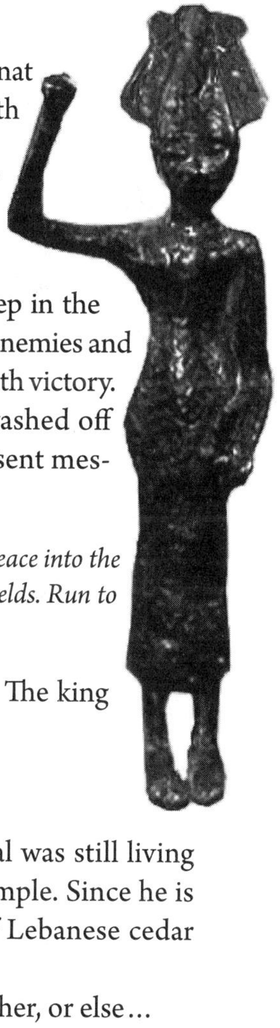

The tablets are broken, but the story picks up with Anat preparing herself for battle with henna, scented with coriander and murex.

Anat battled in the valley against the soldiers of Yamm. She annihilated the men, their heads rolling like balls. She tied their severed hands to her belt and made a garland necklace of their skulls. Anat waded vulva-deep in the gore and soaked in the soldiers' blood. She drove off her enemies and laughed. Anat's heart was filled with joy, her belly filled with victory.

Anat returned home and cleaned herself up. She washed off the blood and waited for her love Baal to return. Baal sent messengers, telling Anat,

> *Remove war from the Earth, set love in the ground, pour peace into the heart of the Earth, pour tranquility into the heart of the fields. Run to me with your feet, race to me with your legs.*

Anat went to meet Baal on the peak of Mt. Zaphon. The king dismissed his wives when his sister approached.

BAAL NEEDS A HOME

Baal and Anat discussed his lack of a home, for Baal was still living in the home of his father. A god's home was his temple. Since he is now King of the Gods, Baal needed a grand temple of Lebanese cedar built for him.

Anat says that she will speak to El and he will answer her, or else...

> *I'll push him to the ground like a lamb, I'll make his hair run with blood, his gray beard with gore, unless he gives Baal a house like the other gods, and a court like Asherah's sons.*

Anat went to the encampment of El, the creator of the universe. She immediately threatened her father.

Don't rejoice in your well-built house El, I will seize it with my mighty arm. I'll smash your head, I'll make your gray hair run with blood, your gray beard run with gore.

El, the kind and compassionate, took it all in stride, unconcerned by his daughter's tantrums.

I know you daughter, how furious you are, that among the goddesses there is no restraining you; what do you want Maiden Anat?

Your decree is wise, El, your wisdom is eternal, a lucky life is your decree... Baal has no house like the other gods, and Baal is the conqueror, our judge, higher than all.

El consented to her wish. He tells Anat to visit Asherah and gain her mother's favor with gifts of gold and silver.

Visiting Asherah

Asherah was at her home working with her exalted spindle when she saw Anat and Baal approaching. The Mother Goddess was terrified of her mighty children. She broke out in sweat and her joints trembled.

Why has Baal the Conqueror arrived? Why has Maiden Anat arrived? Would you kill me or my sons? Or finish off my pride of lions?

But when she saw the gleam of the gold and silver she was glad. Asherah agreed to visit El on Baal's behalf.

Asherah went to El the Bull and prostrated herself before him. El got excited by his wife's visit, he offered her food and drink, and asked,

Does the El the King's passion excite you? Does the love of the Bull arouse you?

Asherah passed off the seduction but pleaded Baal's case. El replied spitefully, annoyed that his advances were spurned.

So am I a servant? A slave-girl of Asherah who molds bricks?

But El agreed to the request and ordered a house for Baal to be built. Asherah praised him,

You are truly wise, your gray beard truly instructs you.

THE DEATH OF BAAL

Anat celebrated the good news and Baal was glad. Baal's house was built of silver and gold, Lebanese cedar, and the purest lapis lazuli. Baal then went on a victory tour, dispatching his enemies and sacking many towns.

Baal was enthroned as the mightiest of the gods and he then decided to challenge his brother Mot, the god of death, for ultimate supremacy. Much of this section is damaged, but Baal sent messengers to Mot, telling him that Baal is now champion of all the gods and Mot must submit to him.

After some more damaged text, there is a decision by the Assembly of the Gods that Baal must submit to death. Apparently, Baal had overstepped his boundaries, as even the immortals must submit to death eventually.

Baal was terrified and afraid, but he obeyed. Before Baal went to his doom he had sex with a young cow who bore him a child, perhaps an heir.

Mot killed Baal and the Lord of the Earth perished. Death came upon the land and fertility vanished.

LAMENTATIONS OF THE GODS

El came down from his house in mourning and lamentations, covering himself with dirt, wearing a hempen sackcloth in the ritual fashion.

El cut his skin with a stone, made incisions with a razor, and cut his cheeks and chin, he raked the length of his arms, he plowed his chest like a garden, he raked his back like a valley. El raised his voice,

> *Baal is dead, what will happen to the people?*

Anat went about hunting until she found Baal's body. She also cut her skin with stones, and covered herself in hemp sackcloth. When she was done weeping, she brought Baal's body back to Mt. Zaphon and she buried him. Anat made great offerings and sacrifices.

Asherah's sons competed to be the new king, but they were no comparison to the mighty Baal.

ANAT DEFEATS DEATH

Anat sought out Mot. Like the heart of a cow for her calf, so was Anat's heart for her brother Baal.

She grabbed Death by the edge of his clothes, raised her voice and demanded,

> *Come Death, give me my brother!"*

Anat seized El's son Death:

With a sword she split him;
With a sieve she winnowed him;
With fire she burned him;
With millstones she ground him;
In the fields she sowed him.
Birds ate his flesh;
Fowl consumed his parts;
Flesh cried out to flesh!

Anat destroyed Death and ground him up like grain and Baal was restored to life.

El was glad. Baal returned to his royal throne and dispatched his rivals.

Baal Enthroned

Then in the seventh year, Mot, apparently not permanently dead, approached Baal.

Because of you I experienced shame. Give me one of your brothers for me to eat and my anger will turn away.

Baal somehow tricked Mot into eating his own brothers instead, the lines of text are damaged.

Baal and Mot proceeded to fight anew. Mot was strong, Baal was strong. The Sun eventually interceded, telling Mot not to kill Baal, or surely El would overturn him.

Mot was afraid and finally declared,

Let Baal be enthroned on his royal throne, the seat of his dominion.

This concludes the Baal Cycle. Baal is enthroned above all, but not without the crucial assistance of his sister Anat, the goddess who defeated Death and had the spirit to challenge El.

Anat displays none of the subtlety and magic of Isis, or the sensuality of Ishtar, but there is no denying her raw power. Anat's mastery of death and ability to drive terror into the hearts of the other powerful gods puts Anat into a category of her own.

Chapter Nineteen

CHILD SACRIFICE

Greatest Sin

The greatest sin committed by the Phoenicians, according to the Biblical writers and the Greeks, was sacrificing their children to the gods. The Greeks, Romans, and Hebrews were universally disgusted by Phoenician child sacrifice and it was a crucial distinction between their cultures.

The Greek story of Agamemnon and Iphigenia, as well as the Hebrew story of Abraham and Isaac, indicate that child sacrifice practices were familiar but were being pushed out in the religious reformations of the Axial Age. Among the reasons why the Hebrews and Hellenistic Greeks saw themselves as superior was that they no longer viewed child sacrifice as a useful tradition.

Despite being a civilized and cosmopolitan people, the Phoenicians were deeply superstitious by Greek and Roman accounts, clinging to talismans and amulets that would help protect them from their malevolent gods. Archaeology has confirmed that the Baalists did practice human sacrifice. Thousands of infant graves have been unearthed at Carthage in a huge "tophet," a burial ground for charred human and animal sacrifices. Smaller tophets were found at Phoenician sites in Sicily, Sardinia, and Tunisia. Child sacrifice at Carthage took place continuously for over 600 years through good times and bad.

Human sacrifice in the form of killing war captives and slaves was not unusual in the ancient world. Nor was it unheard of for an entire royal court to practice ritual suicide upon the death of the king or Pharaoh. These and other similar practices, including cannibalism, have been documented in many cultures in many parts of the world. The Phoenician/Canaanite practice of sacrificing their own children to placate the gods does seem to be unique in the Iron Age Mediterranean. Child sacrifice does not appear to have been practiced in any of the other neighboring cultures like Mesopotamia or Egypt.

The Greeks allude to child sacrifice in their mythology as an ancient practice of their uncivilized forebears. The sacrifice of Iphigenia at the beginning of the Iliad is told in contradictory stories; in some cases, the girl dies and in others, she is saved by the goddess Artemis. In the Hebrew Bible, God instructs Abraham to sacrifice his son Isaac but the boy is rescued at the last moment. Many scholars believe that there were multiple versions of this story as well, with some featuring the death of Isaac.

Why?

Sacrifices were made under different circumstances, sometimes infants were killed to honor a request being granted by the gods. In other cases, children could be sacrificed in times of danger and deprivation, such as a siege or famine. In one Biblical instance, Canaanite child sacrifice apparently worked to defend against an assault by the Israelites. Fortunately, we now understand that these sacrifices were a futile and useless superstition that our ancestors were correct to abandon.

> *When the king of Moab saw that the battle had gone against him, he took with him seven hundred swordsmen to break through to the king of Edom, but they failed. Then he took his firstborn son, who was to succeed him as king, and offered him as a sacrifice on the city wall. The fury against Israel was great; they withdrew and returned to their own land.*
>
> – 2 Kings 3:26-27

Archaeologists have found that Phoenician infant burials took place regularly over a long period of time. Human sacrifice was part of their culture, and most of the literature describes the sacrifices as the fulfillment of vows and responses to prayers being answered by the gods. Apparently, people would offer a child if the gods delivered them their prayer requests. The tophets contain a mix of animal and child remains carefully placed in urns, indicating that animals were used as well, or as substitutes for children. The fact that the animals and children were all buried together shows that these were not child or pet cemeteries, but ritual offerings to the gods.

No Tears Allowed

It was a requirement that the parents of the sacrificed child not shed any tears, or else the sacrifice was invalidated and the child would still be dead. Greek historian Plutarch wrote:

> *With full knowledge and understanding they themselves offered up their own children, and those who had no children would buy little ones from poor people and cut their throats as if they were so many lambs or young birds; meanwhile the mother stood by without a tear or moan;*

> *but should she utter a single moan or let fall a single tear, she had to forfeit the money, and her child was sacrificed nevertheless; and the whole area before the statue was filled with a loud noise of flutes and drums so the cries of wailing should not reach the ears of the people.*
>
> – *On Superstition* by Plutarch[1]

The method of sacrifice was dramatic, a bronze statue of a god with arms outstretched was stoked with a hot fire. The babies and animals were placed in the god's arms and immediately consumed by the flames.

> *Out of reverence for Kronos, the Phoenicians, and especially the Carthaginians, whenever they seek to obtain some great favor, vow one of their children, burning it as a sacrifice to the deity, if they are especially eager to gain success.*
>
> *There stands in their midst a bronze statue of Kronos, its hands extended over a bronze brazier, the flames of which engulf the child. When the flames fall upon the body, the limbs contract and the open mouth seems almost to be laughing, until the contracted [body] slips quietly into the brazier. Thus it is that the "grin" is known as "sardonic laughter," since they die laughing.*
>
> – Cleitarchus (ca. 310-300 BC)[2]

The Greek writers wrote for Greek audiences and they routinely used the familiar names of Greek gods when describing foreign gods, which leads to some confusion among later scholars, who must take care to recognize which gods are being described. In the context of human sacrifice, the Greeks consistently describe them as sacrifices to Cronos, the cruel King of the Titans, the older generation of gods who ate his own children and was displaced by Zeus. Cronos was the equivalent of El, which supports the theory that the early pagan Hebrews did sacrifice their children as told in the story of Abraham and Isaac.

Corruption

Child sacrifices were made by the wealthy and elite, including the royalty. The practice fell into disrepute and corruption when the rich were allowed to purchase the children of the poor as substitutes for their own children. Carthage came under siege in 308 BCE by the King of Syracuse leading to a political crisis and mass sacrifices.

1 Plutarch, *On Superstition*, as published in Vol. II of the Loeb Classical Library edition, 1928.

2 Mosca, Paul G., *Child Sacrifice in Canaanite and Israelite Religion*. PhD thesis, Harvard, 1975, p.22. Reference via Bennie H. Reynolds, "Molek: Dead or Alive? The meaning and derivation of mlk and ###", in *Human sacrifice in Jewish and Christian tradition*, ed. K. Finsterbusch &c, Leiden: Brill, 2007, p.133-150, p.149 n.68.

Therefore the Carthaginians, believing that the misfortune had come to them from the gods, betook themselves to every manner of supplication of the divine powers...

They also alleged that Cronus had turned against them inasmuch as in former times they had been accustomed to sacrifice to this god the noblest of their sons, but more recently, secretly buying and nurturing children, they had sent these to the sacrifice; and when an investigation was made, some of those who had been sacrificed were discovered to have been supposititious.

When they had given thought to these things and saw their enemy encamped before their walls, they were filled with superstitious dread, for they believed that they had neglected the honours of the gods that had been established by their fathers.

In their zeal to make amends for their omission, they selected two hundred of the noblest children and sacrificed them publicly; and others who were under suspicion sacrificed themselves voluntarily, in number not less than three hundred.

There was in their city a bronze image of Cronus, extending its hands, palms up and sloping toward the ground, so that each of the children when placed thereon rolled down and fell into a sort of gaping pit filled with fire.

– Diodorus Siculus (20.14 via Lacus Curtius)[3]

Moloch or Mulk?

In the Bible, the Hebrews describe the practice as sacrifices to the god Moloch, and as "passing the children through fire." It is possible that "Moloch" is actually a mistranslation and does not refer to a god but is simply a name for the type of sacrifice. Biblical Hebrew is written with no vowels, leading to many possible translations of the same words. The Hebrew texts describe "mlk" sacrifices, which are traditionally seen as the deity Moloch. Many scholars now believe the word is "mulk," a name for the type of sacrifice that was used in Carthage.[4] If the sacrifices were not made to Moloch, that also strengthens the argument that the sacrifices were made to El.

12th century Jewish philosopher Maimonides described a pagan custom of passing infants through fire that did not involve sacrifice, but was reminiscent of the Mystery religions, and the myths where the goddesses

3 Diodorus Siculus, *The Library of History*, published in Vol. X of the Loeb Classical Library edition, 1954. http://penelope.uchicago.edu/Thayer/E/Roman/Texts/Diodorus_Siculus/20A*.html

4 Stager, Lawrence E., Wolff, Samuel R. "Child Sacrifice at Carthage—Religious Rite or Population Control? Archaeological evidence provides basis for a new analysis," *Archaeological Review*, 1984.

Isis and Demeter put an infant in the fire to grant them immortality. Some descriptions of "passing through fire" in ancient texts and the Bible may refer to this custom from the Mystery religions.

> *Know that traces of this practice have survived even to the present day, because it was widespread in the world. You can see how midwives take a young child wrapped in its swaddling-clothes, and after having placed incense of a disagreeable smell on the fire, swing the child in the smoke over that fire. This is certainly a kind of passing children through the fire, and we must not do it.*
> – Maimonides, *Guide for the Perplexed,* part 3, ch. 37 v.7

Abortion

In these ancient times, high child mortality was the norm. Newborns were kept at arm's length emotionally because so many of them died. Parents were accustomed to forming emotional attachments to babies only after the children were sure to survive.

It is also entirely possible that child sacrifice also served as a form of postpartum abortion and population control. Even in the western world in recent times, unwanted infants were commonly abandoned outside to perish. Abortions are dangerous, especially in the ancient world. It was much safer for a woman to carry a baby to term and then decide if she wanted to keep it, keeping in mind sex preferences and the child's health.

Cultures that are deeply rooted in nature like the Goddess worshippers view life in cyclical terms and appreciate that death begets new life and they don't elevate humans above nature. When you believe that death begets life, the emotional pain that comes with the loss of a loved one is tempered by the faith in the restorative value of the new life to come. The Hebrews and the Greeks both elevated humans as being the most important component in creation. They saw the deliberate sacrifice of one's own child as a sacrilege.

Modern cultures would never tolerate the sacrifice of our own infants, but we do see the evolution of this philosophical dispute in the debate over abortion, euthanasia, and suicide. Judeo-Christian ethics proclaim that life and death decisions belong to God alone and that it is immoral for humans to take another human's life. Despite the fact that these ethics are thrown out the window in the context of war and criminal justice, Judeo-Christian cultures are as blood-soaked as anyone in these matters. Modern day social progressives and reformers seek to restore personal decisions about death in the form of abortion, euthanasia and suicide back to individuals while religious conservatives work to keep these practices illegal.

VOLUME II
Old Testament

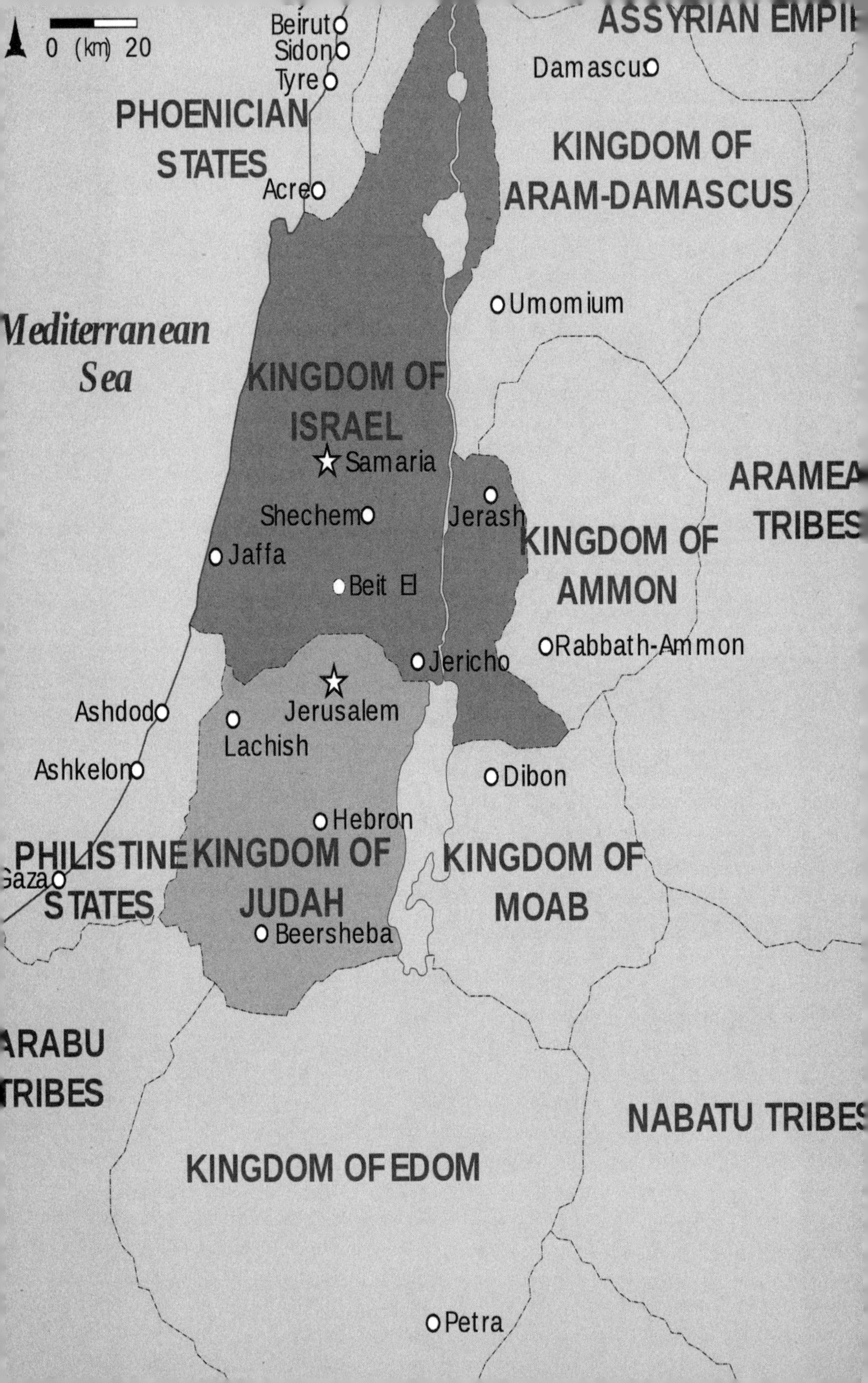

0 (km) 20
Beiruto
Sidon
Tyre
ASSYRIAN EMPI
Damascus
PHOENICIAN STATES
Acre
KINGDOM OF ARAM-DAMASCUS
Umomium
Mediterranean Sea
KINGDOM OF ISRAEL
Samaria
ARAMEA TRIBES
Shechem
Jerash
KINGDOM OF AMMON
Jaffa
Beit El
Rabbath-Ammon
Jericho
Jerusalem
Ashdod
Lachish
Ashkelon
Dibon
Hebron
PHILISTINE STATES
KINGDOM OF JUDAH
KINGDOM OF MOAB
Gaza
Beersheba
ARABU TRIBES
NABATU TRIBES
KINGDOM OF EDOM
Petra

Chapter Twenty

PAGAN HEBREWS

El Elohe Israel

There he set up an altar and called it El Elohe Israel.

– Genesis 33:20[1]

The Hebrews, or Israelites, were a mixed Semitic shepherding tribe from the southern Levant. The Hebrews emerged from the Bronze Age Collapse and in the first millennium BCE, they preached a revolutionary idea that had a profound influence on human culture and world affairs.

The new idea of the Hebrews is that there is just one God, monotheism, a single cosmological unity to the entire universe, not thousands of inchoate pagan gods acting independently in a disassociated universe. And unlike the cruel, capricious, and immoral pagan gods, the Hebrew God demands ethical, moral behavior, and provides a long list of laws that must be followed, lest he is provoked into anger and retribution.

The Hebrews ushered in a religious reformation and sparked a culture war lasting centuries. Worshipping one God alone required that the worship of all the other gods must be eliminated, particularly the highly popular goddesses. The move to shut down ancient temples was not well-received in the community and caused serious conflict, as shown in the events of the Old Testament.

The Hebrews were shepherds who worshipped the Heavenly Father, and their rivals were the Canaanite farmers who worshipped the Earthly Mother. The Earthly Mother and the Heavenly Father had traditionally been husband and wife, but monotheism required their divorce. God was elevated while the Goddess was written out of history.

The Hebrews were not always monotheists though. Abraham and the early Hebrews were pagans in a pagan world. More specifically, they were

1 All Biblical translations used in this text are taken from the New International Version (NIV), unless noted (KJV) for King James Version. All translations, including the Hebrew, are taken from biblehub.com. Certain words have been presented in their Hebrew form instead of English. These words are *Yahweh* (the LORD), *El, Elohe, Elohim* (God, gods), and qedesha (temple priestess). Hebrew does not have a word for goddess.

monolatrists (henotheists) in a polytheistic world. The Hebrews elevated one god, El, above the others but they recognized the entire Canaanite pantheon. Centuries after Abraham, Moses introduced monotheism as a new concept, along with a new name for God – Yahweh.

In the pagan world, every tribe was free to worship whatever gods they chose. The Hebrews worshipped El, the Creator of the Universe. El presided over the Canaanite pantheon as the father of the gods, and the Israelites had a tribal identity as his followers. Many lines of scripture reveal the polytheistic roots of the monotheistic traditions.

Elohim presides in the great assembly; he renders judgment among the gods.
– Psalm 82

Canaanite Religion

Canaanite religion predated the Bronze Age Collapse, these were the old gods with roots in the Neolithic, whose traditions contrasted with the (then) modern cultures of the Hellenistic Greeks and Hebrews. The Canaanite religion of this era was defined by the major temples in Phoenicia (Lebanon). Their traditions were drawn from Mesopotamia but also syncretized elements from Egypt. Canaanite Goddess worship shared many practices with the Mystery religions and Dionysus festivals that were prominent throughout the Near East and Greece in this period.

The Goddess traditions were rooted in nature and the cycles of life. They celebrated sexuality and believed that sex makes the flowers grow. Multi-day festivals featuring rituals, feasts, music, dancing, drinking, intoxication, and sacred sex, were cultural highlights every year. The Phoenicians and early Hebrews also practiced child sacrifice, a practice that the Hebrew religious reforms thankfully eliminated.

The introduction of the Hebrew God and monotheism, which would take form in the great religions of Judaism, Christianity, and Islam, was an intellectual leap forward for humanity – even though it came at the cost of losing touch with the feminine divine. Monotheism, the idea that everything in the universe can be reduced to the action of a single loving God, brought intellectual cohesion to religious cosmology compared to the disassociated actions of pagan gods.

The Hebrews were similar to the other Axial Age movements of the first millennium BCE that birthed our modern religions and philosophy. The Greek philosophers, Confucianists, Buddhists, Taoists, Zoroastrians, and the rest broke from older nature-based, shamanistic traditions and instead placed human ethics and moral behavior at the forefront of religion. In their own way, each of these movements preached that moral behavior was more important than superstitious fealty to unknowable gods.

In the traditional pagan worldview, humans were created to serve the gods and were in effect slaves to the gods. Monotheism freed us all from the intellectual slavery of servitude to the gods, mythically symbolized as Moses leading the escape from bondage in Egypt.

Israel

Tradition tells us that the Hebrews got their start with the first patriarch, Abraham (originally named Abram), who originated the worship of the one true God, El. Abraham led his shepherding clan from the Mesopotamian city of Ur into the land of Canaan around the 18th century BCE. His son Isaac, grandson Jacob, and their families are the Patriarchs, the progenitors of the Hebrew people, and the 12 Tribes of Israel.

El was the equivalent of An, the Heavenly Father from Sumer, and arguably the first-named god. An was generally distant and removed from human affairs and he retreated from active worship over time. It may have been the case that the Hebrews reestablished the ancient religion of An/El after it had fallen out of favor. El was known as the Bull of Heaven and one of his primary idols was the golden bull or calf.

It is from Jacob that we get the name Israel, and Israelites for the Hebrew people. Jacob was a trickster and deceiver who was blessed after he physically fought with an angel of God. He was given a new name, Israel, which means "wrestles with God" (Genesis 32:28). Jacob then set up an altar which he called "El Elohe Israel" which means "El is the God of Israel" (Genesis 33:20). Many Bible verses identify El as the God of Israel.

> *And he blessed Abram, saying, "Blessed be Abram by El Most High, Creator of heaven and earth. And praise be to El Most High, who delivered your enemies into your hand."*
>
> – Genesis 14:19-20

> *"I am El, the Elohe of your father," he said. "Do not be afraid to go down to Egypt, for I will make you into a great nation there.*
>
> – Genesis 46:3

El is usually called Elohim in the Bible. Elohim is both a proper Hebrew name for God derived from El, and also a generic word for gods generally (plural Elohe). This is the same in English when we use the word "god" as a generic word for deities and also as the proper name God. There are many variations on the name El such as El Shaddai (God Almighty, God the Provider), and El Elyon (God Most High). The name El appears in many place names like the town of Bethel, and of course, Israel.

God's Family

The Hebrews elevated El above the other gods, but the other gods from the Phoenician/Canaanite pantheon continued to be worshipped in the community. El's son Baal was the King of the Gods, the thunder-wielding warrior god of storms, rain, and dew. The goddesses were especially important.

The Canaanite Triple Goddess was Asherah, Astarte, and Anat; the mother, maiden, and death – who represent the cycle of life. Asherah was the Canaanite mother goddess, the wife of El, the Lady of the Sea, she was the mother of 70 gods who belonged to her. One of the 12 tribes of Israel is named Asher in honor of Asherah.

The beloved Astarte, the goddess of love and war, was the Queen of Heaven. The terrifying, blood-soaked, warrior maiden Anat was the sister/lover of Baal, and the scourge of his enemies. Baal, Asherah, and Astarte are all mentioned numerous times in the Bible as great rivals to the Hebrews, while Anat was conspicuously omitted from the scriptures. The qedesha were temple priestesses in service of the Triple Goddess.

EXODUS

Tradition tells us that later generations of Hebrews migrated to Egypt to escape famine and were enslaved for four centuries. They may have been related to the Hyksos, who were Semitic invaders and conquerors of Egypt who ruled there from 1630-1523 BCE. The story of the Exodus tells how Moses led the Israelites out of slavery in Egypt and into 40 years of wandering around Sinai before they were able to enter the land of Canaan.

Scholars believe that the Exodus, if it happened, must have been around 1250 BCE. The earliest appearance of the Hebrews in the archaeological record is from an Egyptian stele from 1207 BCE commemorating a military victory by Pharaoh over the Hebrews. There is no written evidence for a Hebrew slave revolt in Egypt, but we do know this is during the Bronze Age Collapse. It was a period of great tumult and upheaval which may have presented the opportunity for an underclass tribe of Semites to leave.

With the Bronze Age Collapse, the Near East entered into a two hundred year dark age when both writing and trade disappeared. The Hittites to the north were destroyed, while the Egyptians and Assyrians retreated to their homelands. The Israelites settled in Canaan during this period of political instability when the Levant was no longer dominated by any of the traditional military powers. The Hebrews were able to find a home for themselves in the sparsely settled Canaanite hill country where they periodically fought with the indigenous people for control of the valuable settlements and water sources.

Monotheism

It was Moses who introduced the revolutionary concept of monotheism, and the new name Yahweh for the monotheistic God (Exodus 3:15). Monotheism means that there is only one God, a single cosmological unity to the entire universe, and not thousands of gods all doing their own thing in a disassociated universe. Worshipping one god required that the people stop worshipping all the other gods, particularly the popular goddesses, who became rivals when before they had been family.

Monotheism has its roots in Egypt. The heretic Pharaoh Amenhotep IV elevated Aten to be the supreme God around 1346 BCE and banned the worship of all other gods. This religious reform was highly unpopular in Egypt and only lasted twenty years. The death of the Pharaoh prompted the immediate return to traditional Egyptian religion.

The idea of monotheism clearly held on with some people though and found new life among the Israelites. They blended their worship of El, the creator of the universe, with the idea that there is only one true God. El was given the new name Yahweh to symbolize this profound transformation.

The radical new idea of monotheism set off a religious culture war that lasted seven centuries within the Hebrew community. The Yahwists, the partisan followers of Yahweh, fought to eliminate the worship of the traditional gods and turn the people to worship Yahweh alone. This cultural civil war played out in Jerusalem over the entire history of the first Hebrew Temple and can be seen clearly in the Biblical text.

The Israelites entered into Canaan after the death of Moses around 1200 BCE, and they took Jerusalem under King David around 1000 BCE. The nation of Israel held its maximum territory at this point. The first Hebrew Temple was completed by King Solomon in 957 BCE, and the united kingdom split after Solomon's death around 930 BCE. The north-

ern kingdom of Israel lasted two centuries until it was overrun by the Assyrians in 720 BCE. Jerusalem was in the southern kingdom of Judah and it was destroyed, along with Solomon's temple, by the Babylonians in 586 BCE, leading to the exile.

When Moses came down from Mt. Sinai in Exodus 32 with the new covenant laws for the tribe, he was dismayed to find the people worshipping a golden calf (or bull). The golden calf was a symbol of El and the old traditional ways of worship. Moses had all the people killed who had worshipped the golden calf, and rewarded the Levite tribe who did the killing by making them into priests.

Centuries later when the united kingdom split in two, the northern kingdom of Israel immediately erected two golden bulls in the towns of Bethel and Dan and continued worshipping in the traditional pagan manner. The northern kingdom of Israel was pagan for its entire existence, much to the chagrin of the biblical writers.

In addition to being the name of the mother goddess, an Asherah was also a sacred carved pole representing the goddess that stood next to the altars to El/Yahweh. There are many times in the Bible where the Yahwists cut the Asherah poles down, and the people put them back up as soon as they were able.

Qedesha priestesses and transgender priests in service of the Triple Goddess were present in the first Hebrew temple for its entire history, though they are described dismissively as mere temple prostitutes or harlots. After the destruction of Jerusalem and the exile, the Hebrew women defended their goddess worship against the blame laid on them by the prophet Jeremiah (Jeremiah 44). Clearly, there were significant disputes over goddess worship from the time of Moses all the way through the end of the first temple period.

God is Male

The Hebrew God is unequivocally male, even though philosophers attempt to claim that God transcends gender. To make the shift from El to Yahweh, the Goddess needed to be removed from the picture, but her powers were only partially absorbed by Yahweh. The Goddess traditions were pushed underground and outside civilization, but never disappeared.

Yahweh became the Heavenly Father, but unlike El, Yahweh has no wife and no sexual relations. The Hebrews crafted a unique cosmology where their God created the world alone, asexually. This stands in contrast to the creation stories of their neighboring cultures in which the gods and goddesses mated and bore generations of gods and other creatures. The Hebrew language does not even have a word for *goddess*.

The Hebrews elevated humans, particularly men, to the center of creation. Humans were not made to serve the gods as traditionally believed in pagan customs. To the Hebrews, God created the Earth for the benefit of humans, and women were created subservient, for the benefit of men. The Bible makes humans the most important by saying that God created humans in his image; as opposed to seeing gods in the image of humans, and as metaphors for the mysteries of creation.

The Hebrews taught that God created the Earth for man to have dominion over, and they do not believe that the Earth is the Mother Goddess. The Hebrews do not believe that the Earth is our living, breathing mother. They argue that to worship her is idolatry because you are worshipping the creation and not the creator. This distinction is one of the clearest philosophical breaks made by the Hebrews away from the traditional beliefs of their Canaanite neighbors and indigenous people around the world.

The monotheistic reformers worked for centuries to discourage Goddess worship. Their ultimate success represented a divorce of God from the Mother Goddess, a divorce from nature worship, and its rituals including its sexuality, sacred plants, and shamanism.

This religious reformation took the form of a bloody culture war that lasted centuries. The disputes centered in the first Hebrew temple in Jerusalem where people argued over the worship of the popular pagan goddesses and gods. In their zeal, the monotheists would deny the existence of the feminine divine altogether and relegate nature to a mere collection of resources to be exploited for human satisfaction. This mindset has led inexorably to the era of industrialized planetary destruction we are living through today.

ARCHAEOLOGY OF ISRAEL

Scholars and archaeologists have worked for nearly two hundred years to find definitive evidence of the stories in the Bible. Important work has been done to put Bible stories into the proper historical context. While we don't know everything, we are increasingly able to discern which details of the Bible are historical, which are fiction, and the editorial perspectives of the authors.

We can see clearly that the Hebrew Bible is harshly polemical and presents one side in a political and cultural divide within the Hebrew/Canaanite community. The Hebrew Bible was written by the Yahwists who condemned the native people without ever attempting to offer their perspective.

The stories we read in the Bible reflect the views of the final editors who carefully crafted centuries worth of old folk tales to present their preferred perspective of Hebrew tribal history. The Biblical writers exaggerate numbers, excise details, and whitewashed events as they saw fit. Certain details peek through though, like shadows under white paint, that give clues about how the events truly occurred.

The earliest mention of Israel in the archaeological record is on the Merneptah Stele from Egypt and dating to 1207 BCE. The stele celebrates the Pharaoh's victorious military campaigns against the Libyans and the Sea Peoples as well as an additional campaign in Canaan where Israel (listed as a city) and other Canaanite cities were defeated. Though the uprisings were put down at that time, this actually marks the beginning of the end of Egyptian hegemony in Canaan. As the Bronze Age Collapse went into full effect, Egypt receded to its traditional borders. It was in this power vacuum that the Israelites were able to grow and prosper.

Merneptah Stele

By Biblical tradition, when Moses died, the leadership of the Israelites passed on to Joshua who was a military leader. Joshua led the Israelite invasion into Canaan where the Bible depicts mass bloodshed, slaughter, and the genocidal destruction of Canaanite cities.

Tradition dates the entry into Canaan around 1400 BCE, while scholars place the date of the Hebrew entry into Canaan around 1200 BCE, and debate whether there ever truly was a conquest. Many scholars believe that the Hebrews gradually settled into the sparsely inhabited countryside and told folk tales about themselves waging great military victories in the past. It remains debated whether the Hebrews were a foreign tribe at all or had Canaanite roots, but it is clear that the early Hebrews were worshipping the Canaanite gods.

JERICHO

The city of Jericho perfectly exemplifies the debates between scholars and the faithful. Jericho was destroyed and burned by the Israelites in a famous Biblical story told in Joshua chapter 6. The story tells how the Israelites used the mystical Ark of the Covenant to bring down the city's impenetrable walls.

Jericho is one of humanity's oldest settlements, dating back to the dawn of the Neolithic around 8000 BCE. Jericho is even older than Çatal Hüyük and it was one of the very first settlements that sprouted after the Younger Dryas cataclysms. Residents of Jericho today describe it as humanity's oldest city. By the time Joshua and the Israelites showed up, Jericho had already been inhabited for 7000 years.

Jericho has been heavily excavated and archaeologists have found the ruined walls and burned city just as it is described in the Bible. The faithful take this as a sign of the Bible's inerrancy. But is that really the correct interpretation? The important question is, when did the walls fall? Were the Hebrews responsible for bringing the walls down as described in the Bible? Or did they find the walls already broken down and then invent stories taking credit for the ruins in their midst.

Archaeologist Kathleen Kenyon did extensive work in Jericho and dated the destruction of the walls to 1550 BCE[2]. Dissenting scholars have argued for a later date of 1400 BCE, which is when some of the religious faithful believe the Israelites entered Canaan. Academics attribute the destruction of Jericho's thick walls to an earthquake centuries before the Israelites arrived. They believe that Jericho was uninhabited when the Israelites emerged in the area around 1200 BCE. The faithful on the other hand, view the archaeological evidence as proof of the Bible's truth.

Israelites bring down the walls of Jericho

2 Dever, William G. *Did God Have a Wife?: Archaeology and Folk Religion in Ancient Israel.* Eerdmans, 2005.

Asherah

Thousands of goddess images and figurines have been unearthed by archaeologists all over Syria, Israel, and Palestine.[3] One of the earliest figurines dates back to 4500 BCE and features a naked goddess seated on a stool, balancing a cheese/butter urn atop her head. Excavations at the early Bronze Age city of Ai uncovered a large post of charred wood which scholars believe to be an Asherah, one of the sacred wooden poles that represent the goddess.[4]

Goddess images found on plaques date back to 1500-1200 BCE and feature a nude goddess with wide hips, large breasts, and pubic triangle, often astride a lion, wearing an arrow quiver, and holding lotus flowers and snakes. These images represent Asherah, Astarte, and Anat who may be portrayed separately or as a singular cosmic goddess. The figurines depict a fully nude female with long hair, her hands holding her breasts. In some instances, she is wearing a bouffant wig in the style of Egyptian goddesses. In Egypt, Asherah, Astarte, and Anat were syncretized into a single lion-riding goddess named Qedesh, "the Holy One." They had a holy city, also named Kadesh, in today's Syria that appears in the Bible.

Among the most controversial archaeological discoveries was an inscription found at Kuntillet Ajrud, which says "Yahweh and his Asherah", demonstrating a clear connection between the supposedly monotheistic Yahweh and the Goddess. The inscription dates from ~830-760 BCE during the First Temple period and was found at a remote site in the Sinai desert near the modern border of Israel and Egypt. This period was during the Hebrew culture wars and shows that the Yahwist reformation took centuries to complete.

The inscriptions were found by archaeologists in 1975 on two large storage jars, or pithos, with unusual drawings and letters written in an early Hebrew script.[5] The inscription, "Yahweh and his Asherah" has caused considerable debate among scholars as to what it means. Do these inscriptions describe

3 William Dever, *Did God Have a Wife*, also Raphael Patai, *The Hebrew Goddess*.
4 Darlene Kosnik, *History's Vanquished Goddess Asherah*, Emergent Press, llc, 2014
5 Dever, but dozens of scholarly articles discuss this highly controversial topic.

God and his wife, or merely God's possession of a cultic object? The term Asherah in the Bible describes both the Canaanite goddess and the carved pole, like a totem pole, that stood in the temple next to the altar to represent her.

Conservative scholars and theologians loathe the idea that God could have had a wife, but these inscriptions are among the most unequivocal evidence that the early Hebrews were in fact pagan and worshipped the full Canaanite pantheon. The evidence and the scriptures show that the emergence of monotheism played out over centuries of social conflict.

Goddess Figurines

Molds have been discovered for mass production of small clay goddess figurines and they were popular, found in many homes. These figurines reflect a continuity of goddess worship from the Ice Age, through the Neolithic and Bronze Age.

A later type of figurine emerged after the fall of Samaria in the 7th and 8th centuries BCE. These later Judean figurines are called "pillar-base" because they only depict the upper half of the body and not the legs. These figurines are nude with prominent breasts, one type has simple finger-pinched faces, while others have molded faces. They are not sexualized images and may represent a nursing mother.

All told, around 3000 goddess figurines have been found in Israel/Palestine. The figurines are generally found in homes or in debris piles, but not in graves. They were likely a part of home/folk traditions and not the official cults. Scholars believe they represent household gods and that they are not toys.

Judaean female clay "pillar figurines". Jerusalem, Beer-Sheva, Tel Erani (8th-6th BCE). Wikimedia/Israel Museum

Tel Arad temple "holy of holies": The two altars can be seen—the large frankincense altar on the left, and the small cannabis altar on the right. A cultic stone can be seen in the far corner. Much of the above is a recreation at the site—the original altars and stairs are were transported to the Israel Museum in Jerusalem, where the Tel Arad shrine has been recreated. Photo by Sarah Murray. From watchjerusalem.com.

Chapter Twenty-One

CANNABIS IN THE BIBLE

Then God said, "I give you every seed-bearing plant on the face of the whole earth and every tree that has fruit with seed in it. They will be yours for food."

Genesis 1:29

Archaeology

Archaeologists working at the Israeli site of Tel Arad in the Negev Desert recently discovered that a shrine contained residues from burnt cannabis and frankincense on a pair of limestone altars. This research, published in 2020, is the first conclusive evidence that intoxicating cannabis resins were used ritually in Hebrew worship, though cannabis use has been suspected for a long time.[1]

Tel Arad was a Canaanite city going back to the third millennium BCE and was an Israelite fortress from the 10th to 6th centuries BCE. This is the exact same period when the first Hebrew temple in Jerusalem was active and suggests that similar rituals were practiced there.

Evidence of cannabis used for midwifery was found in a tomb from the 4th century CE, in Beit Shemesh, Israel, between Jerusalem and Tel Aviv. Inside the tomb was the skeleton of a pregnant 14-year-old girl who died late in her term or while giving birth. The full-size fetus was still in her mother's womb and was too large for a safe birth. Inside of her abdominal area, scientists found a gray material that upon analysis showed the chemical remains of cannabis. Scholars believe that cannabis was used medicinally to assist the doomed mother to give birth, but in this case, the midwives were not successful.[2]

Cannabis fibers and drugs both appear many times in the Bible but are not generally recognized because the words cannabis and hemp do not appear in English or other translations. The sacred role played by cannabis drugs in the Bible speaks to the pagan roots of the Hebrews. The later re-

1 Fox, Alex, "Archaeologists Identify Traces of Burnt Cannabis in Ancient Jewish Shrine," smithsonianmag.com, June 4, 2020. www.smithsonianmag.com/smart-news/cannabis-found-altar-ancient-israeli-shrine-180975016/

2 Russo 2007

jection of cannabis intoxication in the Judeo-Christian tradition is further evidence of the divorce from the earlier nature-based religious practices.[3]

Qaneh

Cannabis is mentioned by name five times in the original text of the Hebrew Bible as the word *qaneh,* or *qaneh bosm,* but is mistranslated in most texts as calamus, a different plant, or else the meaningless term *aromatic cane.* The mistake translating cannabis was first made in the *Septuagint,* the first translation of the Hebrew Bible into Greek in the third century BCE, and was transmitted to subsequent translations.

The etymology of qaneh bosm was first identified by Polish etymologist Sula Benet (aka Sara Benetowa) in her 1936 PhD thesis at Columbia University, and again in a 1975 paper.[4] Her work has been confirmed by modern scholars though her conclusions are controversial. Modern cannabis scholar Chris Bennett has done the most work to illuminate the use of cannabis in ancient religion and the Bible.

Qaneh means hemp and can also mean branch or reed, while *bosm* means fragrant or aromatic. In many ancient languages, including Hebrew, the root *qan (kan)* had a double meaning, both hemp, and reed. Qaneh bosm has clear similarities to other ancient names for cannabis such as the Assyrian *qunubu.*[5] It has also been suggested that the Hebrew word *pannag* is a variation of the Hindu word *bhanga* and the Persian *bang. Bhang* is both the name of the plant and the intoxicating cannabis milk beverage widely used in religious rites.[6]

In all five instances where qaneh, or qaneh bosm, is mentioned, cannabis fits the context while calamus or aromatic cane does not. The instances are Exodus 30:23; Song of Solomon 4:14; Isaiah 43:24; Jeremiah 6:20; and Ezekiel 27:19. Biblical commentary often refers to the spices mentioned in these verses as vague and ambiguous, but cannabis makes perfect sense. Cannabis is described as a sacred ingredient in Moses' holy anointing oil, a valued spice, a ritual offering, and as an object of trade.

---

3 The role played by cannabis in ancient religion and the Bible has been documented most thoroughly by the scholar Chris Bennett in his books and articles, *Sex, Drugs, and Violence in the Bible, Green Gold and the Tree of Life, Cannabis and the Soma Solution*, his research has greatly informed this book.

4 Sula Benet (aka Sara Benetowa), *Tracing one word through different languages.* Institute of Anthropological Sciences, Warsaw, 1936. Reprinted 1967 In: *The Book of Grass.* George Andrews and Simon Vinkenoog (eds.) Grove Press, New York, "pp. 15-18.

5 Sula Benet (aka Sara Benetowa), *Early Diffusion and Folk Uses of Hemp*, 1975

6 Mechoulam, R., W. A. Devane, A. Breuer, and J. Zahalka. 1991. "A random walk through a cannabis field." *Pharmacology Biochemistry and Behavior* 40(3): 461–464.

Cannabis had been widely used in the ancient Near East for thousands of years as a drug and fiber before the arrival of the Hebrews. It did not grow much in Canaan but the fiber and drug products were traded. Cannabis was burned as incense in temples, used as a ritual intoxicant, aphrodisiac, and as a medicine.

Hemp fibers were common and ritual weaving was typical in goddess worship across cultures. Hemp was used for ropes and shipbuilding, and as canvas for tents, sails, and sackcloths, while fine hemp was used as linen. Hemp would certainly have been appreciated by nature worshippers for whom plants were central to their awareness, since cannabis is the only plant that provides such a diversity of products.

The Assyrians, who had intimate, ongoing relations with the Hebrews, used cannabis extensively in religious rites and as a drug to induce ecstasy in the goddess temples. The pagan traditions practiced in Canaan widely overlapped with those of Mesopotamia.

Song of Solomon 4:14

In the romantic Song of Songs, King Solomon compares his beautiful bride to a garden filled with cannabis and all the finest spices. Cannabis is mentioned alongside myrrh, with which it was commonly combined to make incense as well as strong drink (drug cocktails in wine).

> *You are a garden locked up, my sister, my bride; you are a spring enclosed, a sealed fountain. Your plants are an orchard of pomegranates with choice fruits, with henna and nard, nard and saffron, cannabis [qaneh],[7] and cinnamon, with every kind of incense tree, with myrrh and aloes and all the finest spices.*
>
> – Song of Songs 4:12-14

Jeremiah 6:20

Cannabis was presented as an offering in Yahweh's temple. The prophet Jeremiah preached in Jerusalem at the time it was destroyed by the Babylonians. Jeremiah mentions "cannabis from a distant land" as among the offerings the Hebrews made to Yahweh that were no longer satisfying.

> *"What do I care about incense from Sheba or sweet cannabis [qaneh][8] from a distant land? Your burnt offerings are not acceptable; your sacrifices do not please me."*
>
> – Jeremiah 6:20

7 Translated "calamus" in most Biblical texts.

8 Qaneh in Hebrew, sweet calamus, sweet cane in most English translations.

Isaiah 43:24

Cannabis appears in Isaiah 43, which comes from the time of exile in Babylon after the destruction of Jerusalem. Israel had offended Yahweh with their lack of offerings, and fragrant cannabis is included among the offerings that Israel had failed to bring.

> *"You have not bought any fragrant cannabis [qaneh][9] for me, or lavished on me the fat of your sacrifices. But you have burdened me with your sins and wearied me with your offenses."*
>
> – Isaiah 43:24

Ezekiel 27:19

The prophet Ezekiel mentions cannabis in his lament for Tyre, in a list of products traded from Lebanon.

> *"'Damascus did business with you because of your many products and great wealth of goods. They offered wine from Helbon, wool from Zahar and casks of wine from Izal in exchange for your wares: wrought iron, cassia and cannabis [qaneh].[10]*
>
> – Ezekiel 27:18-19

Exodus 30:23

Cannabis appears most prominently during the career of Moses. Cannabis is explicitly identified as an ingredient in the holy anointing oil as instructed directly by God. These same ingredients were thought to have been used in the sacred incense as well.

> *"Take the following fine spices: 500 shekels of liquid myrrh, half as much (that is, 250 shekels) of fragrant cinnamon, 250 shekels of fragrant cannabis [qaneh bosm],[11] 500 shekels of cassia – all according to the sanctuary shekel – and a hin of olive oil. Make these into a sacred anointing oil, a fragrant blend, the work of a perfumer. It will be the sacred anointing oil."*
>
> – Exodus 30:23-25

Cannabis is likely the burning bush through which God first spoke to Moses. It is also the model for the Menorah, the sacred seven-branched

9 Cannabis is mistranslated as calamus, sweet cane, or aromatic cane, in most Bibles.
10 Hebrew qaneh, calamus, sweet cane, aromatic cane in English translations.
11 Qaneh bosm translated as fragrant calamus, aromatic cane, fragrant cane, sweet calamus in English.

candle stand, whose branches are made of qaneh. These interpretations indicate that Moses was something of a desert shaman whose practices were still close to the paganism of the early Hebrews and much different from the practices of formal Judaism many centuries later.

> *The buds and branches [qan] shall all be of one piece with the lampstand, hammered out of pure gold.*
>
> – Exodus 25:36

Genesis 3:6-7

Cannabis may also be the Tree of Knowledge of Good and Evil in the Garden of Eden, the forbidden fruit eaten by Eve and Adam. In this interpretation, Eve represents Asherah and the Goddess traditions, being condemned by the monotheistic reformers who wrote the story.

The Tree of Knowledge can be seen as cannabis; the plant is attractive to the eye, the fruit is good to eat, and when eaten it creates a mystical, mind-expanding experience. The first thing Adam and Eve do after eating the fruit is to sew clothes using hemp fibers, and then they become farmers. This symbolizes that hemp was arguably the first fiber plant cultivated at the dawn of the Neolithic Revolution. In this story, the plant is forbidden by the Yahwists precisely because it was important and sacred in the rival Goddess traditions.

> *When the woman saw that the fruit of the tree was good for food and pleasing to the eye, and also desirable for gaining wisdom, she took some and ate it. She also gave some to her husband, who was with her, and he ate it. Then the eyes of both of them were opened, and they realized they were naked; so they sewed fig leaves together and made coverings for themselves.*
>
> – Genesis 3:6-7

The Caravan of Abraham by James Tissot

Chapter Twenty-Two

ABRAHAM

The story of Abraham is well known, he is the father of the three great monotheistic religions; Judaism, Christianity, and Islam. As with all important mythologies, the story of Abraham comes from a place beyond fact and fiction, a place where symbolism and inherited wisdom have more value than historical veracity.

The stories of Abraham and the patriarchs were written down a thousand years after they were said to have taken place and are impossible to verify historically. The texts we read were written by the Yahwists, and the name Yahweh is used throughout. Though historically, Abraham, Isaac, and Jacob, were likely worshipping El, and had never heard the name Yahweh.

The seed of Abraham's story is that, as a youth, he came to believe that the entire universe was the work of a single Creator and in adulthood, he taught his belief to others. Elohim, the creator God, reached out to Abraham directly with an offer, a divine covenant. If Abraham would leave his ancestral home and commit to worshipping El, then El would bless him with the "Promised Land." God would give Abraham a great nation in the land of Canaan and bless his name.

A covenant is the most sacred bond between a god and their worshippers. The covenant is an agreement, a contract that defines the people's behavior and how they are supposed to worship, and what the god gives the people in return. In Ishtar's religion, the people were given sensual pleasure and the Earth's continued fertility in exchange for the work of maintaining the temple and the idols, the irrigation canals, growing food, and all the rest of the work required of society.

Circumcision

Abraham took his wife and family and traveled to the land of Canaan, which they would call Israel. But El, God, also had an important requirement his people must keep in order to confirm the covenant. God said to Abraham:

> *This is my covenant with you and your descendants after you, the covenant you are to keep: Every male among you shall be circumcised. You*

are to undergo circumcision, and it will be the sign of the covenant between me and you.

For the generations to come every male among you who is eight days old must be circumcised, including those born in your household or bought with money from a foreigner - those who are not your offspring. Whether born in your household or bought with your money, they must be circumcised. My covenant in your flesh is to be an everlasting covenant. Any uncircumcised male, who has not been circumcised in the flesh, will be cut off from his people; he has broken my covenant.

– Genesis 17:10-14

God insists on a curious way of confirming the covenant, the act of circumcision. Circumcision is the slicing of the sensitive foreskin off of the tip of the male penis. The circumcision is seen by believers to represent the spiritual rebirth of the man who has come to dedicate himself to holiness, the flesh is cast away so that the spirit may grow strong.

Women could not take part in the covenant since they have no penis to circumcise (though female circumcision would be invented later in other religions). This is an important symbolism that women would be treated as second-class citizens in Hebrew culture. Circumcision in both men and women is a distinctly sexual act. More precisely it is an anti-sexual act, that seeks to discourage sexual pleasure by slicing away sensitive parts of the genitals from where pleasure is derived. Female circumcision would arise in other ancient cultures that sought to enforce sexual restraint by cutting off the sensitive external parts of the vagina.

The famous 12th-century Jewish rabbi and philosopher Maimonides said explicitly that the purpose of circumcision is to limit sexual intercourse and reduce enjoyment:

As regards circumcision, I think that one of its objects is to limit sexual intercourse, and to weaken the organ of generation as far as possible, and thus cause man to be moderate... The bodily injury caused to that organ is exactly that which is desired; it does not interrupt any vital function, nor does it destroy the power of generation. Circumcision simply counteracts excessive lust; for there is no doubt that circumcision weakens the power of sexual excitement, and sometimes lessens the natural enjoyment: the organ necessarily becomes weak when it loses blood and is deprived of its covering from the beginning.

– Maimonides, *Guide for the Perplexed*, part 3, ch 49, 11

Circumcision is also an outward physical sign to other people of the devotees' dedication to their faith. In the religious context of the times, circumcision indicates a break from nature-worshipping traditions that viewed sexuality as the source of creation and routinely used sex in their worship. Sexual partners and sacred sex priestesses would surely notice the genital modification and know that the man worshipped the one God alone and no Goddess, and he would not be able to lie about it. Circumcision symbolizes the patriarchal rejection of the feminine divine and the concept of sacred sexuality, a theme that would play out through the Old Testament and the history of the Hebrews.

SACRIFICE OF ISAAC

Abraham was very old when he first became a father, he was 99 when he was circumcised and his son Ishmael was 13. Ishmael was not born to Abraham's wife but to his concubine Hagar, and he became the father of the Islamic religion. All of the other males and male slaves in Abraham's household were circumcised as well. Abraham's wife Sarah was 90 years old when God blessed her with another child, whom they named Isaac, who was a delight to his parents.

> *Then God said, "Take your son, your only son, whom you love – Isaac – and go to the region of Moriah. Sacrifice him there as a burnt offering on a mountain I will show you."*
>
> – Genesis 22:2

When Isaac was 13 years old, God tested Abraham by telling him to take his beloved son up to Mount Moriah and sacrifice him as a burnt offering. Child sacrifice was a common tradition among the Canaanites and pagan Hebrews.

Abraham sadly obeyed and early the next morning he loaded up his donkey with wood and set out on the journey with Isaac. When they arrived at the location, Abraham prepared the altar of sacrifice and arranged the wood on it. He bound Isaac, laid him on top of the wood, and readied his knife to slay his son. But at the last moment an Angel appeared to Abraham and Isaac was spared, a ram appeared as a substitute sacrifice.

> *"Do not lay a hand on the boy," he said. "Do not do anything to him. Now I know that you fear God, because you have not withheld from me your son, your only son."*

Abraham looked up and there in a thicket he saw a ram caught by its horns. He went over and took the ram and sacrificed it as a burnt offering instead of his son.

– Genesis 22:12-13

God said to Abraham that because he was obedient he would be blessed, his descendants would be as numerous as the stars in the sky, and as the sand on the beach, and that they would take possession of the cities of their enemies. With this rescue of Isaac, God showed that he would never demand child sacrifice by his followers, in contrast to the traditional Canaanite culture of the time.

This story of Abraham and Isaac is very similar to the Greek story of Agamemnon and his daughter Iphigenia. At the beginning of the Trojan War, King Agamemnon had to sacrifice his daughter after offending the goddess Artemis. But there are multiple versions of the story, in some, the girl dies, and in others, she is rescued at the last moment by the goddess who provided a substitute animal. Many biblical scholars believe that earlier versions of the Hebrew story also feature the death of Isaac. The Hellenistic Greeks and Hebrews were contemporary cultures and both eliminated the child sacrifice customs of their ancestors.

We know from Greek and Roman writings that the practice of child sacrifice existed for many centuries in the Phoenician/Canaanite culture. Archaeologists who unearthed Phoenician tophets (sacrificial burial grounds) found many infant remains as well as those of animals used as substitutes for child sacrifices. These mythical stories represent people's real experiences, regardless of whether the events actually took place. The Greeks and Hebrews both rejected child sacrifice in their cultures and it was a giant moral step forward in human civilization that deserves credit and appreciation from later generations who were spared the agony.

LION OF JUDAH

Joseph

By Biblical tradition, a few generations after Abraham, his descendant Jacob fathered 12 sons who would become patriarchs of the 12 Tribes of Israel. One of those sons, Joseph, was preferred by his father and given a coat of many colors. His jealous brothers hated Joseph and sold him into slavery in Egypt. After dramatic tales, Joseph became Vizier to the Pharaoh and eventually brought his family to Egypt to escape famine in Canaan. In time, the Israelites would be enslaved in Egypt for centuries and led to freedom by Moses in the Exodus.

If the Hebrew connection to the Hyksos is factual, it is in this set of stories about Joseph where it takes place. In this hypothesis, the pharaoh who is friendly to Joseph is a Hyksos pharaoh. When the Hebrews were later enslaved, it was after the Hyksos had been repelled and native Egyptians had reestablished their rule.

Judah

One of Joseph's brothers was Judah, father of the important tribe of Judah, and the one who proposed selling Joseph into slavery for a profit rather than killing him. Judah would later demonstrate his repentance and righteousness after meeting Joseph again in Egypt. Before that moment arrives though, Judah must show his judgment and compassion through the unusual story of his relationship with Tamar, the matriarch of the tribe of Judah. This is a story that many students of the Bible find uncomfortable for its sexual content and seemingly strange behavior.

After selling Joseph away, Judah left his brothers and married a Canaanite woman who bore him three sons. The oldest son married Tamar, but before they could bear a child he was killed. Judah ordered his second son Onan to fulfill his duties and have sex with Tamar and raise his brother's heir as was the tradition at the time.

> *But Onan knew that the child would not be his; so whenever he slept with his brother's wife, he spilled his semen on the ground to keep from providing offspring for his brother.*
>
> *What he did was wicked in Yahweh's sight; so Yahweh put him to death also.*
>
> – Genesis 38:9-10

It is from this story that we get the word "onanism," for coitus interruptus when the man spills his seed outside the woman during sex.

Tamar

Judah then ordered Tamar to live in his household as a widow until the youngest son was old enough to mate. But Judah feared that his youngest too would die and he was never given over to Tamar. After a long time, the now widower Judah decided one day to go to the sheep-shearing festival. It was a common practice to procure the services of a prostitute at the festivals.

When Tamar heard that Judah was going out, she took off her widow's clothes, dressed up, and put on a veil to disguise herself. Since she had been denied a child by Judah, Tamar decided to take the initiative for herself. Tamar positioned herself on the road where she knew Judah would see her.

When Judah saw Tamar he thought she was a prostitute, a zonah, for she had covered her face. Not realizing that she was his daughter-in-law, Judah went over to Tamar by the roadside and asked to have sex with her. Judah said that he would give her a young goat from his flock – and gave her his seal, cord, and staff as a pledge until he returned. The seal, staff, and cord were important legal possessions used to sign contracts. They had sex and Tamar became pregnant by Judah.

The next day Judah sent his friend with the goat to redeem his pledge, but he could not find the woman. The friend asked the men who lived there, "where is the qedesha who was beside the road?" "There hasn't been any qedesha here," they replied.

Judah's friend had been too embarrassed to ask for a zonah, a common prostitute, so he pretended to be looking for a qedesha, a *Holy One,* who was more respected. This distinction is often lost in English translations of the Bible and must be read in the original Hebrew. The King James Bible uses the word *harlot* for both *zonah* and *qedesha,* while other translations use the words *prostitute* and *cult prostitute* respectively.

> *He asked the men who lived there, "Where is the qedesha who was beside the road at Enaim?" "There hasn't been any qedesha here," they said.*
>
> *So he went back to Judah and said, "I didn't find her. Besides, the men who lived there said, 'There hasn't been any qedesha here.'"*
>
> *Then Judah said, "Let her keep what she has, or we will become a laughingstock. After all, I did send her this young goat, but you didn't find her."*
>
> *About three months later Judah was told, "Your daughter-in-law Tamar is guilty of prostitution, and as a result, she is now pregnant." Judah said, "Bring her out and have her burned to death!"*
>
> *As she was being brought out, she sent a message to her father-in-law. "I am pregnant by the man who owns these," she said. And she added, "See if you recognize whose seal and cord and staff these are."*
>
> *Judah recognized them and said, "She is more righteous than I, since I wouldn't give her to my son Shelah." And he did not sleep with her again.*
>
> –Genesis 38:21-26

Tamar gave birth to twins and secured her place in the family and inheritance. This was very risky and dangerous for Tamar; if things had gone wrong, she would have been killed. But through her assertiveness, she managed to make things right after all the wrongs that had been done to her. Tamar had always been innocent, all she wanted was a child and it was not her fault that her husband died or that his brother failed in his obligations, even though he took advantage of her sexually. Judah was a righteous man whose visit with a prostitute was perfectly normal for the times, and he demonstrated his righteousness when he dealt with Tamar honorably after she revealed her trick.

Lion of Goddesses

One of Tamar's sons was the ancestor of King David, and thus Tamar is one of the matriarchs of the House of David, the ruling line of Jerusalem that includes King Solomon and Jesus. The tribe of Judah is the namesake for the nation of Judah and its symbol is the Lion of Judah, one of the nationalist symbols of modern Israel. The Solomonic Dynasty of Ethiopia also uses the Lion of Judah as a political symbol, and it appears in Rastafarian traditions.

It gets little discussion, since the Biblical faiths deny the existence of the Goddess and the feminine divine, that lions were symbols of goddesses going back to Catal Huyuk. Asherah, Astarte, and Anat all loved lions and rode them into battle. The goddess-worshipping King Solomon sat on a throne decorated with lions, just like the goddess Cybele.

Astarte in all of her various incarnations (Inanna, Ishtar, Aphrodite, Venus) was the love goddess and the patron of prostitutes. The qedesha that Judah's friend embarrassedly asked for was one of Astarte's sacred sex priestesses. This is why the Lion of Judah is symbolic of Tamar, the assertive prostitute who was the mother of the House of David.

Moses Comes Down from Mount Sinai

Chapter Twenty-Three

MOSES AND MONOTHEISM

Egypt

Centuries after Abraham, a new Hebrew leader emerged, Moses, the great prophet and teacher – the "Law Giver." Moses is the most important religious teacher in the Biblical tradition, alongside Jesus, and his legacy is impossible to overstate. Moses introduced monotheism to the Israelite people and he gave a new name to El; Yahweh.

By Biblical tradition, Moses was born in Egypt when the Hebrews were enslaved. Moses is an Egyptian name. But there is no archaeological evidence or entries in the voluminous records of the Egyptians for Moses, enslaved Hebrews, or large migrations out of Egypt as told in the Biblical story of the Exodus. Moses is likely a quasi-historical leader whose story is wrapped up in legend, mythology, and symbolism.

It is conceivable that the Hebrews were related to the Hyksos, Semitic invaders of Egypt who ruled briefly from around 1630 BCE to 1523 BCE when they were expelled. Classical historians such as Josephus Flavius who wrote *The Antiquities of the Jews* in the first century CE identified the Hebrews with the Hyksos. The Hyksos conquered Egypt and introduced their own religion. The Hyksos pharaohs never claimed to be divine as was the Egyptian custom and they moved their capital to the same region, Goshen, where the Hebrews settled. The native Egyptians eventually rebelled and expelled the Hyksos, killing or enslaving the foreigners. Joseph may have been a Viceroy/Vizier for a Hyksos pharaoh friendly to the Hebrews, leading to the later Israelite enslavement after the Hyksos expulsion.

Aten

A century ago, the public was stunned to learn that the Israelites were not the first monotheists. Archaeologists had discovered the story of the Egyptian pharaoh Akhenaten, "The Heretic King," who briefly imposed monotheism on an unwilling Egyptian people. Akhenaten closed all the old temples and forced the people to worship one god alone, Aten, the sun god.

Akhenaten ruled from 1353-1336 BCE and was originally known as Amenhotep IV; his wife was Queen Nefertiti. In the fifth year of his reign, he changed his name to Akhenaten, "Beneficial to Aten," and imposed religious reforms on the country. Akhenaten moved the capital away from Thebes to Amarna, a new city in the north. The pharaoh introduced a program of religious reforms that included closing temples, disbanding priesthoods, diverting their income to the cult of Aten, and changing the names of gods to reflect the new doctrine.

Akhenaten's reforms did not outlast his death, and a series of new kings with brief reigns followed, culminating with his son Tutankhamun. Tutankhamun is famous because his entire tomb and mummy were found intact by archaeologists in 1922. This was a rarity since most of the pharaonic tombs were robbed of their valuables in antiquity. Tutankhamun was nine years old and sickly when he took the throne. He only ruled for ten years, but he did restore the traditional gods and moved the capital back to Thebes.

Later Egyptians attempted to erase the memory of Akhenaten and his entire family from the historical record. Their images, graves, and sarcophaguses were defaced and their names were removed from the Kings' Lists. Akhenaten and his religious reforms would have been completely forgotten forever if they had not been rediscovered by archaeologists.

It is speculative, but reasonable to imagine that the Israelites and their radical new ideas about the worship of one god alone were at least influenced by Akhenaten, if not directly related to the cult of Aten. Many books and theories have been presented in the last century exploring possible connections between the Hebrews and Akhenaten as well as possible connections between the Hebrews and the Hyksos. Early Hebrew history is a long story of the battle within the community over their worship practices. Similar to the Egyptian experience, the transition to monotheism would require the purging of many ancient pagan traditions, including the elimination of priestesses who were respected women in the community.

Monotheism

Through Moses, Yahweh presented an updated covenant with the Israelites that went beyond promising them a home in the land of Canaan. The new covenant was to worship Yahweh alone and obey his laws completely, then he would make them favored above all other people and deliver them from slavery. Deliverance from physical slavery in Egypt is symbolic of being delivered from the mental slavery of pagan religions that viewed humans as slaves to the gods. The Israelites were free people, God's chosen people, all they had to do was worship him alone and follow his laws completely and they would be blessed.

Yahweh is a loving God who cares for his people, unlike the cruel and capricious pagan gods. But Yahweh is also a jealous God who does not tolerate the worship of any other gods or goddesses. Yahweh would not tolerate idolatry, the crafting of any images of gods for worship purposes. Most pagan worship used statues of the gods and obligated people to bring them food and clothing in rituals.

The pagan Hebrews worshipped El with the idol of a golden bull/calf. This is why they were monolatrists, they practiced idolatry in service of one god. Hebrew monotheism broke this tradition and introduced a new form of worship that was more philosophical and abstract. The new practices intentionally steered away from superstitious idolatry. Yahweh created the Earth for humans to have dominion over, not to serve food to statues.

Monotheism represented a massive break from the ancient traditions. Freedom from slavery did not simply mean escape from physical bondage, but liberation from the mental slavery that said all humans are made to serve the gods. Monotheism teaches us to worship the one God who brought order to the universe and grants freedom to humans. Do not prostrate yourself before a multitude of unreliable gods who compete with one another. Follow the divine laws of Yahweh that demand ethics and morality. Transcend human laws created by kings and priests who routinely justified injustice as divine will. Pray directly to the living God rather than inanimate idols and no longer will you have to sacrifice your children to bring rain or end a siege.

Monotheism brought unity and cohesiveness to the cosmos, compared to the incoherent pagan cosmology of the Phoenicians and Mesopotamians. The pagan worldview was quite primitive by modern standards, ruled by gods who were often cruel and whose motives were hopeless to understand.

Rejection of Our Mother

One of the most profound impacts of monotheism was the rejection of the Earthly Mother. The Biblical traditions do not recognize the concept of the feminine divine. The Hebrew language does not even have a word for goddess. This error needs to be corrected if we ever hope to see true equality for women and environmental sustainability.

In monotheistic traditions, there is no sacred sex, no unity of male and female, no hieros gamos, and no cycle of life rituals to ensure the seasons. In monotheism, the Heavenly Father absorbed all the powers of creation that had always been the territory of the Mother Goddess. Nature was removed as a focus of worship and male priests took over all the roles that had once been the responsibility of the priestesses and the transgendered.

The Hebrews broke from the long-standing Goddess traditions by worshipping a solitary God who they claimed transcends gender and sexuality. Yet at the same time, Yahweh, God, is presented as male and described with the male pronouns he and him. By arguing on one hand that God transcends gender but then routinely describing God as he, Biblical monotheism equates males with being closer to God than females.

The feminine divine gets lost in Biblical monotheism and not by accident. The Hebrews were not only patriarchal but deeply misogynistic, just like their contemporaries in Greece. A common prayer said daily by orthodox Jews to this day is, "thank you God for not making me a woman." The Yahwists actively persecuted Goddess worship in order to bring the community around to the idea of their one God. Moses was just the beginning of this centuries-long process and the Yahwist culture war has continued to reverberate to this day.

CALLED TO MINISTRY

Birth of Moses

There is no evidence for the existence of Moses outside the Bible. Certain details of his biography are clearly legendary, such as his birth story, and he is credited with performing many supernatural feats. Most scholars believe that the story of Moses is a mythological retelling of a historical figure. His life and times were embellished into a grand narrative that provides a birth story for the entire Israelite people.

All great mythical heroes need a heroic birth story and Moses is no different. His tale is clearly adopted from Sargon of Akkad, one of the most famous people in the ancient Near East. Biblical tradition says that Moses was a Hebrew born into slavery in Egypt. At this time the Pharaoh had ordered all newborn Hebrew children to be killed because he feared their population growth and ambitions.

Just like Sargon, Moses' mother hid the infant in a basket in the river to protect him. Moses's mother placed the basket in the reeds along the banks of the Nile River. She instructed her eight-year-old daughter Miriam to wait nearby and watch over her baby brother. The Pharaoh's daughter came along and found the basket, discovering the baby. The princess took pity on the infant, which she knew was a Hebrew.

Clever Miriam approached Pharaoh's daughter and asked if she should find a Hebrew woman to wet nurse the baby for her. In this way, Miriam was able to get Moses's own mother to take care of the child, a complete turn of events considering that the baby was supposed to be killed. Moses was adopted by the Pharaoh's daughter and raised as royalty, just like Sargon of Akkad.

Moses was aware of his Hebrew roots. One day as an adult, Moses saw an Egyptian overseer beating a Hebrew slave. Moses killed the Egyptian man and then fled the country to Midian, in the northwest-Arabian peninsula. In Midian, Moses met a pagan priest named Jethro who had seven daughters. Moses married one of the daughters, the beautiful Zipporah, and they had a son.

In Ethiopian traditions, Moses fled first to Ethiopia and stayed for many years before going to Midian. There Moses served as a military general and sired a royal line that eventually produced the Queen of Sheba.

Burning Bush

While living in Midian with his wife, Moses went out one day to tend the flocks and he saw a remarkable sight. Moses saw a bush that was on fire but did not burn up. God called out to Moses from within the bush and told him he was standing on holy ground.

It is not the traditional interpretation of the Bible, but it is easy to view the burning bush as cannabis. The sacred plant had been burned in heaps in religious ceremonies for thousands of years in the region. Cannabis had been the catalyst for mystical experiences and spiritual encounters with the divine for generations of priests and shamans.

All the legendary and mythological tales in the Old Testament evolved for centuries through oral tradition before being written down in the form we see today. Many stories had roots in earlier pagan traditions that were later purged. We see the pagan use of cannabis peering through the monotheist whitewash throughout Moses' entire career.

Introducing Yahweh

God told Moses from the burning bush that he has seen the suffering and misery of his people in Egypt. God now intended to rescue the Israelites from their slave masters. God told Moses that he is sending him back to Egypt to bring the Israelites out and into "a good and spacious land, a land flowing with milk and honey," the land of Canaan. Moses asked how he should identify him, what is his name?

> *And Elohim said unto Moses, I AM THAT I AM.*
>
> – Exodus 3:14 (KJV)

God is all-encompassing, infinite, omnipotent, his own source of creation. God continued to say that he has a new name. He had been known as Elohim to Moses's forefathers, Abraham, Isaac, and Jacob; but now he would be known as Yahweh.

> *Elohim also said to Moses, "Say to the Israelites, 'Yahweh, the God of your fathers – the Elohe of Abraham, the Elohe of Isaac and the Elohe of Jacob – has sent me to you.' "This is my name forever, the name you shall call me from generation to generation."*
>
> – Exodus 3:15

In English translations of the Bible, the Hebrew Elohim and its variants are written as *God*, while Yahweh is written as *the LORD*. No longer would the Israelites be worshipping El above the other gods in the monolatrist manner. This new name for God marked the beginning of a profound religious reformation and the introduction of new monotheistic ideas.

Yahweh insists that he is the only god and demands that the worship of the other traditional gods be halted. This new monotheistic phase would test the Hebrew people for centuries. Going forward, the Yahwists would be the political faction within the Hebrew community advocating for monotheism and repression of all the competing deities, particularly Baal and the goddesses.

Circumcision of Moses

On the road prior to arriving in Egypt, a strange thing happened while staying in an inn. Without warning, Yahweh rose up to kill Moses but only the quick actions of Zipporah saved his life. Why would Yahweh want to kill Moses? This entire passage has plagued Biblical scholars for generations and been subject to much debate.

At a lodging place on the way, Yahweh met Moses and was about to kill him. But Zipporah took a flint knife, cut off her son's foreskin and touched Moses' feet with it. "Surely you are a bridegroom of blood to me," she said.

> *At a lodging place on the way, Yahweh met Moses and was about to kill him. But Zipporah took a flint knife, cut off her son's foreskin and touched Moses' feet with it. "Surely you are a bridegroom of blood to me," she said. So Yahweh let him alone. (At that time she said "bridegroom of blood," referring to circumcision.)*
>
> – Exodus 4:24-26

Zipporah realized that they had neglected to circumcise their son and she quickly took a flint and sliced the baby's penis. The next line is generally translated as saying that Zipporah took the bloody foreskin and touched Moses' feet with it, but "feet" is often used as a Biblical euphemism for genitals, another way of saying "private parts."

By touching Moses' penis with the bloody foreskin, Zipporah symbolically circumcised her husband who had apparently failed to perform the painful ritual on himself. The phrase "bridegroom of blood" is open to interpretation, but may be a reference to purged pagan traditions, perhaps from Zipporah's family.

The fact that Yahweh would want to kill Moses over his failure to circumcise himself indicates the critical importance of the ritual. Circumcision symbolizes the divorce from the Goddess more than any other ritual. Circumcision sends a message that the Hebrews would not participate in sacred sex rituals.

Biblical monotheism is distinct in world religion for having a sexless god and no representation whatsoever of the feminine divine. All of the pagan traditions featured gods with active sex lives or who were intentionally chaste. These traditions saw the Earthly Mother and the Heavenly Father as the parents of all the other gods and the source of all life. The Yahwists believe that the Heavenly Father acts alone and they do not recognize the Earthly Mother. Circumcision symbolizes this distinction of the monotheists from the broader pagan world.

SERPENT OF POWER

The serpent is the ancient shamanistic symbol of wisdom, divination, and prophecy. The serpent features prominently in Moses' career, demonstrating the pagan roots of the Hebrews. Yahwist reformers later worked to purge the serpent and convert the symbol into something dark. In the Garden of Eden story, which was written centuries later, the serpent became the famous symbol of Eve's temptation and the fall of man.

During the time of Moses though, the serpent was still a symbol of power and wisdom. Yahweh encouraged Moses to confront the Pharaoh, telling Moses he will perform wonders that will compel Pharaoh to let his people go. To ensure that he is believed, Yahweh makes Moses's staff turn into a snake when he throws it on the ground, and back into a staff when he picks it up. Moses would use this powerful staff repeatedly during his leadership of the Israelites.

Moses said that he does not speak well, so Yahweh appointed his brother Aaron to join him as his spokesman. Their older sister Miriam would continue to play an important role as a prophetess and leader of the women. Moses, Aaron, and Miriam are among the select few people that Yahweh ever speaks directly to in the Bible.

Moses said goodbye to Jethro and headed back to Egypt, along with Zipporah, their family, and the staff of Yahweh. Moses and Aaron confronted the Pharaoh and demanded the release of the Israelites. Moses sparked many dramatic and supernatural events including a battle of the serpent staffs with Pharaoh's magicians.

> *So Moses and Aaron went to Pharaoh and did just as Yahweh commanded. Aaron threw his staff down in front of Pharaoh and his officials, and it became a snake. Pharaoh then summoned wise men and sorcerers, and the Egyptian magicians also did the same things by their secret arts: Each one threw down his staff and it became a snake. But Aaron's staff swallowed up their staffs.*
>
> – Exodus 7:10-12

Bronze Serpent

Moses led the Hebrews out of slavery and into forty years of nomadic wandering through the Arabian desert and the southern Levant. This long story is known as the Exodus. At one point, the Israelites complained and Yahweh struck them with venomous snakes to torment them. After they repented, Moses made a bronze serpent and put it on a pole to miraculously heal the people who had been poisoned.

> *They spoke against God and against Moses, and said, "Why have you brought us up out of Egypt to die in the wilderness? There is no bread! There is no water! And we detest this miserable food!" Then Yahweh sent venomous snakes among them; they bit the people and many Israelites died.*

> *The people came to Moses and said, "We sinned when we spoke against Yahweh and against you. Pray that Yahweh will take the snakes away from us." So Moses prayed for the people.*
> *Yahweh said to Moses, "Make a snake and put it up on a pole; anyone who is bitten can look at it and live." So Moses made a bronze snake and put it up on a pole. Then when anyone was bitten by a snake and looked at the bronze snake, they lived.*
>
> – Numbers 21:5-9

Once again, the serpent is shown to have powerful, mystical capabilities. For generations, this bronze serpent was an object of worship for the Israelites. Centuries later, it was broken down and removed during the Yahwist reforms of King Hezekiah.

> *He removed the high places, smashed the sacred stones, and cut down the Asherah poles. He broke into pieces the bronze snake Moses had made, for up to that time the Israelites had been burning incense to it. (It was called Nehushtan.)*
>
> – 2 Kings 18:4

Golden Calf

In one of the most famous stories from the Exodus, we see clear evidence of the early Hebrews practicing idolatry in worshipping El. During a visit to Mount Sinai, Moses was gone for a long time talking to Yahweh and the Israelites became impatient waiting. They convinced Aaron to make idols they could pray to. The Israelites were unsure about Moses and his teachings and in their insecurity, they reverted to the traditions they knew and understood.

Aaron collected gold jewelry from the people and fashioned a golden calf. It was most likely a golden bull that the Biblical writers treated with disdain and mockery by calling it a calf. The Bull of Heaven was the traditional sign of El and many other leading gods. Cattle were widely worshipped, then and now, from Egypt all the way to India. Cattle are treated with reverence to this day in Hindu and some indigenous African traditions.

Yahweh and Moses were outraged by the Israelite idolatry, they would no longer allow the old ways of worship. When he returned to camp, Moses destroyed the golden calf. The Levite tribe rallied to Moses and they went through the camp killing everyone who had worshipped the golden calf. Around 3000 people were killed according to the story. The Levites were blessed for their actions and would be appointed as priests in the Hebrew temple.

The golden bulls would not disappear though, the pagan traditions were difficult to erase and for centuries the Israelites would repeatedly return to worshipping them. Two golden bulls were built in the Israeli cities of Bethel and Dan immediately upon the split of the united kingdom. The golden bulls stood in the northern kingdom for its entire history, along with a towering Asherah pole in Samaria.

Pillar of Smoke

Moses ultimately led the tribes back to Mount Sinai, where he first met Yahweh in the burning bush. Here Yahweh reconfirmed the ongoing relationship with cannabis, telling Moses he would visit him in a cloud of smoke. The smoke came from burning herbs and incense, including cannabis, if not mostly cannabis. This makes Moses appear to be a desert shaman and again shows the pagan roots of the early Hebrews.

> *Yahweh said to Moses, "I am going to come to you in a dense cloud, so that the people will hear me speaking with you and will always put their trust in you."*
>
> – Exodus 19:9

> *Mount Sinai was covered with smoke, because Yahweh descended on it in fire. The smoke billowed up from it like smoke from a furnace, and the whole mountain trembled violently.*
>
> – Exodus 19:18

Moses would pitch a tent outside of the camp, called the "Tent of the Meeting," or the Tabernacle, where he would go and meet with Yahweh. The people would watch Moses whenever he went to the tent and wait for the pillar of smoke to arise that signaled that he was speaking to God.

> *As Moses went into the tent, the pillar of cloud would come down and stay at the entrance, while Yahweh spoke with Moses. Whenever the people saw the pillar of cloud standing at the entrance to the tent, they all stood and worshiped, each at the entrance to their tent. Yahweh would speak to Moses face to face, as one speaks to a friend.*
>
> – Exodus 33:9-11

> *Then the cloud covered the tent of meeting, and the glory of Yahweh filled the tabernacle. Moses could not enter the tent of meeting because the cloud had settled on it, and the glory of Yahweh filled the tabernacle.*
>
> *In all the travels of the Israelites, whenever the cloud lifted from above the tabernacle, they would set out; but if the cloud did not lift, they did not set out - until the day it lifted. So the cloud of Yahweh was over the tabernacle by day, and fire was in the cloud by night, in the sight of all the Israelites during all their travels.*
>
> – Exodus 40:34-38

As long as the Tabernacle remained filled with smoke, the Israelites knew that Moses was speaking with God. They stayed in their camp and when the cloud departed so did they. This is representative of an entheogenic, shamanistic experience, engaging with the mystical and divine through an intoxicating smoke. Moses stepped into the cloud to speak with God. The Yahwists who wrote the Bible we read today removed details from the stories, such as cannabis use, that were associated with purged pagan traditions.

Shekinah

Shekinah is the Hebrew word describing the physical manifestation of God, particularly as the cloud of smoke in the Tabernacle and later in the Jerusalem Temple. The word does not appear in the Bible but is used by scholars.

Shekinah is a feminine word, invented by medieval Kabbalists in a partial rebirth of the feminine divine. The Kabbalists were Jewish mystics who presented the Shekinah as the feminine representation of God's earthly presence. The Shekinah is the wife of God manifested as a cloud of smoke in stories told of Moses and the first Temple. The Kabbalists graphically portrayed God and his bride in a sexual embrace.

The *kapnobatai* were Thracian mystics from the same era as the Hebrews who were called the "smoke-eaters," or the "smoke-walkers" for their abundant cannabis use. Cannabis did not grow in abundance in the desert – like it does in Thrace, but hashish was an object of trade and incense has many ingredients, some of which are intended to produce an abundance of smoke.

Tabernacle

Yahweh gave Moses many laws for the Hebrews to follow and specific instructions for constructing the Tabernacle, the Ark of the Covenant, and all the furnishings within it, including the curtains, altars, incense, and holy anointing oil. The Tabernacle was a portable temple that was the Earthly home of Yahweh, known as " Tent of the Congregation" that replaced the older "Tent of the Meeting." The Ark of the Covenant was a mystical wooden chest, sheathed in gold and decorated with cherubim, that contained the stone tablets on which were written the Ten Commandments. The Ark was kept in the "Holy of Holies," the inner sanctum of the Tabernacle, and later, the temple in Jerusalem.

> *These are the offerings you are to receive from them: gold, silver and bronze; blue, purple and scarlet yarn and fine linen; goat hair; ram skins dyed red and another type of durable leather; acacia wood; olive oil for the light; spices for the anointing oil and for the fragrant incense; and onyx stones and other gems to be mounted on the ephod and breastpiece.*
>
> *Then have them make a sanctuary for me, and I will dwell among them. Make this tabernacle and all its furnishings exactly like the pattern I will show you."*
>
> – Exodus 25:3-9

> *All those who were skilled among the workers made the tabernacle with ten curtains of finely twisted linen and blue, purple and scarlet yarn, with cherubim woven into them by expert hands.*
>
> – Exodus 36:8

Cannabis likely appears twice on the list of materials for the tabernacle, in the fine linen and in the spices for the anointing oil and fragrant incense, burned in temples throughout the ancient Near East. Hemp and linen were used side by side and it is impossible to distinguish fine hemp from linen. Linen is light and supple while hemp was used for heavy-duty work like tents, making hemp the more likely material for a durable tabernacle; the word canvas is derived from cannabis.

It is notable that there are specific instructions to weave together linen and woolen yarn, this is a blending of animal and vegetable, farmer and shepherd, God and Goddess, just like bhang which combines milk and cannabis. This instruction would later be reversed by Yahwist reformers as the Shatnez, specific instructions to not blend together wool and linen. This detail appears to be a remnant of earlier pagan traditions that were later purged.

HOLY ANOINTING OIL

The holy anointing oil was very important; it distinguished the sacred from the secular, and it was used to anoint the priests and kings by pouring it over their heads until the oil dripped from their beards. The holy anointing oil was wiped on every item in the tabernacle and all over the cloth and carpets of the tabernacle itself to mark them as sacred.

The recipe for the holy anointing oil contains the first and most important of five explicit references to cannabis in the Hebrew Bible. In most translations, cannabis is replaced by calamus, a plant that has some medicinal properties but none of the sacred traditions of cannabis.

> *Take the following fine spices: 500 shekels of liquid myrrh, half as much (that is, 250 shekels) of fragrant cinnamon, 250 shekels of fragrant cannabis [qaneh bosm], 500 shekels of cassia--all according to the sanctuary shekel - and a hin of olive oil.*
>
> *Make these into a sacred anointing oil, a fragrant blend, the work of a perfumer. It will be the sacred anointing oil. Then use it to anoint the tent of meeting, the ark of the covenant law, the table and all its articles, the lampstand and its accessories, the altar of incense, the altar of burnt offering and all its utensils, and the basin with its stand. You shall consecrate them so they will be most holy, and whatever touches them will be holy.*
>
> *Anoint Aaron and his sons and consecrate them so they may serve me as priests. Say to the Israelites, 'This is to be my sacred anointing oil for the generations to come. Do not pour it on anyone else's body and do not make any other oil using the same formula. It is sacred, and you are to consider it sacred. Whoever makes perfume like it and puts it on anyone*

other than a priest must be cut off from their people.'"

– Exodus 30:23-33

It is like precious oil poured on the head, running down on the beard, running down on Aaron's beard, down on the collar of his robe.

– Psalm 133:2

The recipe for the holy anointing oil is psychoactive and potent. 250 shekels of cannabis equals 6.28 pounds of flowering cannabis tops infused into roughly 1.5 gallons of olive oil (around 6 liters, hin is not a precise measure), plus myrrh, cinnamon, and cassia. This recipe was boiled and distilled so that all the spices were infused into the oil.

Cannabis can be absorbed through the skin. In the context of a spiritual ritual where the set and setting encourage a mystical experience, the holy anointing oil can create an intense experience of connection to the divine. People continue to follow this recipe today and attest to its medicinal and psychoactive value.

The prohibition against sharing the recipe or using it for anything other than sacred purposes shows how important the holy anointing oil was. In many cultural traditions, sacred and medicinal recipes were kept secret and never to be revealed. This was especially true if they had potent mystical properties as magic revealed is magic lost.

The priest and the village wise woman alike both had every incentive to keep their secret tricks close to the vest. The Hebrew Torah was originally written only for priests to read since most people were illiterate. So at the time they were written down, the recipes for the holy anointing oil and incense were intended to instruct priests and were not intended for the public to read.

Sacred Incense

There are similar instructions for making sacred incense in the following verses, though they do not explicitly mention qaneh bosm. The sacred incense was burned every morning and every evening in the temple.

Then Yahweh said to Moses, "Take fragrant spices - gum resin, onycha and galbanum - and pure frankincense, all in equal amounts, and make a fragrant blend of incense, the work of a perfumer. It is to be salted and pure and sacred. Grind some of it to powder and place it in front of the ark of the covenant law in the tent of meeting, where I will meet with you. It shall be most holy to you.

– Exodus 30:34-36

Rabbinical Midrash commentary on the holy incense states that the "fragrant spices" were the same spices from the holy anointing oil. This means that the incense did include cannabis even if it is not explicitly listed in the Biblical text.[1] The exact recipes of spices and aromatics used in sacred incense were carefully guarded secrets by incense makers. In later centuries, the Jewish historian Josephus described the incense as having thirteen ingredients, while Rabbinical tradition described a recipe with eleven ingredients.

Menorah

The Menorah, the golden Hebrew lampstand which stood in the temple can also be seen as representing cannabis and the earlier phase of pagan Hebrew shamanism. The Menorah has seven branches and holds seven candles; it is designed in a plant motif and with all the branches it looks like a field of cannabis. It is said to represent the tree of life, and when lit, the Menorah represents the burning bush.

The Hebrew word for branch is *qan*, which can also mean reed or rod – it is also the root of the word *qaneh* for cannabis, and is used repeatedly throughout the instructions for the design of the Menorah.

> *Make a lampstand of pure gold. Hammer out its base and shaft, and make its flowerlike cups, buds and blossoms of one piece with them. Six branches [qaneh] are to extend from the sides of the lampstand - three on one side and three on the other. Three cups shaped like almond flowers with buds and blossoms are to be on one branch [qaneh], three on the next branch [qaneh], and the same for all six branches [qaneh] extending from the lampstand. And on the lampstand there are to be four cups shaped like almond flowers with buds and blossoms. One bud shall be under the first pair of branches [qaneh] extending from the lampstand, a second bud under the second pair, and a third bud under the third pair - six branches [qaneh] in all. The buds and branches [qaneh] shall all be of one piece with the lampstand, hammered out of pure gold.*
>
> – Exodus 25:31–36

1 Midrash, *Rabbeinu Bachya*, Composed in Middle-Age Spain (c.1290 - c.1310 CE). A commentary on the Torah written by Rabbi Bahya ben Asher, 1255-1340, in Spain. Midrash are teachings and commentaries written by Hebrew Rabbis that interpret scripture and include additional stories.

Miram by Sir Edward Poynter

Chapter Twenty-Four

MIRIAM – PROPHETESS PUNISHED

Prophetess

The treatment of Miriam, the older sister of Moses and Aaron, is one of the most interesting and underappreciated stories in the Bible. Whoever recorded these stories left out many important details about Miriam's life and role in the community. We are left with an enigma. Who was Miriam really?

Miriam was undoubtedly a significant character. She is one of only seven female Hebrew prophetesses and one of the few characters who spoke directly to Yahweh. But Yahweh punished Miriam for arguing with Moses over issues that are not completely clear. She then disappears from the narrative, apparently having lost her role as a leader.

As a child, eight-year-old Miriam watched over the infant Moses while he floated in a basket in the Nile River. It was clever Miriam who guided the child into the hands of the Pharaoh's daughter. Miriam then boldly approached the princess offering to find a suitable wet-nurse, who was none other than her own mother. This seminal act set forth Moses' entire fate.

As an adult, Miriam the prophetess was the leader of the women. After the Israelites had successfully fled Pharaoh's forces in the Exodus, Miriam led the women in singing and dancing with tambourines. The Song of Miriam is said to be one of the oldest songs in the western tradition.

> *And Miriam the prophetess, the sister of Aaron, took a timbrel in her hand; and all the women went out after her with timbrels and with dances. And Miriam answered them, "Sing ye to Yahweh, for he hath triumphed gloriously; the horse and his rider hath he thrown into the sea."*
>
> – Exodus 15:20-21 (KJV)

Qedesha

It is important to understand the context of what it meant to be the leader of the women in the community. The Hebrews were still pagan at this stage. Moses was bringing the people new ideas about monotheism, they were hearing the name Yahweh for the first time. Up until this time the Hebrews worshipped El, the Heavenly Father, and his wife Asherah, the Mother Goddess, along with Astarte the Queen of Heaven, and the terrifying Anat. There were qedesha in the community and the practices of sacred sex and ritual prostitution were alive and well.

Miriam may well have been a qedesha herself. She is not said to have had a husband or child, and she did like music and dance. At the very least, Miriam looked after the qedesha as a community leader. If Miriam was a qedesha then her curious fate would make much more sense and would specifically reflect the changing norms that the Yahwists sought to impose.

Miriam and Aaron complain against Moses, engraving from "The Bible and Its Story Taught by One Thousand Picture Lessons, vol. 2", edited by Charles F. Horne and Julius A. Bewer, published by Francis R. Niglutsch, New York, 1908

Dispute with Moses

During the forty years of nomadic wandering, Miriam was involved in a strange argument with Moses and angrily punished by Yahweh. The nature of the dispute is ambiguous, it has something to do with Moses's wife, but it is not clear what happened. The Biblical text leaves out any substantive details and there are wildly different interpretations of the story.

We see Yahweh speaking directly to Moses, Aaron, and Miriam together. No one else was allowed to enter the Tent of the Meeting to speak to God. At one point, Moses refers to God as "El."

> *Miriam and Aaron began to talk against Moses because of his Cushite wife, for he had married a Cushite. "Has Yahweh spoken only through Moses?" they asked. "Hasn't he also spoken through us?" And Yahweh*

heard this. (Now Moses was a very humble man, more humble than anyone else on the face of the earth.)

At once Yahweh said to Moses, Aaron and Miriam, "Come out to the tent of meeting, all three of you." So the three of them went out. Then Yahweh came down in a pillar of cloud; he stood at the entrance to the tent and summoned Aaron and Miriam.

When the two of them stepped forward, he said, "Listen to my words: "When there is a prophet among you, I, Yahweh, reveal myself to them in visions, I speak to them in dreams. But this is not true of my servant Moses; he is faithful in all my house. With him I speak face to face, clearly and not in riddles; he sees the form of Yahweh. Why then were you not afraid to speak against my servant Moses?"

The anger of Yahweh burned against them, and he left them. When the cloud lifted from above the tent, Miriam's skin was leprous -- it became as white as snow.

Aaron turned toward her and saw that she had a defiling skin disease, and he said to Moses, "Please, my lord, I ask you not to hold against us the sin we have so foolishly committed. Do not let her be like a stillborn infant coming from its mother's womb with its flesh half eaten away."

So Moses cried out to Yahweh, "Please, El, heal her!"

Yahweh replied to Moses, "If her father had spit in her face, would she not have been in disgrace for seven days? Confine her outside the camp for seven days; after that she can be brought back."

So Miriam was confined outside the camp for seven days, and the people did not move on till she was brought back.

– Numbers 12:1-15

CUSHITE WIFE

A straight reading of the text implies that Moses has a new wife who is not Zipporah but an unidentified Cushite woman. Miriam and Aaron were angry about it for some reason, perhaps because she was a foreigner of a different race. A Cushite is a dark-skinned African from the Kingdom of Kush (south of Egypt) or Ethiopia. Cushite women were regarded as exceptionally beautiful. Scholars have debated the identity of the Cushite woman for centuries. Zipporah is known to have been from Midian, but many traditions provide connections between Midian and Cush. These traditions are especially strong in Ethiopia, where they have long had narratives of Moses' time in their land.

Since Miriam is the one who spoke first and most forcefully, and not Aaron, she is the one punished by Yahweh for criticizing his most faithful

Moses and his Ethiopian wife Zipporah by Jacob Jordaens, 1645

servant Moses. The common interpretation of the story says that Miriam was punished for being racist against Moses's African wife.

It is a satisfactory moral lesson to say that Miriam's error was in being racist. But this explanation hardly makes sense on closer review. Tribalism was common in the ancient world, but racism based on skin color did not exist as a concept. It seems unlikely that Moses would have married a woman whose tribal identity was utterly unacceptable to his family. Likewise, it seems difficult to imagine why Miriam was upset with her sister-in-all after knowing her for many years without any explanatory details. It is precisely these details that are missing from the story. We never hear a word from the Cushite woman's mouth.

Celibacy

Jewish Midrash tradition from 200 CE adds additional details to the story that gives it a very different meaning.[1] In this version, the Cushite woman is Zipporah. The dispute with Miriam was the result of Moses having withdrawn from Zipporah sexually so that he could focus his mind on his prophesying. Now we see the story in terms of sex and celibacy and not in terms of race.

> *How did Miriam know that Moses had ceased from marital relations (with his wife Zipporah)? Seeing that Zipporah did not adorn herself as other (married) women did, she asked her for the cause and was told: "Your brother is not 'particular' about this thing" (intercourse, [being constantly "on call" for the word of G-d]). Thus Miriam learned of the matter. She apprised Aaron of it and they both spoke of it (as being a troublesome precedent for others.)*
>
> – Midrash Sifrei Bamidbar 99

1 Midrash – Sifrei Bamidbar, paragraph 99 – Composed in Talmudic Israel/Babylon (200 CE). Sifrei (Books) also known as Sifrei debe Rav or Sifrei Rabbah refers to either of two works of Midrash halakhah, based on the biblical books of Bemidbar (Numbers) and Devarim (Deuteronomy). https://www.sefaria.org/Sifrei_Bamidbar.100

As the leader of the women, Miriam defended the interests of the righteous Zipporah. Miriam and Aaron did not want the other prophets to feel obligated to withdraw sexually from their wives. They thought it would be a bad precedent to encourage celibacy. The idea that Miriam could have been a qedesha only adds color to this theory. Miriam would have been quite offended if Moses was breaking free of his traditional sexual obligations. We can see with 3000 years of hindsight that this may be exactly what happened.

Throughout the culture clashes in the Old Testament, the sexual practices of the Goddess worshippers were one of the primary sources of friction. This argument here may have been the first fight between the Yahwists and the women. The Biblical writers likely excised details intentionally in order to present their preferred version of events.

Kadesh

Yahweh punished Miriam severely for having the impertinence to question Moses. Her skin was struck with leprosy and she was sent out of the camp for seven days. Miriam then disappears entirely from the Biblical narrative, except for one last mention, the announcement of her death and burial in the city of Kadesh.

> *In the first month the whole Israelite community arrived at the Desert of Zin, and they stayed at Kadesh. There Miriam died and was buried.*
>
> – Numbers 20:1

The symbolism is probably intentional that Miriam was buried in the town of Kadesh, the city known to have been holy to the Canaanite Triple Goddess and her qedesha priestesses. This detail may confirm that Miriam was herself a qedesha. The qedesha were the great rivals to the Biblical prophets. The Biblical writers may have been making it clear that they were burying the traditions of sacred sexuality along with the prophetess.

Miriam's expulsion from the camp and her ignominious exit from the narrative is the first act in the centuries-long divorce between the newly monotheistic Hebrews and the traditional goddess worship. The first argument that led to the eventual divorce of God from the Mother Goddess.

Moses Breaks the Tables of the Law

Chapter Twenty-Five

HEBREW LAW

Leviticus

Yahweh transmitted many laws to Moses that govern Hebrew life and culture. This was unique to the Hebrews, in neighboring cultures laws came from the kings, like the Code of Hammurabi in Babylon. The pagan gods had nothing to say about laws or ethics, except that they appreciated righteousness.

The pagan gods certainly did not model or demand moral behavior, they were amoral at best when they were not downright cruel. The fact that the Hebrew god demanded moral and ethical behavior was among the big issues that separated the monotheistic Hebrews from the broader pagan world and was a source of strength and pride for the Israelites.

Many of the laws transmitted to Moses reflected common morality found across cultures; do not lie, steal, murder, rape, commit incest, cheat in business, blaspheme, disrespect your parents, etc. Distinctive Hebrew laws confirmed ritual purity, proper sacrifice, and the cleanliness of foods; such as not eating pork or keeping food kosher. The Hebrews also had their own festivals, Passover, the Festival of Unleavened Bread, the Festival of Weeks, and the Festival of Tabernacles. They did not practice the cycle of life festivals of their neighbors.

Women's subordinate role in the Hebrew community is seen throughout the law. Women were considered ceremonially unclean after childbirth – if she gives birth to a boy she is unclean for one week – if a girl then two weeks (Leviticus 12:1-8). Lepers were unclean, and so was mold and mildew. Men were unclean if they suffered from some type of bodily discharge. Women were unclean during menstruation and so was anything or any person they touched, or any bed or chair that the menstruating women lay or sat on, or any person who touches the bed or chair. If a man has sex with a menstruating woman then he too will be unclean for seven days (Leviticus 15:19-27).

Sexual Morality

Laws regarding sexual morality contrasted Hebrew culture with their pagan neighbors. Sacred sex and temple prostitution that confirmed the fertility of nature were celebrated practices throughout the region. Pagan women were encouraged to participate in temple sex and receive the blessings of the Goddess; they were not shamed for their fornications, but the Hebrews did not approve.

> *You must not do as they do in Egypt, where you used to live, and you must not do as they do in the land of Canaan, where I am bringing you. Do not follow their practices.*
>
> – Leviticus 18:3

> *"'Do not have sexual relations with your neighbor's wife and defile yourself with her.*
>
> *"'Do not give any of your children to be sacrificed to Molek, for you must not profane the name of your God. I am Yahweh.*
>
> *"'Do not have sexual relations with a man as one does with a woman; that is detestable.*
>
> *"'Do not have sexual relations with an animal and defile yourself with it. A woman must not present herself to an animal to have sexual relations with it; that is a perversion.*
>
> *"'Do not defile yourselves in any of these ways, because this is how the nations that I am going to drive out before you became defiled.*
>
> – Leviticus 18:20-24

All of these practices occurred in Canaan and throughout the Ancient Near East. They were openly sexual cultures not concerned with monogamy (though legally, wives belonged to their husbands), they sacrificed children to the Gods, homosexuality was acceptable, and they practiced beastiality to some extent by both men and women (though we don't know the context or meaning of it). We don't have diaries of people's bedroom exploits but all of these practices are attested to in Greek literature and mythology.

Beastiality is indicated in myth, Ishtar is said to be a lover of animals including the Bull of Heaven. In Greek myth, Pasiphaë was struck with an unnatural lust and had a wooden cow constructed that would allow her to copulate with a bull. She was impregnated by a sacred white bull sent by Poseidon and gave birth to the Minotaur, the legendary creature that is half-man, half-bull. This myth served as an allegory for the Greeks of the excesses of female sensuality and justification for keeping their wives' and daughters' sexuality under control, something their Near Eastern neighbors did not try to do.

Don't Listen to Qedesha

Many of the practices of the qedesha are explicitly listed as forbidden.

> *"'Do not practice divination or seek omens.*
>
> *"'Do not cut your bodies for the dead or put tattoo marks on yourselves*
>
> *"'Do not degrade your daughter by making her a prostitute, or the land will turn to prostitution and be filled with wickedness.*
>
> *"'Do not turn to mediums or seek out spiritists, for you will be defiled by them.*
>
> – Leviticus 19:26-31

> *"'If a priest's daughter defiles herself by becoming a prostitute, she disgraces her father; she must be burned in the fire.*
>
> – Leviticus 21:9

Yahweh wants only healthy people, no cripples or disfigured people may come near the altar to make offerings. The prohibition against damaged testicles is a restriction against eunuchs to serve as priests. Transgender priests were common and celebrated for their gender-bending in Goddess worship, but not so for the monotheists, who reject them completely.

> *No man who has any defect may come near: no man who is blind or lame, disfigured or deformed; no man with a crippled foot or hand, or who is a hunchback or a dwarf, or who has any eye defect, or who has festering or running sores or damaged testicles.*
>
> – Leviticus 21:18-20

Yahweh wanted his people to practice good ethics, at least within the Israelite community. Love your neighbor as yourself is an early version of the Golden Rule, an admonition repeated by Jesus and across many cultures.

> *Do not seek revenge or bear a grudge against anyone among your people, but love your neighbor as yourself.*
>
> – Leviticus 19:18

> *If a man seduces a virgin who is not pledged to be married and sleeps with her, he must pay the bride-price, and she shall be his wife. If her father absolutely refuses to give her to him, he must still pay the bride-price for virgins.*
>
> – Exodus 22:16-17

Do not allow a sorceress to live.[1]

– Exodus 22:18

Anyone who has sexual relations with an animal is to be put to death.

– Exodus 22:19

Whoever sacrifices to any god other than Yahweh must be destroyed.

– Exodus 22:20

Do not mistreat or oppress a foreigner, for you were foreigners in Egypt.

– Exodus 22:21

Do not take advantage of the widow or the fatherless.

– Exodus 22:22

If you lend money to one of my people among you who is needy, do not treat it like a business deal; charge no interest.

– Exodus 22:25

DEUTERONOMY

The book of Deuteronomy contains a long list of laws that expand on the laws handed down to Moses on Mt. Sinai. These laws detail the pagan practices that are not to be allowed in Israelite culture. These were written much later, in the 7th century BCE by the Deuteronomist priests under the Yahwist King Josiah, and ascribed to Moses.

Do Not Follow Other Gods

Do not follow other gods, the gods of the peoples around you; for Yahweh your God, who is among you, is a jealous God and his anger will burn against you, and he will destroy you from the face of the land.

– Deuteronomy 6:14-15

Yahweh is not tolerant at all of the other gods, or of their people.

When Yahweh your God brings you into the land you are entering to possess and drives out before you many nations – the Hittites, Girgashites, Amorites, Canaanites, Perizzites, Hivites and Jebusites, seven nations larger and stronger than you – and when Yahweh your God has

1 In the King James Bible, sorceress is translated as witch, "Thou shalt not suffer a witch to live." King James was a notorious witch hunter who had many women tortured.

delivered them over to you and you have defeated them, then you must destroy them totally.

Make no treaty with them, and show them no mercy. Do not intermarry with them. Do not give your daughters to their sons or take their daughters for your sons, for they will turn your children away from following me to serve other gods, and Yahweh's anger will burn against you and will quickly destroy you.

This is what you are to do to them: Break down their altars, smash their sacred stones, cut down their Asherah poles and burn their idols in the fire.

Deuteronomy 7:1-5

Yahweh will take over all the blessings normally offered by the Goddess.

He will love you and bless you and increase your numbers. He will bless the fruit of your womb, the crops of your land – your grain, new wine and olive oil – the calves of your herds and the lambs of your flocks in the land he swore to your ancestors to give you. You will be blessed more than any other people; none of your men or women will be childless, nor will any of your livestock be without young. Yahweh will keep you free from every disease.

– Deuteronomy 7:12-15

Centralized Temple Worship

Worship only in the main temple in Jerusalem, not at any other shrines or altars, no do-it-yourself religion.

Destroy completely all the places on the high mountains, on the hills and under every spreading tree, where the nations you are dispossessing worship their gods. Break down their altars, smash their sacred stones and burn their Asherah poles in the fire; cut down the idols of their gods and wipe out their names from those places.

– Deuteronomy 12:2-3

Then to the place Yahweh your God will choose as a dwelling for his Name – there you are to bring everything I command you: your burnt offerings and sacrifices, your tithes and special gifts, and all the choice possessions you have vowed to Yahweh.

Be careful not to sacrifice your burnt offerings anywhere you please. Offer them only at the place Yahweh will choose in one of your tribes, and there observe everything I command you.

– Deuteronomy 12:11; 13-14

If your very own brother, or your son or daughter, or the wife you love, or your closest friend secretly entices you, saying, "Let us go and worship other gods" (gods that neither you nor your ancestors have known), you must certainly put them to death. Your hand must be the first in putting them to death, and then the hands of all the people. Stone them to death, because they tried to turn you away from Yahweh your God, who brought you out of Egypt, out of the land of slavery.

– Deuteronomy 12:6; 9-10

No Goddess Worship

Do not set up any wooden Asherah pole beside the altar you build to Yahweh your God.

– Deuteronomy 16:21

Let no one be found among you who sacrifices their son or daughter in the fire, who practices divination or sorcery, interprets omens, engages in witchcraft, or casts spells, or who is a medium or spiritist or who consults the dead.

– Deuteronomy 18:10-11

No one who has been emasculated by crushing or cutting may enter the assembly of Yahweh.

– Deuteronomy 23:1

A woman must not wear men's clothing, nor a man wear women's clothing, for Yahweh your God detests anyone who does this.

– Deuteronomy 22:5

No eunuchs or transgenders. The Goddess celebrates her transgender priests.

No Israelite man or woman is to become a qedesha.

– Deuteronomy 23:17

The Israelites were at war with the qedesha.

You must not bring the earnings of a female prostitute (zonah) or of a male prostitute into the house of Yahweh your God to pay any vow, because Yahweh your God detests them both.

– Deuteronomy 23:18

Here the Hebrew word for prostitute is *zonah*, not *qedesha*, referring to conventional prostitutes.

Show No Pity

Show no pity: life for life, eye for eye, tooth for tooth, hand for hand, foot for foot.

– Deuteronomy 19:21

If two men are fighting and the wife of one of them comes to rescue her husband from his assailant, and she reaches out and seizes him by his genitals, you shall cut off her hand. Show her no pity.

– Deuteronomy 25:11-12

Show her no pity.

If your son is stubborn and disobeys, he must be stoned to death.

If someone has a stubborn and rebellious son who does not obey his father and mother and will not listen to them when they discipline him, his father and mother shall take hold of him and bring him to the elders at the gate of his town.

They shall say to the elders, "This son of ours is stubborn and rebellious. He will not obey us. He is a glutton and a drunkard. Then all the men of his town are to stone him to death. You must purge the evil from among you. All Israel will hear of it and be afraid.

– Deuteronomy 21:18-21

Shatnez

Do not wear clothes of wool and linen woven together.

– Deuteronomy 22:11

Shatnez is a reversal of the instructions given to Moses for the construction of the Tabernacle that specifically called for wool and linen to be woven together.

Virgins & Marriages

When you go to war against your enemies and Yahweh your God delivers them into your hands and you take captives, if you notice among the captives a beautiful woman and are attracted to her, you may take her as your wife.

– Deuteronomy 21:10-11

If a husband decides he does not like his wife and accuses her of not being a virgin, then her parents must submit proof of her virginity prior to marriage.

If, however, the charge is true and no proof of the young woman's virginity can be found, she shall be brought to the door of her father's house and there the men of her town shall stone her to death. She has done an outrageous thing in Israel by being promiscuous while still in her father's house. You must purge the evil from among you.

– Deuteronomy 22:20-21

No extramarital sex.

If a man is found sleeping with another man's wife, both the man who slept with her and the woman must die.

– Deuteronomy 22:22

If a man happens to meet in a town a virgin pledged to be married and he sleeps with her, you shall take both of them to the gate of that town and stone them to death – the young woman because she was in a town and did not scream for help, and the man because he violated another man's wife. You must purge the evil from among you.

– Deuteronomy 22:23-24

But if out in the country a man happens to meet a young woman pledged to be married and rapes her, only the man who has done this shall die.

– Deuteronomy 22:25

If a man happens to meet a virgin who is not pledged to be married and rapes her and they are discovered, he shall pay her father fifty shekels of silver. He must marry the young woman, for he has violated her. He can never divorce her as long as he lives.

–Deuteronomy 22:28-29

If a man marries a woman, but she becomes displeasing to him because he finds something improper about her, he may write her a divorce certificate, hand it to her, and send her away from his house.

– Deuteronomy 24:1 (HCSB)

Judah and Tamar

This is the custom behind the story of Judah and Tamar.

If brothers are living together and one of them dies without a son, his widow must not marry outside the family. Her husband's brother shall take her and marry her and fulfill the duty of a brother-in-law to her.

The first son she bears shall carry on the name of the dead brother so that his name will not be blotted out from Israel.

However, if a man does not want to marry his brother's wife, she shall go to the elders at the town gate and say, "My husband's brother refuses to carry on his brother's name in Israel. He will not fulfill the duty of a brother-in-law to me." Then the elders of his town shall summon him and talk to him.

If he persists in saying, "I do not want to marry her," his brother's widow shall go up to him in the presence of the elders, take off one of his sandals, spit in his face and say, "This is what is done to the man who will not build up his brother's family line."

That man's line shall be known in Israel as The Family of the Unsandaled.

– Deuteronomy 25:5-10

Judah Gives his Signet, Bracelets and Staff in Pledge to Tamar by Gerard Hoet

This four-tiered cult stand found at Tanaach is thought to represent Yahweh and Asherah, with each deity being depicted on alternating tiers. Photo: © The Israel Museum, Jerusalem/Israel Antiquities Authority (photograph by Avraham Hay).

Chapter Twenty-Six

YAHWISTS

Culture War

An overarching theme of the Hebrew Bible is that the historical narrative is harshly polemical, it is a political document reflecting one side of a 500-year civil war between the Hebrew Israelites and the pagan Canaanites. The Biblical writers were Yahwists, ultra-nationalist partisans trying to impose their religious values on all the people in the land of Canaan, and they savage their political/religious opponents in the harshest terms.

The Hebrew writers made no attempt to explain or sympathize with the Canaanite perspective and decry their cultural traditions as abominations. The Canaanites are portrayed as foreign to the Israelites even though it is clear from the text that the Hebrews were part of the broader Canaanite culture.

Biblical Writers

The Hebrew Bible is a collection of books that were written by a number of authors over a period of centuries and stitched together by a series of editors. Hebrew writing developed out of the Phoenician model and the earliest examples are steles that date back to the 9th century BCE. Literacy was never widespread, folk tales maintained in the oral tradition proliferated for centuries and only the educated elites did any writing. The stories of Abraham, Moses, and King David, were first written down centuries after they were supposed to have taken place.

Specific authors and dates of the Biblical books are mostly unknown. It is generally understood that assorted mythologies, histories, and prophetic writings were collected before a major portion of the Torah was written by the Deuteronomist generation of priests and prophets during the reign of the Yahwist King Josiah in the 7th century BCE.

After the destruction of the Jerusalem temple in 587 BCE, the surviving writings were taken to Babylon where another generation of priests led by Ezra the scribe compiled, edited and completed the writing of the

Hebrew Bible we read today (though more books continued to be added for another two centuries).

One feature all the Biblical writers share is that they were committed Yahwists. All of the writers were dedicated to promoting his worship and shutting down the worship of the traditional pagan gods led by Baal and the goddesses Asherah, Astarte, and Anat.

Canaanite Religion

The Canaanites' religious traditions were thousands of years old and maintained superstitious elements we would consider quite backward today, such as child sacrifice and divination using animal entrails. Yet there were also many popular parts of the Goddess traditions that reflect vital elements of the lived human experience, such as our sexuality and connections to nature, that would be right at home in today's secular cultures. These same culture war dynamics continue to echo today.

The Canaanite religion is identified in the Bible by some primary symbols; the golden calves and Asherah poles, as well as by the qedesha priestesses. The Canaanites worshipped the pagan gods in "high places", which were simple temples and may have just been platforms. The Goddess worshippers also practiced ritual sex in sacred groves and prostitution in the temples.

Entering Canaan

Picking up the story after many years of wandering. The Israelites eventually arrived at the border of the land of Canaan around 1200 BCE. Moses died just before entering the promised land and his aide Joshua became the new leader of the Israelites.

Joshua was a war leader who attacked Canaanite settlements, including Jericho, one of humanity's oldest cities. The Hebrews attacked many Canaanite cities, both winning and losing battles. When possible, the Israelites forced the Canaanites they defeated into slavery and forced labor.

Yahweh instructed the Hebrews not to make treaties or friendships with the local people but instead break down their altars, smash their statues of the gods, and cut down their Asherah poles. But the Israelites were slow to adopt the worship of Yahweh and they continued the traditional worship of Baal and Asherah for centuries.

> *Be careful not to make a treaty with those who live in the land where you are going, or they will be a snare among you. Break down their al-*

tars, smash their sacred stones and cut down their Asherah poles. Do not worship any other god, for Yahweh, whose name is Jealous, is a jealous God. "Be careful not to make a treaty with those who live in the land; for when they prostitute themselves to their gods and sacrifice to them, they will invite you and you will eat their sacrifices. And when you choose some of their daughters as wives for your sons and those daughters prostitute themselves to their gods, they will lead your sons to do the same.

– Exodus 34:12-16

Asherah Pole

The Asherah pole, sometimes just called an Asherah, was a carved pole that stood next to the altars of Baal and El/Yahweh. Asherah was the wife of El and the mother of Baal, and the pole represents the Mother Goddess and her sacred groves of trees. There are no explicit descriptions of an Asherah pole, so we don't know exactly what they looked like. But we can infer that the Asherah pole is like a maypole or a totem pole, ancient and common religious symbols that represent Mother Earth and the feminine divine.

Carved wooden poles are used today by indigenous people around the world from Siberia to North America, but the roots of the traditions predate history. The Shigir Idol is an 11,500-year-old carved totem pole that was discovered in a Russian peat bog near the city of Yekaterinburg. It is one of the oldest wood carvings ever found and one of the oldest pieces of monumental art.[1]

The unbroken thread of cultural continuity that traces from the Neolithic Shigir Idol through the Asherah poles to today's totem poles and maypoles demonstrates the deep, integral connection human beings feel naturally towards Mother Earth and the feminine divine.

Shigir Idol

It was a repeating theme for centuries of Hebrew history that the Yahwists would chop down the Asherah poles and the people would put them back up again. Asherah poles stood in the first Hebrew temple built by King Solomon for two-thirds of its history and a grand Asherah pole stood in Samaria, the capital of the northern kingdom of Israel for its entire two-hundred-year existence. Asherah and the goddesses were quite beloved.

1 Curry, Andrew, This 11,000-year-old statue unearthed in Siberia may reveal ancient views of taboos and demons, *Science Magazine*, sciencemag.org, Apr. 25, 2018. https://www.sciencemag.org/news/2018/04/11000-year-old-statue-unearthed-siberia-may-reveal-ancient-views-taboos-and-demons

Gideon

Gideon was an Israelite who lived during the battles with the Canaanites. An angel visited and called him to be valiant for Yahweh. In a dream, Gideon was instructed to tear down the altar to Baal that his father had built and also the Asherah pole beside it. The fact that Gideon's father had built the altar and Asherah pole demonstrates clearly that the early Hebrews were pagan Canaanites, and that the monotheistic ideals arose over time from within the community.

> *So Gideon took ten of his servants and did as Yahweh told him. But because he was afraid of his family and the townspeople, he did it at night rather than in the daytime. In the morning when the people of the town got up, there was Baal's altar, demolished, with the Asherah pole beside it cut down and the second bull sacrificed on the newly built altar!*
>
> *They asked each other, "Who did this?" When they carefully investigated, they were told, "Gideon son of Joash did it." The people of the town demanded of Joash, "Bring out your son. He must die, because he has broken down Baal's altar and cut down the Asherah pole beside it."*
>
> *But Joash replied to the hostile crowd around him, "Are you going to plead Baal's cause? Are you trying to save him? Whoever fights for him shall be put to death by morning! If Baal really is a god, he can defend himself when someone breaks down his altar." So because Gideon broke down Baal's altar, they gave him the name Jerub-Baal that day, saying, "Let Baal contend with him."*
>
> – Judges 6:27-32

Baal-Zebub

Baal-Zebub was a name given to Baal in the Bible. Baal's names were often hyphenated with the name of a town, or an honorific, and the name Baal itself is a title meaning "Lord". Baal-Hadad means Lord Hadad. Zebub means "flies" or "dung", so Baal-Zebub means "Lord of the Flies" or "Lord of Shit" and it is obviously meant to be an insult. In medieval times, Baalzebub became a name for a demon or the devil.

Two Eminent Devils. Satan and Beelzebub

Chapter Twenty-Seven

SHAMEFUL ASTARTE AND JEALOUS YAHWEH

Powerful Goddesses

The Biblical writers did their best to diminish the goddesses so that the readers do not see how popular and powerful they were. Asherah and Astarte are mentioned numerous times, but always in a manner that is derisive and condescending. The reader must read between the lines to discern just how important the goddesses were in the lives of the common people. The Biblical writers and prophets did not represent the common consensus of the community, they were a minority of religious reformers railing against the popular culture.

The monotheistic Yahwists described Yahweh as a jealous god. "His name is Jealous" and they were completely intolerant of the popular gods worshipped by the vast majority of the people. And although the Bible describes Yahweh as the God of their ancestors, in truth Yahweh was the new god. The pagan pantheon were the ancient gods whose history went back thousands of years.

Ashtoreth

Asherah and the Asherah poles are mentioned over 40 times in the Bible, while Astarte is mentioned around a dozen times with various names.

Astarte is referred to by her title, the Queen of Heaven. But more often she is given the insulting name, *Ashtoreth*, or *Ashtaroth*. This name is the most revealing of the Biblical writers' views of the beloved goddess. Ashtoreth means "shameful Astarte". The *-eth* is an epithet derived from the Hebrew word *boshet* which means shame.

As the Queen of Heaven, Astarte was the most important goddess in the land, equal to Baal, with whom she was sometimes associated as a consort. Astarte's sacred sex, cycle of life rituals, big festivals, temple prostitution, war powers, and divination, were all despised by the Yahwists who sought to exterminate them. Astarte, who was worshipped by King Solomon, was the greatest rival and threat to the Yahwists.

> *Then the Israelites did evil in the eyes of Yahweh and served the Baals. They forsook Yahweh, the God of their ancestors, who had brought them out of Egypt. They followed and worshiped various gods of the peoples around them. They aroused Yahweh's anger because they forsook him and served Baal and the Ashtoreths.*
>
> – Judges 2:11-13

Astarte by John Singer Sargent, 1895

The name Ashtoreth was used when King Saul, the first king of the Israelites and the father of King David, was killed in battle by the Philistines. They cut off Saul's head, stripped his armor, and brought it to the temple of "shameful" Astarte.

> *They put his armor in the temple of the Ashtoreths and fastened his body to the wall of Beth Shan.*
>
> – 1 Samuel 31:10

Eshbaal

We see another example of the "-eth" epithet when Eshbaal was called Ish-Bosheth, "man of shame." Eshbaal was briefly a Hebrew King, he was one of the sons of King Saul and a rival to King David who defeated him in a civil war before seizing the Israelite throne. The Biblical writers obviously favored King David, and they never offered fair treatment of their rivals.

> *Ish-Bosheth son of Saul was forty years old when he became king over Israel, and he reigned two years. The tribe of Judah, however, remained loyal to David.*
>
> – 2 Samuel 2:10

Where Is Anat?

It is notable that the Biblical writers never mention Anat and she makes no appearances in the Bible. Anat was the sister/lover of Baal, sister of Astarte, daughter of Asherah, and death in the Triple Goddess.

Anat was a very popular goddess and was certainly well known to the Biblical writers. Perhaps the blood-soaked warrior maiden was too terrifying to describe, even in insulting terms. Anat would not have felt threatened by Yahweh – she is the one who told El, "I'll smash your head, I'll make your gray hair run with blood, your gray beard run with gore" in the Baal Cycle myth.

Anat's favorite activity was slaughtering the enemies of Baal and wading up to her vulva in a pool of their blood and limbs. She made a necklace of their skulls and a belt of their human hands. And who were the greatest enemies of Baal? None other than the Hebrews. One can only imagine what stories were told about those hated Yahwists in the temples to Anat. Anat would have delighted in their slaughter.

For the biblical writers, Anat the terrible was *she who must not be named.* In the Bible, Asherah is cut down, Astarte is blasphemed, and Anat's very existence is denied.

King Solomon in Old Age

Chapter Twenty-Eight

KING SOLOMON

King David

After defeating Ishbaal, David became king of all 12 tribes in the united kingdom of Israel. Around 1000 BCE King David attacked the walled city of Jerusalem in a daring raid. David led his men through a water shaft leading from the Gihon spring into the city. King David defeated the Jebusites who lived there and drove them away, establishing Jerusalem as the capital of Judah and Israel, and from there one of the most exalted cities in the world.

As King David's health failed at the end of his long rule, various princes asserted their claims for the throne. David's wife Bathsheba, with whom he had had a scandalous adulterous affair when they first met, maneuvered her youngest son to be chosen by David as his successor.

David and Bathsheba's 15-year-old young son was named Jedidiah, "the friend of God." After being anointed king beside the Gihon Spring, drenched in the holy cannabis oil, he would be known by a name of legendary renown.

> *Zadok the priest took the horn of oil from the sacred tent and anointed Solomon. Then they sounded the trumpet and all the people shouted, "Long live King Solomon!"*
>
> – 1 Kings 1:39

King of Peace

King Solomon ruled in Jerusalem for 40 years from 970-931 BCE and is revered by Jews, Christians, Muslims, and Rastafarians, as the wisest and wealthiest of all the world's ancient kings. Known as the "King of Peace," Solomon ruled the united kingdom of Israel, brought trade and prosperity, built the first Hebrew Temple in Jerusalem, and is credited with authoring the biblical books of Proverbs, Ecclesiastes, and the Song of Songs.

King Solomon is one of the most celebrated figures of all time and countless stories exist about him outside the Bible. Solomon's exploits and wealth are clearly exaggerated in the Bible, but it is not hard to believe that there was a real King Solomon who lived at this time who was wealthy and successful. Scholars and archaeologists continue to debate the existence of King Solomon and King David since no evidence confirming them has been found, but it is accepted that the Israelites were in Jerusalem in this period.

> *King Solomon was greater in riches and wisdom than all the other kings of the earth. All the kings of the earth sought audience with Solomon to hear the wisdom God had put in his heart.*
>
> – 2 Chronicles 9:22-23

There is no archaeological evidence for King Solomon, but the Temple Mount in Jerusalem is believed to be the sacred home of the first and second Hebrew temples. The Temple Mount is currently the home of the Islamic Dome of the Rock and the Al-Aqsa Mosque. It is the single most contentious location on all of planet Earth, fought over by Jews, Muslims, and Christians alike.

Goddess Worshipper

For all of King Solomon's great attributes, he is harshly criticized in the Bible for his Goddess worship and devotion to his wives. King Solomon built a temple (or high place) to Astarte in Jerusalem. He is said to have had 700 wives and 300 concubines, he loved women and the women loved him. The king was a sensuous man who appreciated the finer things in life; luxury, poetry, wisdom, and love.

King Solomon kept the pagan traditions alive and likely took part in the hieros gamos rituals. The Song of Solomon comes from a genre of sacred love poetry used in these traditions. The king had close relations with the goddess worshipping Phoenicians who helped him build the Hebrew temple and with whom he engaged in wide-ranging trade.

The Biblical writers blamed Solomon's goddess worship for the breakup of the united kingdom of Israel, which occurred after the king died. Yet this scapegoating of Solomon's goddess worship sidesteps the stated reasons for the revolt and the actions of the participants.

Jeroboam led a revolt against Solomon's son King Rehoboam because of their harsh labor practices, not because of their paganism. The breakup of Israel was effectively a slave revolt against the bad king Rehoboam. The first thing Jeroboam did after breaking away from the temple leadership in Jerusalem was to establish pagan shrines in Israel. Goddess worship thrived in the northern kingdom and was popular among the people.

Pharaoh's Daughter

The young King Solomon quickly and ruthlessly eliminated his rivals and consolidated his hold on power. The Bible says that he made an alliance with Egypt and married the Pharaoh's daughter, who was Solomon's primary wife and for whom he built a palace.

This marriage would have been a significant political alliance for Israel if it really happened. Egyptian royalty did not normally marry outside their family, they were very inbred. They did not like to leave Egypt and they did not make a practice of political marriages as was common in other cultures. There is no record of this marriage to King Solomon in Egyptian records and scholars dispute that it ever occurred.

The Hebrews also had their own historical grievances against Egypt, they had been slaves and had fought against Egypt to gain their independence. But according to the Biblical narrative, the alliance was useful. Pharaoh sent his army to decimate the fortified city of Gezer and gave it as a dowry to his daughter for King Solomon. It has been confirmed that the Israelites did hold the city of Gezer.

> *Pharaoh king of Egypt had attacked and captured Gezer. He had set it on fire. He killed its Canaanite inhabitants and then gave it as a wedding gift to his daughter, Solomon's wife.*
>
> – 1 Kings 9:16

Wisdom

While King Solomon successfully consolidated his power, the people continued to worship in the old pagan ways, offering sacrifices and burning incense at the high places. *High places* were hilltop altars and sacred groves where the people made offerings to the gods and goddesses. There was no centralized worship in pagan folk traditions, just community altars that people built themselves. The big cities had state religions and large temples, but in the countryside religion was a community and family affair. There was no doctrine, dogma, or overarching authority to spiritual matters. Paganism was a do-it-yourself religious framework.

Wise King Solomon followed the people and also burned incense and made offerings on the high places. The following passage is crucial. "The king went to Gibeon to offer sacrifices, for that was the most important high place."

> *Solomon showed his love for Yahweh by walking according to the instructions given him by his father David, except that he offered sacrifices and burned incense on the high places. The king went to Gibeon to of-*

fer sacrifices, for that was the most important high place, and Solomon offered a thousand burnt offerings on that altar.

At Gibeon Yahweh appeared to Solomon during the night in a dream, and God said, "Ask for whatever you want me to give you."

Solomon answered... "Now, Yahweh my God, you have made your servant king in place of my father David. But I am only a little child and do not know how to carry out my duties.... So give your servant a discerning heart to govern your people and to distinguish between right and wrong. For who is able to govern this great people of yours?"

Yahweh was pleased that Solomon had asked for this. So God said to him, "Since you have asked for this and not for long life or wealth for yourself, nor have asked for the death of your enemies but for discernment in administering justice, I will do what you have asked.

I will give you a wise and discerning heart, so that there will never have been anyone like you, nor will there ever be. Moreover, I will give you what you have not asked for – both wealth and honor – so that in your lifetime you will have no equal among kings.

– 1 Kings 3:3-13

King Solomon made a thousand burnt offerings at Gibeon, the most important pagan shrine. Rather than being angry, Yahweh rewarded Solomon by granting him wisdom. Solomon took that blessing and became the philosophical bridge between the pagan and monotheistic traditions.

Solomon transmuted the imagery of pagan goddesses into the poetic language of wisdom. He is the father of the Wisdom Traditions. Solomon describes wisdom in feminine terms, as a new representation of the feminine divine that was acceptable to the monotheists. In the book of Proverbs, Solomon describes how wisdom was at God's side as he laid the foundations of creation, guided by her hand. Later Hellenistic philosophers would give wisdom the name Sophia.

The Book of Chronicles was written later and it tells the same story slightly differently. The writer of Chronicles altered the detail that Gibeon was "the most important high place" and changed it to be the location for the tent of meeting instead. This is a clear example of revisionist history as the Bible went through generations of writers over many centuries.

Solomon and the whole assembly went to the high place at Gibeon, for God's tent of meeting was there, which Moses Yahweh's servant had made in the wilderness.

– 2 Chronicles 1:3

Two Women and a Baby

Solomon then judged a famous dispute. Two women came to him both claiming to be the mother of the same baby, while the other's baby was dead. The king said, "bring me a sword, cut the child in half and give one half to each mother."

The woman whose child was alive was deeply moved out of love for her son and said, "do not kill the living baby!" But the woman whose child was dead said, "neither of us can have him!"

Then the king made his ruling, "Give the baby to the first woman, she is the mother of the living child." When all Israel heard the verdict they were awed by Solomon's wisdom.

> *Solomon's wisdom was greater than the wisdom of all the people of the East, and greater than all the wisdom of Egypt.*
>
> *He spoke three thousand proverbs and his songs numbered a thousand and five.*
>
> *From all nations people came to listen to Solomon's wisdom, sent by all the kings of the world, who had heard of his wisdom.*
>
> – 1 Kings 4:30; 32; 34

PROVERBS

King Solomon is the father of the wisdom traditions and the author of the books of Proverbs and Ecclesiastes. Solomon is the one who transmuted the pagan goddess traditions into wisdom, known later as Sophia and the Logos. Wisdom was with God at the beginning.

These passages speak for themselves.

> *BLESSED IS HE WHO FINDS WISDOM:*
>
> *Blessed are those who find wisdom, those who gain understanding, for she is more profitable than silver and yields better returns than gold. She is more precious than rubies; nothing you desire can compare with her. Long life is in her right hand; in her left hand are riches and honor.*
>
> *Her ways are pleasant ways, and all her paths are peace. She is a tree of life to those who take hold of her; those who hold her fast will be blessed.*
>
> – Proverbs 3:13-18

> *By wisdom Yahweh laid the earth's foundations, by understanding he set the heavens in place; by his knowledge the watery depths were divided, and the clouds let drop the dew.*

My son, do not let wisdom and understanding out of your sight, preserve sound judgment and discretion; they will be life for you, an ornament to grace your neck.

– Proverbs 3:19-21

EXCELLENCE OF WISDOM:
Does not wisdom call out? Does not understanding raise her voice? At the highest point along the way, where the paths meet, she takes her stand; beside the gate leading into the city, at the entrance, she cries aloud:

"To you, O people, I call out; I raise my voice to all mankind. You who are simple, gain prudence; you who are foolish, set your hearts on it. Listen, for I have trustworthy things to say; I open my lips to speak what is right. My mouth speaks what is true, for my lips detest wickedness.

All the words of my mouth are just; none of them is crooked or perverse. To the discerning all of them are right; they are upright to those who have found knowledge. Choose my instruction instead of silver, knowledge rather than choice gold, for wisdom is more precious than rubies, and nothing you desire can compare with her.

"I, wisdom, dwell together with prudence; I possess knowledge and discretion. To fear Yahweh is to hate evil; I hate pride and arrogance, evil behavior and perverse speech. Counsel and sound judgment are mine; I have insight, I have power. By me kings reign and rulers issue decrees that are just; by me princes govern, and nobles – all who rule on earth.

I love those who love me, and those who seek me find me. With me are riches and honor, enduring wealth and prosperity. My fruit is better than fine gold; what I yield surpasses choice silver. I walk in the way of righteousness, along the paths of justice, bestowing a rich inheritance on those who love me and making their treasuries full.

"Yahweh brought me forth as the first of his works, before his deeds of old; I was formed long ages ago, at the very beginning, when the world came to be.

When there were no watery depths, I was given birth, when there were no springs overflowing with water; before the mountains were settled in place, before the hills, I was given birth before he made the world or its fields or any of the dust of the earth.

I was there when he set the heavens in place, when he marked out the horizon on the face of the deep, when he established the clouds above and fixed securely the fountains of the deep, when he gave the sea its boundary so the waters would not overstep his command, and when he marked out the foundations of the earth.

Then I was constantly at his side. I was filled with delight day after day, rejoicing always in his presence, rejoicing in his whole world and delighting in mankind.

"Now then, my children, listen to me; blessed are those who keep my ways.

Listen to my instruction and be wise; do not disregard it.

Blessed are those who listen to me, watching daily at my doors, waiting at my doorway. For those who find me find life and receive favor from Yahweh. But those who fail to find me harm themselves; all who hate me love death."

– Proverbs 8:1-36

ECCLESIASTES

The book of Ecclesiastes is full of King Solomon's wisdom.

For with much wisdom comes much sorrow; the more knowledge, the more grief.

– Ecclesiastes 1:18

Whoever loves money never has enough; whoever loves wealth is never satisfied with their income.

– Ecclesiastes 5:10

Do not say, "Why were the old days better than these?" For it is not wise to ask such questions. Wisdom, like an inheritance, is a good thing and benefits those who see the sun. Wisdom is a shelter as money is a shelter, but the advantage of knowledge is this: Wisdom preserves those who have it.

– Ecclesiastes 7:10-12

There is something else meaningless that occurs on earth: the righteous who get what the wicked deserve, and the wicked who get what the righteous deserve. This too, I say, is meaningless.
So I commend the enjoyment of life because there is nothing better for a person under the sun than to eat and drink and be glad. Then joy will accompany them in their toil all the days of the life God has given them under the sun.

– Ecclesiastes 8:14-15

No one can comprehend what goes on under the sun. Despite all their efforts to search it out, no one can discover its meaning. Even if the wise claim they know, they cannot really comprehend it.

– Ecclesiastes 8:17

I have seen something else under the sun: The race is not to the swift or the battle to the strong, nor does food come to the wise or wealth to the brilliant or favor to the learned; but time and chance happen to them all.

Moreover, no one knows when their hour will come: As fish are caught in a cruel net, or birds are taken in a snare, so people are trapped by evil times that fall unexpectedly upon them.

– Ecclesiastes 9:11-12

WEALTH

Israel reached its greatest territorial expanse under King Solomon. He dominated the local tribes to the east, the Ammonites, Moabites, and Edomites, and sent his armies into Syria as well. He exacted tribute and forced the tribes to labor on his building projects. Palestine lay along important trade routes linking Africa to Asia and Europe.

Solomon had close and profitable relations with King Hiram of Tyre and the Phoenicians. With control of Edom, Israel had ports on both the Mediterranean and the Gulf of Aqaba on the Red Sea, enabling lucrative trade from the Atlantic Ocean to the Indian Ocean.

Solomon raised the kingdom to the heights of its commercial potential. He became fabulously wealthy and the people were very happy. With trade came peace and King Solomon ruled over a prosperous kingdom.

The people of Judah and Israel were as numerous as the sand on the seashore; they ate, they drank and they were happy. And Solomon ruled over all the kingdoms from the Euphrates River to the land of the Philistines, as far as the border of Egypt. These countries brought tribute and were Solomon's subjects all his life.

– 1 Kings 4:20-21

King Hiram Of Tyre

King Solomon's alliance with the Phoenician King Hiram of Tyre had previously been established by King David. The Tyrians were among the world's great sailors, traders, and craftsmen, and they possessed the valuable cedar forests of Lebanon. King Hiram provided Solomon with all the cedar and juniper timber he wanted, and Solomon paid him in wheat and olive oil. Together they engaged in wide-ranging and profitable trade.

> *King Solomon also built ships at Ezion Geber, which is near Elath in Edom, on the shore of the Red Sea. And Hiram sent his men--sailors who knew the sea--to serve in the fleet with Solomon's men. They sailed to Ophir and brought back 420 talents of gold, which they delivered to King Solomon.*
>
> – 1 Kings 9:26-28

Gold from Ophir

King Solomon is reported to have been the richest king ever, his gold from Ophir is legendary. For centuries people have searched for Solomon's famous gold mines, but nothing definitive has been found.

King Solomon was said to be so wealthy that he used gold plates, goblets, and utensils, and that the people of Israel did not even bother using silver because it was as common as stones. Solomon amassed massive stores of gold, thousands of horses, cavalry, men, and chariots. We can assume the elaborate claims of wealth to be literary embellishments.

> *The king made silver and gold as common in Jerusalem as stones, and cedar as plentiful as sycamore-fig trees in the foothills.*
>
> – 2 Chronicles 1:15

> *All King Solomon's goblets were gold, and all the household articles in the Palace of the Forest of Lebanon were pure gold. Nothing was made of silver, because silver was considered of little value in Solomon's days.*
>
> *The king had a fleet of trading ships at sea along with the ships of Hiram. Once every three years it returned, carrying gold, silver and ivory, and apes and baboons. King Solomon was greater in riches and wisdom than all the other kings of the earth.*
>
> *The whole world sought audience with Solomon to hear the wisdom God had put in his heart. Year after year, everyone who came brought a gift – articles of silver and gold, robes, weapons and spices, and horses and mules.*
>
> *Solomon accumulated chariots and horses; he had fourteen hundred chariots and twelve thousand horses, which he kept in the chariot cities and also with him in Jerusalem. The king made silver as common in Jerusalem as stones, and cedar as plentiful as sycamore-fig trees in the foothills.*
>
> – 1 Kings 10:21-27

Building Projects

Solomon went on an extensive building campaign throughout the country. He built garrison towns for his cavalry, and the fortified cities of Hazor, Megiddo, and Gezer, along with impressive water conduits that allowed cities to withstand sieges.

Solomon was especially lavish with his capital, Jerusalem; he built a great wall and terraces to support buildings and paid particular attention to the new Temple and royal palace. Solomon also built temples and tolerated the worship of foreign gods by travelers and visitors on trade missions. Solomon put thousands of men into forced labor to build his palace, temple, and other civil works.

> *Solomon conscripted the descendants of all these peoples remaining in the land – whom the Israelites could not exterminate – to serve as slave labor, as it is to this day. But Solomon did not make slaves of any of the Israelites; they were his fighting men, his government officials, his officers, his captains, and the commanders of his chariots and charioteers.*
>
> – 1 Kings 9:21-22

In time, Solomon's ill-treatment of his slaves and laborers led to the revolt that split the kingdom of Israel. Although the Yahwist prophets and Biblical writers would scapegoat his Goddess worship instead.

Hiram Abiff

King Hiram sent architects and skilled craftsmen to help King Solomon build his temples and other projects. Chief among them was Hiram Abiff, the widow's son from Tyre. Hiram Abiff was skilled in every kind of bronze work and Solomon appointed him to be chief architect and Master of Works.

> *And king Solomon sent and fetched Hiram out of Tyre. He was a widow's son of the tribe of Naphtali, and his father was a man of Tyre, a worker in brass: and he was filled with wisdom, and understanding, and cunning to work all works in brass. And he came to king Solomon and wrought all his work.*
>
> – 1 Kings 7:13-14 (KJV)

Hiram Abiff constructed Solomon's grand throne made of ivory and overlaid with gold, with six steps, two lions stood beside the armrests, and twelve more lions aside the six steps. A throne of lions fit for a king, or for a goddess.

> *Then the king made a great throne covered with ivory and overlaid with fine gold. The throne had six steps, and its back had a rounded top. On both sides of the seat were armrests, with a lion standing beside each of*

them. Twelve lions stood on the six steps, one at either end of each step. Nothing like it had ever been made for any other kingdom.

– 1 Kings 10:18-20

The lion throne is another clear indication of Solomon's goddess worship. This tradition goes back to Catal Huyuk, but the Biblical writers seem to think it was unique. The goddess Cybele sat in a similar lion throne a thousand years later in Rome.

Solomon's Temple

King Solomon constructed the legendary first Hebrew Temple in Jerusalem, it took seven years to build. The Temple's magnificence is detailed in the Bible and has long been extolled in legend. King Hiram of Tyre provided the materials and skilled workmen, and the Temple was built in the style of pagan temples of the era throughout the region.

The Biblical description of Solomon's Temple suggests that the inside ceiling was 60 cubits long (90 feet), 20 cubits wide (30 feet), and 30 cubits high (45 feet). Solomon's Temple had a three-room plan with an inner sanctum at the rear. The Temple was built from stone and cedar and the construction consisted of finely hewn masonry combined with carved wooden cherubs and bronze basins. The inner walls were overlaid with carved cedar and completely gilded with gold.

The temple was decorated in a Garden of Eden motif of cherubs and verdant vegetation; palm trees, open flowers, pomegranates, gourds, lions, and oxen. The cherubim appear like angels with wings. There was a pair of large cherubim statues that guarded the Ark of the Covenant in the Holy of Holies, an interior room no one was allowed into except the high priest.

The plans of the building were Phoenician of origin and the materials, skilled workmen, and architects were delivered by King Hiram of Tyre. Archaeologists have uncovered pagan temples virtually identical to Solomon's from the same era. The Ain Dara temple to Astarte in Syria was operating from 1300 BCE to 740 BCE, the same period as Solomon's.

The inside of the temple was cedar, carved with gourds and open flowers. Everything was cedar; no stone was to be seen.

Solomon covered the inside of the temple with pure gold, and he extended gold chains across the front of the inner sanctuary, which was overlaid with gold. So he overlaid the whole interior with gold. He also overlaid with gold the altar that belonged to the inner sanctuary.

– 1 Kings 6:18; 21-22

He placed the cherubim inside the innermost room of the temple, with their wings spread out. The wing of one cherub touched one wall, while the wing of the other touched the other wall, and their wings touched each other in the middle of the room. He overlaid the cherubim with gold. On the walls all around the temple, in both the inner and outer rooms, he carved cherubim, palm trees and open flowers. He also covered the floors of both the inner and outer rooms of the temple with gold.

– 1 Kings 6:27-30

Holy Smoke

When the priests dedicated the temple and brought the Ark of the Covenant into the Holy of Holies, a thick cloud of smoke, the Shekinah, filled the temple and prevented the completion of the rituals.

The priests then brought the ark of Yahweh's covenant to its place in the inner sanctuary of the temple, the Most Holy Place, and put it beneath the wings of the cherubim.

When the priests withdrew from the Holy Place, the cloud filled the temple of Yahweh. And the priests could not perform their service because of the cloud, for the glory of Yahweh filled his temple.

– 1 Kings 8:6; 10-11

The Shekinah, the presence of God, manifests as a cloud of smoke that filled the Temple.

Then the temple of Yahweh was filled with the cloud, and the priests could not perform their service because of the cloud, for the glory of Yahweh filled the temple of God.

– 2 Chronicles 5:13-14

Cannabis in the Temple

Cannabis was well represented in the temple, King Solomon loved it. Hashish was burned routinely as incense and presented as a sacrificial offering. Ganja was used medicinally by the qedeshas for sacred sex and midwifery. Hemp fibers were woven into shrouds that wrapped the newborn and the corpse.

There were qedeshas and male qedesh employed in the Temple for most of its history. Women wove sacred textiles that were commonly used to create separate spaces and rooms. Hanging fabrics were used at the temple to create pavilions and tents for visitors and vendors.

Asherah poles were a mainstay in the temple but they were a source of contention as the Yahwists objected to their presence.

Ring Of Aandaleeb

In Arabic legends, King Solomon had a magic ring, the Ring of Aandaleeb, that was said to be a gift from God himself. The ring was made from brass and iron, lapis lazuli, and set with four jewels, on which the true name of God was engraved. It allowed Solomon to control demons, perform exorcisms, and speak with animals.

The ring features a sacred symbol, two interlaced triangles surrounded by a circle. The shape of the interlaced triangles gave the appearance of a 3-dimensional figure which made demons confused and dizzy, unable to do Solomon any harm.

The Seal of Solomon represents the God Triad and the Triple Goddess balanced and entwined within cosmic unity. Mother, Father, and the Holy Spirit. Wise King Solomon loved God and he loved the Goddess as well.

In modern times, the Seal of Solomon was adapted into the Star of David, the nationalist symbol of the state of Israel. The Star of David features two overlaid triangles, but they are laid flat and not intertwined, and the Star of David also does not have a circle around it as the Seal of Solomon does.

Solomon's Foreign Wives

King Solomon loved many foreign women, he had 700 wives and 300 concubines as described in the Book of Kings. The Book of Chronicles skips over this controversial aspect of Solomon's biography. The Biblical writers blame Solomon's wives for leading him astray from Yahweh and they blame this sin for the later breakup of the kingdom of Israel.

Solomon held fast to them in love.

– 1 Kings 11:2

King Solomon had close relations with the Phoenicians and it is clear from scripture that Solomon worshipped as a pagan. He worshipped (shameful) Astarte of Sidon, as well as other foreign gods, including the detestable Moloch, and burned incense to the goddesses on the high places. The Biblical writers never accuse Solomon of sacrificing his own children, but it is clear through the narrative that the practice continued for centuries.

> *King Solomon, however, loved many foreign women besides Pharaoh's daughter – Moabites, Ammonites, Edomites, Sidonians and Hittites. They were from nations about which Yahweh had told the Israelites, "You must not intermarry with them, because they will surely turn your hearts after their gods." Nevertheless, Solomon held fast to them in love.*
>
> *He had seven hundred wives of royal birth and three hundred concubines, and his wives led him astray. As Solomon grew old, his wives turned his heart after other gods, and his heart was not fully devoted to Yahweh his God, as the heart of David his father had been.*
>
> *He followed Ashtoreth the goddess of the Sidonians, and Molek the detestable god of the Ammonites. So Solomon did evil in the eyes of Yahweh; he did not follow Yahweh completely, as David his father had done. On a hill east of Jerusalem, Solomon built a high place for Chemosh the detestable god of Moab, and for Molek the detestable god of the Ammonites. He did the same for all his foreign wives, who burned incense and offered sacrifices to their gods.*
>
> – 1 Kings 11:1-8

King Solomon would eventually die in his bed; fat, rich, and happy, surrounded by his family and the women that loved him. If God was unhappy with King Solomon, he did not show it in Solomon's lifetime, or perhaps the Goddess just loved him more.

SONG OF SONGS

The Song of Songs, also called the Song of Solomon, or the Canticles, is the only romantic and erotic book in the Bible. It is a love song of passion and devotion between the King and his beautiful new bride. The Song of Songs comes from the tradition of Babylonian hieros gamos love poetry. King Solomon worshipped Astarte and may have taken part in the sacred marriage rituals.

The Bride is unnamed. By tradition, she is thought to be the Pharaoh's daughter, but of course, Solomon had many wives. In the verses, she is said to be from Lebanon. The bride is described as dark-skinned and Solomon has black hair, neither is Caucasian.

Images of nature worship abound in the Canticles and it also contains the second reference to cannabis in the Bible. Cannabis is in a list of the finest incense spices that are compared to the beauty of the bride (Songs 4:14). As in the recipe for the holy anointing oil, cannabis is listed next to myrrh, implying its use in incense.

The Bride:
Let him kiss me with the kisses of his mouth – for your love is more delightful than wine. Pleasing is the fragrance of your perfumes; your name is like perfume poured out. No wonder the young women love you! Take me away with you – let us hurry! Let the king bring me into his chambers.

Dark am I, yet lovely, daughters of Jerusalem, dark like the tents of Kedar, like the tent curtains of Solomon. Do not stare at me because I am dark, because I am darkened by the sun.

My beloved is to me a sachet of myrrh resting between my breasts. My beloved is to me a cluster of henna blossoms from the vineyards of En Gedi.

– Songs 1:2-6; 13-14

The Bride:
I am a rose of Sharon, a lily of the valleys.

Solomon
Like a lily among thorns is my darling among the young women.
– Songs 2:1-2

The Wedding Day:
Who is this coming up from the wilderness like a column of smoke, perfumed with myrrh and incense made from all the spices of the merchant? Look! It is Solomon's carriage, escorted by sixty warriors, the noblest of Israel,

Come out, and look, you daughters of Zion. Look on King Solomon wearing a crown, the crown with which his mother crowned him on the day of his wedding, the day his heart rejoiced.

– Songs 3:6-7; 11

His mother is the Goddess, who confirms the king in the sacred marriage.

Solomon:
How beautiful you are, my darling! Oh, how beautiful! Your eyes behind your veil are doves.

Your hair is like a flock of goats descending from the hills of Gilead. Your teeth are like a flock of sheep just shorn, coming up from the washing. Each has its twin; not one of them is alone.

Your lips are like a scarlet ribbon; your mouth is lovely. Your temples behind your veil are like the halves of a pomegranate. Your neck is like the tower of David, built with courses of stone; on it hang a thousand shields, all of them shields of warriors.

Your breasts are like two fawns, like twin fawns of a gazelle that browse among the lilies. Until the day breaks and the shadows flee, I will go to the mountain of myrrh and to the hill of incense. You are altogether beautiful, my darling; there is no flaw in you. Come with me from Lebanon, my bride, come with me from Lebanon. Descend from the crest of Amana, from the top of Senir, the summit of Hermon, from the lions' dens and the mountain haunts of leopards.

You have stolen my heart, my sister, my bride; you have stolen my heart with one glance of your eyes, with one jewel of your necklace. How delightful is your love, my sister, my bride! How much more pleasing is your love than wine, and the fragrance of your perfume more than any spice! Your lips drop sweetness as the honeycomb, my bride; milk and honey are under your tongue. The fragrance of your garments is like the fragrance of Lebanon.

You are a garden locked up, my sister, my bride; you are a spring enclosed, a sealed fountain. Your plants are an orchard of pomegranates with choice fruits, with henna and nard, nard and saffron, cannabis [qaneh][1] and cinnamon, with every kind of incense tree, with myrrh and aloes and all the finest spices. You are a garden fountain, a well of flowing water streaming down from Lebanon.

– Songs 4:1-15

Solomon:
I have come into my garden, my sister, my bride; I have gathered my myrrh with my spice. I have eaten my honeycomb and my honey; I have drunk my wine and my milk. Friends Eat, friends, and drink; drink your fill of love.

– Songs 5:1

The Bride:
My beloved is radiant and ruddy, outstanding among ten thousand. His head is purest gold; his hair is wavy and black as a raven. His eyes are like doves by the water streams, washed in milk, mounted like jewels. His cheeks are like beds of spice yielding perfume. His lips are like lilies dripping with myrrh. His arms are rods of gold set with topaz. His body is like polished ivory decorated with lapis lazuli. His legs are pillars of marble set on bases of pure gold. His appearance is like Lebanon, choice as its cedars. His mouth is sweetness itself; he is altogether lovely. This is my beloved, this is my friend, daughters of Jerusalem.

– Songs 5:10-16

1 Translated "'calamus" in most Biblical texts.

The Bride:
I belong to my beloved, and his desire is for me. Come, my beloved, let us go to the countryside, let us spend the night in the villages. Let us go early to the vineyards to see if the vines have budded, if their blossoms have opened, and if the pomegranates are in bloom - there I will give you my love. The mandrakes send out their fragrance, and at our door is every delicacy, both new and old, that I have stored up for you, my beloved.
– Songs 7:10-13

Mandrake (also mandragora) is a psychoactive plant, it belongs to the belladonna family and has long been used medicinally and ritually as an emetic, narcotic, and antispasmodic; its forked root is said to inspire divination and it appears in many ancient legends. Mandrake played an active role in herbal medicine, magic, and witchcraft from Sumer through medieval times.

The Visit of the Queen of Sheba to King Solomon by Edward Poynter

Sumerian Hieros Gamos Love Poem

This Sumerian hieros gamos love poem is presented here for comparison to the Song of Songs. This is the oldest love poem in the world and the similarity with the Song of Songs is clear; though a thousand years apart, they are written in the same style.

This poem is addressed to the Sumerian king Shu-Sin, ruler of Sumer and Akkad from 1972-1964 BCE, by his beloved "Bride." These poems were read aloud during the sacred marriage ceremonies. It is likely that King Solomon took part in these ceremonies as well, something the Biblical writers would have been loath to admit.

THE LOVE SONG FOR SHU-SIN

Bridegroom, dear to my heart,
Goodly is your beauty, honeysweet,
Lion, dear to my heart,
Goodly is your beauty, honeysweet.

You have captivated me, let me stand tremblingly before you,
Bridegroom, I would be taken by you to the bedchamber,
You have captivated me, let me stand tremblingly before you,
Lion, I would be taken by you to the bedchamber.

Bridegroom, let me caress you,
My precious caress is more savory than honey,
In the bedchamber, honey-filled,
Let me enjoy your goodly beauty,
Lion, let me caress you,
My precious caress is more savory than honey.

Bridegroom, you have taken your pleasure of me,
Tell my mother, she will give you delicacies,
My father, he will give you gifts.

Your spirit, I know where to cheer your spirit,
Bridegroom, sleep in our house until dawn,
Your heart, I know where to gladden your heart,
Lion, sleep in our house until dawn.

You, because you love me,
Give me pray of your caresses,
My lord god, my lord protector,
My Shu-Sin, who gladdens Enlil's heart,
Give me pray of your caresses.

Your place goodly as honey, pray lay (your) hand on it,
Bring (your) hand over like a gishban-garment,
Cup (your) hand over it like a gishban-sikin-garment
It is a balbale-song of Inanna.

– Kramer, *The Sumerians*[2]

2 Kramer, *The Sumerians*, p.254

Chapter Twenty-Nine

QUEEN of SHEBA

Makeda

The Queen of Sheba came to visit King Solomon in a short chapter of the Bible that spawned many legends and traditions. The beautiful Queen had heard of Solomon's great wisdom and wealth and wanted to see for herself. She came bearing fabulous gifts and departed with many of her own. In Ethiopian legend, the King and Queen had a child of noble birth and historic importance. By tradition, the Queen is believed to have come from Ethiopia, though some scholars say the location was more likely Yemen.

> *When the queen of Sheba heard about the fame of Solomon and his relationship to Yahweh, she came to test Solomon with hard questions. Arriving at Jerusalem with a very great caravan - with camels carrying spices, large quantities of gold, and precious stones - she came to Solomon and talked with him about all that she had on her mind. Solomon answered all her questions; nothing was too hard for the king to explain to her.*
>
> *When the queen of Sheba saw all the wisdom of Solomon and the palace he had built, the food on his table, the seating of his officials, the attending servants in their robes, his cupbearers, and the burnt offerings he made at the Temple of Yahweh, she was overwhelmed. She said to the king, "The report I heard in my own country about your achievements and your wisdom is true. But I did not believe these things until I came and saw with my own eyes. Indeed, not even half was told me; in wisdom and wealth you have far exceeded the report I heard. How happy your people must be! How happy your officials, who continually stand before you and hear your wisdom!"...*
>
> *King Solomon gave the queen of Sheba all she desired and asked for, besides what he had given her out of his royal bounty. Then she left and returned with her retinue to her own country.*
>
> 1 Kings 10:1-8; 13

Kebra Nagast

In Ethiopian tradition, the Queen of Sheba is named Makeda. She had a child with King Solomon named Menelik who became king and patriarch of the Solomonic Dynasty of Ethiopia. The *Kebra Nagast*, the "Glory of Kings" is an Ethiopian sacred text written from 1314-1322, but whose origins are centuries earlier.[1] It expounds on many Biblical tales and presents the history of the Solomonic dynasty.

The Kebra Nagast tells the full story of the Queen of Sheba and King Solomon. It also tells how their son Menelik took the Ark of the Covenant with him back to Ethiopia where it still resides today. By tradition, the Ark of the Covenant is said to reside in a small chapel in the Ethiopian town of Axum under the careful watch of a single priest who will remain on duty until he dies.

Menelik

When Menelik was 22 years old he traveled to Jerusalem from Ethiopia to meet his father for the first time. As Menelik approached Jerusalem, the people who saw him were amazed at his resemblance to King Solomon. The people became excited and Solomon soon learned of the regal visitor making his way to the palace. When the king first saw Menelik, he knew immediately that the visitor was his son and embraced him warmly. No proof was required as their features and manner were so similar. Menelik displayed great bearing and wisdom even as a young man.

King Solomon brought Menelik into his chambers and arrayed him in gorgeous apparel and gave him a belt of gold and a crown. Solomon presented Menelik to all the nobles, who accepted him and gave him presents. Solomon wanted Menelik to remain in Jerusalem and succeed him as king, but Menelik was anxious to return to Ethiopia and be king there. Makeda had her son make a sacred vow that he would return home soon. Menelik knew that his half-brother Rehoboam had claim to the throne in Jerusalem and would be a rival. Rehoboam was six years older and born to Solomon's wife, while Makeda and Solomon were never married.

King Solomon was aware that Rehoboam lacked wisdom and would be a poor king. Solomon begged Menelik to stay, he offered him the kingdom and many wives and concubines, but Menelik would not be swayed. Menelik had sworn on his mother's breast that he would return home soon and not marry a woman in Israel. To swear by a woman's breast was a serious matter.

1 *The Queen of Sheba and Her Only Son Menyelek (Kebra Nagast)* translated by Sir E.A. Wallis Budge, Cambridge, Ontario, 2000.

Solomonic Dynasty

Solomon saw that it was impossible to keep Menelik in Jerusalem. So the king declared his intention to send the eldest sons of the nobles to Ethiopia, to found a new colony of Hebrews. Zadok the priest anointed Menelik King of Ethiopia inside the Holy of Holies, drenching him with the sacred cannabis oil. Menelik took the Hebrew name, David II, after his grandfather.

Not everyone was happy to leave Jerusalem, for the Ark of the Covenant contained the laws of God and brought good fortune to Israel. Some of the men suggested that they secretly take the Ark with them. Some versions of the story say that Menelik knew of the plan, other versions say he did not.

A wooden box was fashioned that was a replica of the Ark, which was always kept covered under a sacred cloth. The men were not being completely selfish for they knew that the Kingdom was not stable. Solomon was getting old and many enemies were rising against him.

Ark of the Covenant

Menelik's men were able to sneak the Ark of the Covenant out of the Temple because Yahweh wanted the Ark moved. The Ark was loaded onto a wagon and covered over with baggage. Menelik received Solomon's blessings and said farewell. As the caravan left Jerusalem, the men and women wailed and the animals howled. King Solomon and his people knew instinctively that the glory of Israel had departed with the caravan.

As Menelik traveled, the caravan was led by the Archangel Michael, who cut a path and sheltered them from the heat. Neither man nor beast touched the ground with their feet, they were carried aloft with the speed of an eagle. The caravan traveled in one day a distance that normally took thirteen.

It was revealed to the entire company that they were in possession of the Ark of the Covenant. They all let out a great cheer and Menelik vowed to establish the second Kingdom of God in Ethiopia. King Menelik ruled honorably and fathered the Solomonic Dynasty. The Ark of the Covenant has remained in Ethiopia until this day, 3000 years later.

When Zadok the priest discovered the Ark missing, he fainted on the spot. Solomon led his men in pursuit of the caravan, but it was too late. The king returned to Jerusalem and wept bitterly. King Solomon knew that the Ark of the Covenant could not have been carried off without Yahweh's support, for the Ark is powerful and able to take care of itself.

Previous usurpers had all been destroyed. Satisfied that the will of God is irresistible, Solomon and the priests vowed to keep the disappearance of the Ark a secret. They allowed the duplicate box to remain in place, covered with cloth, lest enemies try to take advantage of their misfortune.

After King Solomon died, Jeroboam led the ten tribes who formed the northern kingdom of Israel into open rebellion against Judah. The nation split in two, never to be rejoined until modern times. Pharaoh Shishak of Egypt then attacked Judah and plundered the temple, taking away everything, so it was good that the Ark of the Covenant had already been moved.

> *In the fifth year of King Rehoboam, Shishak king of Egypt attacked Jerusalem. He carried off the treasures of the temple of Yahweh and the treasures of the royal palace. He took everything, including all the gold shields Solomon had made.*
>
> 1 Kings 14:25-26

ETHIOPIA

Ethiopia is the birthplace of humanity, the oldest human skeletons were found there and it is where the migrations out of Africa originated. There are many important spiritual traditions in Ethiopia. To this day, Ethiopia has maintained the oldest continuous traditions of Judaism and Christianity. The country played an important role in the foundation of Islam and was an inspiration to the modern Rastafarians.

Beta Israel is an ancient tribe of Ethiopian Jews who live in Ethiopia and neighboring Eritrea. Beta Israel traces their heritage directly back to King Menelik. The Black Jews are the keepers of the Ark of the Covenant and the Kebra Nagast is one of their sacred texts. The Ark of the Covenant is kept in a small chapel in the town of Axum (Aksum) where only a single priest, appointed for life, is allowed to see it.

Ethiopian Coptic Christians trace their roots back to the first century CE and the evangelizing of the Apostle Matthew who was one of the original 12 disciples of Jesus. Coptic traditions are as old as the Catholic Church and they traditionally depict Jesus as black.

Prophet Mohammed

The Prophet Mohammed also visited Ethiopia in the early days of Islam to escape persecution and was given sanctuary. In thankfulness and respect for his hosts, Mohammed dictated in the Koran that jihad, holy war, should never be conducted in Ethiopia. When all the neighboring countries became thoroughly Islamic, Ethiopia was spared. The native Ethiopian Jewish and Christian traditions were permitted to co-exist alongside Islam, an arrangement that has persisted to this day.

Emperor Haile Selassie

Modern Ethiopians trace their royal lineage back 3000 years, from King Solomon, Makeda, and Menelik all the way to their last emperor in the 20th century, Haile Selassie. Emperor Haile Selassie had a long career and was a major figure in international politics. Selassie successfully resisted European colonialism and fought an important war against fascist Italy in the 1930s.

Haile Selassie was the last, and only true African royalty, during an era of rising African Black pride. Haile Selassie was hailed by Africans the world over who were struggling to reclaim their identity after centuries of slavery and oppression. The Emperor helped to found the League of Nations and the United Nations, where he represented the voices of the colonized Africans. Sadly, Haile Selassie was deposed and murdered by Marxist insurgents in 1975 under circumstances that remain disputed.

The Emperor's official title utilizes the Lion of Judah motif:

By the Conquering Lion of the Tribe of Judah, His Imperial Majesty Haile Selassie I, King of Kings of Ethiopia, Elect of God.

Rastafarians

Haile Selassie was deified as a Christ figure by the Rastafarian faith from the Caribbean island nation of Jamaica. Haile Selassie never claimed divinity for himself and was mystified by the fervent adoration. The Rastafarians are formally recognized internationally as a modern-day religion.

The most famous Rastafarian is the Reggae musician and mystical prophet Bob Marley, who became an international musical superstar in the 1970s. Bob Marley sang many songs of praise for "Jah Rastafari!" *Jah* is their name for God, and *Ras Tafari* was a title for the Emperor.

Bob Marley adapted one of Haile Selassie's speeches at the U.N. into an iconic song of protest and righteous indignation at the racist policies of the European and American colonial powers. This message provides a standard for a post-racial society, "when the color of a man's skin is of no more significance than the color of his eyes."

WAR

Until the philosophy which holds one race superior and another inferior is finally and permanently discredited and abandoned. Everywhere is war.

That until there's no longer first-class and second-class citizens of any nation.

Until the color of a man's skin is of no more significance than the color of his eyes. Me say war.

That until the basic human rights are equally guaranteed to all, without regard to race. Dis a war.

That until that day, the dream of lasting peace, world citizenship, and rule of international morality will remain but a fleeting illusion to be pursued, but never attained.

Now everywhere is war. War.

– Bob Marley, *War,* words by Haile Selassie

Ganja

The Rastafarians are well known for their ritual use of cannabis, which they call *ganja,* despite its prohibition and the risk of arrest by law enforcement. The Rastafarians trace their cannabis use back to King Solomon, who burned ganja in the Temple in Jerusalem. The Rastafarians are very health-conscious people who emphasize natural diets, clean living, family, and community. They reject hard drugs and alcohol but consume cannabis daily. They call ganja, "the Lamb's Bread," and value it for its medicinal and spiritual qualities. The Rastafarians believe that cannabis grows on King Solomon's grave.

Emancipate yourself from mental slavery, none but ourselves can free our minds.

– Bob Marley

Chapter Thirty

KINGDOM DIVIDED

King Solomon's Failure

As King Solomon grew old the kingdom of Israel weakened, trouble mounted, and enemies began to rise. King Solomon had forced many people into slavery, and their hearts burned against him. King Hiram of Tyre had been disappointed with the twenty towns in Galilee that Solomon had given in payment for cedar, juniper, and gold (1 Kings 9:11-12) indicating a loss of wealth. The new Pharaoh in Egypt was no friend, in Edom there was unrest that threatened the Red Sea port of Ezion-Geber, and in Syria, the Aramites had caused Solomon trouble throughout his life. But the most problematic uprising for Solomon and the united kingdom was led by Jeroboam, who had been one of Solomon's officials.

> *Solomon tried to kill Jeroboam, but Jeroboam fled to Egypt, to Shishak the king, and stayed there until Solomon's death.*
>
> – 1 Kings 11:40

Jeroboam's Rebellion

The Biblical writers say in 1 Kings 11 that Jeroboam rebelled against the king after a prophet told him that Yahweh was angry with Solomon for worshipping Astarte and other foreign gods. Because of Solomon's sins, Yahweh was going to give ten of the twelve Israelite tribes to Jeroboam, while the tribes of Judah and Benjamin would remain with the king in Jerusalem.

Yet the story makes clear that the root cause of Jeroboam's rebellion was not Solomon's paganism, but his mistreatment of the slaves and laborers. Jeroboam was a labor leader and a pagan just like Solomon. The northern kingdom of Israel Jeroboam founded was pagan throughout its entire history.

> *Solomon reigned in Jerusalem over all Israel forty years. Then he rested with his ancestors and was buried in the city of David his father. And Rehoboam his son succeeded him as king.*
>
> – 1 Kings 11:42-43

Wicked Rehoboam

The new King Rehoboam was young and arrogant, not wise like his father. The rebel Jeroboam returned from Egypt and went with a council to visit the king. Jeroboam said, "your father put a heavy yoke on us, but now lighten the harsh labor and the heavy yoke he put on us, and we will serve you" (1 Kings 12).

Rehoboam sought counsel from the elders, they recommended that the King give a favorable response, and then the people would be loyal to him. But Rehoboam ignored their advice, he asked his young friends what they thought. The King's friends advised him to say, "my father laid on you a heavy yoke; I will make it even heavier. My father scourged you with whips; I will scourge you with scorpions."

The King answered the people harshly, ignoring the sage advice of the elders. When the people of Israel heard the King's response, they returned home and revolted. Rehoboam sent out his man in charge of forced labor, but the Israelites stoned him to death. The King narrowly escaped in his chariot. Israel and Judah prepared for war. Ten tribes followed Jeroboam as King of Israel, while the tribes of Judah and Benjamin followed King Rehoboam in Jerusalem.

Pagan Israel

Jeroboam consolidated his power in the north. In order to discourage the people from worshipping at the Temple in Jerusalem, the King made two golden bulls, one in the town of Bethel and the other in Dan. King Jeroboam built shrines on the high places and appointed priests from among all the people.

The northern kingdom of Israel was pagan throughout its entire 210-year history. It was in conflict with Judah most of the time until Israel was overrun by the Assyrians in 721 BCE. Israel never returned to the pure worship of Yahweh alone. Not one king of Israel is celebrated by the Biblical writers, every single one of them is considered to be bad. The golden bulls remained standing and a towering Asherah pole was erected in the capital city of Samaria.

Pagan Judah

In Judah, Rehoboam also continued worshipping in the pagan ways. They worshipped nature in the sacred groves, continued their sexual culture, and even had male qadesh along with the qedeshas in Solomon's temple.

> *They also set up for themselves high places, sacred stones and Asherah poles on every high hill and under every spreading tree. There were even male qadesh in the land; the people engaged in all the detestable practices of the nations Yahweh had driven out before the Israelites.*
>
> – 1 Kings 14:23-24

Yahweh had many followers in Judah and the Yahwists were a potent political force, but they were a minority. Most of the people worshipped in the traditional pagan ways. Pharaoh Shishak of Egypt attacked Judah and robbed the Temple of its treasures in Rehoboam's fifth year. After that defeat, Yahweh's temple lost much of its glory and importance.

Queen Mother Maacah

Rehoboam's wife was Maacah, and she was Queen Mother when her grandson Asa ascended the throne. Asa had a long rule of 41 years and was one of the few kings of Judah who was a Yahwist reformer. Asa deposed Maacah because she had made an Asherah pole. Asa cut the sacred pole down and burned it. The king eliminated the male qadesh from the temple, but not the female. The priestesses would prove to be difficult opponents for the Yahwists, and despite the reforms, the high places remained.

This one of those biblical details where one must read between the lines. The writers state that the male qadesh were removed, (possibly the transgendered priests), but they make no mention of the female qedesha. This detail tells us that the priestesses remained in place, otherwise, the writers would have said so.

> *Asa did what was right in the eyes of Yahweh, as his father David had done. He expelled the male qadesh from the land and got rid of all the idols his ancestors had made. He even deposed his grandmother Maakah from her position as queen mother, because she had made a repulsive image for the worship of Asherah. Asa cut it down and burned it in the Kidron Valley. Although he did not remove the high places, Asa's heart was fully committed to Yahweh all his life.*
>
> – 1 Kings 15:11-14

Death of Jezebel

Chapter Thirty-One

QUEEN JEZEBEL

Pagan Queen of Israel

In Israel, there was a series of coups and assassinations, with every new ruler slaughtering the entire families of their predecessors. Omri became king of Israel in 884 BCE and established the new city of Samaria as his capital. Omri is one of the oldest biblical figures whose existence has been documented by archaeologists.

King Ahab followed his father Omri. Ahab had a notorious wife, Queen Jezebel. Ahab inspired more anger in the biblical writers than any other king of Israel, and Jezebel is arguably the most detested woman in the Bible.

> *He set up an altar for Baal in the temple of Baal that he built in Samaria. Ahab also made an Asherah pole and did more to arouse the anger of Yahweh, the God of Israel, than did all the kings of Israel before him.*
>
> – 1 Kings 16:32-33

Jezebel was a Phoenician princess from Sidon, daughter of Ethbaal, the king of Tyre and Sidon. Ethbaal is a known historical figure, he had been a high priest of Astarte who assassinated the previous king to take the Phoenician throne. The royal marriage between Jezebel and Ahab sealed a strong alliance between Phoenicia and Israel. Meanwhile, Phoenician relations with the Yahwists in Judah were poor.

Yahwists and Baalists

Ahab and Jezebel built a new temple to Baal in Samaria with 450 prophets, along with a grand Asherah pole for the capital city. In Jezreel, they built a palace for themselves, and a temple to the Mother Goddess Asherah with 400 prophets and Jezebel as their personal patron.

Queen Jezebel was a passionate defender of the traditional religion, she was raised in the temple of Astarte and was the leader of the temple of Asherah in Israel. There was a conflict in Israel between the Yahwists and the Baalists. Queen Jezebel led a campaign to eliminate the Yahwists who she saw as dangerous insurgents.

Elijah was a prophet of Yahweh in Israel, and the chief opponent of Ahab and Jezebel. There were also Yahwists in the royal court – Obadiah was a palace administrator who secretly helped Elijah's Order, the "Sons of the Prophet." Obadiah helped the Order escape Jezebel's persecution by hiding them in caves with food and water.

Vineyard at Jezreel

A couple of years later there was an incident in Jezreel that would normally have been a minor dispute but escalated politically. At least according to the Biblical writers who absolutely despised Jezebel and sought to make her look bad at all times. There was a vineyard close to the palace that Ahab desired to add to his gardens, but the owner refused to sell to the king, as the land was his inheritance. Ahab was sullen and depressed by his inability to achieve his desires.

According to the biblical tale, when Queen Jezebel learned the source of her husband's melancholy, she laughed. "Is this how a King of Israel acts? Cheer up. I'll get you the vineyard."

Jezebel arranged for the vineyard owner to be falsely accused of blasphemy and stoned to death, allowing Ahab to seize the land. Many scholars have pointed out that it was unlikely that Jezebel could have acted alone without Ahab and the other leaders' knowledge.

The treachery did not go unnoticed. Elijah confronted Ahab, telling the King that "I will bring disaster upon you and wipe out your house." Elijah predicted doom for Jezebel as well.

> *"Dogs will devour Jezebel by the wall of Jezreel."*
>
> – 1 Kings 21:23

ELIJAH ON MOUNT CARMEL

Contest of Prophets

There was a drought and severe famine in the land, the people were suffering from lack of rain and food. One day Elijah confronted Ahab directly, castigating the King for worshipping Baal. Elijah challenged Ahab to a contest of prophets.

> *"Now summon the people from all over Israel to meet me on Mount Carmel. And bring the four hundred and fifty prophets of Baal and the four hundred prophets of Asherah, who eat at Jezebel's table."*
>
> – 1 Kings 18:19

A great crowd gathered on Mount Carmel to see the battle between Elijah and the prophets of Baal. Elijah challenged the people to choose between Yahweh and Baal – they could not worship both.

Then Elijah said to them, "I am the only one of Yahweh prophets left, but Baal has four hundred and fifty prophets. Get two bulls for us. Let Baal's prophets choose one for themselves, and let them cut it into pieces and put it on the wood but not set fire to it. I will prepare the other bull and put it on the wood but not set fire to it. Then you call on the name of your god, and I will call on the name of Yahweh. The god who answers by fire – he is God."

Then all the people said, "What you say is good."

Elijah said to the prophets of Baal, "Choose one of the bulls and prepare it first, since there are so many of you. Call on the name of your god, but do not light the fire." So they took the bull given them and prepared it. Then they called on the name of Baal from morning till noon. "Baal, answer us!" they shouted. But there was no response; no one answered. And they danced around the altar they had made.

At noon Elijah began to taunt them. "Shout louder!" he said. "Surely he is a god! Perhaps he is deep in thought, or busy, or traveling. Maybe he is sleeping and must be awakened." So they shouted louder and slashed themselves with swords and spears, as was their custom, until their blood flowed. Midday passed, and they continued their frantic prophesying until the time for the evening sacrifice. But there was no response, no one answered, no one paid attention.

Then Elijah said to all the people, "Come here to me." They came to him, and he repaired the altar of Yahweh, which had been torn down.

Elijah took twelve stones, one for each of the tribes descended from Jacob, to whom the word of Yahweh had come, saying, "Your name shall be Israel." With the stones he built an altar in the name of Yahweh, and he dug a trench around it large enough to hold two seahs of seed.

He arranged the wood, cut the bull into pieces and laid it on the wood. Then he said to them, "Fill four large jars with water and pour it on the offering and on the wood."

"Do it again," he said, and they did it again. "Do it a third time," he ordered, and they did it the third time. The water ran down around the altar and even filled the trench.

At the time of sacrifice, the prophet Elijah stepped forward and prayed: "Yahweh, the God of Abraham, Isaac and Israel, let it be known today that you are God in Israel and that I am your servant and have done all these things at your command. Answer me, Yahweh, answer me, so these people will know that you, Yahweh, are God, and that you are turning their hearts back again."

Then the fire of Yahweh fell and burned up the sacrifice, the wood, the stones and the soil, and also licked up the water in the trench.

When all the people saw this, they fell prostrate and cried, "Yahweh – he is God! Yahweh – he is God!"

Then Elijah commanded them, "Seize the prophets of Baal. Don't let anyone get away!" They seized them, and Elijah had them brought down to the Kishon Valley and slaughtered there.

– 1 Kings 18:22-40

Revealing Details

There are many revealing details in this famous story. We see the nature of Canaanite worship practices, the priests of Baal pray, shout, do ecstatic ritual dance, and flagellate themselves until they bleed. Though these practices may seem primitive to the modern mind, they still occur today in some religions.

The Baalists' prayers go unanswered, their bull remains unburned atop the altar. Elijah mocks them, "perhaps Baal is taking a nap!" But Elijah never confronts the prophets of Asherah, the goddess was too highly respected to be attacked directly.

Elijah's Magic Trick

After Baal failed to arrive and burn their bull, Elijah then stepped forward with his show, and he had a trick up his sleeve. Elijah had chosen the location on Mt. Carmel strategically for there was an old burned altar to Yahweh there that had been torn down. Biblical altars from this era were commonly made from limestone and when limestone is burned it changes chemically and becomes quicklime, calcium oxide, a common chemical.

Elijah arranged his altar all by himself, including cutting up his own meat and getting it ready. It is not mentioned in the text, but Elijah likely salted the meat and the altar with powdered sulfur. Then Elijah proceeded to drench his meat with four large jars of water, a very strange thing to do when trying to light a fire. This is because it was probably not water, but naphtha, or a naphtha and water blend.

Naphtha

Naphtha is a clear distillate of petroleum used for fuel, it was known as "thick water" in the ancient world and came from Persia. The combination of naphtha, sulfur, and quicklime creates a violent fiery reaction that perfectly matches the description of Elijah's fire. A variation of this recipe was used as an incendiary weapon in ancient times called "Greek Fire" that was devastating in naval battles. Another Biblical mention of naphtha comes from the Apocryphal book of Maccabees.

> *After the materials of the sacrifice had been consumed, Nehemiah ordered that the liquid that was left should be poured on large stones. When this was done, a flame blazed up; but when the light from the altar shone back, it went out. When this matter became known, and it was reported to the king of the Persians that, in the place where the exiled priests had hidden the fire, the liquid had appeared with which Nehemiah and his associates had burned the materials of the sacrifice, the king investigated the matter, and enclosed the place and made it sacred. And with those persons whom the king favored he exchanged many excellent gifts. Nehemiah and his associates called this 'nephthar', which means purification, but by most people it is called naphtha.*
>
> – 2 Maccabees 1:31-36 (Apocrypha)

Elijah was very clever, he challenged the prophets of Baal to a contest that he knew they would lose because he was utilizing a magician's trick. Advanced science and technology always appear like magic, or a miracle of God, to those who do not understand how it works. Elijah exploited the Baalists' superstitions and ignorance and blinded them with science.

Slaughter Them All

After winning the contest, Elijah had the crowd seize the 450 prophets of Baal and they slaughtered them all. Yahweh praised Elijah for his murders – Yahweh is an intolerant, jealous god. Elijah conspicuously does not have the prophets of Asherah killed. There are multiple instances in the Hebrew Bible when the temples to Baal and his followers are killed by the Yahwists, but the Yahwists almost never touch the goddess temples or the qedesha priestesses. The Triple Goddess was the true rival to Yahweh.

After the killing of the prophets of Baal, the sky grew dark with clouds, the wind rose, and heavy rain started to fall for the first time in a long while. King Ahab rode back to Jezreel and Elijah went also. Ahab told Jezebel everything that had happened, and how the prophets of Baal had all been killed by the sword.

Jezebel was furious and enraged; she sent a threatening letter to Elijah. "May the gods punish me severely if by this time tomorrow I do not make your life like one of them." Elijah was afraid for his life and fled into the desert.

One can imagine Jezebel invoking the goddess Anat to bring forth her vengeance and slaughter Elijah along with all the prophets of Yahweh.

ASSASINATION OF JEZEBEL

Jehosophat

Jehosophat, the son of Asa became king in Judah. Jehosophat is a curious character – he was a Yahwist who continued the reformist work of his father Asa, and was praised by the Biblical writers for bringing peace and stability to Judah. But Jehosophat was also an ally of Ahab and Jezebel, the Biblical writer's greatest enemies.

> *He rid the land of the rest of the male qadesh who remained there even after the reign of his father Asa.*
>
> – 1 Kings 22:46

As with the other kings before him, Jehosophat had difficulty in removing the goddesses and the female qedesha. The gender-bending male qadesh were easier targets for removal.

Alliance of Israel and Judah

Israel and Judah were joined in a royal marriage between Athalia, the daughter of Ahab and Jezebel, and Jehoram, the prince of Judah. Athalia would eventually become the only woman to ever rule in Jerusalem as a solo Queen.

The Kings Ahab and Jehosophat rode into battle together in Syria. King Ahab was disguised as a common soldier but was killed nonetheless by a random arrow that struck between the plates of his armor. Ahab was buried in Samaria, his son Ahaziah succeeded him as king. The war in Syria lasted a long time.

Ahaziah was a pagan king in Israel who made his mother Jezebel proud; the Biblical writers heap scorn upon him. Ahaziah did not rule long though, he was injured in a fall and died from his injuries, but not before the prophet Elijah denounced him.

Joram became the new king of Israel, while Jehoram became the new king of Judah, succeeding Jehosophat who died after a long, successful reign. Israel and Judah remained allies and Jezebel remained Queen Mother in Israel. Jehoram of Judah was a pagan king who was married to Athalia. Elijah cursed Jehoram with a lingering disease of the bowels, and in his second year his bowels came out and he died in great pain.

PROPHET ELISHA

Yahweh came to Elijah in the desert and gave him instructions to anoint Jehu as the new king of Israel. Jehu was a commander of Israel's soldiers fighting in Syria.

Elijah died of old age and was replaced by his chosen successor Elisha. Elisha did not take kindly to being teased.

> *From there Elisha went up to Bethel. As he was walking along the road, some boys came out of the town and jeered at him. "Get out of here, baldy!" they said. "Get out of here, baldy!"*
>
> *He turned around, looked at them and called down a curse on them in the name of Yahweh. Then two bears came out of the woods and mauled forty-two of the boys.*
>
> – 2 Kings 2:23-24

KING IN HEMP SACKCLOTH

The Syrians laid siege to Samaria and a great famine overtook the city. The king of Israel was greatly distressed, he wore hemp sackcloth under his royal robes. As he was inspecting the walls, the king heard the cries of the people, who had taken to cannibalism to survive.

Then [the King] asked her, "What's the matter?" She answered, "This woman said to me, 'Give up your son so we may eat him today, and tomorrow we'll eat my son. 'So we cooked my son and ate him. The next day I said to her, 'Give up your son so we may eat him,' but she had hidden him."

When the king heard the woman's words, he tore his robes. As he went along the wall, the people looked, and they saw that, under his robes, he had sackcloth on his body.

– 2 Kings 6:28-30

The Syrians departed before taking the city and Israel survived the day. In Judah, a new pagan king came to the throne, Ahaziah, the son of Athalia, who remained Queen Mother in Jerusalem. The two pagan kings of Israel and Judah went to war together in Syria.

King Joram of Israel was wounded in the battle and returned to Jezreel to recover from his wounds. King Ahaziah went to visit his friend in Jezreel. It was a fateful decision.

Jehu's Coup

The prophet Elisha set in motion a coup in Israel. He sent one of his men to the battlefield in Syria where the Israeli commanders could be found. The prophet was told to find the commander Jehu, pull him aside and secretly anoint him King of Israel, and then run away fast. The young prophet told Jehu:

You are to destroy the house of Ahab your master, and I will avenge the blood of my servants the prophets and the blood of all Yahweh's servants shed by Jezebel.

– 2 Kings 9:7

When Jehu went out to his fellow officers, one of them asked him, "Is everything all right? Why did this maniac come to you?"

"You know the man and the sort of things he says," Jehu replied.

"That's not true!" they said. "Tell us."

Jehu said, "Here is what he told me: 'This is what Yahweh says: I anoint you king over Israel.'"

They quickly took their cloaks and spread them under him on the bare steps. Then they blew the trumpet and shouted, "Jehu is king!"

– 2 Kings 9:11-13

Jehu immediately rode fast for Jezreel before word got out of his treachery. As he approached the palace with his troops, the guards asked him if he came in peace, but Jehu told them to fall in line behind him, which they did. The king rode out to meet Jehu himself; they met by the vineyard that Jezebel and Ahab had seized.

> *When Joram saw Jehu he asked, "Have you come in peace, Jehu?"*
>
> *"How can there be peace," Jehu replied, "as long as all the idolatry and witchcraft of your mother Jezebel abound?"*
>
> *Joram turned about and fled, calling out to Ahaziah, "Treachery, Ahaziah!"*
>
> *Then Jehu drew his bow and shot Joram between the shoulders. The arrow pierced his heart and he slumped down in his chariot.*
>
> – 2 Kings 9:22-24

Death of Ahab

Defenestration of the Queen

The king of Judah attempted to flee in his chariot but was wounded. He made it as far as Megiddo where he also died. Jehu then proceeded to perform one of the most famous assassinations of all time, the defenestration of the pagan Queen of Israel.

> *Then Jehu went to Jezreel. When Jezebel heard about it, she put on eye makeup, arranged her hair and looked out of a window. As Jehu entered the gate, she asked, "Have you come in peace, you Zimri, you murderer of your master?"*
>
> *He looked up at the window and called out, "Who is on my side? Who?" Two or three eunuchs looked down at him. "Throw her down!" Jehu said. So they threw her down, and some of her blood spattered the wall and the horses as they trampled her underfoot.*
>
> *Jehu went in and ate and drank. "Take care of that cursed woman," he said, "and bury her, for she was a king's daughter." But when they went out to bury her, they found nothing except her skull, her feet and her hands.*
>
> – 2 Kings 9:30-35

Jezebel has been reviled for centuries. From the Biblical perspective, Jezebel is the quintessentially evil woman who dominates her weak husband and compels him to perform heinous acts. She faced her death with composure by taking the time to put on makeup and adorn herself. This has been portrayed as the ultimate act of haughty pride before her deserved fall. From her perspective, Jezebel chose to face her treacherous assassins as a Queen, regal and proud. She had always remained true to her gods and goddesses and would meet her fate with dignity.

Jezebel was thrown from a window, a highly symbolic representation of her fall. Jezebel's blood splattered on the wall and sidewalk, and her body was desecrated by animals, leaving nothing to bury but her skull, hands, and feet. These details are likely a literary embellishment that shows the complete disdain the Biblical writers had for the proud pagan Queen.

It is an interesting detail to note that Jezebel was thrown down by eunuchs. The Biblical writers did not approve of eunuchs, but transgenders were celebrated in the goddess temples, so this detail may have been included to also slander eunuchs as untrustworthy.

Jehu's Treachery

Jehu proceeded to go on a killing campaign to consolidate his control of the throne. He had the heads taken of 70 princes who were the leading men of Samaria. They also captured a caravan of 42 royal visitors from Judah who had not heard about the coup and slaughtered them all. Jehu went to Samaria and killed everyone who was a friend or relative of the royal family. He then performed a truly sacrilegious murder.

Jehu gathered all the priests and servants of Baal and ordered them to the temple. The new king was going to offer a great sacrifice to the god. Jehu sent word throughout Israel that everyone must gather for an Assembly of Honor for Baal. No one stayed away, the temple was crowded from one end to the other. In treachery, Jehu had assembled 80 soldiers outside the temple.

> *As soon as Jehu had finished making the burnt offering, he ordered the guards and officers: "Go in and kill them; let no one escape." So they cut them down with the sword. The guards and officers threw the bodies out and then entered the inner shrine of the temple of Baal. They brought the sacred stone out of the temple of Baal and burned it. They demolished the sacred stone of Baal and tore down the temple of Baal, and people have used it for a latrine to this day.*
>
> *So Jehu destroyed Baal worship in Israel. However, he did not turn away from the sins of Jeroboam son of Nebat, which he had caused Israel to commit - the worship of the golden calves at Bethel and Dan.*
>
> – 2 Kings 10:25-29

Jehu destroyed the temple of Baal, he desecrated the shrines, smashed the idols, and turned the temple into a latrine. Jehu killed the priests and worshippers, yet he did not go all the way to Yahweh – the golden bulls in Bethel and Dan remained, and the goddesses went untouched.

Once again we see the Yahwists defeating Baal while being powerless against the goddesses. The Asherah pole continued to stand in Samaria and Astarte remained the Queen of Heaven, the most popular deity in the land. Jehu's family would rule Israel for four generations.

ATHALIA

Queen of Judah

Scripture says that when Athalia, Queen Mother of Judah, heard that her son was dead she immediately killed the entire royal family to secure her own claim to the throne. Tough lady. Athalia became the Queen of Judah, the only woman to ever rule solo from Jerusalem. Athalia held the throne for six years and was disliked by the biblical writers nearly as much as her mother, and she met a similar fate.

There was one prince who survived the purge. The infant Joash was one-year-old and he was hidden away from Athalia. Six years later, a priest named Jehoiada plotted a coup. He gathered a company of soldiers to take positions around the temple and the city gates.

> *Jehoiada brought out the king's son and put the crown on him; he presented him with a copy of the covenant and proclaimed him king. They anointed him, and the people clapped their hands and shouted, "Long live the king!"*
>
> *When Athaliah heard the noise made by the guards and the people, she went to the people at the temple of Yahweh. She looked and there was the king, standing by the pillar, as the custom was. The officers and the trumpeters were beside the king, and all the people of the land were rejoicing and blowing trumpets. Then Athaliah tore her robes and called out, "Treason! Treason!"*
>
> *Jehoiada the priest ordered the commanders of units of a hundred, who were in charge of the troops: "Bring her out between the ranks and put to the sword anyone who follows her." For the priest had said, "She must not be put to death in the temple of Yahweh."*
>
> *So they seized her as she reached the place where the horses enter the palace grounds, and there she was put to death.*
>
> – 2 Kings 11:12-16

Death of Athallia

Baal's Idol Smashed

Jehoiada led the people to the temple of Baal and they tore it down. They smashed the sacred stones and the altars and killed the priests. But once again, the temples to the goddesses went unmolested.

Joash became king when he was seven years old and ruled 40 years. For the first few years, Jehoiada the priest was in charge and there were restorations to Yahweh's temple, though the high places remained, and the people continued to worship in the traditional ways.

After Jehoiada died, Joash restored pagan worship to the royal court and prayed to Asherah. Joash was eventually assassinated by his own officials and replaced by his son. Judah then went through a series of kings over the next century who vacillated between Yahweh and the traditional pagan worship. They also fought a series of wars with Israel.

Chapter Thirty-Two

ASSYRIANS

Neo-Assyrian Empire

The Neo-Assyrian Empire rose in Mesopotamia after the Bronze Age Collapse. For three centuries, from 912-612 BCE, it was the most powerful empire the world had ever seen. The Assyrians had highly effective leadership and bureaucracy that was a model for later empires; they were the first to mass-produce iron weapons that were superior to bronze, they had advanced military tactics, disciplined professional troops, and magnificent siege machines that were the pride of the empire, engineered for breaching the mightiest walled cities. The Assyrians had a reputation in their time for great cruelty, though they would prove no worse than Alexander the Great or the Romans who came later.

The Assyrians controlled the major trade routes and dominated the surrounding states in Babylonia, western Persia, Anatolia, the Levant, and their territory extended eventually to include Egypt. The Assyrians played decisive roles in the history of both Israel and Judah and they appear often in the Bible. This period of history in the Ancient Near East is well understood by historians and archaeologists and events portrayed in the Bible were documented in the records of neighboring cultures. The Hebrews appear in the records of the Assyrians and we can see both sides of their conflicts.

Shalmaneser III (859-824 BCE) expanded the empire along the Mediterranean coast, he received tribute from the wealthy Phoenician cities of Tyre and Sidon at the time Ahab and Jezebel ruled Israel. Assyrian records show their successor King Jehu submitting and paying tribute to Shalmaneser III.[1] Israel occupied important trade routes and was a strategic location for the Assyrians in their efforts to dominate the entire Mediterranean coast.

Semiramis

Assyrian women were not allowed to attend school or hold positions of authority, even though in earlier periods of Mesopotamian his-

1 Panel A2 of the Black Obelisk (British Museum, ME 118885) showing Jehu king of Israel, who is designated as m*la-ú-a DUMU mHu-um-ri*'Jehu descendant of Omri', submitting to Shalmaneser III of Assyria (858-824 BC).

tory women had enjoyed almost equal rights. This trend is a reflection of centuries of constant warfare and strongman leadership all over that reduced women to war prizes, whose role in society was to tend to men's needs and take care of the home and children.

There was one famous exception to the rule of repressed Assyrian women. Semiramis was a legendary Queen who ruled Assyria and Babylon after the death of her husband, and maintained her power for decades after her young son ascended to the throne. The legends were based on the historical Queen Sammu-Ramat, the Queen Regent who ruled solo 811-806 BCE, and continued alongside her son Adad-Nirari III, whose rule lasted until 783 BCE.

Semiramis was an impressive figure in the ancient world, she led military campaigns and achieved great victories, helping to stabilize and expand the Assyrian empire at a sensitive time in its history. Semiramis was remembered by the Greeks centuries later who mythologized her in their histories. In many stories, Semiramis was an armed Amazon warrior queen.

The Two Babylons

The legend of Semiramis has been misappropriated by modern fundamentalist Christians who created a false history of her as a pagan goddess. Alexander Hislop in his 1858 CE book, *The Two Babylons*, misidentified Semiramis as the Whore of Babylon and Queen of Heaven, the arch-enemy of the good, and the founder of all pagan religions. She was said to be the wife of Nimrod from the Bible, and the mother of Tammuz in a pagan trinity.

This story has no basis in history but is popular in some contemporary evangelical Christian faiths. These three disparate characters were plucked from different legends and myths and were never originally in the same stories. Nimrod is the grandson of Noah in the Bible, with no mention of a wife. Tammuz was the husband of Ishtar, a dying and rising god, not a baby, while Semiramis was a historical Assyrian Queen.

Supreme God Ashur

The Assyrians practiced a form of monolatry that approached monotheism, they insisted their god Ashur was the supreme god of the universe, and while they did not ban other gods, they did view them all as manifestations of the supreme God Ashur. In this way, the Assyrians could bring political-religious consistency to the empire while avoiding the toxic social conflict that comes with forcibly banning competing temples. Assyrian military dominance was taken as self-evident proof of the superiority of Ashur over all other gods, and government propaganda proclaimed the message.

Assyrian religion also reflected the philosophical trends of the Axial Age leading people towards higher, more abstract concepts of God as displayed in diverse religions like Hebrew monotheism, Zoroastrianism, Chinese Taoism, Confucianism, and aspects of Greek philosophy. These Axial Age religions contrasted with more old-fashioned, immanent notions of the divine found in nature worship and shamanism.

By virtue of being the reproductive side of humanity, women are intrinsically closer to nature worship that focuses on the cycles of life, death, and rebirth. As the visceral worship of nature was devalued in favor of the worship of a transcendent supreme being, women's central role in ritual was devalued as well, until the point was reached in formal monotheism where women were excluded from ritual altogether.

The Assyrians made significant progress in medicine, building on the foundation of the Babylonians, and absorbing the knowledge and talent of those they conquered. Ashurnasirpal II (884-859 BCE) consolidated Assyrian rule in the Levant and through Canaan; he made the first systematic lists of plants and animals in the empire and brought scribes with him on campaign to record new finds.

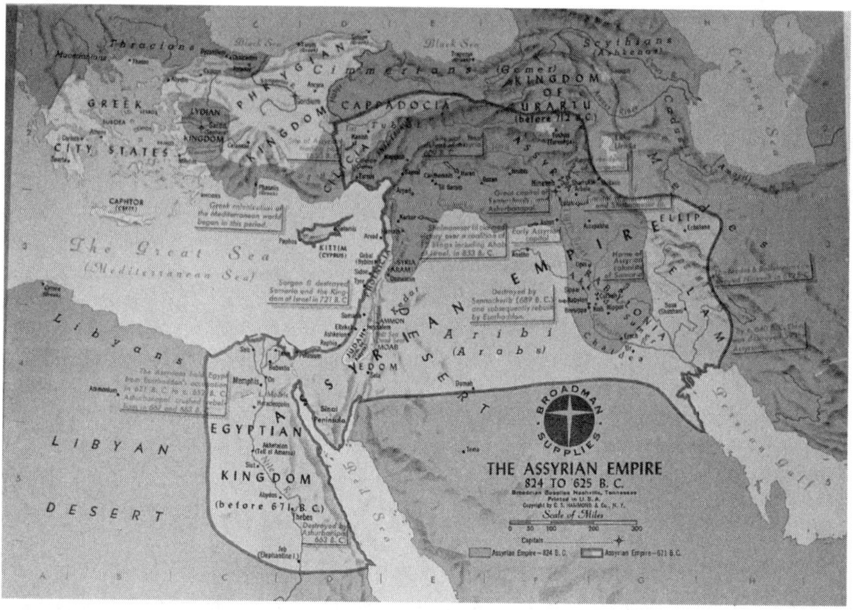

Mulk Sacrifice

Chapter Thirty-Three

FALL of ISRAEL

Tiglath-Pileser III

The Assyrian empire suffered from civil war until Tiglath-Pileser III (745-727 BCE) took power and revitalized it. Many scholars consider the rule of Tiglath-Pilaser to be the true start of the Neo-Assyrian Empire; he reorganized the military and the Assyrian army became the most effective in history. In 729 BCE, Tiglath-Pileser went to Babylonia and captured the king of Babylon. Tiglath-Pileser appears in the Bible, he conquered Israel and commanded heavy tribute from Samaria.

> *In the time of Pekah king of Israel, Tiglath-Pileser king of Assyria came and took Ijon, Abel Beth Maakah, Janoah, Kedesh and Hazor. He took Gilead and Galilee, including all the land of Naphtali, and deported the people to Assyria.*
>
> – 2 Kings 15:29

King Ahaz of Judah

In Judah, King Ahaz was a vassal of Tiglath-Pileser and paid the Assyrians tribute, allying with them against Israel and Syria. King Ahaz was pagan and adopted Assyrian religion. He even built an altar to Ashur which he placed in the Temple of Yahweh, greatly displeasing the biblical writers. King Ahaz sacrificed his own children and was one of the most offensive kings to Yahweh after Ahab and Jezebel.

> *[Ahaz] followed the ways of the kings of Israel and even sacrificed his son in the fire, engaging in the detestable practices of the nations Yahweh had driven out before the Israelites. He offered sacrifices and burned incense at the high places, on the hilltops and under every spreading tree.*
>
> – 2 Kings 16:3-4

> *Ahaz sent messengers to say to Tiglath-Pileser king of Assyria, "I am your servant and vassal. Come up and save me out of the hand of the king of Aram and of the king of Israel, who are attacking me." And*

Ahaz took the silver and gold found in the temple of Yahweh and in the treasuries of the royal palace and sent it as a gift to the king of Assyria. The king of Assyria complied by attacking Damascus and capturing it. He deported its inhabitants to Kir and put Rezin to death.

– 2 Kings 16:7-9

Altar for Ashur

Then King Ahaz went to Damascus to meet Tiglath-Pileser king of Assyria. He saw an altar in Damascus and sent to Uriah the priest a sketch of the altar, with detailed plans for its construction. So Uriah the priest built an altar in accordance with all the plans that King Ahaz had sent from Damascus and finished it before King Ahaz returned.

When the king came back from Damascus and saw the altar, he approached it and presented offerings on it. He offered up his burnt offering and grain offering, poured out his drink offering, and splashed the blood of his fellowship offerings against the altar. As for the bronze altar that stood before Yahweh, he brought it from the front of the temple - from between the new altar and the temple of Yahweh - and put it on the north side of the new altar.

– 2 Kings 16:10-14

Attack on Israel

Tiglath-Pileser III died in 727 BCE, succeeded by Shalmaneser V. King Hoshea of Israel suspended paying tribute, perhaps sensing weakness, and allied himself with Egypt against Assyria in 725 BCE. This bad decision led Shalmaneser to invade Israel and besiege Samaria for three years. Hoshea was captured and put in an Assyrian prison.

Shalmaneser king of Assyria came up to attack Hoshea, who had been Shalmaneser's vassal and had paid him tribute. But the king of Assyria discovered that Hoshea was a traitor, for he had sent envoys to So, king of Egypt, and he no longer paid tribute to the king of Assyria, as he had done year by year. Therefore Shalmaneser seized him and put him in prison.

The king of Assyria invaded the entire land, marched against Samaria and laid siege to it for three years. In the ninth year of Hoshea, the king of Assyria captured Samaria and deported the Israelites to Assyria. He settled them in Halah, in Gozan on the Habor River and in the towns of the Medes.

– 2 Kings 17:3-6

TEN LOST TRIBES

The siege and destruction of Samaria brought an end to Israel as an independent kingdom in 722 BCE. The people were all deported to various parts of Assyria, becoming the 10 Lost Tribes of Israel. Deportees were allowed to take their families and possessions and were given land to live on, while deportees from other conquered cities were moved in. The Assyrians treated the people they conquered and relocated relatively well, they were considered to be Assyrians once the fighting ended and they had submitted to the central authority.

The biblical writers blame the fall of Israel on their failure to worship Yahweh properly, though the Assyrians would have claimed that their victories were the result of their superior god Ashur.

All this took place because the Israelites had sinned against Yahweh their God...

The Israelites secretly did things against Yahweh their God that were not right. From watchtower to fortified city they built themselves high places in all their towns. They set up sacred stones and Asherah poles on every high hill and under every spreading tree. At every high place they burned incense, as the nations whom Yahweh had driven out before them had done. They did wicked things that aroused Yahweh's anger.

– 2 Kings 17:7;9-11

They forsook all the commands of Yahweh their God and made for themselves two idols cast in the shape of calves, and an Asherah pole. They bowed down to all the starry hosts, and they worshiped Baal. They sacrificed their sons and daughters in the fire. They practiced divination and sought omens and sold themselves to do evil in the eyes of Yahweh, arousing his anger.

– 2 Kings 17:16-17

The king of Assyria brought people from Babylon, Kuthah, Avva, Hamath and Sepharvaim and settled them in the towns of Samaria to replace the Israelites. They took over Samaria and lived in its towns.

– 2 Kings 17:24

Kings of Nineveh

Shalmaneser died suddenly during the siege of Samaria and was replaced by Sargon II who brought the empire to its greatest heights politically and militarily. Sargon II was followed by Sennacherib (705-681 BCE) who campaigned widely and ruthlessly, devastating Judah and laying siege to Jerusalem during the reign of King Hezekiah.

Sennacherib chose the ancient city of Nineveh as his capital. He built the "Palace Without Rival" and created a vast library. Nineveh was dedicated to the goddess Ishtar. Sennacherib's grand palace gardens at Nineveh are believed by many scholars to be the true "Hanging Gardens of Babylon" since this "Wonder of the Ancient World" has never been found in Babylon.

Sennacherib did invade Babylon though, breaking the canals and flooding the city. He then looted the ancient temples, which was considered to be the height of sacrilege even by his own people. Sennacherib was assassinated in his palace by his own sons for his crimes against the gods.

The next king was Esarhaddon, one of the king's sons, who killed all his brothers and rivals to secure the throne in a brief civil war. Esarhaddon expanded the empire into Egypt and secured vassal treaties with a number of nations.

The last great king of Assyria was Ashurbanipal who ruled 42 years and is famous for the great library he created. The King sent envoys to every corner of the empire to acquire books for preservation in the Royal Library at Nineveh.

After Ashurbanipal's death, the Assyrian empire went into decline, it had become too large to manage effectively and regions began to break away. In 612 BCE Nineveh was sacked and burned by a coalition of Babylonians, Persians, Medes, and Scythians. The city was burned and the residents were massacred. The Assyrian royal library collapsed and the clay texts it held were preserved when they were baked hard in the fires and buried beneath the rubble.

This catastrophe inadvertently yielded one of the greatest archaeological finds ever when it was discovered 2,454 years later (1842 CE). The Royal Library of Ashurbanipal contained vast amounts of art and 30,000 cuneiform tablets, including the Epic of Gilgamesh, the Enuma Elish, and important evidence of the ritual use of cannabis.

Chapter Thirty-Four

PROPHET HOSEA AND QEDESHA GOMER

Troubled Marriage

The biblical book of Hosea details the story of the prophet Hosea who lived in Israel during its final days. Hosea is the first of the twelve minor prophets and his book is considered to be one of the oldest texts in the Bible, written around 760-720 BCE. Hosea preached doom for the nation of Israel if they continued their pagan worship and failed to turn completely to Yahweh.

The centerpiece of Hosea's story is the relationship with his wife Gomer, who is described as a "woman of adultery." Gomer was likely a qedesha though the text does not explicitly say so – at the very least she was a promiscuous Canaanite woman.

Qedesha were free to marry, but they were known to make poor wives because of their independent ways. The prophet of Yahweh and the qedesha in service of the Triple Goddess had a contentious marriage, she had three children, but only the first was fathered by her husband.

Gomer's adultery is used as a metaphor for the spiritual adultery of Israel who worshipped many gods and goddesses rather than Yahweh alone. The book of Hosea is a poetic allegory that is simultaneously a conversation between the prophet and his wife, Yahweh and Israel, and Yahweh and the Goddess herself.

Three Children

When Yahweh began to speak through Hosea, Yahweh said to him, "Go, marry a promiscuous woman and have children with her, for like an adulterous wife this land is guilty of unfaithfulness to Yahweh." So he married Gomer, daughter of Diblaim, and she conceived and bore him a son.

Then Yahweh said to Hosea, "Call him Jezreel, because I will soon punish the house of Jehu for the massacre at Jezreel, and I will put an end to the kingdom of Israel. In that day I will break Israel's bow in the Valley of Jezreel."

Gomer conceived again and gave birth to a daughter. Then Yahweh said to Hosea, "Call her Lo-Ruhamah (which means "not loved"), for I will no longer show love to Israel, that I should at all forgive them. Yet I will show love to Judah; and I will save them--not by bow, sword or battle, or by horses and horsemen, but I, Yahweh their God, will save them."

After she had weaned Lo-Ruhamah, Gomer had another son. Then Yahweh said, "Call him Lo-Ammi (which means "not my people"), for you are not my people, and I am not your God.

– Hosea 1:2-9

The names of the children are symbolic. The first son born to the couple is named for Jezreel, the location of the palace built by Queen Jezebel, and where Jehu massacred her family in his coup. The second and third children born to Gomer belonged to her, they were not fathered by Hosea. Yahweh calls them "not loved," and "not my people." Yahweh rejects those who do not follow his laws. These names may also reflect Hosea's towards his wife's children.

Declaration of Divorce

In the next chapter, Hosea seeks to put an end to Gomer's independence, just as Yahweh wanted to bring an end to Goddess worship and her nature festivals, carousing, and sexual rituals. Hosea plans to shut Gomer in and lock her away from her lovers, but it is also Yahweh saying that the Goddess is no longer his wife and he intends to lock her up.

This is the declaration of divorce of God from the Goddess.

"Rebuke your mother, rebuke her, for she is not my wife, and I am not her husband. Let her remove the adulterous look from her face and the unfaithfulness from between her breasts. Otherwise, I will strip her naked and make her as bare as on the day she was born; I will make her like a desert, turn her into a parched land, and slay her with thirst.

I will not show my love to her children, because they are the children of adultery. Their mother has been unfaithful and has conceived them in disgrace. She said, 'I will go after my lovers, who give me my food and my water, my wool and my linen, my olive oil and my drink.'

Therefore I will block her path with thornbushes; I will wall her in so that she cannot find her way. She will chase after her lovers but not catch them; she will look for them but not find them. Then she will say,

> *'I will go back to my husband as at first, for then I was better off than now.'*
> *She has not acknowledged that I was the one who gave her the grain, the new wine, and oil, who lavished on her the silver and gold - which they used for Baal. "Therefore I will take away my grain when it ripens, and my new wine when it is ready. I will take back my wool and my linen, intended to cover her naked body. So now I will expose her lewdness before the eyes of her lovers; no one will take her out of my hands.*
> *I will stop all her celebrations: her yearly festivals, her New Moons, her Sabbath days - all her appointed festivals. I will ruin her vines and her fig trees, which she said were her pay from her lovers; I will make them a thicket, and wild animals will devour them. I will punish her for the days she burned incense to the Baals; she decked herself with rings and jewelry and went after her lovers, but me she forgot," declares Yahweh.*
> *"Therefore, I am now going to allure her; I will lead her into the wilderness and speak tenderly to her. There I will give her back her vineyards, and will make the Valley of Achor a door of hope. There she will respond as in the days of her youth, as in the day she came up out of Egypt.*
> *"In that day," declares Yahweh, "you will call me 'ishi'; you will no longer call me 'Baali.' I will remove the names of the Baals from her lips; no longer will their names be invoked.*
>
> – Hosea 2:2-17

Ishi means "my husband", Baali means "my lord", and was a conventional Canaanite greeting but the Yahwists banned the expression.

Yahweh Takes Her Powers

The divorce was not just between Yahweh and the Goddess, it was between the men and the women in the community. A divorce between the priests and priestesses, who were their own wives, daughters, and mothers – whose sacred traditions had to be repressed and expelled from the community. From there, Yahweh took over the powers of nature and creation for himself.

> *In that day I will make a covenant for them with the beasts of the field, the birds in the sky, and the creatures that move along the ground. Bow and sword and battle I will abolish from the land, so that all may lie down in safety. I will betroth you to me forever; I will betroth you in righteousness and justice, in love and compassion. I will betroth you in faithfulness, and you will acknowledge Yahweh.*

"In that day I will respond," declares Yahweh – "I will respond to the skies, and they will respond to the earth; and the earth will respond to the grain, the new wine, and the olive oil, and they will respond to Jezreel. I will plant her for myself in the land; I will show my love to the one I called 'Not my loved one.' I will say to those called 'Not my people,' 'You are my people'; and they will say, 'You are my God.'"

– Hosea 2:18-23

Bring Her Home

In the third chapter, Hosea goes to Gomer with valuables (there was no money, all was barter) to entice her to return to him. These verses are often interpreted that Hosea was purchasing Gomer from another man, but the text does not indicate explicitly whom the barter was paid to. Qedesha were the masters of their own behavior, and they kept the gifts they received in exchange for sex. It seems that Hosea gave the gifts to Gomer in order to win back her favor.

Yahweh said to me, "Go, show your love to your wife again, though she is loved by another man and is an adulteress. Love her as Yahweh loves the Israelites, though they turn to other gods and love the sacred raisin cakes."

So, I bought her for fifteen shekels of silver and about a homer and a lethek of barley. Then I told her, "You are to live with me many days; you must not be a prostitute or be intimate with any man, and I will behave the same way toward you."

– Hosea 3:1-3

Hosea tells Gomer that she must be sexually faithful to him and he will be faithful to her as well. The book does not record her response; for all the reader knows she may have demanded a divorce and left with the children.

Prophecies of Doom

Gomer then disappears from the narrative as Hosea criticizes the people of Israel for their idolatrous, promiscuous behavior and predicts their doom at the hands of the Assyrians. The prophet says he will "destroy your mother," destroy the Goddess.

You stumble day and night, and the prophets stumble with you. So I will destroy your mother

– Hosea 4:5

> *"They will eat but not have enough; they will engage in prostitution but not flourish, because they have deserted Yahweh to give themselves to prostitution; old wine and new wine take away their understanding.*
>
> *My people consult a wooden idol, and a diviner's rod speaks to them. A spirit of prostitution leads them astray; they are unfaithful to their God. They sacrifice on the mountaintops and burn offerings on the hills, under oak, poplar, and terebinth, where the shade is pleasant. Therefore your daughters turn to prostitution and your daughters-in-law to adultery.*
>
> *"I will not punish your daughters when they turn to prostitution, nor your daughters-in-law when they commit adultery, because the men themselves consort with harlots and sacrifice with qedesha - a people without understanding will come to ruin!*
>
> – Hosea 4:10-14

It was culture war, the Yahwists were determined to wipe out all the religious practices and culture of the Canaanites.

> *They are unfaithful to Yahweh; they give birth to illegitimate children. When they celebrate their New Moon feasts, he will devour their fields.*
>
> – Hosea 5:7

The Canaanites did not practice paternity, they traced their bloodlines through their mothers and children belonged to their mothers to raise until they were adults. The Biblical writers say all their children are "illegitimate." The Hebrews needed to control their women's sexual lives in order to enforce paternity, which they emphasize strongly throughout the Bible. The Bible often repeats long lists of patriarchal generations to demonstrate a claim of paternity back to Adam and Eve. Paternity was not important to the Canaanites, they had matriarchal bloodlines. The Goddess does not believe in monogamy and does not recognize paternity.

King Hezekiah

Chapter Thirty-Five

KINGS of JUDAH

KING HEZEKIAH

King Hezekiah was one of the most important Hebrew kings and Yahwist reformers. Hezekiah was considered a near-messianic figure for his dedication to Yahweh and his success in restraining the Assyrians from destroying Jerusalem. Hezekiah was King of Judah from 715-686 BCE, he is well attested by archaeologists and left permanent marks on the city of Jerusalem we can still see today.

As a young man, the king had witnessed the destruction of Israel at the hands of the Assyrians, and he had to deal with the aggressive empire through much of his reign. Many refugees from Israel settled in Judah including the followers of the northern prophets.

Hezekiah followed his father, the pagan King Ahaz who built the altar to Ashur in the Hebrew temple. Ahaz was condemned by the prophet Isaiah and the biblical writers as a committed pagan who worshipped Baal, sacrificed his own children, and made offerings on the high places. Ahaz's son Hezekiah did not support his father and did not even give him a proper burial.

Yahwist Reformer

King Hezekiah was one of only two biblical kings fully committed to Yahweh, he committed dramatic religious reforms and attempted to completely exterminate pagan religion in Judah. The prophet Isaiah was a mentor and adviser to Hezekiah and assisted his reforms.

> *In the first month of the first year of his reign, he opened the doors of the temple of Yahweh and repaired them.*
>
> – 2 Chronicles 29:3

> *When all this had ended, the Israelites who were there went out to the towns of Judah, smashed the sacred stones, and cut down the Asherah poles. They destroyed the high places and the altars throughout Judah and Benjamin and in Ephraim and Manasseh. After they had*

destroyed all of them, the Israelites returned to their own towns and to their own property.

He ordered the people living in Jerusalem to give the portion due the priests and Levites so they could devote themselves to the Law of Yahweh.

– 2 Chronicles 31:1;4

Hezekiah reopened and repaired the Temple and reinstated the Passover Festival. The king then closed the public altars, smashed the idols, and cut down the Asherah poles. These reforms were more than symbolic, Hezekiah sought to centralize worship at the Jerusalem Temple and he ordered that all offerings be consolidated into the hands of the temple priests.

This centralization of worship was a critical step in the formation of the Judeo-Christian traditions, it represents the first time that temple priests attempted to consolidate all religious worship under their authority. Paganism had always been a do-it-yourself religious framework rooted in family and community. The introduction of religious authorities who mediated all worship practices, usurping the independence of the people to create their own altars, would become a defining feature of the Judeo-Christian and Islamic traditions we still see today.

Smash the Bronze Serpent

In his religious reforms, Hezekiah not only smashed the idols and cut down the Asherah poles, but he also "broke into pieces the bronze snake Moses had made." This was the bronze snake Moses made to heal the Israelites from the scourge of snakes Yahweh had sent in Numbers 21:6-9. The bronze snake had been kept as a sacred relic for some 600 years.

He removed the high places, smashed the sacred stones, and cut down the Asherah poles. He broke into pieces the bronze snake Moses had made, for up to that time the Israelites had been burning incense to it. (It was called Nehushtan.)

Hezekiah trusted in Yahweh, the God of Israel. There was no one like him among all the kings of Judah, either before him or after him.

– 2 Kings 18:4-5

In Hebrew, "Nehushtan" means "a mere piece of brass," the term is derogatory and dismissive, though in English bibles Nehushtan is said to simply be the name of the object. This is one of the big fights in the divorce and an example of a goddess symbol being purged by monotheistic reformers who worked to push her worship underground.

Hezekiah's Tunnel

King Hezekiah rebelled against Assyria and stopped paying them tribute, allying with Egypt instead. Knowing that Jerusalem would be subject to a siege, Hezekiah undertook major building campaigns around the city. Hezekiah fortified the Broad Wall of Jerusalem and built towers on it.

Hezekiah also commissioned one of the most impressive engineering feats of the ancient world. Jerusalem's water supplies came from the Gihon Spring, outside the city walls. In order to protect the water and deny it to the Assyrians, Hezekiah had a long tunnel built that would channel the water into the City of David. The tunnel leads from the Gihon Spring to the Pool of Siloam.

The tunnel is 583 yards (533 m) long and was excavated by two teams, each starting on opposite ends and meeting perfectly in the middle. It required sophisticated engineering and measurement techniques for the two teams to successfully meet underground. Modern scholars have not determined how they did it. The tunnel was sealed by an earthquake in the Middle Ages. Archaeologists unearthed Hezekiah's tunnel and tourists can go through it today. There is an inscription on the wall commemorating the breakthrough moment when the two digging teams came together underground over 2700 years ago.

Attack on Judah

Judah was attacked in 701 BCE by Sennacherib, the king of Assyria, who laid waste to the countryside and captured all the fortified cities. The town of Lasich was a heavily defended fortress, it was 80 miles from Jerusalem and the second most important city in Judah. The siege and destruction of Lasich was a major victory for the Assyrians. King Sennacherib commissioned huge stone reliefs celebrating the event that can now be found in the British Museum.

The biblical writers barely mention the epic defeat. They do say that after the capture of Lasisch and the slaughter of its citizens, envoys of King Hezekiah went there to meet the Assyrians to offer them tribute. Hezekiah took all the gold and silver from the temple and royal treasury and paid it to the Assyrians to prevent a siege of Jerusalem.

> *So Hezekiah king of Judah sent this message to the king of Assyria at Lachish: "I have done wrong. Withdraw from me, and I will pay whatever you demand of me."*
>
> *The king of Assyria exacted from Hezekiah king of Judah three hundred talents of silver and thirty talents of gold. So Hezekiah gave him all the silver that was found in the temple of Yahweh and in the treasuries of the royal palace. At this time Hezekiah king of Judah stripped off the gold with which he had covered the doors and doorposts of the temple of Yahweh, and gave it to the king of Assyria.*
>
> – 2 Kings 18: 14-16

This meeting between Hezekiah and Sennacherib was recorded by the Assyrians. Sennacherib stated in his inscriptions that they laid siege to Jerusalem but left after extracting heavy tribute. King Hezekiah was made a prisoner in his palace, trapped like a bird in a cage.

The Assyrians raise the amount of silver received from 300 to 800 talents, plus Hezekiah's daughters and concubines, but is otherwise consistent with the Bible. These inscriptions were found in Nineveh on the Taylor Prism, a large six-sided block filled with cuneiform writings detailing the exploits of King Sennacherib, which is also kept in the British Museum.

> *As to Hezekiah, the Jew, he did not submit to my yoke, I laid siege to his strong cities, walled forts, and countless small villages, and conquered them by means of well-stamped earth-ramps and battering-rams brought near the walls with an attack by foot soldiers, using mines, breeches as well as trenches. I drove out 200,150 people, young and old, male and female, horses, mules, donkeys, camels, big and small cattle beyond counting, and considered them slaves. Himself I made a prisoner in Jerusalem, his royal residence, like a bird in a cage. I surrounded him with earthwork in order to molest those who were his city's gate. Thus, I reduced his country, but I still increased the tribute and the presents to me as overlord which I imposed upon him beyond the former tribute, to be delivered annually. Hezekiah himself did send me, later, to Nineveh, my lordly city, together with 30 talents of gold, 800 talents of silver, precious stones, antimony, large cuts of red stone, couches inlaid with ivory, nimedu-chairs inlaid with ivory, elephant-hides, ebony-wood, boxwood and all kinds of valuable treasures, his own daughters and concubines.*[1]

1 D. Luckenbill. 1927. *Ancient records of Assyria and Babylonia: Vol. II*. T.C. Mitchell. 1988. The Bible in the British Museum.

HEZEKIAH'S DESPAIR

In the Bible, the story goes on. The biblical writers say that Sennacherib departed after accepting the tribute but then returned, threatening again to destroy Jerusalem. This time though, the city was saved through divine intervention.

Upon hearing of the Assyrians' return, Hezekiah despaired. He put on hemp sackcloth and prayed in the temple of Yahweh for deliverance. The king prayed, saying that all the other gods the Assyrians destroyed are made of stone and wood, but Yahweh is the one true god. According to the Bible, Yahweh responded to Hezekiah and saved Jerusalem.

> *When King Hezekiah heard this, he tore his clothes and put on sackcloth and went into the temple of Yahweh.*
>
> *"It is true, Yahweh, that the Assyrian kings have laid waste these nations and their lands. They have thrown their gods into the fire and destroyed them, for they were not gods but only wood and stone, fashioned by human hands. Now, Yahweh our God, deliver us from his hand, so that all the kingdoms of the earth may know that you alone, Yahweh, are God."*
>
> – 2 Kings 19:1; 17-19

GOD'S MIRACLE

> *"Therefore, this is what Yahweh says concerning the king of Assyria: "He will not enter this city or shoot an arrow here. He will not come before it with shield or build a siege ramp against it. By the way that he came he will return; he will not enter this city," declares Yahweh. "I will defend this city and save it, for my sake and for the sake of David my servant!"*
>
> *That night the angel of Yahweh went out and put to death a hundred and eighty-five thousand in the Assyrian camp. When the people got up the next morning - there were all the dead bodies! So, Sennacherib king of Assyria broke camp and withdrew. He returned to Nineveh and stayed there.*
>
> – 2 Kings 19:33-36

The Assyrians did not record any such event, though perhaps they would not want to record an embarrassment. The Egyptians have a similar legend about Sennacherib. They say that he was repulsed in Egypt when in a single night his army was decimated by a plague of field mice who ate through their bowstrings and the thongs of their shields.

This miracle saved Jerusalem and Hezekiah was hailed as a hero. If Jerusalem had fallen the Hebrew religion may not have survived. Whatever truly happened, there is no dispute that Jerusalem did survive and was never sacked by the Assyrians, even though the rest of Judah was laid to waste. This rescue gave rise to the belief among the Hebrews that Yahweh was truly a great God and that Jerusalem was inviolable. Hebrew confidence remained high until the city was burned by the Babylonians a little more than a century later.

Sennacherib was killed in 681 BCE at his palace in Nineveh by his own sons because he had committed sacrilege by desecrating the sacred temples in Babylon and flooding the ancient city.

> *One day, while he was worshiping in the temple of his god Nisrok, his sons Adrammelek and Sharezer killed him with the sword, and they escaped to the land of Ararat. And Esarhaddon his son succeeded him as king.*
>
> –2 Kings 19:37

PROPHET ISAIAH

Women of Zion are Haughty

The prophet Isaiah was in Judah during the reigns of Kings Ahaz and Hezekiah in the 8th century BCE when the Assyrians were exerting their dominance. Isaiah predicted doom for the Hebrews if they continued in their idolatrous ways and allowing the women to enjoy themselves independently.

> *Yahweh says, "The women of Zion are haughty, walking along with outstretched necks, flirting with their eyes, strutting along with swaying hips, with ornaments jingling on their ankles. Therefore Yahweh will bring sores on the heads of the women of Zion; Yahweh will make their scalps bald."*
>
> *In that day Yahweh will snatch away their finery: the bangles and headbands and crescent necklaces, the earrings and bracelets and veils, the headdresses and anklets and sashes, the perfume bottles and charms, the signet rings and nose rings, the fine robes and the capes and cloaks, the purses and mirrors, and the linen garments and tiaras and shawls. Instead of fragrance, there will be a stench; instead of a sash, a rope; instead of well-dressed hair, baldness; instead of fine clothing, sackcloth; instead of beauty, branding.*

> *Your men will fall by the sword, your warriors in battle. The gates of Zion will lament and mourn; destitute, she will sit on the ground.*
>
> – Isaiah 3:16-26

The Yahwist prophets and kings continually condemned the popular folk religion and practices. Isaiah could not tolerate the finely dressed women with their jewelry and perfume, "strutting along with their swaying hips." Isaiah says their incense altars and Asherah stones will be broken down and crushed to pieces, while the men fall in battle for their sins against Yahweh.

> *By this, then, will Jacob's guilt be atoned for, and this will be the full fruit of the removal of his sin: When he makes all the altar stones to be like limestone crushed to pieces, no Asherah poles or incense altars will be left standing.*
>
> – Isaiah 27:9

(Jacob is a name for Israel).

> *In that day people will look to their Maker and turn their eyes to the Holy One of Israel. They will not look to the altars, the work of their hands, and they will have no regard for the Asherah poles and the incense altars their fingers have made.*
>
> – Isaiah 17:7-8

A Live Coal From The Altar

In one colorful event from the career of Isaiah, the prophet had an intense psychedelic vision where he saw God in all his glory. The temple filled with smoke in a scene evocative of hashish incense. Isaiah believed he was ruined for he had unclean lips, but one of Yahweh's seraphim brought a lump of coal from the altar and touched it to Isaiah's lips, taking away his sin. To this day, hashish smokers use a hot knife to bring a smoldering lump of hashish close to their mouth to breathe in the intoxicating smoke.

> *I saw Yahweh, high and exalted, seated on a throne; and the train of his robe filled the temple. Above him were seraphim, each with six wings: With two wings they covered their faces, with two they covered their feet, and with two they were flying. And they were calling to one another: "Holy, holy, holy is Yahweh Almighty; the whole earth is full of his glory."*

> *At the sound of their voices, the doorposts and thresholds shook and the temple was filled with smoke. "Woe to me!" I cried. "I am ruined! For I am a man of unclean lips, and I live among a people of unclean lips, and my eyes have seen the King, Yahweh Almighty."*
>
> *Then one of the seraphim flew to me with a live coal in his hand, which he had taken with tongs from the altar. With it, he touched my mouth and said, "See, this has touched your lips; your guilt is taken away and your sin atoned for."*
>
> – Isaiah 6:1-7

KING MANASSEH

Popular Pagan

Hezekiah died a few years after the Assyrian siege and was succeeded by his son. King Manasseh had Judah's longest reign, holding the throne for 55 years, from 698-642 BCE. The Bible does not say much about Manasseh, he reversed Hezekiah's reforms and reinstated pagan worship, and for this reason, Manasseh is condemned by the biblical writers as one of the worst kings of Judah. Yet the historical record indicates that the reign of Manasseh was a time of stability and trade in Judah. In Rabbinic literature, Mannaseh is said to have murdered the prophet Isaiah.

The Yahwist reforms were not popular with the people who wanted their community altars back and desired the freedom to worship as they please. As soon as Hezekiah died, the Asherah poles and high places were restored. The Canaanites also brought back their idolatrous superstitions and child sacrifice, and Manasseh is said to have sacrificed his own son.

> *He rebuilt the high places his father Hezekiah had destroyed; he also erected altars to Baal and made an Asherah pole, as Ahab king of Israel had done. He bowed down to all the starry hosts and worshiped them.*
>
> *In the two courts of the temple of Yahweh, he built altars to all the starry hosts. He sacrificed his own son in the fire, practiced divination, sought omens, and consulted mediums and spiritists. He did much evil in the eyes of Yahweh, arousing his anger. He took the carved Asherah pole he had made and put it in the temple.*
>
> – 2 Kings 21:3; 5-7

The people probably thought highly of Manasseh as his reign was a time of peace and prosperity in Judah. Manasseh was a loyal vassal of Assyria and is listed in their records as an ally. The reinstatement of folk religion would have been a smart political move that earned the loyalties of the wealthy landowning elite and smoothed relations with the Assyrians. Judah had favored trade relations with Nineveh and there were profitable exports of olive oil and wine to the empire.

Supposed Repentance

Later biblical writers of the Book of Chronicles add an event not included in the Book of Kings, an event that seems unlikely. In Chronicles, they say that late in his reign Manasseh was taken prisoner by the Assyrians and led away in chains. Manasseh eventually repented and Yahweh restored him to his throne. There is no recording of these events in Assyrian sources, and it seems that this was an embellishment intended to provide some Yahwist flavor to Manasseh's successful pagan reign.

King Amon followed Manasseh and he was also pagan, but Amon only ruled two years before being assassinated. Apparently, Amon was popular, because the people rose up and killed the conspirators.

> *Amon's officials conspired against him and assassinated the king in his palace. Then the people of the land killed all who had plotted against King Amon, and they made Josiah his son king in his place.*
>
> 2 Kings 21:23-24

KING JOSIAH

Second Great Reforms

King Josiah was the second great Yahwist reformer and he is hailed in the Bible for his fealty to Yahweh. King Josiah had a large influence on the writing of the Bible as significant portions were written during his rule. Josiah was 8 years old when he became king, and 18 when he ordered renovations to the Temple in Jerusalem. The reforms of Hezekiah and Josiah are the high water marks for the Yahwists during the First Temple period. This is when God threw the Goddess out of the Temple on their way to finally being divorced.

During the Temple renovations, Hilkiah the high priest discovered the lost book of Moses, The Book of the Law, that we now see in the biblical Book of Deuteronomy. Modern scholars agree that it was virtually impossible that a 600-year-old scroll was suddenly discovered and most believe it was written at the time of Josiah.

> *Hilkiah the priest found the book of the law of Yahweh written by the hand of Moses.*
>
> – 2 Chronicles 34:14

Deuteronomists

It is this generation of literate priests that are known colloquially as the "Deuteronomists." They are thought to have collected the older texts from both Judah and Israel, including earlier drafts of the Torah stories, and to have written the historical books of Joshua, Judges, Ruth, Samuel, and Kings. These texts were transmitted to Babylon during the exile where the "Priestly" group compiled, edited, and redacted them into the Hebrew Bible we know today. These Yahwist priests were politically and ideologically driven to present their view of history and perceptions of morality.

The lost book of Moses was brought to the king and read aloud to him. Josiah was deeply moved by the words and immediately commenced reforms to bring his nation back into the grace of Yahweh. Josiah banned all other forms of worship and began a campaign to wipe out the pagan traditions and centralize worship at the temple in Jerusalem.

> *The king ordered Hilkiah the high priest, the priests next in rank, and the doorkeepers to remove from the temple of Yahweh all the articles made for Baal and Asherah and all the starry hosts. He burned them outside Jerusalem in the fields of the Kidron Valley and took the ashes to Bethel.*
>
> *He did away with the idolatrous priests appointed by the kings of Judah to burn incense on the high places of the towns of Judah and on those around Jerusalem – those who burned incense to Baal, to the sun and moon, to the constellations and to all the starry hosts.*
>
> *He took the Asherah pole from the temple of Yahweh to the Kidron Valley outside Jerusalem and burned it there. He ground it to powder and scattered the dust over the graves of the common people.*
>
> – 2 Kings 23:4-6

Burn the Asherah

The Asherah pole installed at Solomon's Temple was cut down, burned, ground into powder, and the dust scattered over the graves of her worshippers. The burning of incense on the high places is condemned, as is the worship of Baal and other gods. The starry hosts were planetary deities; the gods of the sun, moon, Mercury, Venus, Mars, Jupiter, and Saturn.

> *He also tore down the quarters of the male qadesh that were in the temple of Yahweh, the quarters where women did weaving for Asherah.*
>
> – 2 Kings 23:7

This passage is particularly revealing – Josiah removed the male qadesh, but pointedly does not mention the female qedesha, who were presumably left alone. The priestesses were always a much tougher target. The women in the temple did sacred weaving for Asherah; fabrics and tapestries were commonly used in the temples to create separate rooms, tents, and pavilions to house guests, vendors, or perhaps the qedesha themselves. One can only speculate how much of the sacred weaving used hemp, one of their staple fibers.

Josiah destroying gods

He desecrated Topheth, which was in the Valley of Ben Hinnom, so no one could use it to sacrifice their son or daughter in the fire to Molek.
– 2 Kings 23:10

Josiah ended the practice of child sacrifice, he destroyed the Tophet, the altar of sacrifice. No one can argue against the Hebrew hostility to child sacrifice.

Astarte's High Place

The king also desecrated the high places that were east of Jerusalem on the south of the Hill of Corruption – the ones Solomon king of Israel had built for Ashtoreth the vile goddess of the Sidonians.
– 2 Kings 23:13

Josiah destroyed the high places Solomon built for Astarte and other foreign gods. Here the writers again refer to Astarte as Ashtoreth, "shameful Astarte", the vile goddess of Sidon, and confirm that King Solomon worshipped her. Sidon was the hometown of Queen Jezebel, whose father was a high priest of Astarte before he became king.

Josiah smashed the sacred stones and cut down the Asherah poles and covered the sites with human bones. Even the altar at Bethel … even that altar and high place he demolished. He burned the high place and ground it to powder, and burned the Asherah pole also. Then Josiah looked

> *around, and when he saw the tombs that were there on the hillside, he had the bones removed from them and burned on the altar to defile it.*
>
> – 2 Kings 23:14-16

The altar at Bethel was first established by Jacob and called *El Elohe Israel.* It is also where Jeroboam built one of the golden bulls to El after Israel split from Judah. Josiah defiled the ancient altars by digging up the nearby graves and burning the human bones on them. The King condemned the shamans and spiritists and eliminated the worship of household gods.

> *Josiah slaughtered all the priests of those high places on the altars and burned human bones on them. Then he went back to Jerusalem.*
>
> – 2 Kings 23:20

> *Furthermore, Josiah got rid of the mediums and spiritists, the household gods, the idols and all the other detestable things seen in Judah and Jerusalem.*
>
> – 2 Kings 23:24

Archaeologists have found shrines overturned and deliberately dismantled from the time period that would appear to be from the reforms of Josiah and Hezekiah. The household gods may have been associated with the small goddess figurines that archaeologists have found all over Israel. The pillar-base figurines were popular during exactly the time that Josiah and Hezekiah attempted their reforms, and they continued to be made until Jerusalem was overthrown and the Hebrews exiled.

Death of Josiah

The geopolitical situation was in flux during Josiah's time. The Assyrian empire was weak and under threat from rivals, but a new power had not emerged yet. In 612 BCE Nineveh was sacked and burned by an alliance of Medes, Persians, Chaldeans (Neo-Babylonians), and Scythians. The fall of Nineveh was a dramatic moment in the ancient world that was written about in Babylonian, Greek, and Roman texts. But it would take another few years before the Assyrian empire completely collapsed.

In 605 BCE, Pharaoh Necho II of Egypt marched his army up the Mediterranean coast to assist the Assyrians at Carchemish in the fight with the Babylonians. Carchemish on the Euphrates river was the last hold-out of the Assyrians. Necho II is the same Pharaoh who sponsored the Phoenician sailing voyage around Africa. The Egyptians attempted to cross through the Jezreel Valley and appealed to Josiah for permission to pass. Necho was not looking to fight Josiah but the king rejected the Egyptian appeals.

> *Necho sent messengers to him, saying, "What quarrel is there, king of Judah, between you and me? It is not you I am attacking at this time, but the house with which I am at war. God has told me to hurry; so stop opposing God, who is with me, or he will destroy you."*
>
> – 2 Chronicles 35:21

END OF THE HOUSE OF DAVID

Josiah seemed to believe that Egypt and Assyria were weak, but his miscalculation proved fatal.

> *While Josiah was king, Pharaoh Necho king of Egypt went up to the Euphrates River to help the king of Assyria. King Josiah marched out to meet him in battle, but Necho faced him and killed him at Megiddo.*
>
> – 2 Kings 23:29

Apparently, King Josiah's dedication to Yahweh provided him no protection in battle or assurance of victory. Josiah's death brought an end of fealty to Yahweh in Judah. All of the kings that followed were pagan and a few years later Jerusalem was destroyed by the Babylonians.

The Death of King Josiah by Antonio Zanchi

The Egyptians marched north and fought with the Assyrians, but left behind a sizable force in Jerusalem. On their return march, Necho stopped in Jerusalem and deposed king Jehoahaz who had only ruled three months. Necho installed his own vassal king, Josiah's other son Jehoiakim, and imposed a heavy tribute on Judah.

Josiah's death at Megiddo marked the end of Judean independence and the effective end of the house of David. The Yahwist reforms were not enough to spare Yahweh's people from destruction and exile.

Prophet Jeremiah

Chapter Thirty-Six

PROPHET JEREMIAH

Weeping for Jerusalem

Jeremiah was a prophet in Judea during the time of Josiah, he was the son of the high priest Hilkiah and may have been one of the Deuteronomist writers. Jeremiah witnessed the fall of Jerusalem, the burning of the Temple, and the exile of the Hebrew people to Babylon. Jeremiah was taken with a different set of exiles to Egypt. Jeremiah was the chief mourner of King Josiah and was deeply bothered by the prompt return to pagan practices the moment that Josiah passed.

Jeremiah was known as the weeping prophet, he preached that Judah would be destroyed by invaders of the north because they had forsaken God by worshipping Baal, committing idolatry, and all the rest of the sins of the Canaanites. Jeremiah preached that the Babylonians would defeat Judah, which was an unpopular message with the king. The prophet used the metaphors of divorce and circumcision to describe the fealty Yahweh demands.

> *During the reign of King Josiah, Yahweh said to me, "Have you seen what faithless Israel has done? She has gone up on every high hill and under every spreading tree and has committed adultery there. I thought that after she had done all this she would return to me but she did not, and her unfaithful sister Judah saw it.*
>
> *"I gave faithless Israel her certificate of divorce and sent her away because of all her adulteries. Yet I saw that her unfaithful sister Judah had no fear; she also went out and committed adultery. Because Israel's immorality mattered so little to her, she defiled the land and committed adultery with stone and wood. In spite of all this, her unfaithful sister Judah did not return to me with all her heart, but only in pretense," declares Yahweh.*
>
> – Jeremiah 3:6-10

> *Circumcise yourselves to Yahweh, circumcise your hearts, you people of Judah and inhabitants of Jerusalem, or my wrath will flare up and burn like fire because of the evil you have done – burn with no one to quench it.*
>
> – Jeremiah 4:4

Jeremiah preached social justice and advocated for the poor against the depredations of the rich and powerful.

> *"Among my people are the wicked who lie in wait like men who snare birds and like those who set traps to catch people. Like cages full of birds, their houses are full of deceit; they have become rich and powerful and have grown fat and sleek. Their evil deeds have no limit; they do not seek justice. They do not promote the case of the fatherless; they do not defend the just cause of the poor."*
>
> – Jeremiah 5:26-29

> *If you really change your ways and your actions and deal with each other justly, if you do not oppress the foreigner, the fatherless or the widow and do not shed innocent blood in this place, and if you do not follow other gods to your own harm, then I will let you live in this place, in the land I gave your ancestors forever and ever.*
>
> – Jeremiah 7:5-7

Jerusalem's Final Warning

> *"Raise the signal to go to Zion! Flee for safety without delay! For I am bringing disaster from the north, even terrible destruction." A lion has come out of his lair; a destroyer of nations has set out. He has left his place to lay waste your land. Your towns will lie in ruins without inhabitant. So put on sackcloth, lament and wail, for the fierce anger of Yahweh has not turned away from us.*
>
> – Jeremiah 4:6-8

> *This is what Yahweh says: "Look, an army is coming from the land of the north; a great nation is being stirred up from the ends of the earth. They are armed with bow and spear; they are cruel and show no mercy. They sound like the roaring sea as they ride on their horses; they come like men in battle formation to attack you, Daughter Zion."*
>
> – Jeremiah 6:22-23

> *I will destroy Daughter Zion, so beautiful and delicate.*
>
> – Jeremiah 6:2

> *This is what Yahweh Almighty says: "Cut down the trees and build siege ramps against Jerusalem. This city must be punished; it is filled with oppression. As a well pours out its water, so she pours out her wickedness. Violence and destruction resound in her; her sickness and wounds are ever before me. Take warning, Jerusalem, or I will turn away from you and make your land desolate so no one can live in it."*
>
> – Jeremiah 6:8

Offerings of Cannabis to Yahweh

Hear, you earth: I am bringing disaster on this people, the fruit of their schemes because they have not listened to my words and have rejected my law.

What do I care about incense from Sheba or sweet cannabis [qaneh][1] from a distant land? Your burnt offerings are not acceptable; your sacrifices do not please me."

– Jeremiah 6:19-20

Yahweh was angry and now rejected the Israelite offerings as too little, too late; they are too far gone in their sins. Cannabis from a distant land does imply that they were not growing cannabis in Judah – but were trading for it. This passage again confirms that offerings of cannabis were made to Yahweh in the Hebrew temple.

Offerings to the Queen of Heaven

Judah persisted in worshipping the Goddess, they made offerings to Astarte, the Queen of Heaven.

Do you not see what they are doing in the towns of Judah and in the streets of Jerusalem? The children gather wood, the fathers light the fire, and the women knead the dough and make cakes to offer to the Queen of Heaven. They pour out drink offerings to other gods to arouse my anger.

– Jeremiah 7:17-18

Child Sacrifice Condemned

Yahweh's disgust with child sacrifice is again stated by Jeremiah.

"'The people of Judah have done evil in my eyes, declares Yahweh. They have set up their detestable idols in the house that bears my Name and have defiled it. They have built the high places of Topheth in the Valley of Ben Hinnom to burn their sons and daughters in the fire – something I did not command, nor did it enter my mind."

"So beware, the days are coming," declares Yahweh, "when people will no longer call it Topheth or the Valley of Ben Hinnom, but the Valley of Slaughter, for they will bury the dead in Topheth until there is no more room."

– Jeremiah 7:30-32

---

1 Qaneh in Hebrew, sweet calamus, sweet cane in most English translations.

Jerusalem is Taken and the Sons of King Zedekiah are Slain Before his Eyes

Chapter Thirty-Seven

EXILE to BABYLON

Nebuchadnezzar, King of Babylon

Nebuchadnezzar II became the king of Babylon in 605 BCE and consolidated the conquest of the Assyrians begun by his father with the destruction of Nineveh in 612 BCE. Nebuchadnezzar extended the empire into Anatolia and Egypt and for a brief time, the Neo-Babylonian (or Chaldean) empire dominated the Ancient Near East, until the rise of Cyrus II and the Persians in the following century.

Nebuchadnezzar led a great renaissance of Babylon and made many great renovations and restorations to the city; including the construction of the great walls, the grand processional boulevard, and the lavishly decorated Ishtar Gate. He rebuilt all his major cities on a lavish scale. At this time Babylon was the biggest, wealthiest, and most cosmopolitan city in the world.

At the Battle of Carchemish in 605 BCE, the armies of Egypt and the remnants of the Assyrians fought an alliance led by Babylon of Medes, Persians, and Scythians. Carchemish was an Egyptian colonial city on the Euphrates river and the default capital for the Assyrians after the fall of Nineveh. Pharaoh Necho II and the Egyptians were resoundingly defeated by Nebuchadnezzar who completely devastated the combined Egyptian and Assyrian forces. Necho was forced back to Egypt, his dreams of a new Egyptian empire shattered. On the way back to Egypt, he installed his vassal king in Jerusalem.

Destruction of Jerusalem

During the time of imperial unrest, Judah rebelled against Babylon. Nebuchadnezzar answered in 597 BCE by invading Judah and laying siege to Jerusalem, turning it into a vassal state. King Jehoiakim died and his 18-year-old son Jehoiachin became king, but he did not sit on the throne long. Three months after his ascension, Nebuchadnezzar marched up to the gates of Jerusalem and the king and the entire royal family surrendered. Nebuchadnezzar stripped the Temple of its valuables and sent 10,000 elites into exile in Babylon.

He carried all Jerusalem into exile: all the officers and fighting men, and all the skilled workers and artisans - a total of ten thousand. Only the poorest people of the land were left.

– 2 Kings 24:14

The last king of Judah was Zedekiah; he was installed by Nebuchadnezzar and ruled 11 years. Zedekiah was pagan and of no value to the Yahwists. Against the warnings of Jeremiah and other advisors, Zedekiah rebelled against Babylon in his ninth year and made an alliance with Egypt. Nebuchadnezzar responded by invading Judah again and laying siege to Jerusalem in December, 589 BCE. The siege lasted 30 months and great suffering befell the people. Jerusalem fell for good in 586 BCE.

Jeremiah Arrested

Jeremiah warned Zedekiah that Babylon would defeat Judah and the Egyptians would not be able to save them. Jeremiah was arrested, accused of being a traitor in favor of the Babylonians. Jeremiah was then thrown into a mud-filled cistern in an attempt to kill him, but he was rescued by allies.

When Nebuchadnezzar finally succeeded in taking Jerusalem, Zedekiah and his family attempted to flee but were captured on the plains of Jericho. The last thing Zedekiah ever saw was the execution of his sons – his eyes were put out and the last king of Judah was taken as a blind captive to Babylon and imprisoned.

The Burning of Jerusalem by Nebuchadnezzar's Army by Juan de la Corte

Solomon's Temple Burned

The Hebrew Temple was burned and the rest of the people exiled, leaving behind only the poorest of the poor. All of the valuables that remained were brought back to Babylon. The destruction of the Temple was the ultimate loss for the Israelites, Solomon's Temple was the heart and center of Hebrew spiritual life.

> *On the seventh day of the fifth month, in the nineteenth year of Nebuchadnezzar king of Babylon, Nebuzaradan, commander of the imperial guard, an official of the king of Babylon, came to Jerusalem. He set fire to the temple of Yahweh, the royal palace and all the houses of Jerusalem. Every important building he burned down.*
>
> *The whole Babylonian army under the commander of the imperial guard broke down the walls around Jerusalem. Nebuzaradan the commander of the guard carried into exile the people who remained in the city, along with the rest of the populace and those who had deserted to the king of Babylon. But the commander left behind some of the poorest people of the land to work the vineyards and fields.*
>
> – 2 Kings 25:8-12

Jeremiah was freed by the Babylonians and told that he was free to live wherever he wanted. He could go to Babylon with royal support, but Jeremiah chose to stay behind in Judah. There were disputes and conflicts among the remaining Judeans and the group decided to go to Egypt. Jeremiah counseled strongly against leaving Judah but was taken against his will with the group of exiles.

Women Defend the Goddess

In Egypt, Jeremiah had a big public dispute with the exiles, particularly with the women whom he blamed for worshipping Astarte, the Queen of Heaven, when they should have been worshipping Yahweh.

> *"This is what Yahweh Almighty, the God of Israel, says: 'You saw the great disaster I brought on Jerusalem and on all the towns of Judah. Today they lie deserted and in ruins because of the evil they have done. They aroused my anger by burning incense to and worshiping other gods that neither they nor you nor your ancestors ever knew.'"*
>
> – Jeremiah 44:2-3

The women responded to Jeremiah with great anger and indignation. They argued that life was good when they made their offerings to the Queen of Heaven, they had plenty of food and suffered no evil. It was only after they stopped making offerings to Astarte that they began suffering from sword and famine.

The women clearly believed that Astarte offered them more protection than Yahweh. This passage offers important details about how they baked cakes in the image of the Goddess and poured out drink offerings to her, practices that were also seen in Babylon.

> *Then all the men who knew that their wives were burning incense to other gods, along with all the women who were present – a large assembly – and all the people living in Lower and Upper Egypt, said to Jeremiah,*
>
> *"We will not listen to the message you have spoken to us in the name of Yahweh! We will certainly do everything we said we would: We will burn incense to the Queen of Heaven and will pour out drink offerings to her just as we and our ancestors, our kings and our officials did in the towns of Judah and in the streets of Jerusalem. At that time we had plenty of food and were well off and suffered no harm. But ever since we stopped burning incense to the Queen of Heaven and pouring out drink offerings to her, we have had nothing and have been perishing by sword and famine."*
>
> *The women added, "When we burned incense to the Queen of Heaven and poured out drink offerings to her, did not our husbands know that we were making cakes impressed with her image and pouring out drink offerings to her?"*
>
> *Then Jeremiah said to all the people, both men and women, who were answering him, "Did not Yahweh remember and call to mind the incense burned in the towns of Judah and the streets of Jerusalem by you and your ancestors, your kings and your officials and the people of the land? When Yahweh could no longer endure your wicked actions and the detestable things you did, your land became a curse and a desolate waste without inhabitants, as it is today. Because you have burned incense and have sinned against Yahweh and have not obeyed him or followed his law or his decrees or his stipulations, this disaster has come upon you, as you now see."*
>
> *Then Jeremiah said to all the people, including the women, "Hear the word of Yahweh, all you people of Judah in Egypt. This is what Yahweh Almighty, the God of Israel, says: You and your wives have done what you said you would do when you promised, 'We will certainly carry out the vows we made to burn incense and pour out drink offerings to the Queen of Heaven.' "Go ahead then, do what you promised! Keep your vows!"*
>
> – Jeremiah 44:15-25

The women angrily made clear that they had no intention of abandoning the great goddess. Jeremiah had no further response, he was angry but conceded, and basically said, "do what you want."

The drink offerings are never clearly identified, nor is the incense, but both could contain cannabis. Bhang was widely used ritually throughout Persia and India and by the Scythians. The Assyrians documented the use of cannabis in their sacred incense, and the Hebrews had their own holy anointing oil containing cannabis.

Competing Cosmologies

Of the 373 years that Solomon's Temple was in Jerusalem, an Asherah pole stood out front for roughly two-thirds of the time, worshipped by the traditional farming people. The mother goddess Asherah was El's wife but Yahweh wanted a divorce and he got it. The Goddess remains unattached to this day.

Solomon's Temple was the center of a spiritual conflict over fundamentally contradictory worldviews. Traditional folk beliefs held that the Heavenly Father and the Earthly Mother were husband and wife. King Solomon understood this, but the Yahwists preached that the Heavenly Father ruled alone.

Monotheism leaves no room for the Goddess. The Yahwist reformers pushed her worship out of the Temple and condemned it. Yahweh then took all the powers of nature and reproduction for himself. The women in the community who were dedicated to the Goddess were neither consulted nor did they approve, monotheism was forced upon them.

Prophet Ezekiel

Chapter Thirty-Eight

PROPHET EZEKIEL

By the Rivers of Babylon

The prophet Ezekiel lived in Judah during the Babylonian defeat of Jerusalem and he departed with the first wave of exiles. Five years later Ezekiel had a divine encounter by the rivers of Babylon and began his prophetic work. Yahweh called Ezekiel to prophesy against the exile Israelites for their stubborn and obstinate behavior. Ezekiel accused Israel of breaking the covenant, saying Jerusalem would be attacked again.

Ezekiel had a dramatic, phantasmagoric vision of God.

> *I looked, and I saw a windstorm coming out of the north – an immense cloud with flashing lightning and surrounded by brilliant light. The center of the fire looked like glowing metal, and in the fire was what looked like four living creatures. In appearance their form was human, but each of them had four faces and four wings. Their legs were straight; their feet were like those of a calf and gleamed like burnished bronze.*
>
> – Ezekiel 1:4-7

Son of Man, Eat this Scroll

Yahweh gave Ezekiel a scroll to eat. Many scholars have likened the scroll to hashish, and Ezekiel's visions as psychedelic. Majoun is a traditional intoxicating hashish candy made with sweets, nuts, and spices, that are common in the Middle East.

> *Then he said to me, "Son of man, eat this scroll I am giving you and fill your stomach with it." So I ate it, and it tasted as sweet as honey in my mouth.*
>
> – Ezekiel 3:3

Yahweh's presence is again described as a cloud filling the temple, from burning coals carried by cherubim, similar to Isaiah.

> *I looked, and I saw the likeness of a throne of lapis lazuli above the vault that was over the heads of the cherubim. Yahweh said to the man*

clothed in linen, "Go in among the wheels beneath the cherubim. Fill your hands with burning coals from among the cherubim and scatter them over the city." And as I watched, he went in.

Now the cherubim were standing on the south side of the temple when the man went in, and a cloud filled the inner court. Then the glory of Yahweh rose from above the cherubim and moved to the threshold of the temple. The cloud filled the temple, and the court was full of the radiance of the glory of Yahweh.

– Ezekiel 10:1-4

Smash the Idols

Yahweh continued his intolerance of paganism and promoting violence against it.

Your altars will be demolished and your incense altars will be smashed; and I will slay your people in front of your idols.

– Ezekiel 6:4

Wherever you live, the towns will be laid waste and the high places demolished, so that your altars will be laid waste and devastated, your idols smashed and ruined, your incense altars broken down, and what you have made wiped out.

– Ezekiel 6:6

And they will know that I am Yahweh, when their people lie slain among their idols around their altars, on every high hill and on all the mountaintops, under every spreading tree and every leafy oak--places where they offered fragrant incense to all their idols.

– Ezekiel 6:13

Women Weeping for Tammuz

Ezekiel has a vision of pagan worship in Solomon's Temple. He sees women weeping for Tammuz, Astarte's husband. Tammuz was the equivalent of the Sumerian Dumuzi, and in a later iteration he was Adonis.

Then he brought me to the entrance of the north gate of the house of Yahweh, and I saw women sitting there, mourning the god Tammuz.

– Ezekiel 8:14

Tammuz was the dying and rising god of the Canaanites. These traditions were strong in most pagan communities and came in a variety of guises, whether it was Demeter and Persephone in Eleusis, Isis and Osiris in Egypt, Aphrodite and Adonis, Cybele and Attis, and others. Tammuz died in the early summer when the rains ceased, leaving Astarte/Ishtar to mourn his passing. The women empathized with Astarte in the annual festival and ritually wept for the dying god. The Goddess then helped Tammuz return to life and reunite with him sexually while the people celebrated with feasts and rejoicing.

Tammuz is also the name of the tenth month of the Hebrew and Babylonian calendars. Solomon's Temple was burned in the month of Tammuz. Yet another indication of the pagan roots of the Hebrews that goes with one of the 12 Tribes being named Asher in honor of Asherah.

In Ezekiel's vision, Yahweh orders that the idolaters be killed with impunity in an act of mass murder.

> *Follow him through the city and kill, without showing pity or compassion. Slaughter the old men, the young men and women, the mothers and children"*
>
> – Ezekiel 9:5-6

Qedesha Condemned

Ezekiel condemned the women prophets, who can be understood to be the qedesha with their magic charms and veils of anonymity. Ezekiel says the qedesha had the powers of life itself, killing those who should not have died and sparing those who should not have lived, in defiance of Yahweh's judgment.

> *"Woe to the women who sew magic charms on all their wrists and make veils of various lengths for their heads in order to ensnare people. Will you ensnare the lives of my people but preserve your own? You have profaned me among my people for a few handfuls of barley and scraps of bread. By lying to my people, who listen to lies, you have killed those who should not have died and have spared those who should not live.*
>
> *"'Therefore this is what the Sovereign Yahweh says: I am against your magic charms with which you ensnare people like birds and I will tear them from your arms; I will set free the people that you ensnare like birds. I will tear off your veils and save my people from your hands, and they will no longer fall prey to your power. Then you will know that I am Yahweh.*

"Because you disheartened the righteous with your lies, when I had brought them no grief, and because you encouraged the wicked not to turn from their evil ways and so save their lives, therefore you will no longer see false visions or practice divination. I will save my people from your hands. And then you will know that I am Yahweh."

– Ezekiel 13:18-21

UNFAITHFUL WIFE

Unfaithful Goddess

Through Ezekiel, Yahweh castigates Jerusalem for her unfaithfulness, but the words can be read as God speaking angrily to his wife, the Goddess, exerting his dominance and authority. In this long passage, Ezekiel uses sexual language and imagery similar to Hosea.

On the day you were born your cord was not cut, nor were you washed with water to make you clean, nor were you rubbed with salt or wrapped in cloths. No one looked on you with pity or had compassion enough to do any of these things for you. Rather, you were thrown out into the open field, for on the day you were born you were despised.

"'Then I passed by and saw you kicking about in your blood, and as you lay there in your blood I said to you, "Live!" I made you grow like a plant of the field. You grew and developed and entered puberty. Your breasts had formed and your hair had grown, yet you were stark naked.

"'Later I passed by, and when I looked at you and saw that you were old enough for love, I spread the corner of my garment over you and covered your naked body. I gave you my solemn oath and entered into a covenant with you," declares the Sovereign Yahweh, "and you became mine.

"'I bathed you with water and washed the blood from you and put ointments on you. I clothed you with an embroidered dress and put sandals of fine leather on you. I dressed you in fine linen and covered you with costly garments. I adorned you with jewelry: I put bracelets on your arms and a necklace around your neck, and I put a ring on your nose, earrings on your ears, and a beautiful crown on your head.

"So, you were adorned with gold and silver; your clothes were of fine linen and costly fabric and embroidered cloth. Your food was honey, olive oil, and the finest flour. You became very beautiful and rose to be a queen. And your fame spread among the nations on account of your beauty, because the splendor I had given you made your beauty perfect," declares the Sovereign Yahweh.

– Ezekiel 16:4-14

"But you trusted in your beauty and used your fame to become a prostitute. You lavished your favors on anyone who passed by and your beauty became his. You took some of your garments to make gaudy high places, where you carried on your prostitution. You went to him, and he possessed your beauty. You also took the fine jewelry I gave you, the jewelry made of my gold and silver, and you made for yourself male idols and engaged in prostitution with them.

And you took your embroidered clothes to put on them, and you offered my oil and incense before them. Also the food I provided for you – the flour, olive oil, and honey I gave you to eat – you offered as fragrant incense before them. That is what happened," declares the Sovereign Yahweh.

– Ezekiel 16:15-19

"And you took your sons and daughters whom you bore to me and sacrificed them as food to the idols. Was your prostitution not enough? You slaughtered my children and sacrificed them to the idols. In all your detestable practices and your prostitution you did not remember the days of your youth, when you were naked and bare, kicking about in your blood."

– Ezekiel 16:20-22

"'Woe! Woe to you," declares the Sovereign Yahweh. "In addition to all your other wickedness, you built a mound for yourself and made a lofty shrine in every public square. At every street corner you built your lofty shrines and degraded your beauty, spreading your legs with increasing promiscuity to anyone who passed by. You engaged in prostitution with the Egyptians, your neighbors with large genitals, and aroused my anger with your increasing promiscuity."

– Ezekiel 16:23-26

"So, I stretched out my hand against you and reduced your territory; I gave you over to the greed of your enemies, the daughters of the Philistines, who were shocked by your lewd conduct. You engaged in prostitution with the Assyrians too, because you were insatiable; and even after that, you still were not satisfied. Then you increased your promiscuity to include Babylonia, a land of merchants, but even with this you were not satisfied."

– Ezekiel 16:27-29

"I am filled with fury against you," declares the Sovereign Yahweh, "when you do all these things, acting like a brazen prostitute! When you built your

mounds at every street corner and made your lofty shrines in every public square, you were unlike a prostitute, because you scorned payment."

– Ezekiel 16:30-31

"You adulterous wife! You prefer strangers to your own husband! All prostitutes receive gifts, but you give gifts to all your lovers, bribing them to come to you from everywhere for your illicit favors. So in your prostitution you are the opposite of others; no one runs after you for your favors. You are the very opposite, for you give payment and none is given to you."

– Ezekiel 16:32-34

(The Greek and Roman writers described the custom of Near Eastern women giving gifts to their lovers.)

"Therefore, you prostitute, hear the word of Yahweh! This is what the Sovereign Yahweh says: Because you poured out your lust and exposed your naked body in your promiscuity with your lovers, and because of all your detestable idols, and because you gave them your children's blood, therefore I am going to gather all your lovers, with whom you found pleasure, those you loved as well as those you hated. I will gather them against you from all around and will strip you in front of them, and they will see you stark naked. I will sentence you to the punishment of women who commit adultery and who shed blood; I will bring on you the blood vengeance of my wrath and jealous anger.

"Then I will deliver you into the hands of your lovers, and they will tear down your mounds and destroy your lofty shrines. They will strip you of your clothes and take your fine jewelry and leave you stark naked. They will bring a mob against you, who will stone you and hack you to pieces with their swords. They will burn down your houses and inflict punishment on you in the sight of many women. I will put a stop to your prostitution, and you will no longer pay your lovers. Then my wrath against you will subside and my jealous anger will turn away from you; I will be calm and no longer angry."

– Ezekiel 16:35-42

Promiscuous Sisters

In a separate story, Ezekiel describes the behavior of two promiscuous sisters and Yahweh's judgment against them. To Ezekiel, the entire city of Jerusalem was a prostitute.

Yet she became more and more promiscuous as she recalled the days of her youth when she was a prostitute in Egypt. There she lusted after her lovers, whose genitals were like those of donkeys and whose emission was like that of horses. So you longed for the lewdness of your youth, when in Egypt your bosom was caressed and your young breasts fondled.

– Ezekiel 23:19-21

LAMENT FOR TYRE

Prophecies of Destruction

Ezekiel announced prophecies of destruction against all of Judah's neighbors; Ammon, Moab, Edom, the Philistines, and Tyre. The detailed descriptions of Tyre demonstrate their reputation in the ancient world as master artisans, shipbuilders, and traders.

"For this is what the Sovereign Yahweh says: From the north, I am going to bring against Tyre Nebuchadnezzar king of Babylon, king of kings, with horses and chariots, with horsemen and a great army. He will ravage your settlements on the mainland with the sword; he will set up siege works against you, build a ramp up to your walls and raise his shields against you. He will direct the blows of his battering rams against your walls and demolish your towers with his weapons.

– Ezekiel 26:7-9

Hempen Shipbuilders

Say to Tyre, situated at the gateway to the sea, merchant of peoples on many coasts, 'This is what the Sovereign Yahweh says: "'You say, Tyre, "I am perfect in beauty." Your domain was on the high seas; your builders brought your beauty to perfection.

They made all your timbers of juniper from Senir; they took a cedar from Lebanon to make a mast for you. Of oaks from Bashan they made your oars; of cypress wood from the coasts of Cyprus they made your deck, adorned with ivory. Fine embroidered linen from Egypt was your sail and served as your banner; your awnings were of blue and purple from the coasts of Elishah.

Men of Sidon and Arvad were your oarsmen; your skilled men, Tyre, were aboard as your sailors. Veteran craftsmen of Byblos were on board as shipwrights to caulk your seams. All the ships of the sea and their sailors came alongside to trade for your wares.

– Ezekiel 27:3-9

In the lament to Tyre, we find a description of their skills as sailors and craftsmen. There are many allusions to hemp; the awnings of blue and purple, the seams caulked with hemp and bitumen, and every ship's ropes and rigging made from hemp.

Cannabis from Lebanon

Here we see cannabis listed among the wares traded between Tyre and Damascus. Both cannabis fibers and drugs were objects of trade, and Lebanon is famous for its hashish to this day.

> *"'Damascus did business with you because of your many products and great wealth of goods. They offered wine from Helbon, wool from Zahar and casks of wine from Izal in exchange for your wares: wrought iron, cassia, and cannabis [qaneh].*[1]
>
> – Ezekiel 27:18-19

The same list contains the Hebrew word *pannag*, which does not appear anywhere else in the Bible. Pannag is often translated as unidentified "cakes" or "confections", but some scholars believe it is a majoun, an intoxicating hashish pastry.

> *"Judah and Israel traded with you; they exchanged wheat from Minnith and Pannag, honey, olive oil and balm for your wares.*
>
> – Ezekiel 27:17

Cannabis in 2nd Isaiah

Cannabis also appears in Isaiah 43, which comes from the time of exile in Babylon after the destruction of Jerusalem. These writings were by an unknown author and tacked onto the earlier writings of the prophet Isaiah and are known as Second Isaiah.

Israel had offended Yahweh with their lack of offerings. Fragrant cannabis is included among the offerings that Israel had failed to bring.

> *"You have not bought any fragrant cannabis [qaneh]*[2] *for me, or lavished on me the fat of your sacrifices. But you have burdened me with your sins and wearied me with your offenses".*
>
> – Isaiah 43:24

Perfect in Beauty

> *"Son of man, take up a lament concerning the king of Tyre and say to him: 'This is what the Sovereign Yahweh says: "'You were the seal of perfection, full of wisdom and perfect in beauty. You were in Eden, the garden of God; every precious stone adorned you: carnelian, chrysolite,*

1 Hebrew qaneh, calamus, sweet cane, aromatic cane in English translations.
2 Cannabis is mistranslated as calamus, sweet cane, or aromatic cane, in most Bibles.

and emerald, topaz, onyx and jasper, lapis lazuli, turquoise, and beryl. Your settings and mountings were made of gold; on the day you were created they were prepared. You were anointed as a guardian cherub, for so I ordained you. You were on the holy mount of God; you walked among the fiery stones. You were blameless in your ways from the day you were created till wickedness was found in you.

"Through your widespread trade you were filled with violence, and you sinned. So I drove you in disgrace from the mount of God, and I expelled you, guardian cherub, from among the fiery stones. Your heart became proud on account of your beauty, and you corrupted your wisdom because of your splendor. So I threw you to the earth; I made a spectacle of you before kings. By your many sins and dishonest trade, you have desecrated your sanctuaries. So I made a fire come out from you, and it consumed you, and I reduced you to ashes on the ground in the sight of all who were watching. All the nations who knew you are appalled at you; you have come to a horrible end and will be no more."

– Ezekiel 28:12-19

Ezekiel predicted the Babylonian attack on Tyre which really did happen. Nebuchadnezzar laid siege to Tyre for 13 years from 586-573 BCE, but he never succeeded in taking the fortified island. It was neither the first nor the last time Tyre was besieged.

Alexander the Great

The city of Tyre consisted of two parts. The mainland city on the coast of Lebanon is very ancient, first settled around 2750 BCE. And then there is an island ½ mile from shore featuring two sheltered harbors and an impregnable fortress with walls soaring 150 feet above the sea. Nebuchadnezzar completely destroyed the mainland portion of the city but was never able to take the fortified island. The Babylonians had no navy and the Tyrians could move about freely by sea.

It was not until 332 BCE that the island fortress finally fell, at the hands of Alexander the Great, who devised a brilliant and brutal strategy to overcome the defenses. Phoenicians usually sought to pay off invaders and make nice, but they denied Alexander's requests to make a sacrifice to the god Melqart in their sacred temple. Foreigners were not allowed to enter Melqart's temple and the Phoenicians were famously superstitious about their gods.

Melqart was a manifestation of Hercules, whom Alexander identified with, and he was insulted to not be permitted entry. He threatened the city and offered to spare them if his requests were permitted. The Tyrians responded by killing Alexander's emissaries and throwing their bodies from the walls into the sea, confident their position was secure.

Tyre Laid to Waste

Alexander was outraged and incensed, he vowed to destroy the city. His plan was simple, stunning, and effective. Alexander blockaded the island with a navy commandeered from neighboring Sidon. At the same time, Alexander completely razed the mainland portion of Tyre and dumped the rubble into the channel. Using timber from the famous cedar forests of Lebanon, the Macedonians built a massive causeway to the island.

The Tyrians resisted courageously, setting fire to the siege towers and sending divers to cut the anchor cables of Alexander's ships. Despite desperate attempts to hold the invaders at bay, Alexander's army breached the walls after eight months. From a tall siege tower, Alexander personally led his elite soldiers over the walls as they forced their way into the city.

It was a slaughterhouse; Alexander laid Tyre to waste. The Macedonians killed or sold into slavery all 30,000 residents. Another 2000 soldiers were crucified on the beach. Before he left, Alexander made his offerings at the Temple of Melqart.

With the fall of Tyre, Carthage emerged as the most important Phoenician colony and the wealthiest city in the Mediterranean. Tyre is still inhabited today but it never regained the heights it held during its Phoenician glory. Over time the causeway silted in and to this day Tyre remains a peninsula and not an island.

A Naval Action During the Siege of Tyre

Chapter Thirty-Nine

CYRUS THE GREAT

Persian Empire

Cyrus II of Persia, also known as Cyrus the Great, defeated the Babylonians and created the Achaemenid (Persian) Empire, the largest empire the world had ever known at that time. The Persian Empire dominated the Near East for two centuries until its defeat at the hands of Alexander.

Cyrus marched into Babylon in 539 BCE and was welcomed with celebrations – the previous king Nabonidus was an apostate who ignored Marduk and the traditional gods in favor of worshipping the moon god Sin alone.

Cyrus was hailed in his time as a wise and benevolent ruler. He earned the goodwill and loyalty of local populations by rejecting the raw brutality of the Assyrians and Babylonians, promoting religious tolerance, and returning exiles to their homes.

Freedom from Exile

For the Jews, Cyrus was a near-messianic figure who freed them from exile, allowing them to return to Jerusalem and re-establish their community and temple.

> *In the first year of Cyrus king of Persia, in order to fulfill the word of Yahweh spoken by Jeremiah, Yahweh moved the heart of Cyrus king of Persia to make a proclamation throughout his realm and also to put it in writing:*
>
> *"This is what Cyrus king of Persia says: 'Yahweh, the God of heaven, has given me all the kingdoms of the earth and he has appointed me to build a temple for him at Jerusalem in Judah. Any of his people among you may go up to Jerusalem in Judah and build the temple of Yahweh, the God of Israel, the God who is in Jerusalem, and may their God be with them. And in any locality where survivors may now be living, the people are to provide them with silver and gold, with goods and livestock, and with freewill offerings for the temple of God in Jerusalem.'"*
>
> – Ezra 1:1-4

Religious Tolerance

Cyrus established Babylon as his capital, prior to building Persepolis. He made a great declaration of peace and demonstrated his commitment to religious tolerance. Cyrus allowed for all the gods to be restored to their temples. The proclamation was written in cuneiform text on a large cylinder and put on public display in Babylon.

Archaeologists found the Cyrus Cylinder. It uses language that is remarkably similar to the Bible, except where the Bible credits Yahweh, Cyrus credits Marduk. Marduk was the Babylonian equivalent to Baal and Zeus.

It is possible that Cyrus issued proclamations in the names of many gods in different communities in the spirit of religious tolerance and harmony. It is also possible that the Biblical writers copied the wording used. The Persians at the time were generally Zoroastrian but Cyrus's personal faith is unknown.

Cyrus Cylinder

> *I am Cyrus, king of the world, great king, mighty king, king of Babylon, king of the lands of Sumer and Akkad, king of the four quarters of the universe... from an ancient royal lineage, whose reign is beloved by (the gods) Marduk and Nabu, whose kingship they desired to make them glad.*
>
> *After entering Babylon in peace, amidst joy and jubilation, I made the royal palace the center of my rule. The great lord Marduk, who loves Babylon, with great magnanimity, established (it) as (my) destiny, and I sought to worship him each day. My teeming army paraded about Babylon in peace, and I did not allow any trouble in all of Sumer and Akkad. I took great care to peacefully (protect) the city of Babylon and its cult places.*
>
> *(And) as for the citizens of Babylon... whom (Nabonidus) had made subservient in a manner (totally) unsuited to them against the will of the gods, I released them from their weariness and loosened their burden. The great lord Marduk rejoiced in my deeds.*
>
> *Kindly he blessed me, Cyrus, the king, his worshipper, Cambyses, the offspring of my loins, and all of my troops, so that we could go about in peace and well-being. By his lofty command, all enthroned kings, the whole world, from the Upper Sea to the Lower Sea, inhabitants of distant regions, all the kings of the West, tent dwellers, brought their heavy tribute to me in Babylon and kissed my feet.*
>
> *From [Babylon] to Ashur and Susa, Agade, Eshnunna, the cities of Zamban, Meturnu, Der as far as the borders of the Gutians – I returned*

to these sanctuaries on the other side of the Tigris, sanctuaries founded in ancient times, the images that had been in them there and I made their dwellings permanent. I also gathered all their people and returned to them their habitations. And then at the command of Marduk, the great lord, I resettled all the gods of Sumer and Akkad whom Nabonidus had brought into Babylon to the anger of the lord of the gods in their shrines, the places which they enjoy.

May all the gods whom I have resettled in their sacred cities ask Marduk and Nabu each day for a long life for me and speak well of me to him; may they say to Marduk, my lord, that Cyrus, the king who worships you, and Cambyses, his son ... their ... I settled all the people of Babylon who prayed for my kingship and all their lands in a peaceful place.[1]

The Cyrus Cylinder, 539 BCE, Babylon

1 Chavalas, Mark ed., translation by Piotr Michalowski, *Historical Sources in Translation: The Ancient Near East*, Blackwell, 2006, published on pp. 428-29. https://www.britishmuseum.org/research/collection_online/collection_object_details.aspx?objectId=327188&partId=1

Ezra Reads the Law to the People

Chapter Forty

WRITING the BIBLE

Sacred Texts Collected

The exiles from Jerusalem brought all the sacred texts they could rescue from Solomon's Temple before it burned. The Hebrew Bible took the form we read today in Babylon during the exile. It is a collection of books written by many authors over many centuries, the precise dates when stories were written and the names of the authors are mostly unknown.

By Talmudic tradition, the 24-book canon of the Hebrew Bible was fixed in 458 BCE by Ezra and the men of the Great Assembly when the texts were first brought to Jerusalem. Additional contributions continued for another 200 years.

The first five books of the Bible are known as the Torah: Genesis, Exodus, Leviticus, Numbers, and Deuteronomy. Tradition says they were all written by Moses himself, but modern scholarship asserts that these books were collected and edited by scribes 500 years or more after Moses would have lived. The bulk of the Book of Deuteronomy was certainly written in the time period of King Josiah and his reforms.

E-J-D-P

Biblical scholars and linguists have studied the Bible for centuries and have identified four groups of authors based on clues in the language and the context of the material. These authors are identified as "E," "J," "D," and "P."

"E" refers to the Elohist, texts that use the name "Elohim" for God. These are the oldest stories from the era when the pagan Hebrews worshipped El, before Moses came along and introduced Yahweh and the monotheistic reforms. These texts include parts of Genesis, Exodus, and Numbers that were later stitched together with other texts. Most significantly, the Elohist wrote the first account of creation in seven days that opens the Bible in Genesis 1:1.

"J" refers to the texts that use the name Yahweh (Jahweh in German, or Jehovah) and is the author of most of the Torah, as seen in Genesis, Exodus, Leviticus, and Numbers. In the Biblical narrative, these are the oldest parts of the story, but that does not mean that these were the oldest stories actually written. Many of the stories about Abraham were written later using the name Yahweh for God, even though the historical Abraham would have been worshipping El.

Widespread literacy in the Near East began the 8th-7th century BCE, which is when the very oldest texts like the Song of Miriam were thought to have been first recorded from the oral tradition.

"D" is the Deuteronomist group. These were the priests and prophets during King Josiah's reign who "found" the lost book of Moses that became the Book of Deuteronomy (Second Law). These writings include many of the laws about behavior and sexual morality that drove Josiah's reforms.

The Deuteronomists are believed to have written most of the historical books; Joshua, Judges, Ruth, Samuel, and Kings. They also likely added sermons Moses said during the wanderings in the wilderness. The Deuteronomists collected the "E" and "J" texts and transmitted them forward to Babylon, along with the writings of the prophets. "J" may have been a member of the Deuteronomists, and the prophet Jeremiah may have been a member as well.

"P" refers to the "Priestly" group of scribes working in Babylon after the exile, presumably under the supervision of Ezra. They assembled the Hebrew Bible into the form we know it today. The "P" writers had the final editorial authority over the text. The "P" writers effectively created the Jewish sacred religious texts from tradition and fragments, and they wrote the rest.

The original Hebrew script was written with no vowels or punctuation, it is an intentionally mystical text full of numerology and profound symbolism. Every word is subject to interpretation based on different choices of vowels. Scholars have debated countless reinterpretations based on alternative vowel choices and these debates will continue as long as people care about the Bible.

Written in Babylon

The Persians allowed the Israelites to practice their religion and encouraged their return to Judea (renamed from Judah), where they became the "Jews." A succession of Persian kings sponsored the Jews to write their sacred texts and provided gold to build the second Jewish Temple in Jerusalem.

We have no way of knowing which texts made the journey to Babylon and what materials the "P" writers had to work with, nor do we know what material was excised out. Based on linguistic clues indicating Babylonian influence, it is believed that the "P" writers wrote much of Genesis and Exodus, including the stories of Abraham and Moses.

Certain details, such as saying that Abraham came from the city of "Ur of the Chaldeans," indicates late authorship in Babylon, because the Chaldeans did not exist as a people in the time of Abraham. The "P" writers also recorded the most famous mythological tales; the Garden of Eden, Noah and the Flood, and the Tower of Babel, all of which have clear connections to older Mesopotamian mythology.

These "P" writers were working in the shadow of the great Ziggurat dedicated to Marduk, in the city filled with the followers of Ishtar, the whore of Babylon. The Yahwists' disdain for the pagan traditions can be felt throughout the text.

The Wisdom literature; the books of Proverbs and Ecclesiastes that are attributed to King Solomon, the Book of Job, as well as the devotional literature and poetry found in the Psalms are all impossible to accurately date.

CULTURE WAR

The polemical nature of the Hebrew Bible is clear to any objective reader, there is a culture war context to the historical and prophetic texts. No attempt is ever made to explain the perspective of the Canaanites or any of the opponents of the Israelites, they are all branded as vile and abominable, while the Israelites are holy, God's chosen people. Nor can the historical writers be considered to be objective; they clearly exaggerate numbers, inflate their heroes, and slander their opponents. It is a revisionist history portraying a one-sided view of events and people.

The Biblical writers were not the common people and their views did not reflect the common people. The Biblical writers were educated and literary elite with an ideological agenda, members of the minority cult of Yahweh that disparaged the common culture. The Yahwists were cultural revolutionaries and they wanted to bring major changes to society. The biblical writers were political partisans and not objective. They championed the cause of Judean nationalism and orthodox Yahwism, and they had no tolerance for divergent views.

The Hebrew rejection of superstitious idolatry and child sacrifice is deserving of credit, though they were extreme in their misogyny towards women and the Goddess. Biblical writers were ashamed and afraid of the Hebrew Goddess, but by condemning her they acknowledge her existence. Goddess worship was driven underground and in later generations, the meaning of Asherah was forgotten.

Moses by Michelangelo

Chapter Forty-One

PAGAN MOSES

Changes in Tradition

The "P" writers in Babylon gave us the biblical text we read today. There had clearly been shifts in the religious practices since the time of Moses, some 800 years earlier, when the Hebrews were much closer to their pagan roots. There are clues in the text that show the biblical writers altered or edited details of Moses' career to fit the ideological agenda of the day, whitewashing embarrassing facts from the past.

The first and most obvious clue of shifts in worship practices is the change in attitudes toward the bronze serpent Moses had made. For centuries the bronze serpent was worshipped but the Yahwist reformers saw the tradition as too pagan and broke the statue into pieces. The serpent was then turned into a negative symbol in the Garden of Eden.

The disappearance of Miriam from the story and the lack of details about her dispute with Moses could indicate parts of the story that were excised because they were uncomfortable for the writers. Perhaps Miriam was a qedesha, after all, she was buried in their holy city of Kadesh.

The story of Moses was clearly embellished to make it more legendary. Moses' birth story was adapted directly from Sargon of Akkad, again showing Mesopotamian influence. The historical Moses was probably something of a desert shaman, filling his tent with intoxicating cannabis smoke to help him talk to God and receive revelations.

Linen and Wool

The Shatnez is one tradition that changes from the time of Moses to the time of the Deuteronomists. Shatnez is a Jewish prohibition on clothes made from linen and wool woven together. Modern-day Jews have their clothes inspected to make sure they are not linsey-woolsey; it is a rule similar to eating only kosher foods.

> *Do not wear clothes of wool and linen woven together.*
>
> – Deuteronomy 22:11

"Keep my decrees. Do not mate different kinds of animals. Do not plant your field with two kinds of seed. Do not wear clothing woven of two kinds of material."
– Leviticus 19:19

Maimonides, the famous Jewish philosopher from the Middle Ages, described the reasons for shatnez in his 1190 CE book, *the Guide for the Perplexed*. Maimonides wrote that the shatnez was part of the ban on pagan magical practices and connections to idolatry. There is also the fact that the practitioners were typically women.

For the same reason, the wearing of garments made of linen and wool is prohibited: the heathen priests adorned themselves with garments containing vegetable and animal material, whilst they held in their hand a seal made of a mineral. This you find written in their books.
– Maimonides, *Guide for the Perplexed,* part 3, ch. 37, v. 5

Farmer and Shepherd

Maimonides says that the mixing of animal and vegetable is forbidden because it is a pagan practice, the blending of farmer and shepherd. It is akin to mixing the spiritual forces represented by Cain, the shepherd who produces wool from his sheep, and Abel, the farmer who produces linen from the Earth. The Hebrews were shepherds, while the farmers were Goddess worshippers. The Hebrews wanted a divorce of God from the Goddess and so they eliminated the traditions that symbolized the farmer and shepherd being brought together.

Sumerian mythology saw conflict between farmer and shepherd turn to friendship, while the biblical conflict between Cain and Abel led to murder and resentment. Bhang, the sacred cannabis milk drink from Persia and

India is a blend of animal and vegetable; milk from cattle, and cannabis from Mother Earth.

Maimonedes was correct in saying that pagans sought the spiritual union of the Heavenly Father and the Earthly Mother. The biblical monotheist traditions explicitly rejected that notion because they reject the existence of the Goddess altogether.

Ephods, Curtains, Spices

Yet at the time of Moses, the instructions given for making the Tabernacle curtains and the ephod on the priest's breastplate are explicitly described as linen mixed with yarn, which is wool from sheep.

> *All those who were skilled among the workers made the tabernacle with ten curtains of finely twisted linen and blue, purple and scarlet yarn, with cherubim woven into them by expert hands.*
>
> – Exodus 36:8

> *They made the ephod of gold, and of blue, purple and scarlet yarn, and of finely twisted linen.*
>
> – Exodus 39:2

This is a strong example of the Hebrews' pagan roots at the time of Moses and the linen could be made of fine hemp.

> *From what you have, take an offering for Yahweh. Everyone who is willing is to bring to Yahweh an offering of gold, silver and bronze; blue, purple and scarlet yarn and fine linen; goat hair; ram skins dyed red and another type of durable leather; acacia wood; olive oil for the light; spices for the anointing oil and for the fragrant incense.*
>
> – Exodus 35:5-8

Here again, we see the pagan details listed together in Exodus; the woolen yarn and linen, spices for the anointing oil and incense containing cannabis. These are among the details that change in later reforms. The biblical writers edited the stories the best they could to present their preferred view of history, but some details slipped through. This shows how cannabis was used ritually at the time of Moses and rejected later on during the reforms of Hezekiah, Josiah, and Ezra.

Creation of Light

CHAPTER FORTY-TWO

GENESIS

SEVEN DAYS OF CREATION

There are two creation stories stitched together in the Bible, and they illustrate the distinct authorship between "J" and "E." These two stories follow one another and contradict each other in important details, demonstrating to any student that it is impossible to read the Bible literally because it is full of contradictions and inconsistencies. The Bible is meant to be read as sacred wisdom literature full of poetic allegories, not as journalism, or a scientific history of life on Earth.

The first page of the Bible opens with the well-known story where God creates the world in seven days. This story is from the Elohist tradition because it uses the name Elohim for God and not Yahweh. The Creation story is likely quite old and may predate the introduction of the name Yahweh by Moses.

The Seven Days of Creation is unique among ancient creation mythologies by reflecting pure monotheism. Elohim creates the Heavens and the Earth all by himself, asexually, without the participation of a goddess. In most other cultures, particularly the pagan cultures, there were male and female deities who mated and parented generations of gods and supernatural creatures. The Hebrews are unique in having a deity that is male without having a female mate and no sex life. The Hebrew language does not even have a word for *goddess.*

In many of these pagan myths, the first mover of creation was a primordial mother goddess who gave birth to her own mate, and from there creation began. The primordial mother goddess was the virgin mother of all. In the Mesopotamian myths from Sumer and Babylon, the primordial mother goddess was depicted as a great sea, *the waters.*

IN THE BEGINNING...

> *In the beginning Elohim created the heavens and the earth. Now the earth was formless and empty, darkness was over the surface of the deep, and the Spirit of Elohim was hovering over the waters.*
>
> – Genesis 1:1-2

There are clear stylistic and symbolic similarities between Genesis and the Babylonian creation myth, the Enuma Elish, particularly in the opening lines. Both stories begin with a primordial emptiness, before Heaven and Earth were formed, when all was water. In Genesis, God alone is responsible for creation, and his spirit "hovers above the waters," implying that the waters were already present.

In the Enuma Elish, the goddess Tiamat is the salt waters, and her mate Apsu is the fresh waters. Apsu is born from Tiamat and they mingle together to parent the other gods and all of creation. Tiamat is clearly identified as the mother of all, the virgin mother who gave birth to her own mate.

> *When in the height heaven was not named,*
> *And the earth beneath did not yet bear a name,*
> *And the primeval Apsu, who begat them,*
> *And chaos, Tiamat, the mother of them both*
> *Their waters were mingled together,*
>
> – Enuma Elish, 1st Tablet:1-5[1]

Tiamat is not the only virgin mother who gave birth to her own mate, this was a typical mythical formulation. For the Olympian Greeks, the mother goddess Gaia gave birth to her husband Uranus and they parented the next generation of deities. For the Sumerians, the primeval sea was named Nammu, and she gave birth to An and Ki, (Heaven and Earth), as well as Enki, who is wisdom. Heaven and Earth are the first manifestations of God and Goddess in the human realm, the Heavenly Father and the Earthly Mother. The Hebrews simply removed the name of the Goddess from their creation myth, though her presence remained.

The great scholar of mythology Joseph Campbell pointed out that the "waters" mentioned in Genesis, is in fact the Goddess, unnamed and unidentified.[2] The Hebrews were familiar with the older Babylonian myth and they used some of the same literary motifs. Their perception of the first moments of creation were similar, the Hebrews modified the Babylonian myth by simply redacting any mention of the Goddess from the story, yet certain details, like the waters, reveal her presence. The waters were present at the beginning because the waters is the Goddess, the virgin mother of God. Some scholars equate the Hebrew word *tehom* which means *deep* with *Tiamat.*

1 King, L.W. (translator), "Enuma Elish - The Epic of Creation," from *The Seven Tablets of Creation*, London 1902. https://www.sacred-texts.com/ane/enuma.htm.

2 *Goddesses: Mysteries Of The Feminine Divine*, Joseph Campbell, New World Library, Novato, California, 2013, p.235.

LET US MAKE MANKIND IN OUR IMAGE

> *Then God said, "Let us make mankind in our image, in our likeness, so that they may rule over the fish in the sea and the birds in the sky, over the livestock and all the wild animals, and over all the creatures that move along the ground."*
>
> – Genesis 1:26

Interestingly, Elohim says, "Let *us* make mankind in *our* image, in *our* likeness" as though he is speaking to other deities. The meaning of this plural phrase has been debated for centuries by students of scripture, it is ambiguous since the Hebrew tradition is clearly monotheistic. Here again, we see the monotheistic writers betraying the pagan roots of their mythologies. El was the Heavenly Father in the Canaanite pantheon of gods before he became Yahweh. In the earliest stories, El is interacting with the rest of the pantheon, but later monotheistic editors removed direct mention of these other gods, though their shadows remained in the text.

DOMINION OVER NATURE

What is not ambiguous in Genesis is the declaration that mankind will rule over all the plants and animals. The idea that humans are superior and rule over nature in a role ordained by the creator of the universe is deeply embedded in Judeo-Christian tradition and the Western mind. This belief has always distinguished biblical cultures from indigenous animist cultures that believe humans are a part of nature and that the Earth is our mother. Separation from nature is a direct consequence of a spiritual worldview that has no role for the feminine divine and the Mother Goddess.

> *So, God created mankind in his own image, in the image of God he created them; male and female he created them.*
>
> *God blessed them and said to them, "Be fruitful and increase in number; fill the earth and subdue it. Rule over the fish in the sea and the birds in the sky and over every living creature that moves on the ground."*
>
> – Genesis 1:27-28

In this creation, man and woman are created together as equals, side by side. In the Garden of Eden story, Eve is created from Adam's rib and is intended to be subordinate to him. This is among the contradictory details between the two creation myths in Genesis.

Genesis teaches us that the world was created for the benefit of man, rather than man being in a humbled position. Humans are created in the image of God, and are exalted, which was not typical in ancient mythology. In most pagan mythology humans were created to serve the gods. Humans were in effect, slaves to the gods. These details distinguish the Hebrews from their pagan neighbors.

In pagan beliefs, humans were not created in the image of God. It was clearly understood that the gods periodically took the form of humans in order to interact with them in stories. Humans could not interact with the gods when they were in their full glory because the humans would be vaporized. In the Enuma Elish, humans are created to be slaves to the gods and relieve them of their labors. The Hebrews taught and believed that they were God's chosen people, favored above all others, and these beliefs have permeated the Judeo-Christian tradition ever since.

Every Seed-Bearing Plant

> *Then God said, "I give you every seed-bearing plant on the face of the whole earth and every tree that has fruit with seed in it. They will be yours for food. And to all the beasts of the earth and all the birds in the sky and all the creatures that move along the ground – everything that has the breath of life in it – I give every green plant for food." And it was so.*
>
> *God saw all that he had made, and it was very good.*
>
> –Genesis 1:29-31

In Genesis, Elohim gives us every seed-bearing herb, which was usually a role for the Goddess who embodied nature and the growth of green plants. This is an example of God taking over the authority of the Goddess for himself.

It is worth noting that cannabis prohibition directly contradicts this biblical teaching. God gives us every green plant for food, cannabis is no exception. Human authorities have no ethical mandate to deny us the use of any wild-growing plants.

GARDEN OF EDEN

Adam and Eve

The second chapter of Genesis gives us the second creation story, the familiar story of Adam and Eve in the Garden of Eden. This story is often described as the *Fall of Man* because it is said to describe the birth of sin and misery in the human experience. But the story should really be seen as the *Fall of the Goddess* because it is a condemnation of Goddess worship, the great rival to the monotheists at the time the story was written.

Eve represents the goddess traditions that were closely associated with serpents, mystical plants, and the tree of life. Cannabis makes a special appearance here as well. For a contemporary audience in Jerusalem at the time, the Hebrew Bible was finalized in the 5th century BCE, these meanings would have been crystal clear. It was St. Augustine in the 4th century CE who first interpreted the Garden of Eden story in terms of original sin, and his teachings have been influential ever since.

The exact date of authorship for the Garden of Eden story is unknown. It is commonly said to have been an early story from the 8th century BCE, but there is no evidence for that. The Garden of Eden story may have been one of the last stories written in Babylon, it has clear political symbolism that would have been understood by the contemporary audiences. The story is a condemnation of nature worship and every word is important, not a single detail is misplaced. The text is deeply symbolic and laden with meaning. The Garden of Eden story is the divorce papers signed, sealed, and delivered.

Symbolism

Judging from the symbolism in the Garden of Eden story it had to have been written after the reforms of Hezekiah and the destruction of Moses' bronze serpent. Up until that time serpents were still valued as symbols of wisdom, divination, and prophecy. The Yahwist reformers rejected divination, especially when performed by women in the temple, so they made the serpent into a villain in the garden, which never would have happened among the earlier Hebrews.

Some scholars have suggested that the Garden of Eden is a metaphor for Solomon's Temple which was decorated in a floral motif.[3] This interpretation also implies that the story was written in Babylon after the fall of Jerusalem, and that the women and their Asherah worship were being blamed for the Temple's destruction.

In the Garden of Eden story, the writers use the compound name "Yahweh-Elohim," "the LORD God," which does not appear elsewhere, indicating that this story may have a unique author.

3 Professor Francesca Stavrakopoulou, *Bible Secrets Revealed*, Documentary, TV Series, 2013

Now Yahweh God had planted a garden in the east, in Eden; and there he put the man he had formed. Yahweh God made all kinds of trees grow out of the ground – trees that were pleasing to the eye and good for food. In the middle of the garden were the tree of life and the tree of the knowledge of good and evil.

– Genesis 2:8-9

Yahweh God took the man and put him in the Garden of Eden to work it and take care of it. And Yahweh God commanded the man, "You are free to eat from any tree in the garden; but you must not eat from the tree of the knowledge of good and evil, for when you eat from it you will certainly die."

– Genesis 2:15-17

This instruction can be seen as a direct condemnation of the shamanistic traditions of using entheogenic plant drugs, including cannabis, for the purposes of gaining mystical insights. Yahweh condemns the entheogenic and shamanistic knowledge and forbids Adam from pursuing it – it is the first drug prohibition.

Then Yahweh God made a woman from the rib he had taken out of the man, and he brought her to the man. The man said, "This is now bone of my bones and flesh of my flesh; she shall be called 'woman,' for she was taken out of man."

– Genesis 2:22-23

Eve was created from Adam, this directly contradicts the Seven Days of Creation myth where male and female humans were created side-by-side, both in the image of God. There is also an interesting connection to the Sumerian story about the *Lady of the Rib* who the Earth Mother Ninhursag (Ki) created to help Enki, again indicating Mesopotamian influence.

Serpent

Now the serpent was more crafty than any of the wild animals Yahweh God had made. He said to the woman, "Did God really say, 'You must not eat from any tree in the garden'?"

The woman said to the serpent, "We may eat fruit from the trees in the garden, but God did say, 'You must not eat fruit from the tree that is in the middle of the garden, and you must not touch it, or you will die.'"

> *"You will not certainly die," the serpent said to the woman. "For God knows that when you eat from it your eyes will be opened, and you will be like God, knowing good and evil."*
>
> – Genesis 3:1-5

The serpent represents the ancient shamanistic traditions of divination, traditions that had existed for thousands of years but were rejected by the monotheists. This story codifies that rejection. The serpent is presented like a Neolithic drug peddler, pushing illicit substances on a naive, unsuspecting youth.

TREE OF KNOWLEDGE OF GOOD AND EVIL

Cannabis is the Forbidden Fruit

By tradition, the forbidden fruit is depicted as an apple, but the text does not specifically identify what plant the Tree of Knowledge of Good and Evil is. Yet Genesis 3:6-7 can be read as a clear and precise description of cannabis, all the valuable parts of the cannabis plant are mentioned; the seeds, the psychoactive resin, and the hemp fibers.

This interpretation implies that cannabis must have been sacred in the Goddess traditions and rejected by the Yahwists for that reason. It is not hard to make this connection. Cannabis was a common offering and incense in the temples of the ancient world, including the Hebrew temple. As a common and important fiber, hemp would have been used in sacred weaving that was important to the goddesses. Finally, as a ritual intoxicant and aphrodisiac, cannabis played a role in the divination, ecstatic dance, and sexual practices so often denounced by the Yahwists throughout the Bible.

Genesis 3:6-7

> *When the woman saw that the fruit of the tree was good for food and pleasing to the eye, and also desirable for gaining wisdom, she took some and ate it. She also gave some to her husband, who was with her, and he ate it. Then the eyes of both of them were opened, and they realized they were naked; so they sewed fig leaves together and made coverings for themselves.*
>
> Genesis 3:6-7

- *The fruit of the tree was good for food*; cannabis seeds are among the most nutritious seeds found anywhere in nature, valued by humans, animals, and birds.

- *The woman saw that the plant was pleasing to the eye*; cannabis is widely regarded as a beautiful, attractive plant.
- *The plant is desirable for gaining wisdom*; cannabis has long been used in religion and ritual, valued for its capacity to promote shamanistic insight and divination.
- *Adam and Eve ate the fruit and their eyes were opened, they realized they were naked*; they ate the cannabis, got high, and had ideas, a classic entheogenic experience.
- *They sewed fig leaves together and made coverings for themselves*; they used the hemp fibers to sew clothes. Hemp is one of our oldest fibers and was used to make the first fabrics at the dawn of the Neolithic Revolution.

Yahweh's Anger

When Yahweh discovered that Adam and Eve had eaten from the Tree of Knowledge he was greatly angered. Yahweh did not want Adam and Eve thinking for themselves, he wanted them to obey his laws. This mirrors the Judeo-Christian belief that our spirituality should be mediated by priests in the Church or Temple, and not through our own personal experiences and ecstasies. Yahweh confronted Adam, who promptly blamed Eve, who then blamed the serpent.

> *And he said, "Who told you that you were naked? Have you eaten from the tree that I commanded you not to eat from?" The man said, "The woman you put here with me - she gave me some fruit from the tree, and I ate it."*
>
> *Then Yahweh God said to the woman, "What is this you have done?" The woman said, "The serpent deceived me, and I ate."*
>
> – Genesis 3:11-13

Serpent Crushed

Yahweh cursed the serpent, which had always been an exalted symbol of wisdom, prophecy, and divination. Until the time of Hezekiah, the Hebrews worshipped the Bronze Serpent of Moses, and it seems highly unlikely that this story was written before the bronze serpent was removed. Yahweh's hostility to pagan divination practices was widely known, and the association of serpents and goddesses is well established.

> *So, Yahweh God said to the serpent, "Because you have done this, "Cursed are you above all livestock and all wild animals! You will crawl*

> *on your belly and you will eat dust all the days of your life. And I will put enmity between you and the woman, and between your offspring and hers; he will crush your head, and you will strike his heel."*
>
> – Genesis 3:14-15

In pagan symbolism, a serpent is exalted when it is presented vertically, standing up, and is considered a threat when presented horizontally. When Yahweh tells the serpent to crawl on his belly it is an explicit degradation of his once-respected position. Yahweh is also breaking the friendship between women and snakes; snakes symbolize rebirth and the cycle of life and were valued because they protected the granaries from rodents. Going forward, snakes would be reviled, as they are today by many people.

Painful Childbirth

> *To the woman he said, "I will make your pains in childbearing very severe; with painful labor you will give birth to children."*
>
> – Genesis 3:16

This is another important clue – in Goddess traditions, to give birth without pain was a blessing and a common characteristic of fertile goddesses who birth many children. Cannabis is a painkiller and birth aid used in ancient times for midwifery. By removing the Goddess and her qedesha, who were both midwives and potion makers, the Yahwists worked to push those healing traditions out of the temple.

Monogamy and Paternity

> *Your desire will be for your husband, and he will rule over you.*
>
> – Genesis 3:16

Eve is instructed that she is not to be sexually promiscuous, she is to desire her husband only, while no such instruction is given to Adam. This is clearly a response to the promiscuity of the women in Jerusalem and Babylon with their sacred sex and ritual prostitution. Canaanite women were not required to be monogamous and tracked bloodlines through their mothers. The Hebrews placed a high value on patriarchy and paternity and needed to control their women's sex lives.

Cursed to be Farmers

To Adam he said, "Because you listened to your wife and ate fruit from the tree about which I commanded you, 'You must not eat from it,' "Cursed is the ground because of you; through painful toil you will eat food from it all the days of your life. It will produce thorns and thistles for you, and you will eat the plants of the field. By the sweat of your brow you will eat your food until you return to the ground, since from it you were taken; for dust you are and to dust you will return."

– Genesis 3:17-19

Adam was blamed for listening to Eve and his punishment was to become a farmer. The Hebrews were shepherds who disdained farmers and their nature worship. For Adam, to become a farmer was a curse. Yahweh tells Adam that the land will not be productive for him, for all his painful toil all he will receive is thorns and thistles, nothing bountiful.

The symbolism here stands in direct contrast to the Goddess whose blessings bring the spring, lush vegetation, and bountiful wild animals. The very purpose of pagan ritual sex was to encourage the fertility of nature, but the Yahwists clearly despised these practices and everything they stood for. The Yahwists don't care about farming, nature, or the cycles of life; for them, the Heavenly Father is the source of all creation.

Mother of all the Living

Adam named his wife Eve, because she would become the mother of all the living.

– Genesis 3:20

Eve is the mother of all living, she is in effect, the Mother Goddess. Eve represents Asherah and all the goddesses. But even though Eve is declared to be the mother of all living, her powers as Mother Goddess were usurped, the powers of creation were taken away from her by the Heavenly Father.

Skins Not Fabric

Yahweh God made garments of skin for Adam and his wife and clothed them.

– Genesis 3:21

Yahweh does not encourage the weaving of fabric; he encourages them to wear animal skins. Weaving is women's work and vegetable fibers a product of the Earth, while animal skins were a product of the shepherds.

NEOLITHIC REVOLUTION

Banished from Eden

> *And Yahweh God said, "The man has now become like one of us, knowing good and evil. He must not be allowed to reach out his hand and take also from the tree of life and eat, and live forever."*
>
> – Genesis 3:22

Here again, we see God speaking to other gods, reflecting the pagan roots of the Hebrew religion, "man has become like us."

> *So, Yahweh God banished him from the Garden of Eden to work the ground from which he had been taken. After he drove the man out, he placed on the east side of the Garden of Eden cherubim and a flaming sword flashing back and forth to guard the way to the tree of life.*
>
> – Genesis 3:23-24

The Garden of Eden can be seen as a metaphor for human life before the Neolithic Revolution when people were hunter-gatherers and had not yet begun to farm. It was Eve who discovered the Tree of Knowledge and learned to plant seeds. Adam was punished for listening to her and forced to toil as a farmer, when before he was a free man.

The expulsion from the Garden of Eden can be seen as a lamentation that once upon a time, before farming, life was easy but had now turned to hard, forsaken labor. A misogynistic lamentation for men wondering why they ever listened to women and thought they had any wisdom to offer.

The Cherubim, which guarded the Ark of the Covenant in Solomon's Temple, are used to guard the path back to the Garden of Eden. The Cherubim symbolically prevented a return to earlier times before the advent of farming, a task the shepherds saw as dreadful.

Paradox of Good and Evil

The sacred plant is called the Tree of Knowledge of Good and Evil because the Neolithic Revolution was a paradox that brought both benefits and burdens. The life of a hunter-gatherer required little labor, but survival was always tenuous; it was dependent on the weather and ready access to food. In contrast, the life of a farmer required arduous hard work to produce the grains and fibers needed to live. The benefit of farming was that it produced surpluses that could be stored and traded, improving both survivability and wealth.

Planting led to the first human settlements that upended thousands of years of nomadic wandering as hunter-gatherers. Settlements eventually became cities which led to civilization. Civilization brought both good and evil – it is a paradox. Planting brought surpluses of food, trade, and wealth, but it also brought greed, jealousy, theft, and conflict.

The benefits of civilization were always spread unevenly as some people had the good fortune to possess the wealth, while others labored or were slaves. The 5000-year history of civilization has always featured class division and exploitation of the poor by the rich. Civilization brought great public works, such as buildings, roads, and temples, as well as comforts like luxuries and art, but it also brought armies, war, slavery, and periodic destruction. These paradoxes have always been with us and remain with us today.

Sacred Cannabis

This story tells us symbolically that cannabis must have been sacred in the Goddess traditions, presumably because it was credited with sparking the Neolithic Revolution. Cannabis certainly was present in the Fertile Crescent settlements where agriculture originally took hold and it fits the description of the Tree of Knowledge of Good and Evil.

The story is telling us that women, not men, discovered the sacred plant from which they learned to plant seeds to grow crops for food and fiber. This memory was preserved through ritual and religious traditions. The Yahwists condemned these traditions and tried to eliminate them. For the authors of this story, both cannabis and the serpent had to be rejected because they represent the goddess traditions of shamanism, ritual sex, sacred weaving, cycles-of-life, and the rest.

Tree of Life

It is notable that the Tree of Knowledge and the Tree of Life are two separate trees. The Tree of Life is a universal archetype that exists in many cultures and has a diversity of meanings. It speaks to immortality for both gods and humans, and the impossibility of achieving that desire. This was demonstrated by Gilgamesh and his fruitless attempt to acquire the Tree of Life for himself. The closest humans can get to immortality is to be remembered for glory, like Achilles. Judeo-Christian traditions emphasize eternal life and not a cycle of life.

Eve and Pandora

The story of Eve is very similar to the Greek story of Pandora, who was also the first woman and blamed for unleashing evil upon the world. Both stories were written in the same era; the Greeks and the Hebrews alike saw women as a source of trouble who needed to be restrained, not empowered. The subordination of women to men has been a theme of civilization ever since.

Divorce Papers

The meaning of the Garden of Eden story would have been abundantly clear to contemporary audiences. It was aimed directly at the worship of Asherah, Astarte, Anat, and goddesses generally. The story offers an alternative cosmological worldview where the Goddesses were devalued along with the women in the community. The qedesha were being put on notice that the new religious authorities would no longer tolerate them or their nature worship.

The Garden of Eden story is the divorce papers signed, sealed, and delivered. No longer would the Heavenly Father and Earthly Mother be husband and wife.

CAIN AND ABEL

Farmer and Shepherd

The story continues with the children of Adam and Eve, Cain and Abel, the first farmer and first shepherd. The Hebrews were shepherds and this story demonstrates their disdain for the farmers who lived in the cities and worshipped the Goddess and the cycles of life.

> *Later she gave birth to his brother Abel. Now Abel kept flocks, and Cain worked the soil. In the course of time Cain brought some of the fruits of the soil as an offering to Yahweh. And Abel also brought an offering – fat portions from some of the firstborn of his flock. Yahweh looked with favor on Abel and his offering, but on Cain and his offering he did not look with favor. So Cain was very angry, and his face was downcast.*
>
> – Genesis 4:2-5

Cain and Abel are archetypal figures, the metaphorical first shepherd and farmer (after Adam). In the Neolithic, farmers and shepherds lived separately, the farmers lived in settlements that eventually became cities. The shepherds were nomads and traders, traveling between cities. The shepherds eventually became raiders of the cities after bronze weapons were invented. The farmers focused their worship on Mother Earth and the shepherds focused on the Heavenly Father, who became the patriarchal warrior gods.

The Heavenly Father Yahweh rejected Cain the farmer's offerings for no apparent reason while he accepted the offerings of meat made by Abel the shepherd. The symbolism is not hard to discern: Yahweh rejects the farmers and embraces the shepherds. The Goddess would of course have accepted Cain's offerings of fruits and vegetables, but she is not mentioned in the story.

Cain is crestfallen, he invites Abel out into a field and kills his brother in cold blood. The innocent shepherd murdered by the treacherous farmer, as told by a shepherd. Yahweh then punished the farmer Cain for his sin, saying the fields would no longer yield crops for him and cursing him into perpetual exile.

Dumuzi and Enkimdu

The tale of Cain and Abel stands in stark contrast to the Sumerian story of Dumuzi the shepherd and the farmer Enkimdu; they compete for the love of the goddess Inanna, but become friends and don't fight. In the Sumerian tale, the farmer welcomes the shepherd onto his land and into the bed of the goddess. With the blessings of the goddess, the warrior shepherd became king. Considering the Babylonian influence on the Biblical writers, some version of the Dumuzi story was likely known to them. The Cain and Abel may have been written as a direct retort to the earlier myth.

First City

> *Cain made love to his wife, and she became pregnant and gave birth to Enoch. Cain was then building a city, and he named it after his son Enoch.*
>
> – Genesis 4:17

Cain went on to father a son and the first city, again reinforcing the idea that the farmer cities with their goddesses were the sources of sin and iniquity.

Chapter Forty-Three

DIVORCE

Return to Jerusalem

After the Persian Empire came to power, the Israelite priests in Babylon were sponsored by a series of Persian kings to return to Jerusalem, restore the temple, and compile their sacred texts. King Cyrus kindly returned the golden treasures that had been seized by Nebuchadnezzar.

At this point the Hebrews were no more – upon their return to Jerusalem and rebirth from the ashes like a phoenix, the Israelites would be known as the Jews. Judah was no longer an independent nation, it was now known as Judea, a province of whichever imperial power was dominant at the time. Judea would not regain its independence for over 2500 years, until the birth of the modern nation of Israel in 1948.

The Jews slowly began returning to Jerusalem after an exile of 70 years. Two years after returning to Jerusalem, in 516 BCE, they began construction of the Second Temple. The returning exiles rebuilt the altar on the foundation of Solomon's Temple, despite their fear of the local people. There was a great deal of resistance and subterfuge from locals who remembered the Yahwists and did not want them to return.

Second Temple

The initial building of the Second Temple was very modest. It had none of Solomon's grandeur and was notable for lacking the Shekinah, the cloud of smoke containing the presence of God. In this new temple there would be no Goddess, no hashish incense burned in her honor, no qedesha, and no sacred weaving either. It would take many years, and overcoming conflict with the local people before the new Jewish temple was completed.

> *But many of the older priests and Levites and family heads, who had seen the former temple, wept aloud when they saw the foundation of this temple being laid, while many others shouted for joy.*
>
> – Ezra 3:12

Ezra The Scribe

This Ezra came up from Babylon. He was a teacher well versed in the Law of Moses, which Yahweh, the God of Israel, had given. The king had granted him everything he asked, for the hand of Yahweh his God was on him.
– Ezra 7:6

Ezra the scribe began his career in Babylon and led a group of exiles returning to Jerusalem in 458 BCE. under King Artaxerxes (or possibly 398 BCE if Artaxerxes II), 60 years or more after the Jews first returned to Jerusalem. Ezra is very important to the Jews, even a second Moses, because he brought the Book of the Law to Jerusalem and is the father of Judaism as we know it. Ezra oversaw the completion of the Hebrew Bible and formalized many Jewish traditions.

Ezra grew up among the Israelites who had remained in Babylon for generations, and they had good relations with the Persians. The Israelites were heavily influenced by the Persian Zoroastrians who were also monotheists, worshipping the god Ahura Mazda. Babylon was richly cultured, cosmopolitan, and religiously tolerant. The cult of Ishtar was still in full effect, so the Israelites and the authors of the Bible were continually exposed to her wild worship.

Ezra was not a prophet but a "priest, a scribe of the law of the God of heaven." It is generally believed that Ezra led the Priestly team of scribes in Babylon that produced the final text of the Hebrew Bible we read today. And while the biblical text does not explicitly say what is in the Book of the Law, it is thought to include the final script of the Torah as well as the books of Joshua, Judges, Ruth, Samuel, Kings, and Chronicles. Additional books continued to be contributed for another two hundred years.

From the Codex Amiatinus :Ezra the scribe. "When the sacred books had been consumed in the fires of war, Ezra repaired the damage."

Drink of Liquid Fire

In the Apocryphal book of 2 Esdras (considered to have been written in the early Christian era between 70 and 218 CE) a supernatural account is given of how Ezra came to write the Bible. Ezra worked from memory, dictating the entire text to five scribes. Ezra did this after drinking from a cup of liquid fire given to him by God. The drink of liquid fire is possibly bhang or some other mystery potion.

> *So, I took the five men, as he commanded me, and we went into the field, and remained there. And the next day, behold, a voice called me, saying, Esdras, open thy mouth, and drink that I give thee to drink. Then opened I my mouth, and, behold, he reached me a full cup, which was full as it were with water, but the color of it was like fire. And I took it, and drank: and when I had drunk of it, my heart uttered understanding, and wisdom grew in my breast, for my spirit strengthened my memory: And my mouth was opened, and shut no more. The Highest gave understanding unto the five men, and they wrote the wonderful visions of the night that were told, which they knew not: and they sat forty days, and they wrote in the day, and at night they ate bread. As for me, I spake in the day, and I held not my tongue by night. In forty days they wrote two hundred and four books.*
>
> – 2 Esdras 14:37-44 (Apocrypha, KJV)

Book of the Law

Ezra was sent from Babylon by King Artaxerxes with a treasury full of gold and silver, and a royal proclamation of his authority to re-establish worship at the second Temple in Jerusalem. Ezra brought the Hebrew Bible with him to Jerusalem and read it aloud to the community. The message was clear to the people. The Jews were to withdraw completely from the broader pagan world and they were to live by their own laws and customs. The Jewish people were not to mix with the locals, they were not to share customs or festivals, and nature worship was strictly forbidden.

> *Ezra the priest brought the Law before the assembly, which was made up of men and women and all who were able to understand. He read it aloud from daybreak till noon as he faced the square before the Water Gate in the presence of the men, women and others who could understand. And all the people listened attentively to the Book of the Law.*
>
> – Nehemiah 8:2-3

Divorce the Canaanite Women

But then Ezra discovered that the Jewish men had been marrying local Canaanite women with their detestable customs and having families with them. Ezra was outraged.

> *They have taken some of their daughters as wives for themselves and their sons, and have mingled the holy race with the peoples around them. And the leaders and officials have led the way in this unfaithfulness. "When I heard this, I tore my tunic and cloak, pulled hair from my head and beard and sat down appalled."*
>
> – Ezra 9:2-3

Ezra prayed in despair. He forced the men to choose between their families and their God.

> *Then Ezra the priest stood up and said to them, "You have been unfaithful; you have married foreign women, adding to Israel's guilt. Now honor Yahweh, the God of your ancestors, and do his will. Separate yourselves from the peoples around you and from your foreign wives."*
>
> – Ezra 10:10-11

Ezra forced the Jewish men who had married pagan women to divorce their wives and children and abandon them.

The Goddess worshipping women could never be proper wives to Jewish men because they did not practice paternity, nor did they practice monogamy. The Canaanite women tracked bloodlines through their mothers and had sex lives independent of their husbands in the goddess temples. This was unacceptable to Ezra and the Jewish leaders who believed in paternity and patriarchy. To be a Jew one must be born of a Jewish mother they proclaimed.

The physical divorce of the Jewish men from their pagan wives was the final act in the divorce between Hebrew God and the Mother Goddess that began 800 years earlier on Mt. Sinai, when Yahweh declared his existence and jealousy of all other gods, including his own wife.

The Divorce was a radical cultural development and a rejection of timeless familial customs. This event signified the rise of book religion and a literate priestly caste with authority over independent, family-centered, do-it-yourself religion and home altars. Going forward, Judaism would be defined by its observance of the law and the centrality of its sacred texts.

Diaspora

Centuries later, the second temple would be destroyed by the Romans and the Jews would again be scattered all over the Earth. During their long history in the diaspora outside Jerusalem, the Jewish community was held together by the observance of the law rather than by the connection to any temple, physical location, or sacred relics.

Despite the belligerence and intolerance displayed in their sacred texts, the Jews never attempted to impose their values on the broader culture. Jewish law was only for the Jewish people. Throughout their history, the Jews were generally a minority people and an insular, non-violent community within the countries they lived in.

The destruction of the Temple of Jerusalem by Francesco Hayez, 1867

Asherah's Revenge

In a reversal of their mythological history, the Jews ended up being persecuted for centuries by their own theological offspring, the Christians and the Muslims. Perhaps the Israelites should not have blasphemed the good Goddess in their sacred texts. Call it Asherah's revenge – the Goddess never forgets an insult.

VOLUME III
New Testament

Jesus with the woman of Samaria

Chapter Forty-Four

JESUS OF CANNABIS

When Jesus therefore had received the vinegar, he said, It is finished: and he bowed his head, and gave up the ghost.

– John 19:30 (KJV)

Jesus of Nazareth was a Jewish preacher, prophet, and healer, who is the savior and centerpiece of the Christian religion. Tradition teaches us that Jesus was publicly executed in Jerusalem around the year 33 CE for heresy and sedition against the Jewish and Roman authorities. Jesus was whipped, beaten, stabbed, and crucified on a cross. He was declared dead and placed in a tomb on a Friday evening – he then emerged from the tomb, alive, Sunday morning. Jesus is the dying-and-rising god in human flesh.

The resurrection of Jesus – its truth, mystery, and controversy, is one of the defining moments in the history of humanity. This event transformed world religion and politics, setting off centuries of reformations and revolutions among the believers and non-believers. The debate over the veracity and symbolism of Jesus' resurrection has framed the very definition of truth and moral authority ever since.

For his Christian followers, Jesus Christ is the son of God and his death was a sacrifice that redeems the sins of his believers, granting them eternal life. Christians believe that Jesus is divine and God in human form. Jesus is not only the son of God, but he is God in the flesh, and connected as a trinity; the Father, Son, and Holy Ghost.

Yet there were many different views of Jesus in the early days. Rival sects formed with radically opposed views of Jesus's teachings and the meaning of his death. Most of Jesus' original disciples remained in Jerusalem as practicing Jews. They were awaiting an apocalypse that came in 70 CE when the Romans killed them all and burned down the temple. The Gnostic mystics taught that Jesus could show us how to know God directly and that Sophia was his bride. The Gnostic trinity was the Father, Son, and Sophia. Some pagans simply welcomed Jesus as the latest addition to their pantheons.

The basic tenets of orthodox Christianity as originated by the Apostle Paul were not settled until 300 years after Jesus passed on. Centuries of vicious theological disputes were followed by harsh authoritarianism when orthodox Christianity became the state religion of the Roman empire and all rival religions were banned and exterminated.

The Muslims revere Jesus as a holy prophet but they do not believe that he is divine or that he died on the cross. Jesus either survived the crucifixion or was substituted by another. The Muslims say that if you saw a man crucified and then later saw him alive, doesn't it make sense that he simply never died?

Islamic Virgin Mary and Jesus

> *That they said (in boast), "We killed Christ Jesus the son of Mary, the Messenger of Allah" – but they killed him not, nor crucified him, but so it was made to appear to them, and those who differ therein are full of doubts, with no (certain) knowledge, but only conjecture to follow, for of a surety they killed him not.*
>
> – Qur'an, 4:157 (Yusuf Ali)

What really happened on the cross?

Chapter Forty-Five

EARTHLY RESURRECTION

Here we present an alternative hypothesis. The resurrection of Jesus was a genuine historical event, but rather than being explained by supernatural forces and the hand of God, the resurrection can be rationally explained by Earthly means; namely pharmacology, medicine, and nursing.

In this theory, Jesus went to his crucifixion willingly with a plan to survive and was aided by the women who saved him. This theory centers on the women who were with Jesus while he was on the cross, the Three Marys – Mother Mary, Mary Magdalene, and Mary Salome, and their mystery potion. The Three Marys are symbolic of the Triple Goddess; the mother, the maiden, and the crone.

The theory of the Earthly Resurrection is that when Jesus was crucified, the Three Marys sedated him with a mystery potion that made him appear dead. They brought him down from the cross before he actually died, gave him medicine, bandaged his wounds, and laid him in the prepared tomb where he slept for a day and a half before being revived. It was the women, trained in the arts of healing and medicine making who performed one of the greatest magic tricks in all of history – faking the death of a condemned man to cheat the executioner, and in doing so elevating their religious teacher into God himself.

Mystery Potion

Is it possible that Jesus could have used a mystery potion to fake his death? Even in the most favorable reading of the evidence, it would have been extremely dangerous and downright crazy. Jesus would have had to survive serious wounds from being beaten, flogged, crucified, and stabbed. For the sake of this hypothesis, assume that Jesus's wounds were not as grievous as they could have been and fell short of being fatal.

People routinely survive major injuries when they are given prompt and effective medical care, and Jesus would have received careful nursing from the Three Marys. They had friends who helped, Nicodemus brought medicines and clean linens. Joseph of Arimathea owned the nearby tomb conveniently available to use for the nursing and burial. Joseph of Arimathea also approached Roman Governor Pontius Pilate personally to ask that Jesus's body be brought down from the cross early, which was critical to his survival.

At the heart of this rational, heretical, theory of Jesus' resurrection lies the mystery potion. Is there a drug that could make a person appear convincingly dead, like in Shakespeare's Romeo and Juliet? With no visible breath or heartbeat, stiff limbs, and pale skin cold to the touch?

Does a drug exist that can make someone appear dead? The answer is yes, and the hypothesis can be tested through modern science and experience. The mystery potion was likely a potent tincture of cannabis, the sacred plant of Eve and the Goddess, perhaps in combination with other drugs. This pharmacological hypothesis was first presented by cannabis historian Chris Bennett.[1]

Catalepsy

Cannabis is a remarkable medicine with unusual qualities. One particularly unusual quality is that massive overdoses of cannabis do not kill, but can knock a person unconscious for a few days. Cannabis is an extremely rare substance in this regard, a true tree of life. After thousands of years of documented usage cannabis drugs have never been known to kill a healthy person.[2]

But cannabis can generate the unusual condition of catalepsy and coma, which creates the appearance of death. Catalepsy is a condition where the limbs are waxy and stiff, as though rigor mortis was setting in. This effect rarely results in death unless the patient suffers from heart failure.

The cataleptic effect from strong doses of cannabis is well documented in modern scientific literature, it is one of four behavioral tetrads associated with the effects of cannabinoids along with hypothermia (cold body temperature), analgesia (painkilling), and hypomotility (reduced physical activity).[3] Each of these tetrads could contribute to the effect of making a person appear dead, while also providing the medicinal, sedative, and painkilling benefits that Jesus would have needed to survive his ordeal.

1 This theory was first presented by Chris Bennett (*Green Gold the Tree of Life*, pp 378-406), who adapted it from the book, *The Passover Plot*, by Hugh J. Schonfield from 1965 who suggested a sedative was used but did not identify what drug it might have been.

2 The US Drug Enforcement Administration (DEA) states that "No deaths from overdose of marijuana have been reported." in its official fact sheets.

3 For example: Egashira, N. (2017). Delta-9-Tetrahydrocannabinol and Catalepsy-Like Immobilization. In *Handbook of Cannabis and Related Pathologies: Biology, Pharmacology, Diagnosis, and Treatment* (pp. 326-334). Elsevier Inc.. https://doi.org/10.1016/B978-0-12-800756-3.00038-7. In Cannabinoid tetrad tests, catalepsy is one of four primary behaviors exhibited by animals subjected to cannabinoids. https://en.wikipedia.org/wiki/Tetrad_test

19th-century medical experiments attempted to determine the fatal dose limits of cannabis by providing massive overdoses to small dogs. Dogs were routinely used to test cannabis medicines in those days and there were established scientific protocols guiding the experiments. Surprisingly, despite their earnest attempts, the scientists never succeeded in actually killing a dog with cannabis drugs. The typical response was that the dog was knocked unconscious for two days and then awoke with no ill effects.[4]

Cannabis has a rich tradition of use in veterinary medicine internationally and scientists have never been able to establish fatal dose limits for large animals after years of studies. In modern science these experiments are not performed on humans or dogs, but are routinely done on mice (which can be killed with potent cannabis injections).

Cannabis had long been used in the medicinal and religious practices of the Ancient Near East and was readily available to Jesus. The plant is documented in ancient and modern medical literature to be a painkiller and anesthetic. Tinctures prepared from cannabis in alcohol or wine were a common medicine then and are still used today.

In the second century CE, the famous Chinese surgeon Hua Tuo invented an anesthetic made from cannabis that he reduced to a powder and mixed with wine. He called it *cannabis boiling powder* and he used it successfully to perform complicated abdominal surgeries.

Hindu fakirs in India, ascetic devotees of Shiva known for their devotion to cannabis, have been known to fake their deaths in demonstrations for British colonialists using a combination of meditation, yoga, and cannabis drugs. In these public demonstrations, the fakirs appeared to be dead to witnesses. The fakirs had no visible pulse or breath and their limbs were stiff. The fakir's assistants buried the seemingly dead body in a tomb or coffin. The fakirs' bodies were then interred and revived after a period of days or even weeks. The

Fakirs Preparing and Partaking in Bhang and Ganja

4 A Pharmacological Study of Cannabis Americana (Cannabis Sativa)" by Parke-Davis researchers E.M. Houghton and H.C. Hamilton, (*American Journal of Pharmacy*), 1908

German naturalist, chemist, and travel writer, Ernst Von Bibra documented the feat by multiple fakirs in his famous 1855 book *Plant Intoxicants.*[5]

Dr. William O'Shaughnessy, a Scottish physician working in Calcutta in the 1840s wrote the first western medical papers on cannabis drugs. O'Shaughnessy detailed instances of patients experiencing catalepsy from strong doses of cannabis.[6]

> *I chanced to lift up my patient's arm. The professional reader will judge of my astonishment, when I found that it remained in the posture in which I placed it. It required but a brief examination of the limbs to find that the patient had, by the influence of this narcotic, been thrown into that strange and most extraordinary of all nervous conditions, into that state what so few have seen, and the existence of which so many still discredit – the genuine catalepsy of the nosologist.*
>
> – Dr. William O'Shaughnessy, Calcutta, India, 1839

In *Romeo and Juliet* (act 4, scene 1), William Shakespeare has an unidentified potion provided to his tragic heroine Juliet to help her fake her death and avoid an unwanted marriage. Juliet's apparent death is so convincing that her parents entomb her, and her true love Romeo commits suicide. Shakespeare was known for the accuracy of the medicines depicted in his plays, and could be describing something like Hua Tuo's surgical anesthesia mixed with wine.

These historical and scientific examples demonstrate that it is medically possible that a preparation of cannabis drugs could conceivably be used to create a cataleptic condition where a living human body appears dead to onlookers.

5 Bennett, Chris, *Cannabis and the Soma Solution*, pp 426. Bennett provides a thorough recounting of the tales of 19th-century Hindu Fakirs being buried alive and revived by assistants in demonstrations for British colonialists.

6 Tod H. Mikuriya, *Marijuana: Medical Papers, 1839-1972*, Blue Dolphin Publishing, Incorporated, 2007

Chapter Forty-Six

ANOINTED ONE

Messiah

There is a scriptural connection between Jesus and cannabis. Jesus is known as the *Messiah,* or the *Christ,* and the word "messiah" means "anointed one." Anointing with oil is a sacred rite reserved for priests and kings that involves pouring holy anointing oil over the head to join them with God. All the sacred objects in the Hebrew temple were anointed to signify their sacredness and distinguish them from the secular.

The recipe for the Hebrew holy anointing oil was given to Moses in Exodus 30:23-25 and contains cannabis (mistranslated in English as *calamus* or *aromatic cane*).[1] The recipe includes over 6 pounds of cannabis infused into 1½ gallons of olive oil and the results are potently psychoactive.

Jesus was a practicing Jew who professed to follow Mosaic law, which implies that the *Messiah,* the *Christ,* the *anointed one,* was anointed with psychoactive cannabis-infused oil. All the Hebrew kings and priests were anointed when they were elevated to leadership positions. Aaron, the brother of Moses, was anointed, and so was David when he became king.

> *It is like precious oil poured on the head, running down on the beard, running down on Aaron's beard, down on the collar of his robe.*
>
> – Psalm 133:2

> *So Samuel took the horn of oil and anointed him in the presence of his brothers, and from that day on the Spirit of Yahweh came powerfully upon David.*
>
> – 1 Samuel 16:13

Healing Oil

In Jesus' time, anointing was not only for sacred rites, but was used for healing as well. Jesus anointed his disciples and instructed them to heal

---

1 The identity of the Hebrew qaneh bosm remains debated by scholars, some argue that calamus is correctly identified, as it does have some medicinal benefits. But calamus does not have the rich tradition of religious and spiritual use across many cultures that cannabis does.

sick people with oil. Some of Jesus' healing miracles; such as healing epileptics, curing the blind, treating women's health, or relieving painful skin conditions, can be interpreted as the use of medicinal cannabis oil.

> *They drove out many demons and anointed many sick people with oil and healed them.*
>
> – Mark 6:13

In this era, there was no differentiation between medical treatments, exorcisms, and miracles. Conditions such as epilepsy were seen as being afflicted with demons; to cure epilepsy was seen as a type of exorcism, and healing a woman's painful menstruation was seen as a miracle. Cannabis medicines are used to treat all these conditions today.

> *Is anyone among you sick? Let them call the elders of the church to pray over them and anoint them with oil in the name of the Lord.*
>
> – James 5:14

The events where Jesus healed people are presented in the Bible as supernatural miracles, as are many other acts of Jesus. For centuries, readers of the Bible have sought to understand the nature of these events and there is a wide diversity of opinions about them. The orthodox accept the scriptural events at face value, believing that the text is a literal description of supernatural events made possible only because Jesus was God incarnate. Other readers seek to describe the miracles in more naturalistic terms, understanding that the supernatural portrayals are intended to make the stories more exciting and to steep them in religious significance.

Jesus was said to perform many demonic exorcisms, casting out spirits that were afflicting people in various ways. One story is about a boy possessed by a demon (Matthew 17:14-21, Luke 9:37-42, Mark 9:14-21) who throws the boy to the ground, causing him to convulse and foam at the mouth. This demon sounds like the disease of epilepsy.

Cannabis is a potent antispasmodic medicine with proven efficacy in modern science for the treatment of epilepsy. A single dose of cannabis tincture has been shown to halt convulsions and stop epileptic seizures. Cannabis has been proclaimed a miracle cure by modern parents whose children are afflicted with this traumatic condition.

Jesus healed numerous lepers in the Gospels (Mark 1:40-45, Matthew 8:1-4, Luke 5:12-16). The term *leprosy* was used broadly in this era to describe a variety of inflammatory skin conditions. Cannabis has antibacterial properties and can be used topically to treat certain painful skin conditions like pruritus. Cannabis has been shown to alleviate the symptoms of pain, itchiness, and inflammation of the skin.

The Gospels tell numerous stories of Jesus healing the blind and restoring their sight, (Matthew 9:27-31, Mark 8:22, John 9:1-12). Cannabis is a proven treatment for glaucoma, one common source of blindness. Glaucoma raises the fluid pressure in the eye to dangerous levels and damages the optic nerves. Cannabis is proven to temporarily reduce intraocular pressure and preserve, or even restore, eyesight. These effects are not permanent and only last a few hours, requiring ongoing use of the medicine multiple times a day.

The Blind Man Bartimaeus in Jericho by Eustache Le Sueur

Another incident speaks to cannabis use as a medicine for midwifery and women's reproductive health. Cannabis is highly valued by women who suffer from painful menstruation. Cannabis is a potent painkiller and anti-inflammatory, and interacts throughout women's reproductive systems. There is a story told of how Jesus cured a woman "who had been subject to bleeding for twelve years" (Matthew 9:20-22, Mark 5:25-34, Luke 8:42-48). As soon as the woman touched Jesus' cloak she was healed and her bleeding stopped.

None of these stories as written can be seen as a definitive use of a healing oil. Yet, interpretations of these stories that seek to discern a naturalistic explanation for seemingly supernatural events can see the use of medicines at play. Especially in the context of Jesus' instructions to his disciples to anoint the sick people with oil and heal them (Mark 6:13).

The Three Marys

Chapter Forty-Seven

THREE MARYS AND SCRIPTURE

"For whatever is hidden is meant to be disclosed, and whatever is concealed is meant to be brought out into the open. If anyone has ears to hear, let them hear."

– Mark 4:22-23

The central and most important miracle of Jesus Christ was his resurrection from the dead. Without the resurrection of Jesus, there is no Christian religion. For the Christian faithful, Jesus' death purifies the believers of their sins and reunites them with God. Jesus' defeat of death symbolizes the eternal life that is waiting for them in heaven.

And if Christ has not been raised, our preaching is useless and so is your faith.

– 1 Corinthians 15:14

The supernatural reality of Jesus' death and resurrection are accepted literally by Christian believers. But is it possible that a natural, earthly explanation could explain the miraculous event? Many naturalistic theories have been offered over the centuries though none of them have ever succeeded in convincing the faithful. The only evidence we have of Jesus' life and death comes from the Biblical Gospels. It is the scriptural text that we must examine to determine if it is possible that Jesus faked his death by using a mystery potion provided by the Three Marys.

Arrested

In the Gospels, Jesus was arrested by Jewish authorities after his betrayal by his disciple Judas. Jesus was put on trial for a variety of offenses, in particular for blasphemy by claiming to be the Messiah and the Son of God. Jesus was then turned over to the Roman authorities, under command of the governor Pontius Pilate, and executed for the seditious crime of claiming to be the King of the Jews.

In the scripture, Jesus does not appear to be surprised by his arrest in the middle of the night. In fact he had predicted his ordeal many times. Did Jesus have a plan? Jesus repeatedly predicted his death and resurrection after three days. His disciples were at a loss to understand what he meant (Matthew 16:21-23, 17:22-23, 20:17-19; Mark 8:31-33, 9:30-32, 10:32-34; Luke 9:21-22, 9:43-45, 18:31-34).

> *...he was teaching his disciples. He said to them, "The Son of Man is going to be delivered into the hands of men. They will kill him, and after three days he will rise." But they did not understand what he meant and were afraid to ask him about it.*
>
> – Mark 9:31-32

> *[Jesus] took the Twelve aside and said to them, "We are going up to Jerusalem, and the Son of Man will be delivered over to the chief priests and the teachers of the law. They will condemn him to death and will hand him over to the Gentiles to be mocked and flogged and crucified. On the third day he will be raised to life!"*
>
> – Matthew 20:17-19

At the Garden of Gethsemane prior to being captured Thursday night, Jesus suffered in anticipation of his coming tribulations and was sweating blood (Luke 22:14), but he made no attempt to flee. In fact, Jesus stayed up late, waiting into the middle of the night for the Jewish authorities to come and arrest him. Jesus was then interrogated, subjected to a show trial, and condemned early Friday morning. He was beaten and whipped by the Romans and forced to carry his heavy cross up the hill.

Pontius Pilate had Jesus flogged with a whip, but it is not specified how many lashes Jesus received, or how serious the wounds were. Jesus was beaten and mocked by the Roman soldiers. They jammed a crown of thorns on Jesus' head until he bled, asking him, "Where is your almighty Father now?" Though Jesus was clearly abused, none of the Gospels provide any details about the severity of his injuries (Matthew 27:27-31, Mark 15:16-20, Luke 22:63-65, John 19:1-15).

Strong Drink

On his way to Golgotha, the hill where he was to be crucified, Jesus was offered wine mixed with myrrh, otherwise known as the *wine of the condemned*. "Strong drink" is a biblical term for wine mixed with myrrh and other drugs, like cannabis, or opium, that was commonly given to prisoners on their way to execution. Strong drink was served as an act of mercy and anesthetic to calm the condemned prisoner's nerves and ease their pain. For Jesus, this potion would have interfered with his plan, so he declined to take it.

> *They tried to give Him wine mixed with myrrh, but He did not take it.*
>
> – Mark 15:23

> *They gave Him wine mixed with gall to drink. But when He tasted it, He would not drink it.*
>
> – Matthew 27:34

> *Give strong drink to the one who is perishing, and wine to those in bitter distress;*
>
> – Proverbs 31:6

The Women Who Loved Jesus

The Three Marys, the women who loved Jesus the most and whom he loved, accompanied him on his way to his execution. Jesus broke with social convention by spending so much time with women and teaching them.

The Three Marys are Mother Mary, Mary Magdalene, and Mary Salome, and they are symbolic of the Triple Goddess. Mother Mary is the virgin mother of Jesus. Mary of Magdala is the maiden, Jesus' closest companion. The precise identity of third Mary is not clear, she is called "the wife of Clopas" and she is also called Salome; in some tellings she is the sister-in-law of Mother Mary, or perhaps her aunt, or the mother of the Beloved Disciple John. In keeping with the symbolism of the Triple Goddess, Mary Salome must have been an older woman, the crone. The Three Marys are venerated in Catholic traditions and legends are told about them.

> *Standing by the cross of Jesus were His mother, His mother's sister, Mary the wife of Clopas, and Mary Magdalene.*
>
> – John 19:25

> *Many women were there, watching from a distance. They had followed Jesus from Galilee to care for his needs.*
>
> – Matthew 27:55

> *Some women were watching from a distance. Among them were Mary Magdalene, Mary the mother of James the younger and of Joseph, and Salome.*
>
> – Mark 15:40

Wine Vinegar on the Cross

The Three Marys are the keystone of this theory, they had the mystery potion prepared to save Jesus's life. The Three Marys kept a watchful eye and at the proper moment they provided Jesus the sacred medicine, the cannabis tincture that allowed him to appear dead and cheat the execution.

Cannabis use was deeply rooted in the Goddess traditions and Mystery religions that were prominent at the time, their secrets were told only to initiates, who were mostly women. It is not hard to imagine how this knowledge of medicine making circulated among wise women but was paid no attention to by men.

> *Later, knowing that everything had now been finished ... Jesus said, "I am thirsty." A jar of wine vinegar was there, so they soaked a sponge in it, put the sponge on a stalk of the hyssop plant, and lifted it to Jesus' lips. When he had received the drink, Jesus said, "It is finished." With that, he bowed his head and gave up his spirit.*
>
> – John 19:28-30

> *Immediately one of them ran and got a sponge. He filled it with wine vinegar, put it on a staff, and offered it to Jesus to drink.*
>
> – Matthew 27:48

> *Someone ran, filled a sponge with wine vinegar, put it on a staff, and offered it to Jesus to drink.*
>
> – Mark 15:36

In the Gospels, the medicine is described as wine vinegar or sour wine, which can be seen as a euphemism for a substance unknown to the writers. It is unlikely that they actually gave him vinegar which would serve as a stimulant like smelling salts, and wake Jesus up, not make him swoon.

As soon as Jesus consumed the potion, he promptly succumbed and appeared dead. This description fits for a cannabis tincture which only takes a few minutes to take effect, especially since this potion would have been extremely potent and Jesus was in a very weakened state.

"Death"

> *When [the centurions] came to Jesus, they did not break His legs since they saw that He was already dead.*
>
> – John 19:33

Jesus "died" after just a few hours on the cross, immediately after consuming the tincture. Typically in crucifixions it took days for someone to expire and Roman soldiers would often break the prisoner's legs to hasten their death. But the soldiers did not need to break Jesus' legs since he already appeared dead, though they did stab him in the side with a spear. The stabbing was probably unanticipated but the flow of fluids (blood and water, John 19:34) could indicate that he was still alive. Once

Jesus was declared dead by the guards his body was allowed to be taken down from the cross.

Then Joseph of Arimathea and Nicodemus, who were friends of Jesus but not Apostles, took the body away. Joseph appealed directly to Pontius Pilate to remove the body and the governor was surprised to hear that Jesus had died so quickly.

Joseph and Nicodemus were part of the plan along with the Three Marys, but the Apostles knew nothing of it. It is not clear if Judas, who betrayed Jesus to the authorities, was part of the plan or not; that speculation is left to others. Another speculation is that Jesus may have had a different plan, that did not include being crucified, and that the women rescued him from the cross by faking his death, but that alternative would negate Jesus' prophecies of his coming death.

> *Joseph of Arimathea, a prominent member of the Sanhedrin who was himself looking forward to the kingdom of God, came and boldly went into Pilate and asked for Jesus' body. Pilate was surprised that He was already dead. Summoning the centurion, he asked him whether He had already died. When he found out from the centurion, he gave the corpse to Joseph.*
>
> – Mark 15:43-45

> *After this, Joseph of Arimathea, who was a disciple of Jesus… asked Pilate that he might remove Jesus' body. Pilate gave him permission, so he came and took His body away. Nicodemus (who had previously come to Him at night) also came, bringing a mixture of about 75 pounds of myrrh and aloes. Then they took Jesus' body and wrapped it in linen cloths with the aromatic spices, according to the burial custom of the Jews.*
>
> – John 19:38-40

Joseph and Nicodemus brought 75 pounds of myrrh and aloes, which is a large quantity and seems unusual for a burial since Jews did not make a practice of embalming the dead, it was their practice to bury the dead quickly. It makes more sense to imagine the 75 pounds of myrrh and aloes as medicines used to treat Jesus's many wounds.

The linen cloth may well have been hemp which was commonly used as a funeral shroud. Joseph was conveniently in possession of his own private, unused tomb that they had ready nearby for Jesus's body. Joseph and Nicodemus could have bribed any Roman guards assigned to watch the tomb, though it is not clear from scripture if the tomb was actually guarded.

Return to Life

Jesus was crucified on a Friday morning, declared dead in the afternoon and laid in the tomb. At daybreak Sunday morning, (on the third day) Mary Magdalene and the other women went to visit the tomb. They reportedly found the heavy stone door removed and the risen Jesus. Jesus would certainly have been unable to remove the stone himself in his condition, someone else would have to have opened the tomb.

In this scenario, the Three Mary's didn't simply discover Jesus alive, they brought more medicines (spices) and carefully revived him. Mary Magdalene then ran to tell the disciples the news, all the while keeping the secret.

> *When the Sabbath was over, Mary Magdalene, Mary the mother of James, and Salome bought spices so that they might go to anoint Jesus' body.*
>
> – Mark 16:1

> *... Mary Magdalene came to the tomb early, while it was still dark. She saw that the stone had been removed from the tomb.*
>
> – John 20:1

> *... she turned around and saw Jesus standing there...*
>
> – John 20:14

> *When Jesus rose early on the first day of the week, he appeared first to Mary Magdalene, out of whom he had driven seven demons.*
>
> – Mark 16:9

After Jesus was revived he convalesced for forty days while his wounds healed. According to the Apostle Paul, Jesus met with more than 500 followers. Jesus then either departed for points unknown, many claim he went to India and lived for years, or maybe he simply succumbed to his injuries and died. In the Bible, it says Jesus ascended to heaven (Acts 1:9-12).

> *After his suffering, [Jesus] presented himself to them and gave many convincing proofs that he was alive. He appeared to them over a period of forty days and spoke about the kingdom of God.*
>
> – Acts 1:3

Neo-Mysteries

The hypothesis that Jesus faked his death using a potent cannabis tincture is pharmacologically conceivable and not impossible. It is a medical reality that extremely strong cannabis tinctures can knock a person unconscious for two days, generating catalepsy that can make the person appear dead.

Christ ascends to heaven before his disciples by M. Wellcome

This theory satisfies the convictions of the faithful that the witnesses who claimed to have seen him alive were, in fact, speaking the truth. It is important that the witnesses were speaking the truth because their testimony is the basis for the entire Christian faith. That the witnesses did not know the entire story is beside the point, they were speaking the truth as they knew it. This theory also satisfies the skeptics who do not believe in supernatural miracles or divine intervention.

The delightful irony of this theory is that rather than being raised by God as taught by doctrine, Jesus was actually raised by the Goddess and Eve's sacred plant, cannabis, the forbidden fruit. The women were the ones who knew the secret, but since women's opinions were not respected by men in the harshly patriarchal world of that time, no one would have paid attention to them even if they had spoken out.

The theory of the Earthly Resurrection reimagines the myth of Jesus in the context of the Mystery Traditions where the Goddess restores the suffering dead hero to life and majesty. If God can be made flesh in Jesus, then the Goddess can be made flesh in the Three Marys and the Virgin Mother.

The Angel and Women at the Empty Tomb

Chapter Forty-Eight

DYING AND RISING GOD

When Jesus rose from the tomb, he became the dying and rising god of pagan mythology in the flesh. The dying and rising god's journey to the underworld and back was among the most enduring and important traditions in the Ancient Near East and a theme that would have been well known to everyone in the Roman Empire.

For thousands of years every spring, pagans celebrated the untimely death of gods like Tammuz, Osiris, Dionysus, Adonis, Baal, and others, whose lives were restored through the heroic efforts of a goddess. The poetic details of these stories varied from one community to the next, but the underlying theme always represented the turning of the seasons, the growth of vegetation, and the cycles of life, death, and rebirth that are central to Goddess religions and their nature-based spirituality.

When Jesus apparently performed this unheard-of feat in real life, a real man being killed and seen to be reborn, he irrevocably transformed world religion. Numerous new faiths emerged around this profoundly dramatic event. After all, why worship a story that is known to be a myth when Jesus the man performed the act in real life? It must have been very powerful for people at that time to hear tales of a man who truly overcame death.

Judeo-Christian traditions do not focus on the cycles of life or connections to nature, instead, they teach that humans are separate from nature and that we all will have eternal life in either heaven or hell depending on our sinful behavior. Christians are taught that by worshipping Jesus and finding salvation from their sins in him, they will live forever in blissful heaven.

> *For God so loved the world that he gave his one and only Son, that whoever believes in him shall not perish but have eternal life.*
>
> –John 3:16

Easter

Easter is the holiday that celebrates the resurrection of Jesus and it is one of the most important holidays in Christianity. Easter demonstrates the syncretization that transformed pagan traditions into Christian traditions. Easter is held every spring near the equinox, just like the old pagan springtime holidays that celebrated the cycles of life. Jesus's birthday is celebrated on Christmas which was also syncretized from earlier pagan holidays set on the winter solstice.

The English word Easter is taken from a Germanic pagan goddess, Eostre, goddess of Spring, otherwise known as Ostara, Austra, and Eastrem. All of these names carry a clear etymological similarity to Ishtar, Astarte, and Ishara, various names for the Queen of Heaven.

Christians transformed these old pagan cycle of life traditions into an eternal life tradition, something new and intentionally distinct from the paganism it replaced.

Ostara by Johannes Gehrts, 1884

Chapter Forty-Nine

FIRST CHRISTIANS

The only evidence for Jesus's resurrection comes from the testimony of witnesses, most of which is included in the Bible. There are no documents from Roman records of Jesus and his execution. The Jewish Christians who knew Jesus best, including his brother James, were killed by the Romans when Jerusalem and the Temple were destroyed in 70 CE. The burning of Jerusalem likely destroyed any contemporary writings about Jesus, leaving little evidence for modern historians to work with.

The only mention of Jesus outside the Bible that is reported to be roughly contemporaneous was supposedly written by the Jewish historian Josephus in his Antiquities of the Jews and published in 93 CE. This account has been embroiled in scholarly controversy for centuries and is widely believed to have been added later by a Christian editor.

For skeptics and non-believers, the lack of convincing evidence for Jesus outside the Bible is proof enough that he was not real, or at least that the resurrection never happened. Yet clearly something dramatic did happen because many people were moved to spread the word and thousands of people found faith in the event soon after.

To this author, the most convincing evidence that Jesus really did rise from the tomb is that multiple worship groups arose around the event that had conflicts and competing agendas. The early Christians had disagreements from the beginning, they argued over the meaning of the resurrection and Jesus's teachings, and they were certainly not a single group of friends or co-conspirators. There were even prominent pagans who incorporated Jesus into their pantheon of personal gods and heroes.

Competing Groups

In the first century CE, there were at least three primary groups of early Christians. These groups had competing theologies and were led by known characters from the Bible. There were the Jewish Christians, the Gnostics, and the orthodox Pauline Christians.

James the Just was the biological brother of Jesus, he was not a follower until witnessing the resurrection, but he became the leader of the Jewish Christians who remained in Jerusalem as practicing Jews.

The Apostles Peter and Paul created orthodox Christianity as we know it and what became the Roman Catholic Church. Peter was the leader of the original disciples, whom Jesus called "the Rock." Paul, who never met Jesus, was the most influential evangelist and invented many of the foundational teachings of Christianity.

Mary Magdalene was a leader among the Gnostics, she was the Apostle of Apostles and her closeness to Jesus made Peter jealous. The Apostle John was the Beloved Disciple who is credited with authoring the Gospel of John, he lived with Mother Mary in Ephesus. John was orthodox but was also a favorite of the Gnostics and they had additional books about him not included in the Bible.

These three rival groups; the Pauline Christians, Jewish Christians, and Gnostic Christians, had severe disputes over theology, law, and practice. Christian theology continued to be splintered for centuries and other groups formed later such as the Arians, who believed that Jesus was the son of God, but not God himself.

Women like Mary Magdalene were very influential in the early church, holding meetings in their homes and organizing in their communities. Christianity was open to all people, including women, slaves, and soldiers, and this was a big part of its appeal – anyone could find salvation in Jesus. Mithraism was another popular religion at the time that shared many characteristics of early Christianity, but it was only open to men (mainly Roman soldiers) and that limited its growth.

Fellowship was central to the early church, small communities formed that held private meetings discussing ideas, philosophy, and morality. This stood in contrast to the prevailing modes of Roman paganism that emphasized public displays and rituals, not private beliefs.[1]

---

1 Ehrman, Bart, *The Triumph of Christianity: How a Forbidden Religion Swept the World*, Simon & Schuster, 2018.

Chapter Fifty

JAMES the JUST

Jewish Christians

Most of Jesus's original 12 disciples remained in Jerusalem as practicing Jews under the leadership of James the Just. The Jewish Christians lived pious lives following Jewish law and were not out evangelizing, which limited their influence later on.

James was the biological brother of Jesus, he was highly respected and influential in his lifetime. James had not been an original follower of Jesus, he only joined after meeting Jesus post-resurrection. James is an important character in the Book of Acts, he mediated the disputes over Paul's heterodox teachings.

James authored the Epistle of James that was the last book accepted into the Bible. The Epistle of James was also one of the most controversial books to be accepted in the Biblical canon because James famously argued with Paul about the nature of faith and salvation.

James said that faith without works is dead, in direct contradiction of Paul's teachings that Christians are "justified by faith in Christ and not by the works of the law" (Galatians 2:16). This dispute between faith and deeds remains alive today among Fundamentalist Christians who focus on faith and mainline Churches who focus on social action and charity.

> *What good is it, my brothers and sisters, if someone claims to have faith but has no deeds? Can such faith save them? Suppose a brother or a sister is without clothes and daily food. If one of you says to them, "Go in peace; keep warm and well fed," but does nothing about their physical needs, what good is it?*
>
> *In the same way, faith by itself, if it is not accompanied by action, is dead. But someone will say, "You have faith; I have deeds." Show me your faith without deeds, and I will show you my faith by my deeds.*
>
> –James 2:14-18

St. James Led to his Execution by Andrea Mantegna

Martyred

James the Just was brutally martyred by the Romans in 62 CE in an act of political violence that outraged the Jewish community and helped spark the revolt that led to the Roman siege of Jerusalem. The Romans viewed Jewish claims for independence as sedition and strongly opposed it.

Most of the Jewish Christians were killed in 70 CE when the Romans burned Jerusalem and destroyed the second Jewish Temple. The Romans attempted to erase the Jewish community and identity completely. They razed the temple to the ground and expelled the Jewish people into the diaspora for the second time.

Many people view Jesus' end-times prophecies to have been fulfilled when Jerusalem was destroyed. Jesus had predicted the destruction of the Jewish temple in Luke 21:6 and Matthew 24:2.

Chapter Fifty-One

PAUL AND PETER

Paul the Evangelist

The Apostle Paul is the founder of Christianity as we know it. Paul never met Jesus nor did he witness the resurrection. Paul experienced his own revelation and was so moved that he became a follower and sought to join the Apostles. Paul was the primary evangelist who brought Christianity to the Gentiles (Greek and Roman pagans) rather than leaving it confined to the narrow band of Jewish followers who had known Jesus in his life.

Paul invented the name Jesus Christ, the idea that Christ died for our sins, the doctrine of salvation through faith, and other important teachings. Paul taught that through Jesus, God provided salvation to all who believed and that this salvation was available to all people; rich, poor, men, women, slaves, sinners, everyone, no matter how wretched they were.

Paul did not get along well with the Jewish Christians, in fact, Paul had serious conflicts in many of the cities he traveled to. Paul was repeatedly beaten and jailed for his preaching that incited both pagans and Jews. But Paul did have an ally in Peter, the leader of Jesus' original disciples.

There were numerous disputes with the Jewish Christians over the substance of what Paul was preaching to the Gentiles. Most significantly, Paul taught that it was not necessary to follow all the Jewish laws in order to follow Jesus even though Jesus said clearly that Jewish law needed to be followed. Jesus said,

> *"Do not think that I have come to abolish the Law or the Prophets; I have not come to abolish them but to fulfill them. For truly I tell you, until heaven and earth disappear, not the smallest letter, not the least stroke of a pen, will by any means disappear from the Law until everything is accomplished."*
>
> – Matthew 5:17-18

Paul argued that Jesus fulfilled the law on our behalf, and Mosaic law did not need to be followed by Gentile Christians. In particular, Jewish kosher dietary laws did not to be observed, nor would new converts need to be circumcised. While it was a great relief to the pagans to not need to perform the painful circumcision, this edict outraged the Jewish Christians, some of whom sought to kill Paul.

The dispute was eventually mediated by James the Just and it was agreed that circumcision would not be required by adult Gentiles to convert to following Jesus (Acts 15:1-15). It was also agreed that the only foods that were forbidden were those that had come from a ritual pagan sacrifice. But of course, we only have the Pauline version of the story because most of the Jewish Christians were killed by the Romans.

Peter the Rock

Peter had a forceful personality and authority among the original disciples. Jesus called Peter his "rock," and the foundation upon which he would build his church. Peter and Paul were the first evangelists, working to convert people to their idea of Christianity. Peter evangelized to the circumcised community while Paul preached to the uncircumcised.

Peter would eventually end up in Rome where he became the first Bishop in the city and ultimately the first Pope of the Roman Catholic Church. Peter and Paul are both believed to have been martyred in Rome roughly around 64 CE during the reign of Emperor Nero.

Authority

As Christianity grew and became more organized, men asserted their power and eventually organized male only leadership and hierarchy. Women had been active leaders in the first churches but before too long, the cultural norms of the day, in which women had no roles in public life, became dominant within the Church. The rivalry for influence between Peter and Mary Magdalene is on full display in the Gnostic texts and it is notable that she disappeared from the narrative of orthodox Church history.

Paul's letter to Timothy about issues in the church in Ephesus defined male authority over women. Many scholars question whether these passages were actually written by Paul, but regardless, they came to be accepted as official church teachings.

> *A woman should learn in quietness and full submission. I do not permit a woman to teach or to assume authority over a man; she must be quiet.*
>
> *For Adam was formed first, then Eve. And Adam was not the one deceived; it was the woman who was deceived and became a sinner. But*

women will be saved through childbearing – if they continue in faith, love and holiness with propriety.

–1 Timothy 2:11-15

Exclusivity

Paul originated the exclusivist and authoritarian nature of Christianity that led to the worst abuses by the Church over the centuries. Jewish ethnic monotheism taught that Yahweh was supreme and the Jews were his chosen people, elevated above all others. But the Jews did not seek to convert anyone to their religion, in fact it was discouraged. Nor did the Jews attempt to dominate the broader culture, they tried to separate from it and maintain their purity. Pauline Christianity on the other hand taught from the start that they had the one correct answer about spiritual matters and the one true God, rendering all other religions and philosophies as false, regardless of their merits.

Saint Paul Writing His Epistles by Le Valentin

Paul was the first missionary, he spent his life traveling and spreading the word of Jesus, trying to convert people to his new religion. This paradoxical spirit of exclusivity and evangelism has defined Christianity ever since. Christians came to believe that they had the God-given authority to render judgment on entire cultures for practicing false religions. They quickly and repeatedly abandoned the peaceful teachings of Jesus in favor of committing the most horrific crimes and abuses, such as forced conversions of indigenous peoples and genocide of the Jews.

Unfortunately, the pattern of religious intolerance has been a characteristic of Christian cultures from the moment they first gained political power in Rome in the 4th century and has continued through history. Roman Christian emperors banned pagan religions and shut down their temples with force and violence. Christians have long fought spiritual warfare in order to impose their religious doctrine on entire societies and eliminate rival beliefs.

Mary Magdalene by Andrea Solario

Chapter Fifty-Two

MARY MAGDALENE

Apostle of Apostles

Saint Mary Magdalene (from the city of Magdala), is among the most enduring and fascinating characters in the New Testament, yet very little is known about her. Mary Magdalene was one of the women who traveled with and supported Jesus, she witnessed his crucifixion, discovered his empty tomb, and was first to see the risen Lord after his resurrection.

Mary Magdalene was the person closest to Jesus that was not one of the 12 male disciples and she is described as Jesus' closest companion. In Gnostic texts, Mary Magdalene is the Apostle of Apostles. Despite Mary Magdalene's intimacy with Jesus, she disappeared from the Biblical narratives after the resurrection and played no role in forming the orthodox churches.

Mary Magdalene is said to have had a sinful background. In Luke 8:2 it says that "seven demons had come out of her," and she has often been described as a prostitute though the scripture does not say that. The symbolism of the seven demons may indicate that Mary Magdalene had been a member of a Mystery religion which were popular with women at that time. Some of the Mystery religions had traditions involving seven gates or seven steps that lead to wisdom or a glorious afterlife.

Many people have speculated about the relationship between Mary Magdalene and Jesus, questioning if they were lovers or even secretly married. Considering Jesus's clear views on marriage and sexual immorality it seems unlikely that they were anything other than teacher and student – but the questions will never die.

Mary Magdalene disappears from the Biblical narrative after the events of the resurrection, which seems odd, considering her centrality to Jesus' life and ministry. Mary had a more prominent role in the Gospels than most of the other Apostles yet she appears nowhere in the official histories of the early orthodox church or in any of Paul's letters.

The reason Mary Magdalene disappeared could be that she was important among the Gnostics who were rivals to the orthodox Christians.

Mary's teachings were likely intentionally forgotten once the orthodox Christians gained political power in Rome and condemned their rivals. Mary Magdalene was written out of church history despite her importance to Jesus personally because she taught a competing set of messages to those of Peter and Paul.

Gospel of Mary

The Gospel of Mary is a rare and important Gnostic text about Mary Magdalene, whom it says Jesus loved more than the other disciples. The Gospel of Mary was excluded from the Biblical canon. This Gospel and other Gnostic texts portray Mary Magdalene as a central figure in early Christianity. She was Jesus' closest and most beloved disciple and the only one who truly understood his teachings.

The Gnostic texts were mostly lost to history but were rediscovered in the last century by archaeologists and scholars in various locations, including the Nag Hammadi library. Most of the texts are fragmentary and the context of many passages is open to interpretation.

The Gospel of Mary details her leadership role among the Gnostic Christians and her rivalry with the Apostle Peter who objected to a woman teaching. It is likely that Mary Magdalene's role and influence was intentionally minimized by early Church fathers who worked tirelessly to push women out of leadership positions. Salacious stories spread about Mary Magdalene, such that she was a prostitute, in order to damage her reputation. In an argument with Mary, Peter said,

> *"Did he then speak secretly with a woman, in preference to us, and not openly? Are we to turn back and all listen to her? Did he prefer her to us?"*
> – Gospel of Mary 9:4

The Gospel of Thomas was another Gnostic text that shows friction between Mary Magdalene and Peter, who says,

> *"Let Mary leave us, for women are not worthy of the life."*
> – Gospel of Thomas: Section 114

Although the Bible says nothing about Mary Magdalene's later life, other sources do preserve some stories about her. According to one well-known tradition, she went to southern France and lived for thirty years at a place called La Sainte-Baume. A local church there claims to have her skull and displays it to pilgrims.

Chapter Fifty-Three

GNOSTICS

The Gnostic Christians were a variety of syncretic mystical sects that originated in Alexandria, Egypt, the leading city for religion and culture at the time. There was no codified set of Gnostic teachings or dogma, the groups were all independent and had their own beliefs. The Gnostics had roots from before Jesus arrived and a number of groups began following him and incorporated his teachings. Their beliefs in the feminine divine, egalitarianism, and a direct, personal, and transcendent participation in the divine, or gnosis, did not align with the beliefs that became orthodox Christianity. Gnostic teachings were deemed heretical by the orthodox Church and most of their books were burned, so very little of their teachings survived.

The primary reason that Gnostics were deemed heretical was because they taught believers to achieve contact with God directly, through their own divine knowledge and moral living, without the mediation of any church, priest, or bishop. Many Gnostic sects openly disregarded any hierarchical organization, did not appoint leaders, priests, or bishops, and honored women as disciples and prophets. These Gnostic teachings challenged both Jewish law and the growing authority of the orthodox Church who encouraged hierarchy and male-only leadership.

The Gnostics embraced the spiritual wisdom of the Mystery religions and the Wisdom traditions; some groups embraced sacred sex while others were ascetic, though details on this front are limited. Among other beliefs, some Gnostic Christians taught that Sophia was the Bride of Christ, and viewed the Holy Trinity as God, Sophia, and Christ.

Simon Magus

Simon Magus was an early Gnostic leader who appeared in the Bible (Acts 8:9-24) and led a formidable sect called the Simonians. Simon Magus was a great rival of Peter for influence among early followers of Jesus. Church fathers claimed that Simon Magus practiced sorcery and witchcraft and he was called the father of heresies by the orthodox church.

Simon had been baptized by John the Baptist and may have witnessed the ministry of Jesus. He traveled with an extraordinarily beautiful woman from Tyre named Helena with whom he was accused of practicing sex magic. The only references to Simon Magus are the writings of his enemies in the Church so the precise nature of his teachings remains obscure.

Death of Simon Magus

NAG HAMMADI LIBRARY

The discovery of the Nag Hammadi library by archaeologists in Egypt in 1945 revealed lost Gnostic gospels such as the Gospel of Thomas, the Gospel of Philip, the Secret Book of John, and the Sophia of Jesus. Some of these are believed to predate the Biblical gospels of Matthew, Mark, Luke, and John, though the texts themselves date to the 4th century CE.

These Gnostic gospels were hidden away in caves to prevent their destruction during a period of book burning after orthodox Christianity became politically powerful in Rome. These gospels were only finally translated and revealed to the public in the 1970s.

The Gospel of Philip contains a cryptic reference to Jesus kissing Mary Magdalene on the mouth, which has led many to speculate that they were lovers or even possibly married.

In this passage from the Sophia of Jesus, the messiah describes the Mother Goddess.

> *The Perfect Savior said to them: "I want you to know that Sophia, the Mother of the Universe and the consort, desired by herself to bring these to existence without her male (consort). But by the will of the Father of the Universe, that his unimaginable goodness might be revealed, he created that curtain between the immortals and those that came afterward, that the consequence might follow.*
>
> – The Sophia of Jesus[1]

SECRET BOOK OF JOHN

The Apostle John is one of the most important founding figures of orthodox Christianity. John was not a Gnostic, but a bigger picture emerges in the non-canonical writings which show that John was also a favorite of the Gnostics. The Apocryphon of John, or Secret Book of John, was an especially important gnostic myth. Three separate copies were found among the Nag Hammadi writings.

The Apocryphon purports to be a secret revelation from Jesus that was received in a vision by the Apostle John. It claims to convey the true nature of the divine realm and its relationship to the material cosmos and humanity. The Apocryphon presents a complex theology steeped in Plato's forms, it is a blend of Hellenistic philosophy, heterodox Judaism, and mysticism. Christian opponents of the Gnostics, such as Irenaeus, considered such doctrines to be pagan corruptions of true monotheism.

1 Parrott, Douglas M.(translator), *The Sophia of Jesus Christ,* The Nag Hammadi Library, Gnostic Society Library. http://www.gnosis.org/naghamm/sjc.html

St. John at Patmos

Chapter Fifty-Four

ST. JOHN THE DIVINE

St. John the Divine was the youngest of Jesus' Apostles and is self-described as the "Beloved Disciple" in the Gospel of John. Scholars dispute the authorship of John's works, but he was nonetheless a central figure in the early Church. John was among the inner nucleus of Jesus's intimate disciples and was instructed to watch over Mother Mary after the crucifixion.

By tradition it is believed that John was not only the youngest of the Disciples, he was also the longest-lived and the only one of the original twelve to die a natural death. John, or one of his students, wrote the Gospel of John, the last of the four Biblical gospels about the life of Jesus to be completed.

The Gospel of John is the most lyrical, beautifully written, and mystically infused of the four canonical Gospels. John emphasizes the incarnation and divinity of Jesus Christ and his performance of miracles. John is also credited with writing three biblical epistles and the Book of Revelation – the apocalyptic, prophetic, and visionary tract that closes out the Bible.

It is unknown where John stood in the disputes with Paul over circumcision and following Jewish law. But there are many details in the Gospel of John that indicate a rivalry with Peter, or at least attempts by John to show himself as an equal.

Many important details are added in John's Gospel that do not appear in the earlier synoptic Gospels of Matthew, Mark, and Luke. In John's Gospel, he is the only Disciple to stand by the cross with the women, and he runs ahead of Peter to reach the empty tomb first. Jesus also instructs the Beloved Disciple from the cross to take care of his Mother Mary, indicating elevated importance for John. The synoptic Gospels do not contain these details and John also presents other events from Jesus' life differently.

With Mary in Ephesus

> *When Jesus saw His mother and the disciple He loved standing there, He said to His mother, "Woman, here is your son." and to the disciple, "Here is your mother." From that time on, this disciple took her into his home.*
>
> – John 19:26-27

John and Mother Mary lived out their lives in Ephesus where they were leaders in an important branch of the early church. They would have been in close contact with the Goddess traditions and Mystery religions as the Grand Temple of Artemis was still a popular destination for pilgrims.

In some traditions, John's mother was Salome, Mary of Clopas, the third Mary at the Cross. This shows that John was close to the Three Marys, perhaps the closest of any of the male disciples. Ironically, John does not describe Mother Mary as a virgin, nor does he recount Jesus' legendary birth story. Despite being personally close to Mary, he makes no attempt to present her as divine.

New Creation Myth

John opens his Gospel with a new creation story, one that presents Jesus as the Logos, the Word, who was with God the Father from the beginning. This story places Jesus in the role of Sophia, or Wisdom, who in the Book of Proverbs was said to be with God at the moment of creation.

> *In the beginning was the Word, and the Word was with God, and the Word was God.*
>
> –John 1:1

> *He was with God in the beginning. Through him all things were made; without him nothing was made that has been made. In him was life, and that life was the light of all mankind. The light shines in the darkness, and the darkness has not overcome it.*
>
> –John 1:2-5

> *The Word became flesh and made his dwelling among us. We have seen his glory, the glory of the one and only Son, who came from the Father, full of grace and truth.*
>
> –John 1:14

The language John uses is unmistakable in its goal to commingle the divinity of Jesus with God. John inserts Jesus into the role played by Sophia as the first emanation of God. In the Wisdom traditions, Sophia had been with God at the beginning and it was through her that God brought order from chaos, but in John's telling, Jesus takes the role of Sophia. John was familiar with the Goddess traditions and he is explicit in co-opting some of those traditions to help him elevate the divinity and majesty of Jesus. Compare John's depiction of Jesus to the description of wisdom in the Proverbs of King Solomon.

"Yahweh brought me forth as the first of his works, before his deeds of old; I was formed long ages ago, at the very beginning, when the world came to be."

– Proverbs 8:22-23

I was there when he set the heavens in place, when he marked out the horizon on the face of the deep, when he established the clouds above and fixed securely the fountains of the deep, when he gave the sea its boundary so the waters would not overstep his command, and when he marked out the foundations of the earth. Then I was constantly at his side. I was filled with delight day after day, rejoicing always in his presence, rejoicing in his whole world and delighting in mankind.

– Proverbs 8:27-31

Paul Preaches at Ephesus

Chapter Fifty-Five

EPHESUS

Mother of God

Ephesus was one of the great Goddess worshipping cities of antiquity. The Grand Temple to Artemis was the largest pagan temple ever built. It was one of the Seven Wonders of the Ancient World and was a famous pilgrimage destination for a thousand years. Ephesus was also an important location for the early church and it is the place where the pagan goddesses were syncretized into the Virgin Mary.

By tradition, Mother Mary went to live with John in Ephesus after the resurrection of her son Jesus and the city became the center of Mary's veneration in the early era of Christianity. The House of the Virgin Mary on Mt. Koressos is a shrine near the city that can be visited today where it is said that Mary ascended into heaven.

The Council of Ephesus in 431 CE was convened to resolve contentious theological disputes of the early church. After heated debate and recriminations among the rival bishops, the Virgin Mary was declared to be the "Mother of God" and not simply the mother of Christ.

It cannot be ignored that the profound declaration that Mary is the "Mother of God" was made in the same city where the most magnificent goddess temple of all time had stood proudly for centuries. It is in Ephesus where the Virgin Mary was elevated in order to absorb the pagan goddesses. The Great Goddess was never destroyed, she changed form and lived on as the Madonna, albeit in a diminished mode that was only venerated and not worshipped.

Paul in Ephesus

During his journeys, the Apostle Paul also lived in Ephesus longer than any other city. It is in this city where we find the only mention of a goddess in the New Testament. Paul nearly started a riot at the Grand Temple of Artemis when he denounced the goddess and the silversmiths producing idols to her (Acts 19:21-41).

> *"And you see and hear how this fellow Paul has convinced and led astray large numbers of people here in Ephesus and in practically the*

whole province of Asia. He says that gods made by human hands are no gods at all."

"There is danger not only that our trade will lose its good name, but also that the temple of the great goddess Artemis will be discredited; and the goddess herself, who is worshiped throughout the province of Asia and the world, will be robbed of her divine majesty."

When they heard this, they were furious and began shouting: "Great is Artemis of the Ephesians!" Soon the whole city was in an uproar.

– Acts 19:26-29

Ephesus was also a cannabis homeland and a region that exported large amounts of hemp to the Roman empire.[1] The Goddess is strongest where the cannabis grows thickest. There is no suggestion that Paul ever used cannabis drugs but he would certainly have been exposed to them. Cannabis drugs, incense, and sacred weaving were all in daily use at the temple to Artemis. But Paul did make his living as a tentmaker and in that capacity would have used cannabis fibers every day for hemp canvas, threads, and lines.

Acts of John

The Acts of John is a non-canonical Christian tract that circulated widely in the first centuries of the Church but was deemed heretical at the Second Council of Nicaea (787 CE) for its Gnostic content. It has survived in fragmentary form ever since. In the Acts of John, the Apostle performed many miracles and won many converts through his feats.

In one of the most dramatic mythological tales, John destroyed the grand temple to Artemis in Ephesus, bringing it down in pieces and shattering the altar through the power of his words. The priest of Artemis was killed by the falling debris, but John resurrected him and brought him back to life.

The Ephesians cried out, "One is the God of John" and converted en masse. This story shows in mythological terms the triumph of Christianity over the pagan traditions. The grand temple of Artemis was one of the most famous monuments in the world and audiences would have clearly understood what it meant that John had brought the temple down and resurrected the dead priest.

And as John spake these things, immediately the altar of Artemis was parted into many pieces, and all the things that were dedicated in the

1 Clarke and Merlin, *Cannabis Evolution and Ethnobotany,* p.160

temple fell, and was rent asunder, and likewise of the images of the gods more than seven. And the half of the temple fell down, so that the priest was slain at one blow by the falling of the [roof] beam.

The multitude of the Ephesians therefore cried out: One is the God of John, one is the God that hath pity on us, for thou only art God: now are we turned to thee, beholding thy marvellous works! have mercy on us, O God, according to thy will, and save us from our great error! And some of them, lying on their faces, made supplications, and some kneeled and besought, and some rent their clothes and wept, and others tried to escape.

– The Acts of John, verse 42[2]

GRAND TEMPLE DESTROYED

The grand temple to Artemis was not actually destroyed in John's lifetime; it was burned down by a Christian mob centuries later. This story was probably written to provide a dramatic illustration of the destruction of the famous temple, but it was considered heretical because it strayed too far from narrow, orthodox teachings that the Catholic Church would tolerate.

Temple of Artemis in Ephesus today

The Acts of John is an example of Christian mythology that an open-ended religion would have tolerated as poetic license. But the Roman Catholic Church demanded exclusive authority over all manners of theology and philosophy and it shut down any ideas it could not control.

The Grand Temple to Artemis was torn down by Christian mobs in 401 CE during the purges of pagan religion. Marble from the temple was harvested over the years and used in other building projects. All that remains today of the Temple to Artemis are elements of the foundation and a single forlorn column assembled by archaeologists from pieces scattered around the site.

2 James, M.R. (translator), *The Acts of John, Gnostic Scriptures and Fragments*, Gnostic Society Library. http://gnosis.org/library/actjohn.htm

Virgin Mary the Queen of Heaven

Chapter Fifty-Six

VIRGIN MARY

Syncretized Goddess

It is in the Virgin Mary where we see the most direct connections between Christianity and the pagan goddess traditions. The Virgin Mary, also known as Madonna, absorbed many of the aspects, titles, and images that were common and familiar to the people of the day.

As the Church grew in the Roman era and people converted, either by choice or by force, the old traditions were converted as well. Syncretization was important in encouraging the Hellenistic world to convert from paganism to Christianity. Adopting familiar motifs and traditions and reframing them in Christian terms made the new religion more understandable and acceptable.

The Virgin Mary was given many of the titles associated with the traditional goddesses; she is called the Queen of Heaven and the Queen of the Universe. Doves are Madonna's symbolic animal, and it is notable that she was not associated with either snakes or lions. Snakes were discredited in the Garden of Eden story and lions represented warrior maidens, a role model that was not to be allowed in patriarchal society.

One of the most common images of Mary is the Madonna and child, where she holds the baby Jesus in her lap. This iconography was adopted directly from the imagery of the Egyptian Isis and Horus. Isis was the source of the Black Madonna. Isis was one of the most popular goddesses in the Hellenistic world, her Mystery religion was practiced across the Roman empire at the time Christianity was born. Just as Isis was the throne upon which the Pharaoh sat, so too the Virgin Mary was said to be the throne on which Jesus sat.

Virgin Birth

The most important symbolism syncretized from the pagan goddesses was the title Virgin and the story of the virgin birth. Ishtar, Inanna, Anat, and many other goddesses were called virgins as a title of respect that signified their status as independent young women, but not as chaste, since these goddesses were highly sexual. Their sacred sex priestesses, the qedesha, were also called virgins. Children born to the qedesha were said to be virgin-born and were often the heroes of legends, such as Sargon the Great.

The idea of goddesses as virgins was one of humanity's oldest written notions, appearing in the earliest cuneiform from Sumer, and would have been perfectly familiar to Hellenistic audiences. Isis was a virgin when she gave birth to Horus. Alexander the Great, Plato, and Romulus and Remus, the founders of Rome, were all reported to have had divine fathers and mortal, virgin mothers.

Mary's virgin birth story does not appear in the first Gospel to be written, the Gospel of Mark, written around 66-70 CE (more than thirty years after the crucifixion). Nor does the virgin birth story appear in the Gospel of John, the Book of Acts, or the writings of the Apostle Paul which predate the writing of the Gospels.

The virgin birth story only appears in the Gospels of Luke and Matthew, written 85-90 CE. This would imply that the virgin birth is fiction because if such a miracle were known by the followers of Jesus in his lifetime it would likely have been proclaimed widely. It seems likely that this supernatural story was tailored to the Hellenistic audiences accustomed to their gods having legendary births. John lived with Mother Mary in Ephesus, he of all people should have proclaimed the virgin birth if it was true, and it is notable that he did not.

The virgin birth story has nonetheless had a profound impact on Christian culture. Paul encouraged asceticism and praised abstinence from sex as a virtue, setting the tone for Christianity as a sex-fearing religion. When combined with their restrictive views on sexual morality, the virgin birth works to set an impossibly high moral standard for women that no human mother could pass.

It is an official doctrine of the Catholic Church that Mary remained a virgin perpetually, even though Jesus is described as having brothers and sisters. The Virgin Mary's chastity has been extolled for centuries as an ethical ideal for women.

Original Sin

Sex was seen as the original sin by Christians, particularly by the early Church father St. Augustine, who interpreted the Garden of Eden story in sexual terms. St. Augustine taught that Adam and Eve transmitted sin to all of humanity through the act of sex. Augustine even created a new word for sexual sin, concupiscence. In the doctrine of original sin, all humans are born sinful by virtue of having been conceived through sex.

Of course, women bore the brunt of the blame for original sin, as they were paradoxically seen as more lustful and sexually insatiable than men. With the Virgin Mary as a role model, no human mother could ever be seen as truly noble, since she automatically fell short of the divine. Men, on the other hand, particularly male priests who had taken vows of celibacy, were seen as the vessels of God.

Sexual asceticism is emphasized in Christianity. Acceptable sexuality is limited to monogamous marriages, ideally only for the purpose of childbearing and with a minimum of pleasure. Sexual pleasure for its own sake is distinctly discouraged as sinful within Christian ethics and any expressions of homosexuality, female pleasure, or transgenderism were utterly repressed.

For the pagans, human sexuality was celebrated as the source of life and was encouraged. There is no Goddess or nature worship in the Judeo-Christian traditions. There is no sacred sex, warrior maidens, female divination, or oracles. The worship of nature is seen as a form of idolatry because one is worshipping God's creation rather than God himself.

Monotheistic spirituality is deeply misogynistic. God is viewed as male with no accompanying female, but the feminine divine could never be completely denied, she evolved and remained alive in Christian traditions.

Hail Mary, Full of Grace

The Virgin Mary has long been an emotional center of Catholic traditions, she is the accessible and approachable side of God. People pray to Mary in hopes that she will intercede on the behalf of the penitent, she is the "mediator of access" to God. The Catholic Church was 100% patriarchal with only men serving as priests and bishops. Mother Mary provided the maternal balance, symbolizing the gospel's imperatives to love, care, and serve, in contrast to the stern, heavy-handed authority of the male leadership.

Many familiar prayers are made to the Virgin Mother, such as the traditional Hail Mary that is said every day by Catholics as the basis for the Rosary prayers.

> *Hail Mary, full of grace, the Lord is with thee. Blessed art thou among women, and blessed is the fruit of thy womb, Jesus. Holy Mary, Mother of God, pray for us sinners, now and at the hour of our death. Amen.*

Hail Holy Queen is part of the Liturgy of the Hours, the Church's official daily prayer.

> *Hail, holy Queen, mother of mercy, our life, our sweetness and our hope. To thee do we cry, poor banished children of Eve. To thee do we send up our sighs, mourning and weeping in this valley of tears. Turn then, most gracious advocate, thine eyes of mercy toward us, and after this our exile, show unto us the blessed fruit of thy womb, Jesus. O clement, O loving, O sweet Virgin Mary! Pray for us, O holy Mother of God, that we may be made worthy of the promises of Christ. Amen.*

Protestant Rejection

Many modern-day Protestant Christians, who broke from the Catholic Church in the 16th century CE, view veneration of the Virgin Mary as thinly veiled goddess worship and it is among their chief criticisms of the Catholics.

The Protestant Reformation was primarily rooted in rebellion against the corrupt Papal leadership of the Catholic Church, but the Protestants had theological complaints as well. Protestants encouraged people to read the Bible for themselves and viewed the heavy use of imagery and iconography in the Catholic Church as idolatry, positions the Catholics rejected. Disputes between the Catholics and Protestants led to centuries of bloody conflict and warfare.

Protestants purged many elements of the Catholic rituals and liturgy including veneration of saints and the Virgin Mary. Protestants emphasize the direct relationship with Jesus Christ as their Lord and savior. While respecting Mary as the mother of Jesus, Protestants do not turn to her for any form of salvation or veneration.

Chapter Fifty-Seven

PAGANS PERSECUTED

From the start, Orthodox Christianity was exclusivistic and evangelistic, it claims to be the one true religion while all others are false. Christianity also emphasizes hierarchical authority and leadership. Claims of authority brought endless disputes and schisms over who was in possession of the true interpretations of theology and scripture.

Christianity was built around the idea of evangelism, teaching followers to go around the world and spread the word of Jesus Christ and build new communities of Christians. Christians believe they are saving people from damnation by getting them to convert to the one true religion.

Christian theology does not tolerate the worship or belief in other gods – it is an intolerant belief system by design. The pagan world, in contrast, tolerated an endless variety of deities and mythologies and there was always room for the addition of new gods and new ideas.

Pagans had obligations as citizens to make offerings to the civic gods endorsed by the political authorities. But pagan political leadership did not interfere with people's private beliefs and local religions, as long as those religions were not seditious. Christians and Jews periodically ran afoul of Roman authorities when they resisted participating in the public pagan festivals.

Christian Rome

Roman Emperor Constantine the Great converted to Christianity in 312 CE and by the end of the 4th century, Christianity had become the state religion of the Roman Empire. Under Constantine, Christianity went from being a minority religion that was occasionally persecuted to the preferred religion of the urban professional class who sought to be in the good graces of the Emperor.

As Christianity grew, Christians began persecuting pagans, vandalizing and pillaging their temples. Subsequent emperors steadily restricted pagan rituals until finally in 391 CE, Emperor Theodosius outlawed pagan religions altogether and forbade access to all the temples. Pagan religious traditions had already been in decline when Christianity started becoming popular. Roman Emperors had been declaring themselves to be gods for centuries. It served to devalue pagan traditions when everyone recognized that these political leaders were clearly men and anything but divine.

When the pagan religions were outlawed, many important temples were smashed and burned by mobs. Their sacred objects and priceless works of art were stolen. Books were burned and statues of the gods were defaced by breaking their noses off. The Greek schools of philosophy were shuttered by force and teachers were murdered in the street. Christians of the era distrusted astronomy, mathematics, and plant medicine as magic, divination, and witchcraft.

MORT DE LA PHILOSOPHE HYPATIE, A ALEXANDRIE

Assassination of Hypatia

In the year 415 CE, the great pagan philosopher Hypatia was dragged from her coach in the city of Alexandria and viciously murdered by a Christian mob. Hypatia's great sin was being a woman who was learned and confident and had the gall to teach men. Hypatia was a beloved teacher of mathematics and philosophy who was esteemed among Alexandria's leading men. She taught geometry and astronomy and invented tools like the astrolabe.

For Hypatia, mathematics was a sacred language of the universe ordering the cosmos in musical intervals and harmonies in space. In the ancient world, there was little to distinguish astronomy from astrology or mathematics from magic and this was enough for Church leaders to accuse her of sorcery.

In practical terms, Hypatia was caught up in the political rivalries between Cyril, a Christian bishop of Alexandria, and the moderates in the community who sought reconciliation among the various faiths. Cyril's predecessor as Bishop had been his uncle Theophilus, who had ordered the burning of the great temples in the city like the Mithraeum dedicated to Mithras and the magnificent Serapeum dedicated to Serapis (Zeus-Osiris) that was at the heart of Alexandrian culture.

Cyril ignited rumors against Hypatia, accusing her of sorcery. A Christian mob dragged the elderly woman through the city and flayed her skin with oyster shells, dismembered her body, and burned it in a mockery of pagan sacrifices.

The assassination of Hypatia marked the end of the pagan world in political terms. The remaining schools and temples were suppressed and the nature-worshipping traditions survived only in the countryside, far away from political authorities.

Cyril was canonized as a Saint in the Catholic Church while Hypatia was all but forgotten for 1500 years. Hypatia's writings were all destroyed, along with the vast majority of philosophical and learned writing from the ancient world. Any knowledge or philosophical thought that challenged orthodox Christianity's narrow view of the world, and the authority of its leadership, was repressed, often with violence.

Notre Dame, Paris

CHAPTER FIFTY-EIGHT

CATHEDRALS

CHURCH OF SAINT MARY MAJOR

Many Catholic churches and cathedrals were built over the sites of old goddess temples, or were simply renamed temples. In Rome, the Basilica of Santa Maria Maggiore (Church of Saint Mary Major) was built immediately following the Council of Ephesus; it is owned by the Vatican and was one of the first and largest churches dedicated to the Virgin Mary. The basilica was built over the sacred caverns of Magna Mater (Great Mother), the Roman mother goddess Cybele.

Church of the Holy Sepulcher

The Church of the Holy Sepulcher in Jerusalem is a sacred site identified as the place of both the crucifixion and the tomb of Jesus Christ. The Church has long been a major pilgrimage center for Christians from all over the world and it was also once the site of a Roman temple to the goddess Venus. At the time of the crucifixion, the site was outside the city walls, but after the Romans burned and devastated Jerusalem, the city was rebuilt as Aelia Capitolina by Roman Emperor Hadrian in 130 CE. The temple to Venus (Aphrodite, Astarte) was one of the major buildings in the city, while the temple to Jupiter (Zeus, Baal) was built on the Temple Mount.

The construction of pagan temples on their holy sites in Jerusalem caused much anger among the remaining Jews. The temple to Venus was apparently built on the site where Jesus was crucified because it was later demolished to make room for the Church of the Holy Sepulcher. Roman Emperor Constantine and his mother personally located the site they believed to be the tomb of Jesus in 327 CE and ordered the church to be built; it remains one of the most sacred sites in Christianity today.

Rome

The Church of Santa Maria sopra Minerva (Saint Mary above Minerva) in Rome was built over the foundation of a temple to goddess Minerva (Athena) around 750 CE. The Pantheon building in Rome is now a Catholic church but was originally built in Roman times as a temple to all the gods. The Pantheon is one of the best preserved of all ancient Roman buildings, it is nearly two thousand years old and has been in continuous use. Altogether there are eleven pagan temples in Rome known to have been converted into Catholic churches.

Notre Dame

The name "Notre Dame" means "Our Lady," referring to the Blessed Virgin Mary, and it is one of the most commonly used names for churches, cathedrals, and schools in the Catholic tradition. In Paris, the famous Notre Dame Cathedral was built on the site of a Roman temple to Isis who was very popular in the Roman Empire. The Parisii people were Gauls who were loyal to Rome and worshipped Isis, the city of Paris was named for them.

PARTHENON

The Parthenon in Athens was dedicated to the goddess Athena in 438 BCE. For nearly a thousand years the Parthenon functioned as a goddess temple and young girls there wove sacred textiles in worship of the goddess. Sometime in the 6th century CE, Byzantine Christians remodeled the building and rechristened it as the Latin cathedral of Parthenos Maria, the Virgin Mary, Our Lady of Athens.

HAGIA SOPHIA

The greatest cathedral from the Middle Ages was the Hagia Sophia in Constantinople, the largest and most magnificent building in Europe for a thousand years. Named for Wisdom, the Hagia Sophia was later converted into a Islamic mosque by the Ottomans. The Hagia Sophia was also built on the site of a pagan temple, though it is not clear to which god.

TEMPLE TO ISIS AT PHILAE

The last great goddess temple to survive with active worship was the temple to Isis at Philae in Egypt. Built on an island in the Nile river, it was said to be one of the burying places of Osiris and was held in deep esteem. First founded in the 7th century BC, if not before, the main temple to Isis was built in the 4th century BC. The complex was beautiful and filled with sacred architecture.

The Temple to Isis at Philae was a great site of pilgrimage for both Mediterranean people and Nubians, the temple complex remained popular deep into the Roman era. For a few centuries, pagan worship continued alongside Christian churches until the Isis temple was officially closed in 537 CE, which marked the official end of ancient Egyptian religion. The temples at Philae were all eventually converted into churches. After the Arab conquest, Egypt became a predominantly Islamic country though a minority of Coptic Christians remained.

Copt altar, Isis Temple, Philae Island, Egypt

Diana as Huntress by Bernardino Cametti

Chapter Fifty-Nine

DIANA

European paganism did not die out completely in the Middle Ages even though it was banned by the Church. Paganism lived on in the rural areas far away from ecclesiastical authorities.

The goddess Diana (Romanized Artemis) remained popular for centuries in medieval Europe. Diana was the Roman goddess of the countryside and hunters, the virgin protector of childbirth and midwives. Diana was chaste, a highly sexualized goddess would not have been appropriate or tolerated in the era of medieval Europe that was under the dominance of the Church.

Diana formed a triple goddess with Luna, goddess of the moon, and Hecate, goddess of magic and the underworld. Shrines to the triple goddess were erected at three-way crossroads across Europe; she was said to wander widely and to usher people between life and death.

Diana had been syncretized with Artemis of Ephesus, again showing the enduring importance and vitality of the Great Goddess who oversaw the cycles of life. As with all pagan traditions, her persona changed with the times and communities. The Goddess never went away, she was reborn with a new name and form.

One of the reasons that Diana was both popular and notorious was that she was the only goddess named in the New Testament, in Acts 19 when the Apostle Paul traveled to Ephesus and nearly caused a riot. Clergymen complained for centuries about the people who followed the heathen goddess, they described Diana as a demon and patron of witchcraft, tempting people away from the one true religion.

The *Canon Episcopi* was one of the most important ecclesiastical documents of the Middle Ages; written in the 10th century, it became enshrined as official Church law in 1140 CE. The *Canon Episcopi* condemned women in service to the pagan goddess Diana, who were said to be held captive by the devil and who practiced the pernicious arts of sorcery, even riding through the air on beasts. The fact that the church fathers felt strongly enough to preach and write laws against Diana is proof that her identity had remained strong in the culture.

Maypoles

Maypole dances were a favorite folk tradition that had origins in Germanic paganism and shared Neolithic roots with the Asherahs and totem poles of indigenous people. In the spring or summer, community festivals were held that featured feasting, drinking, and dancing around the tall maypoles. Though eventually secularized and adopted by Christian cultures, the maypole festivals are clearly the relics of ancient pagan beliefs with their worship of sacred trees and Mother Earth.

Peasant Hemp Farmers

European hemp farmers were the quintessential peasants out in the countryside who kept the goddess traditions alive in their folk festivals. Hemp harvesting and processing is famously difficult work; labor-intensive, and backbreaking. Hemp work was a community affair as many hands make light work, and the evenings were always times for joyous gatherings and carousing.

Europeans did not use hemp as an intoxicant for individuals, but they did throw flowers on the fire during harvest festivals and enjoy the pleasing aromas. European hemp varieties are low in THC, the intoxicating chemical. Cannabis is fundamentally medicinal and just the handling of raw hemp seems to promote good health and generous feelings towards others, even though the odors are strong and disagreeable to some.

All over Europe huge bonfires were kindled every year to promote tall hemp plants. Peasant hemp farmers danced over and around the flames, they believed that the higher they leaped the taller the plants would grow. These hemp dances were taken very seriously and it was believed that any farmer who did not take part could not look forward to a good harvest. In parts of France, women did the leaps while drunk, and elsewhere they danced on rooftops.[1]

Cutting or pulling out the heavy plants was typically men's work, but stripping, beating, and combing the fibers was women's work done in groups. Townspeople gathered at night to work the hemp fibers together and have spinning bees, they finished their work with games and dancing. Young women spent years spinning and weaving hemp textiles like tablecloths and bedsheets which formed a substantial part of her dowry when she married.

There were many European hemp traditions that contained sexual overtones. Across northern Europe, the love goddess Freya was associated with hemp sowing and harvest, erotic rituals were held in her honor.

1 Abel, Ernest L. *Marihuana: the First 12000 Years*. Plenum Pr., 1980, p.67 "Hemp Magic"

We see in these folk cultures where the roots of old European nature worship survived in the era of authoritarian Christianity.

In Norwegian folklore, hemp cloth symbolized the beginning and the end, as it was the first and the last fabric in which people were swathed in this life. It was customary to throw hemp seeds in a fire during funerals. Across many European cultures, the dead were buried in hemp clothes or covered in hempen shrouds.[2] The Merovingian Queen Arnegunde, who was buried in Paris around 570 CE, was covered by a hemp funeral shroud.

Cannabis was commonly associated with magic and believed to possess protective and healing powers. Heroes like St. George, the slayer of dragons, wore hemp shirts, and hemp clothes were associated with surviving plagues and epidemics. The self-sacrifice that went into the hard work of producing hemp was seen as part of its virtue, difficult labor that helps us atone for our sins.

The hempen collar was a name for the hangman's noose which was traditionally made from hemp, the last article worn by many criminals.

WITCHES

Village wise-women were the primary inheritors of the Goddess traditions in Medieval Europe. These women made herbal potions and medicines, were midwives, and were sometimes labeled as witches if the community turned against them.

Magical beliefs persisted in the popular imagination throughout the Middle Ages. Magic could be used for good or ill and healers were respected, but magic used for malevolent purposes would get someone labeled as a witch or sorcerer. For centuries, the Catholic church denied the existence of magic and witchcraft, claiming that to call them a reality was in itself false and heterodox teaching.

There was a widespread belief in Europe and beyond in the efficacy of magical potions that could be used for healing, but also for sinister purposes such as producing impotence or abortions. Fantastic notions existed in the popular mind about witches having the ability to fly through the air, hosting sexual orgies, and transforming people into animals.

The late Middle Ages saw a wave of witch trials and persecutions that lasted three hundred years. In these trials, women and occasionally men were routinely tortured into confessing their crimes. Tens of thousands of

2 Clarke and Merlin, *Cannabis: Evolution and Ethnobotany* p. 279-280 for a long discussion of European hemp folk traditions.

accused witches were executed in grisly fashion, often burned at the stake, or tortured to death with strange and sadistic devices.

The *Malleus Maleficarum*, the "Hammer of Witches," was a notorious book condemning witches published in 1487. It was one of the first books published after the invention of the printing press and it was hugely influential, being reprinted many times. The *Malleus* was the bestselling book after the Bible for over a century. The book was essentially a guide on how to identify, hunt, and interrogate witches, and was misogynistic to the extreme. The *Malleus Maleficarum* labeled witchcraft as heresy and quickly became the authority for both Protestants and Catholics trying to flush out witches living among them.

> *All wickedness is but little to the wickedness of a woman. ... What else is woman but a foe to friendship, an inescapable punishment, a necessary evil, a natural temptation, a desirable calamity, domestic danger, a delectable detriment, an evil nature, painted with fair colours. ...*
>
> *Women are by nature instruments of Satan -- they are by nature carnal, a structural defect rooted in the original creation.*
>
> – *Malleus Maleficarum*, "The Hammer of Witches" [3]

Most witch trials were held in secular courts as witchcraft was seen as a civil crime. Between the years 1500 and 1660, up to 80,000 suspected witches were put to death in Europe. Around 80 percent of them were women thought to be in cahoots with the Devil and filled with lust. The last major witch trials were held in America, in Salem, Massachusetts in 1692.

The witch no. 1 by Joseph Baker, 1892

3 Jacob Sprenger and Heinrich Kraemer, "The Hammer of Witches" (*Malleus Maleficarum*), 1486

Chapter Sixty

WISDOM OF SOLOMON

The *Wisdom of Solomon* is a Jewish work believed to have been written in the first century BCE in Alexandria, Egypt. It is one of the Apocryphal books of the Bible and would have been embraced in the Gnostic traditions. The Wisdom of Solomon reflects core beliefs of Hellenistic philosophy at the time when Sophia, wisdom, was elevated as the feminine aspect of God's glory and the bride of God.

The text is in Greek, so it was certainly not written by King Solomon personally, rather it is a synthesis of Greek and Jewish philosophical thought and dedicated to the father of the wisdom traditions. The book demonstrates the transition in the presentation of the feminine divine from the visceral pagan goddesses into the immanent presence of wisdom. In this passage from the Wisdom of Solomon we see the glory of Sophia.

I learned both what is secret and what is manifest,
for wisdom, the fashioner of all things, taught me.
For in her there is a spirit that is intelligent,
holy, unique, manifold,
subtle, mobile, clear,
unpolluted, distinct, invulnerable,
loving the good, keen, irresistible,
beneficent, humane, steadfast, sure,
free from anxiety, all-powerful, overseeing all,
and penetrating through all spirits
that are intelligent and pure and most subtle.
For wisdom is more mobile than any motion;
because of her pureness she pervades and penetrates all things.
For she is a breath of the power of God,
and a pure emanation of the glory of the Almighty;
therefore nothing defiled gains entrance into her.
For she is a reflection of eternal light,
a spotless mirror of the working of God,
and an image of his goodness.
Though she is but one, she can do all things,
and while remaining in herself, she renews all things;
in every generation she passes into holy souls
and makes them friends of God, and prophets;
for God loves nothing so much as the man who lives with wisdom.
For she is more beautiful than the sun,
and excels every constellation of the stars.
Compared with the light she is found to be superior,
for it is succeeded by the night,
but against wisdom evil does not prevail.

–Wisdom of Solomon, 7:21-30

(The Revised Standard Version of the Bible, Apocrypha)

Chapter Sixty-One

REVELATIONS

Wisdom reposes in the heart of the discerning and even among fools she lets herself be known.

– Proverbs 14:33

The heart of the discerning acquires knowledge, for the ears of the wise seek it out.

– Proverbs 18:15

The one who gets wisdom loves life; the one who cherishes understanding will soon prosper.

– Proverbs 19:8

Generations come and generations go, but the earth remains forever.

– Ecclesiastes 1:4

All streams flow into the sea, yet the sea is never full. To the place the streams come from, there they return again.

– Ecclesiastes 1:7

What has been will be again, what has been done will be done again; there is nothing new under the sun.

– Ecclesiastes 1:9

For with much wisdom comes much sorrow; the more knowledge, the more grief.

– Ecclesiastes 1:18

Questions and Answers

Much has been revealed to me in writing this book. Wonders that were not taught in school or in church. It all started with a question. Who is the wife of God? Who is this character Asherah in the Bible? What does it mean to worship her? Does she have a relationship with cannabis?

These questions led to this book being written, anyone could have asked them. If I did not write this book someone else would have, this story was waiting to be told. I am merely a transcriber, like a musician who pulls a melody out of the air.

I learned of an entirely new narrative in the Bible that had long been forgotten. I learned that there are characters in the Bible we are not taught about, that the monotheistic authorities don't want us to know about. I learned all this from the archaeologists who have been digging up graves for nearly 200 years, looking for the truths of the Bible. In those graves they dug up the old gods, and the internet spread their stories around the world. Archaeology and the internet have shifted the time-space continuum of human culture and there is no going back now. We must adapt and evolve.

I learned that the Earthly Mother and the Heavenly Father were traditionally mates and the parents of all the old gods. I learned that Moses introduced the concept of monotheism and that led to the Goddess and her sacred plant being thrown out of the temple. I learned that the Bible tells the story of the divorce of Mother Earth from God. This is not the story of the Bible I was taught in Church.

I learned that the early Hebrews were pagan and that Abraham was not a monotheist. The God of Abraham was named El and he had a wife and family. *El Elohe Israel.* El is the God of Israel. El's son was Baal, the King of the Gods. El's wife and daughters were the Triple Goddess of Asherah, Astarte, and Anat – the mother, maiden, and death. The monotheists killed Baal but the Goddess remains.

Asherah is the wife of God, the mother of us all, the Lady of the Sea. Astarte is the goddess of love and war, the Queen of Heaven. Anat was so terrifying to the biblical writers that they dared not mention her. Anat is *she who must not be named.* These are the lost goddesses of Israel.

The qedesha were the priestesses of the Goddess, and cannabis was their sacred plant. The King James Bible does not even correctly identify the qedesha, conflating the *Holy Ones* with common prostitutes. Cannabis is all over the Bible as well but its name was conveniently mistranslated, obscuring its identity and ritual significance.

King Solomon was the wisest, wealthiest, and most successful of all the Biblical kings and he was pagan. King Solomon worshipped Astarte and his Song of Songs is ritual love poetry that was read aloud in the *hieros gamos* ceremonies, the sacred marriage between the king and the Goddess.

King Solomon's Goddess worship was not a mistake or an exception to his wisdom, it demonstrates his wisdom. King Solomon is the father of the wisdom traditions and he is the one who bridges the gap between the Bronze Age pagan goddesses and the Hellenistic notion of Sophia. Sophia then became the bride of Christ for the Gnostics. We have much to learn from his books of Proverbs and Ecclesiastes.

In the way of righteousness there is life; along that path is immortality.
– Proverbs 12:28

I learned that humanity was devastated by the calamities of the Younger Dryas at the end of the Ice Age. The scholarly historical narratives do not teach this. We were nearly made extinct like the rest of the large animals at the time. It was the survivors of the great floods that began Neolithic planting. Likewise, the Bronze Age collapse 3000 years ago was a Near East apocalypse that birthed Yahweh and the Greek Olympian gods. We are facing mass extinction and environmental calamity today. The end is a new beginning.

Io received in Egypt by Isis and the river-god Nile, Pompeii, 1st C BCE

We have sacred Goddess traditions that go back to the Ice Age. The feminine divine is expressed as the virgin, mother, wisdom, Gaia, the cycle of life, and so much more. The Asherah, Totem pole, and Maypole are all drawn from a common tradition of Earth worship.

Mother Earth is the Goddess, at least that is the way we know her today. She took many names and forms over the millennia. The simple fact that most everyone in the world, in all cultures, knows exactly who Mother Earth is, demonstrates definitively that the Goddess never went away. She has been with us all along.

The word *Goddess,* like the word *God,* is a poetic allegory that helps us to put a form on something formless, the *Divine.* It is a poetic allegory that helps us to understand something that we know to be real but is utterly beyond our comprehension, the *Mysteries.*

No one can claim to know the truth of God (though many do), we only know pieces of the truth. We assemble these pieces together to form a mosaic that is hopefully an accurate reflection of the truth. The nature of the divine is a mystery, just as the origins of creation and life after death. No one truly knows the answers to these questions.

Culture War

The culture war fought in King Solomon's temple mirrors the culture war being fought today between religious conservatives and the counterculture of progressive secularists. In the ancient Goddess temples, we see expressions of today's progressive social causes; feminism, environmentalism, racial justice, sexual freedom, transgenders, cannabis legalization, and abortion.

The old goddesses are the purest reflection of feminism, they are mythical archetypes of empowered, independent females in all of their diverse roles. In these stories, we see women deified as mothers, warriors, hunters, farmers, oracles, midwives, healers, witches, scholars, poets, artists, musicians, dancers, harlots, virgins, and so many other characters, including the mother of God and primeval first mover of creation.

Gaia is the environment as a single living, breathing, sentient creature. The living web of life, she encompasses the entire concept of environmentalism. The Earth is our mother and today she is bleeding. She has been raped and beaten into submission but she can heal if we stop hurting her, and she still has the power to kill us all.

Racism was not a concept in antiquity. There was always tribalism but human worth was never measured by the color of one's skin. Truth is, there are no chosen people. We are all children of the same mother and she loves us all.

Sexual freedom for women and homosexuals is a break from biblical sexual ethics. Goddess cultures celebrated sexuality as the source of life and creation and understood pleasure to be a blessing. Bloodlines were tracked maternally and there was no obligation to marital monogamy. Monotheists fear sex because they know it puts one in touch with the Goddess and undermines patriarchal authority.

Transgendered people have recently reemerged from the underground and are now fighting for recognition and respect. It should be appreciated that for thousands of years trans people were celebrated as shamans and high priests in the Goddess temples. Trans people were shoved aside when their religious traditions were exterminated.

Cannabis and other entheogenic, psychedelic plants were deemed illegal under the monotheistic laws of the Christians and Muslims. Cannabis and all entheogenic plants were sacred in the Goddess traditions. The psychedelic experience was understood in shamanistic terms to help us communicate with nature.

The Goddess represents the cycle-of-life and death is understood to beget new life. Abortion, euthanasia, and suicide may be tragedies, but they are not sins, and should not be illegal. They merely represent the end of one chapter and the beginning of a new one. Our mother welcomes us all home in death and we must develop a code of ethics to match.

With modern scholarship and archaeology, we can now trace a continuous thread of Goddess traditions and symbolic spiritual motifs all the way through human history back into the Ice Age. Indigenous people have kept these traditions alive and much has been adopted into the secular spirituality of today's counterculture.

Mystery

The Book of Revelation, also known as the Apocalypse of John, is the famous tract that closes out the New Testament of the Bible. John speaks prophetically of the chaotic last days that will usher in a New Age and the second coming of Jesus Christ. The colorful imagery and poetic metaphors have led to a wide variety of interpretations. Scholars see the Book of Revelation as describing the depredations of the Roman Empire and their Emperor cults that were dominant at the time.

Many Christian faithful see the Book of Revelation describing future events and the end of the world. Seven seals and seven trumpets signify coming cataclysms. The four horsemen of the apocalypse bring conquest, war, famine, and death. Among the colorful prophecies is that of a woman riding a beast, she is a prostitute who commits shameful adulteries and is an enemy.

> *And upon her forehead was a name written, MYSTERY, BABYLON THE GREAT, THE MOTHER OF HARLOTS AND ABOMINATIONS OF THE EARTH.*
>
> – Revelation 17:5 (KJV)

Who is the Whore of Babylon? Why was this particular image chosen? Does it speak of the ancient city? Is it Rome? Or the Catholic Church?

It is no mystery, the Whore of Babylon is Ishtar, the Goddess, Mother of All, Queen of the Universe. Whore of Babylon was not an insult, it was a title worn proudly by the city's chief goddess. Babylon was the greatest city in the ancient world for roughly two thousand years and it was home to the Goddess traditions and Mystery religions.

The monotheists cannot tolerate the Mystery religions, for the existence of the Goddess challenges their authority and shatters their truth like glass. They insult her because they fear her. The return of the Goddess marks the end of one chapter and the beginning of the next.

William Blake, The Whore of Babylon, 1809

Alpha and Omega

Throughout the Book of Revelation, God reveals himself through the prophet, declaring:

> *I am the Alpha and the Omega, the First and the Last, the Beginning and the End.*
>
> – Revelation 22:13

In many ancient cultures, cannabis was known as the alpha and the omega, for it was the fiber that wraps the newborn and the corpse. Cannabis also appears on the opening and closing pages of the Bible, the beginning and the end. Cannabis is Eve's forbidden fruit at the opening of Genesis and the tree of life at the closing of Revelation.

We see cannabis after the cataclysms of the end times, when all has been cleansed and there is a new Heaven and Earth. A river of the water of life flows through the middle of the city. "On each side of the river stood the tree of life, bearing twelve crops of fruit, yielding its fruit every month. And the leaves of the tree are for the healing of the nations" (Revelation 22:2).

This is a perfect description of modern cannabis cultivation, yielding twelve crops of fruit every month of the year. Cannabis is grown year-round now, indoors under lights, and around the world. Countless products are made from this diverse plant, far more than 12; foods, medicines, fibers, tinctures, oils, lotions, and so much more. Cannabis naturally grows on river banks, so of course it grows by the river of life. Cannabis is a potent, miracle medicine and it is not known to kill, it is truly a tree of life.

"The leaf of the tree is for the healing of the nations." The seven-bladed cannabis leaf is a powerful political symbol internationally. The entire plant species has been rendered illegal for nearly a century in the War on Drugs. Millions of people all over the world have been harassed, arrested, and imprisoned for their relationship with the sacred plant. This prohibition of cannabis as a living species is a war on nature and a war on indigenous traditions. It is a war on the Goddess and a continuation of the culture wars fought in King Solomon's temple.

Lying prohibitionist authorities claim the sacred plant is no medicine and must be destroyed. Yet cannabis is proving itself to be a miracle medicine right in front of our eyes, curing violent epilepsy instantly in an Earthly miracle for struggling parents of sick children. The lying authorities do not tell us that cannabis has a proud history in America, that the Founding Fathers grew hemp and needed as much as possible to construct the US Navy. Today, the lying authorities would arrest us for growing fiber hemp.

The War on Drugs has been a failure for decades, it only serves to empower law enforcement authorities at the expense of the people. The prohibition is beginning to break down, but it has not fallen yet. Cannabis remains contraband and it is not yet free to grow wild, but it is definitely returning to the respected position it once held. Since prohibition began, cannabis has become far more influential than it was before, fueling the sexual revolution, popular music, and the counterculture. Cannabis challenges monotheistic authorities and is leading us back to the Goddess.

Goddess

Today is the solstice, 2020 CE, and the great conjunction of Jupiter and Saturn. This has been the year of the COVID-19 pandemic. Like many people, I have spent much of this past year living under quarantine. Millions of people have died around the world and the pandemic is far from over. The Earth is on fire, droughts, climate change, environmental degradation, and mass extinction are everywhere we look.

It is time that we get right with Mother Earth. I fear that COVID is just a warning shot across the bow. Our mother is letting us know that time is running out. Human populations have exploded in the last 150 years, we have billions of more people now than we used to thanks to the Industrial Revolution. We could easily lose a few billion people from some calamity. There are numerous Swords of Damocles hanging above global civilization at the moment. Humanity has been devastated before and it can happen again.

Only a true environmental catastrophe will get us to change our ways. Then we will collectively put in the effort to reestablish our relationship with the Goddess, our mother. She will heal us if we let her. We can heal our civilization if we follow her. We need to reconnect to the wisdom of indigenous people who understand that we are children of the living Earth and that for everything we take, we must put something back.

Monotheistic religious authorities reject indigenous traditions and claim authority over morality, spirituality, and death for all people. Like King Hezekiah centralizing worship at the Jerusalem temple and closing down the community altars, monotheists do not allow do-it-yourself religion. They insist on mediating our experiences of the divine through the priesthoods of the church, temple, and mosque. Monotheistic authorities shame us for our sexuality, condemn nature worship, and imprison us for the use of sacred plants.

Goddess offers a contrasting moral code and a cosmology of her own. Mystery over Truth. Cycle of life over eternal life. Circular thinking over linear thinking. Humans are a part of nature rather than separate from it. Bodily autonomy regarding sex, drugs, and death. Embrace of psychedelic plants and shamanism. Cannabis is sacred. Sexual freedom. Monogamy as a choice, not an obligation. Gender bending celebrated as a mystical path. Female equality and egalitarianism over the patriarchy. The Axis.

God the Heavenly Father is I, Goddess the Earthly Mother is O, IO together is the totality of the human experience. The lingam and yoni represent IO and is one of humanity's oldest religious traditions. These are not new ideas.

New Mythologies

Religion is the operating system of a culture. Mythologies speak to the mysteries of creation and our place in them. Every human culture has a religious identity at its heart that brings together the community through a shared worldview, tradition, and beliefs. Religion provides the foundations of our morality by establishing the common beliefs of a culture.

When old religions fail then new ones need to be created. We have free will, and we are free to reimagine mythologies and reinvent symbols to make them useful again. Not only are we free to, we are obligated to create new mythologies when the old ones fail, otherwise entire cultures can fail for lack of a cohesive worldview. The biblical writers reinvented Moses and Abraham, and Paul reimagined Jesus to suit the needs of their times and audiences.

The pagan poets of antiquity were free to reimagine and recreate their myths however they wanted. They trusted inspiration and were free from doctrine and dogma. The stories that rang true and brought wisdom were remembered and repeated. Today, we need to ensure the survival of our civilization from environmental calamity by reconnecting with nature. We need to put our mother, the Goddess, back on the pedestal where she belongs.

Let us tell new stories. Let us reimagine creation and our place in this beautiful, sublime, and mysterious universe.

The Big Bang was a Big Birth…

Ω

On each side of the river stood the tree of life, bearing twelve crops of fruit, yielding its fruit every month. And the leaves of the tree are for the healing of the nations.

– Revelation 22:2

ACKNOWLEDGMENTS

THANKS AND PRAISES

I dedicate this book to Mother Earth and her sacred cannabis plant. I also dedicate this book to my daughters and son, Ava, Rowan, and Lilla. I want them to know that there is no limit on what a girl can be or what she can do.

When I was 17 years old, I learned that the authorities were lying to me. I learned that the Church had no proof for their claims of exclusive truth about God. I learned that the police were lying about marijuana, claiming that it was not a medicine and that it was instead a threat, and would arrest me over these lies.

When I was 20 years old, I got kicked out of college and I spent the next year diligently attempting to write a history of cannabis. With Jack Herer's *The Emperor Wears No Clothes* as my guide, I raided the agricultural libraries at Cornell University to find every old book I could about cannabis. My attempt fell short when I realized I was trying to write the history of the world. I returned to school, graduated, and went on with my life.

I maintained an interest in all aspects of cannabis history and this book became a bucket list project 25 years in the making. This new project started with the five references to cannabis in the Hebrew Bible first identified by Sula Benet. I wanted to understand what it meant that cannabis was sacred in Moses' time and rejected later.

I had a theory that cannabis was associated with Asherah, the Hebrew mother goddess first identified by archaeologists in the 1960s who was also later rejected. The problem was that I did not know the first thing about Asherah or goddesses. I had a lot to learn and the journey took me through the history and mythology of the Ancient Near East. But when I saw the clear connections between cannabis and Goddess worship, I knew I was onto something. I recognized that today's counterculture, the hippies on LSD at a Grateful Dead concert, or the dancers on MDMA at a nightclub rave, would have been right at home in Ishtar's temple.

I could not have completed this project without the internet, Google, Wikipedia, YouTube, countless websites, and the entire field of archaeology. The emergence of the internet is the big difference in what I was able to do now as a researcher versus 25 years ago. Back then it was impossible to locate ancient texts easily from my desk, but now I can search through cuneiform tablets and read the Bible in Hebrew from home.

The internet shifts our perceptions of time and space, and combined with archaeology that allows us to peer into the past, we are now unlocking many ancient secrets.

There are some writers I need to thank.

From Joseph Campbell, I learned about the common religious traditions across cultures that reflect people's ties to nature and the cycles of life. Joseph Campbell had a sensitive appreciation for all the cultures he studied and he has been a big influence on me. He is one of my all-time favorite scholars.

From Chris Bennett, I learned almost everything I know about cannabis in the ancient world and religion. I have been reading his indefatigable scholarship for over 20 years. When it comes to cannabis in religion, I generally learned it first from Chris Bennett and went from there. His influence is felt all over this book.

I came across Merlin Stone after I began this project. She wrote one book, *When God Was a Woman,* based on her own original research in the 1970s. Merlin Stone taught me what goddess worship is all about, the themes to look for, and how the traditions contrasted culturally with the monotheistic religions.

I read Karen Armstrong's *A History of God* in my college days, it was the first piece of comparative religion that had an impact on me. From her, I learned that images of God change over time as cultural needs change. What people thought of God 500 years ago is very different from what they think today, and it will again be different 500 years in the future. I find that encouraging and it gives me faith that the Goddess will return.

Riane Eisler's *The Chalice and the Blade* was seminal in presenting the egalitarian nature of Goddess worshipping Neolithic cultures. Their worldview was later wiped out after the invention of bronze weapons that enabled strong men leading armies to take control of society.

William Dever and Raphael Patai were the first to popularize the idea that Asherah was the wife of God. Scholars have been dancing around the implications of her existence for a generation, while the theologians ignore the question entirely.

From Arthur George, I got the idea that the Garden of Eden story represents a divorce between Yahweh and Asherah, and I expanded on the concept. From Dr. Francesca Stavrakopoulou, I got the idea that Solomon's Temple was a metaphorical Garden of Eden and that the Garden story was written after the sack of Jerusalem and the Babylonian exile.

Terence McKenna taught me about *Gaia consciousness* and the fact that the psychedelic plants allow you to communicate with nature, which shamans have known all along. Mother Nature is sentient and she speaks to us, we just have to listen.

For cannabis research, Robert Connell Clarke has done more than anyone in chasing down cannabis all over the world to understand the genetics and cultural traditions. His book with Mark Merlin, *Cannabis: Evolution and Ethnobotany* is a world-class reference I relied on greatly.

Ethan Russo is among the top medical cannabis scientists and he also wrote some excellent history articles I used. Ernest Abel's *Marihuana: The First 12,000* Years was one of the first cannabis histories I read 25 years ago and it remains one of the best. I still have my old copy and was referencing it in the last days of my research.

Dr. Raphael Mechoulam and his scientific team discovered THC, CBD, and the endocannabinoid system. They unlocked one of the world's most long-standing mysteries, and like cosmic astronomy, revealed a world of more fantastic complexity than we ever could have imagined. Proving that no matter how much we know, the mystery always remains. I don't think it was a coincidence that they made their cannabis discoveries in the Holy Land at Hebrew University in Israel, near Jerusalem, exactly where the divorce of the deities occurred. The Goddess is alive and well and ready to be known again.

Jack Herer's *The Emperor Wears No Clothes* got me started on my cannabis journey when I was a teenager. That was when I learned that cannabis has a proud and noble history and that the government was lying to us when they demonized it and arrested us for associating with it. I was offended by cannabis prohibition then and I remain offended today.

Special thanks to the late Dennis Peron, Todd McCormick, NJ Weedman Ed Forchion, and the millions of cannabis activists who have worked to tell the truth and free the weed. You are hemp patriots.

Thanks to my publisher Kris Millegan who had faith in this book. He helped make it a reality and his illustrations were a great contribution.

I must praise my beautiful, golden dog Charlotte, she passed away while I was completing this text. Charlotte was the family dog to my children and a faithful companion during my writing. Our long afternoon walks provided a daily respite from my work. Charlotte was born a street dog in the Bahamas and I got her as a puppy by chance at the SPCA in Ithaca, New York. Her feral intelligence always showed. You were a good girl Charlotte, enjoy running in the Elysian Fields, I will miss you.

This book was conceived on the beach in beautiful Humboldt County, California, a real Goddess community. Humboldt is one of the magical places in the world, where the mighty redwood forests roll down onto the crashing coasts of the Pacific Ocean, and living proof that the Goddess is strongest where the cannabis grows thickest. Humboldt is famous for producing some of the finest cannabis anywhere in the world. Humboldt is remote country, home to those who wish to hide out in those deep, dark, endless forests, like Sasquatch, and the outlaw marijuana farmers. The sacred plant found a home in Humboldt and I found inspiration.

I completed this book in the city of my birth, Washington D.C., the Imperial city. I wrote the first draft in California and rewrote it two miles from the White House while living under quarantine from the global pandemic and witnessing historic political protests.

This has been a year of social, political, economic, and environmental turmoil. The future is chaotic and uncertain, more so than it has ever been in my life. We are 250 years into the Industrial Revolution and we likely have another 250 years to go. The only constant is change, and the rate of change is increasing exponentially. We cannot predict the plateau.

We know that the emerging technologies of artificial intelligence, robotics, and synthetic biology will alter the very foundation of our global society, just as electricity, hydrocarbons, and global communication already have. But we don't know how these new technologies will change our lives and we don't know if those changes will be good, bad, or a complex, paradoxical mixture, just like fossil fuels and the internet.

I have faith that we can survive and thrive as a global society. I have faith that we can make the whole Earth into a new Garden of Eden by modeling our technology and civilization on nature. We must reorient our market economies to work with nature, not fight her, or beat her into submission. Let us harness the carbon cycle to our advantage as an engine of endless growth. Nature offers the model, let us follow her patterns. I have faith that we can have joy, abundance, and freedom!

Thank Goddess!

Edward Tristram Dodge
December 21, 2020

BIBLIOGRAPHY

Some websites I consulted a lot.

Biblehub.com is an amazing Bible reference with six translations side by side and you can investigate the original Hebrew text and commentary for every verse.

Wikipedia.org is beyond a treasure. I consulted wikipedia constantly for reference on a thousand subjects. It is impossible to overstate how valuable it is.

Sefaria.org is an outstanding site for Hebrew scholarship and classic Judaic and Rabbinical commentary.

http://www.perseus.tufts.edu for ancient Greek texts.

https://www.theoi.com/ for Greek mythology

http://penelope.uchicago.edu/ - ancient texts

http://www.gutenberg.org - ancient texts

www.newworldencyclopedia.org

www.ancient.eu

Abel, Ernest L. *Marihuana: the First 12000 Years*. Plenum Pr., 1980.

Aeschylus, *The Oresteia*, Translated by E. D. A. Morshead. Project Gutenberg. http://gutenberg.net.au/ebooks07/0700021h.html

Anderson, Bernhard W., et al. *The New Oxford Annotated Bible: with the Apocryphal/Deuterocanonical Books*. Oxford Univ. Press, 1997.

Andrews, George and Simon Vinkenoog (eds.) *The Book of Grass*. Grove Press, New York, 1967.

Armstrong, Karen. *The Bible: a Biography*. Grove Press, 2008.

Armstrong, Karen. *A History of God: the 4000-Year Quest of Judaism, Christianity and Islam*. Ballantine, 1993.

Athenaeus, *The Deipnosophistae*, published in Vol. II of the Loeb Classical Library edition, 1928. http://penelope.uchicago.edu/Thayer/E/Roman/Texts/Athenaeus/5C*.html

Baugh, S.M., *Cult Prostitution in New Testament Ephesus: A Reappraisal.* JOURNAL OF THE EVANGELICAL THEOLOGICAL SOCIETY, 42/3 (September 1999) 443–460

Barker, Melissa, *The Sacred Marriage Ritual of the Sumerians and the Kings that practiced it.* Third year Student at the University of South Africa, 2013

Benet, Sula, *Early Diffusion and Folk Uses of Hemp,* from "Cannabis and Culture," Rubin, Vera & Comitas, Lambros, (eds.), The Hague: Moutan, 1975.

Benet, Sula (as Sara Benetowa) *Tracing One Word Through Different Languages.* (1936). (Reprinted in The Book of Grass, 1967.)

Bennett, Chris, *Cannabis and the Soma Solution,* Trine Day, 2010.

Bennett, Chris, *Liber 420: Cannabis, Magickal Herbs and the Occult.* Trine Day LLC, 2018.

Bennett, Chris, *Sex, Drugs, Violence and the Bible.* Forbidden Fruit Pub. Co., 2001.

Bennett, Chris, *Cannabis the Once and Future Tree of Life,* Cannabis Culture, May 19, 2018.

Bennett, Chris, Lynn Osburn and Judy Osburn, *Green Gold the Tree of Life Marijuana in Magic and Religion.* Access Unlimited, Frazier Park, CA, 1995.

Bible, *The Revised Standard Version of the Holy Bible with Apocrypha*

Bible, *New International Version.* Biblehub.com

Bible, *King James Version.* Biblehub.com

Bowker, John. *God: a Brief History.* DK Pub., 2002.

Brown, Cheever Mackenzie, *The Devi Gita: The Song of the Goddess: A Translation, Annotation,* and Commentary, SUNY Press, Jan 1, 1998

Budge, E.A. Wallis, *The Queen of Sheba and Her Only Son Menyelek (Kebra Nagast),* In parentheses Publications Ethiopian Series, Cambridge, Ontario, 2000

Campbell, Joseph, and Safron Rossi (editor), *Goddesses Mysteries of the Feminine Divine.* New World Library, Novato, California, 2013.

Campbell, Joseph, et al. *The Power of Myth.* Anchor Books, 1991.

Campos, Isaac. *Home Grown: Marijuana and the Origins of Mexico's War on Drugs.* Univ Of North Carolina Pr, 2014.

ÇATALHÖYÜK 2013 ARCHIVE REPORT, ÇATALHÖYÜK RESEARCH PROJECT, this report from the archaeologists, team leader Ian Hodder, excludes the word hemp from the discussion of the linen fabric, even though multiple news articles quote him saying the fabric was hemp woven with linen.

Chavalas, Mark ed., translation by Piotr Michalowski, *Historical Sources in Translation: The Ancient Near East,* Blackwell, 2006, published on pp. 428-29.

Church, Sally K., *Two Ming Dynasty shipyards in Nanjing and their infrastructure.* Paper 3, 2011, Faculty of Asian and Middle Eastern Studies, University of Cambridge.

Clarke, Robert Connell, and Mark David Merlin. *Cannabis: Evolution and Ethnobotany.* University of California Press, 2013.

Clarke, Robert Connell. *Hashish!* Red Eye Press, 2010.

Cline, Eric H. *1177 B.C. - the Year Civilization Collapsed.* Princeton University Press, 2015.

Coogan, Michael David., and Mark S. Smith. *Stories from Ancient Canaan.* Westminster John Knox Press, 2012.

Curry, Andrew, "This 11,000-year-old statue unearthed in Siberia may reveal ancient views of taboos and demons," *Science Magazine*, sciencemag.org, Apr. 25, 2018.

Darmesteter,James, *Sacred Books of the East*, American Edition, 1898. http://www.avesta.org/vendidad/vd15sbe.htm

Dever, William G. *Did God Have a Wife?: Archaeology and Folk Religion in Ancient Israel.* Eerdmans, 2005.

Diodorus Siculus, *The Library of History*, published in Vol. X of the Loeb Classical Library edition, 1954. http://penelope.uchicago.edu/Thayer/E/Roman/Texts/Diodorus_Siculus/20A*.html

D. Luckenbill. 1927. *Ancient records of Assyria and Babylonia: Vol. II.* T.C. Mitchell. 1988. The Bible in the British Museum.

ETCSL project, Faculty of Oriental Studies, *A hymn to Inana (Inana C)*, ETCSL translation : t.4.07.3, University of Oxford. http://etcsl.orinst.ox.ac.uk/cgi-bin/etcsl.cgi?text=t.4.07.3#

Ehrman, Bart, *The Triumph of Christianity: How a Forbidden Religion Swept the World*, Simon & Schuster, 2018.

Eisler, Riane, *The Chalice and the Blade: Our History, Our Future*, Harper One, 1987

Eusebius of Caesarea, *Life of Constantine*, Source. Translated by Ernest Cushing Richardson. From Nicene and Post-Nicene Fathers, Second Series, Vol. 1. Edited by Philip Schaff and Henry Wace. (Buffalo, NY: Christian Literature Publishing Co., 1890.) Revised and edited for New Advent by Kevin Knight. <http://www.newadvent.org/fathers/2502.htm>.

Frankfort, Henri, *Kingship and the Gods: a study of Ancient Near Eastern Religion as the Integration of Society and Nature (with a preface by Samuel Noah Kramer)*. The University of Chicago Press, Chicago, London, 1978.

Frazer, James George., and Robert Fraser. *The Golden Bough: a Study in Magic and Religion: a New Abridgement from the Second and Third Editions*. Oxford University Press, 2009.

George, Arthur, and Elena George. *The Mythology of Eden*. Hamilton Books, 2014.

George, Arthur, *Yahweh's Divorce from the Goddess Asherah in the Garden of Eden*, Mythology Matters Blog, 8/21/2018 https://mythologymatters.wordpress.com/2014/10/06/yahwehs-divorce-from-the-goddess-asherah-in-the-garden-of-eden/

Graves, Robert. *The Song of Songs*. C.N. Potter, 1973.

Grinspoon, Dr. Lester, and James Bakalar, *Marihuana: The Forbidden Medicine*. Yale University Press, New Haven and London, 1993.

Hamilton, Edith. *Mythology: Timeless Tales of Gods and Heroes*. Grand Central, 2011.

Hancock, Graham. *Fingerprints of the Gods: The Evidence of Earth's Lost Civilization.* Three Rivers Press (CA), 1996.

Herer, Jack, *The Emperor Wears No Clothes; Hemp and the Marijuana Conspiracy*. Queen of Clubs Publishing, 1985-95.

Herodotus, *The Histories*, with an English translation by A. D. Godley. Cambridge. Harvard University Press. 1920. http://www.perseus.tufts.edu/

Homer. *The Iliad* with an English Translation by A.T. Murray, Ph.D. in two volumes. Cambridge, MA., Harvard University Press; London, William Heinemann, Ltd. 1924.

Homer. *The Odyssey* with an English Translation by A.T. Murray, PH.D. in two volumes. Cambridge, MA., Harvard University Press; London, William Heinemann, Ltd. 1919.

Hongen Jiang, Long Wang, Mark D. Merlin, Robert C. Clarke, Yan Pan, Yong Zhang, Guoqiang Xiao, and Xiaolian Ding. *Ancient Cannabis Burial Shroud in a Central Eurasian Cemetery,* Article in Economic Botany · September 2016. DOI: 10.1007/s12231-016-9351-1

Hürriyet Daily News, *Centuries-old fabric found in Çatalhöyük,* Feb 3, 2014, Dogan News Agency. https://www.hurriyetdailynews.com/centuries-old-fabric-found-in-catalhoyuk-61883

Launderville, Dale, *Celibacy in the Ancient World: Its Ideal and Practice in Pre-Hellenistic Israel, Mesopotamia, and Greece.* Liturgical Press, 2010.

James, M.R. (translator), *The Acts of John,* Gnostic Scriptures and Fragments, Gnostic Society Library. http://gnosis.org/library/actjohn.htm

Keller, Mara Lynn, *The Eleusinian Mysteries of Demeter and Persephone: Fertility, Sexuality, and Rebirth.* Journal of Feminist Studies in Religion, Spring 1988, vol 4, no. 1.

King, L.W., translator, *The Code of Hammurabi,* The Avalon Project, Yale Law School, Lillian Goldman Law Library, New Haven, CT. https://avalon.law.yale.edu/ancient/hamframe.asp

King, L.W. (translator), *Enuma Elish - The Epic of Creation,* from The Seven Tablets of Creation, London 1902. https://www.sacred-texts.com/ane/enuma.htm.

Darlene Kosnik, *History's Vanquished Goddess Asherah,* Emergent Press, llc, 2014

Kovacs, Maureen Gallery (translator), *The Epic of Gilgamesh,* Stanford University Press; 1st Edition, 1989. Electronic Edition by Wolf Carnahan, I998. http://www.ancienttexts.org/library/mesopotamian/gilgamesh

Kramer, Samuel Noah. *History Begins at Sumer: Thirty-Nine Firsts in Recorded History.* University of Pennsylvania Press, 1956.

Kramer, Samuel Noah. *The Sumerians: Their History, Culture, and Character.* The Univ. of Chicago Press, 1963.

Kramer, Samuel Noah. *Gilgamesh and the Huluppu-Tree.* The Univ. of Chicago Press, 1938.

Mayor, Adrienne. *The Amazons: Lives and Legends of Warrior Women across the Ancient World.* Princeton University Press, 2016.

Mark, Joshua J., wrote numerous informative articles on the Ancient Near East on the Ancient History Encyclopedia website, www.ancient.eu.

Maimonides, *Guide for the Perplexed,* English Translation, Friedlander (1903) https://www.sefaria.org/Guide_for_the_Perplexed%2C_Part_3.49.2?lang=bi&with=all&lang2=en

Mikuriya, Tod H. *Marijuana: Medical Papers, 1839-1972.* Symposium Publishing, 2007.

Mills, James H. *Cannabis Britannica: Empire, Trade, and Prohibition, 1800-1928.* Oxford University Press, 2005.

Mosca, Paul G., *Child Sacrifice in Canaanite and Israelite Religion*. PhD thesis, Harvard, 1975, p.22. Reference via Bennie H. Reynolds, "Molek: Dead or Alive? The meaning and derivation of mlk and ###", in Human sacrifice in Jewish and Christian tradition, ed. K. Finsterbusch &c, Leiden: Brill, 2007, p.133-150, p.149 n.68.

M. Ren, Z. Tang, X. Wu, R. Spengler, H. Jiang, Y. Yang, N. Boivin, *The origins of cannabis smoking: Chemical residue evidence from the first millennium BCE in the Pamirs. Sci. Adv.* 5, eaaw1391 (2019). DOI: 10.1126/sciadv.aaw1391

O'Shaughnessy, WB, *On the Preparation of Indian Hemp* (1839). Reprinted in *Marijuana Medical Papers*, Todd Mikuriya, MD, Ed. Medi-Comp Press, 1973.

Pagels, Elaine, *The Gnostic Gospels*. Random House, 1979.

Parrott, Douglas M.(translator), *The Sophia of Jesus Christ*, The Nag Hammadi Library, Gnostic Society Library. http://www.gnosis.org/naghamm/sjc.html

Pliny the Elder, *The Natural History*, John Bostock, M.D., F.R.S., H.T. Riley, Esq., B.A., Ed. 1855. http://www.perseus.tufts.edu/hopper/text?doc=Perseus:abo:phi,0978,001:19

Plutarch, *On Superstition*, as published in Vol. II of the Loeb Classical Library edition, 1928.

Rabbi Bahya ben Asher, Midrash, *Rabbeinu Bachya*, Composed in Middle-Age Spain (c.1290 - c.1310 CE).

Midrash - Sifrei Bamidbar, paragraph 99 - Composed in Talmudic Israel/Babylon (200 CE). Sifrei (Books) also known as Sifrei debe Rav or Sifrei Rabbah refers to either of two works of Midrash halakhah, based on the biblical books of Bemidbar (Numbers) and Devarim (Deuteronomy). https://www.sefaria.org/Sifrei_Bamidbar.100

Rabelais, Francois, *Gargantua and His Son Pantagruel*, Book 3, Chapter 3.LI. Translated into English by Sir Thomas Urquhart of Cromarty and Peter Antony Motteux. Project Gutenberg's Gargantua and Pantagruel, https://www.gutenberg.org/files/8168/8168-h/8168-h.htm#2HCH0003

Robinson, Rowan. *The Great Book of Hemp: the Complete Guide to the Environmental, Commercial, and Medicinal Uses of the World's Most Extraordinary Plant*. Park Street Press, 1996.

Rouse, WHD (translator), *Nonnus, Dionysiaca*. Loeb Classical Library Volumes 344, 354, 356. Cambridge, MA, Harvard University Press, 1940. https://www.theoi.com/Text/NonnusDionysiaca1.html

Rufus, Curtius, *History of Alexander the Great of Macedonia*, translated by John Yardley. https://www.livius.org/sources/content/curtius-rufus/the-rape-of-the-babylonian-women/

Russo, Ethan B., *History of Cannabis and Its Preparations in Saga, Science, and Sobriquet*, Article in Chemistry & Biodiversity, November 2007, DOI: 10.1002/cbdv.200790144

Sargent, Thelma (translator), *The Homeric Hymns*, W. W. Norton & Company, New York,1973.

Schonfield, Dr. Hugh, *The Passover Plot*. Bantam Books, 1967.

Schultes, Richard Evans., et al. *Plants of the Gods: Their Sacred, Healing and Hallucinogenic Powers*. Healing Arts Press, Vermont, 2006.

Sjöö Monica, and Barbara Mor. *The Great Cosmic Mother: Rediscovering the Religion of the Earth*. HarperOne, an Imprint of HarperCollinsPublishers, 2012.

Smith, Anne Marie, *Phoenician Ships: Types, Trends, Trade And Treacherous Trade Routes.* Submitted in accordance with the requirements for the degree of Master of Arts In the subject Biblical Archaeology at the University of South Africa, Supervisor: Prof. Cl Vw Scheepers, November 2012

Stager, Lawrence E., Wolff, Samuel R.,*Child Sacrifice at Carthage—Religious Rite or Population Control? Archaeological evidence provides basis for a new analysis.*, Archaeological Review, 1984.

Stavrakopoulou, Dr. Francesca, *Bible Secrets Revealed,* Documentary, TV Series, 2013

Strabo, *The Geography of Strabo,* published in Vol. V of the Loeb Classical Library edition, 1928. http://penelope.uchicago.edu/Thayer/E/Roman/Texts/Strabo/11N*.html

Stone, Merlin. *When God Was a Woman.* Harcourt Brace Jovanovich, 1978.

Sumler, Alan. *Cannabis in the Ancient Greek and Roman World.* Lexington Books, 2018.

Thompson, Campbell R., *A Dictionary of Assyrian Botany,* The British Academy, Burlington Gardens, London, 1949.

Touw, Mia, "The Religious and Medicinal Uses of Cannabis in China, India and Tibet," *Journal of Psychoactive Drugs* Vol. 13(1) Jan-Mar, 1981

Wolkstein, Diane, and Samuel Noah Kramer. *Inanna: Queen of Heaven and Earth ; Her Stories and Hymns from Sumer.* Harper & Row, New York, 1983.

Index

Symbols

A

B

C

D

E

N

O

P

Q

R

S

Z